Wealth, Income Inequalities, and Demography

Luigi Paganetto
Editor

Wealth, Income Inequalities, and Demography

The Long-Term Policy View

Springer

Editor
Luigi Paganetto
Tor Vergata Foundation for Economic
Research
Rome, Italy

ISBN 978-3-319-05908-2 ISBN 978-3-319-05909-9 (eBook)
DOI 10.1007/978-3-319-05909-9
Springer Cham Heidelberg New York Dordrecht London

Library of Congress Control Number: 2014948211

Printed on acid-free paper

Springer is part of Springer Science+Business Media (www.springer.com)

Contents

Introduction

Luigi Paganetto

Five years after the 2008 crisis, economic growth is still anaemic in many countries. Public debt continue to increase in advanced countries. The combined quantitative easing programmes by Japan, the US and the UK and the liquidity injections in EU are now of an unprecedented scale.

Emerging countries are driving world's economic growth. The Eurozone and US business cycles seems to have decoupled.

US GDP growth tends to show a positive rate around 2 %. EU growth by contrast seems to be on a negative trend, recently including Germany.

Unemployment and excess capacity in EU are high relative the postwar experience. IMF forecasts indicate that current unemployment rates will be probably unchanged in 2015.

EU Commission in 2012 put in evidence the emergence of the increasing phenomenon of long-term unemployment. One year or more is retained as the criteria for measuring this phenomenon. In 2011 those unemployed for more than 1 year were almost 10 million. The reduction of this phenomenon is a priority for citizens and policy makers. The EU Commission pointed out that there is evidence that long periods of unemployment create a negative impact on personal health and well-being. Moreover, the longer people remain unemployed, the harder it becomes for them to find a job.

Data suggest that we have to face a malaise most similar to the depression instead of continuing to talk about recession. Mediterranean countries exhibit a continuing lack of International competitiveness. Austerity policies manifested their limits. Under quantitative easing the new money does not get into the real economy. The main beneficiaries of these policy are the investors, traders and speculators that have a very low propensity to consume goods and services.

L. Paganetto (✉)
Tor Vergata Foundation for Economic Research, Rome, Italy
e-mail: luigi.paganetto@uniroma2.it

L. Paganetto (ed.), *Wealth, Income Inequalities, and Demography*,
DOI 10.1007/978-3-319-05909-9_1,

J. Stiglitz said that the big lesson of the crisis is that economies are not necessarily efficient, stable or self-correcting. What is needed therefore is to correct the economy.

The crisis can't be faced using tools able to fight recession. Indeed the crisis has been accompanied by important structural changes as increasing income inequality, population ageing and shifting wealth from advanced to emerging countries.

OECD estimated that, after two decades of shifting wealth, developing and emerging countries are likely to account for nearly 60 % of world GDP by 2030. At the G20 table are participating the leaders of the countries of the heart of the shifting wealth story: Brazil, China, India, Indonesia and South Africa.

OECD secretary general pointed out that large emerging market economies have helped to soften the impact of the most serious global recession since the 1930s. Through their trade and investment links they have also mitigated the impact of the crisis on the rest of the developing world. And now in the recovery phase they are a major source of growth.

An important consequence of the shifting wealth phenomenon is the coming out of a new competitiveness environment and the new role of demand of emerging countries for advanced economies, European especially.

Europe and Italy have not completed so far the structural adjustments needed to face the new phase opened by shifting wealth.

Income inequalities increased in the recent years. OECD stated that today in the area, the average income of the richest 10 % of the population is about nine times that of the poorest 10 %—a ratio of 9 to 1.

However, the ratio varies widely from one country to another. It is much lower than the OECD average in the Nordic and many continental European countries, but reaches 10 to 1 in Italy, Japan, Korea, and the United Kingdom; around 14 to 1 in Israel, Turkey, and the United States; and 27 to 1 in Mexico.

The latest trends in the 2000s showed a widening gap between the rich and the poor not only in some of the already high inequality countries like Israel and the United States, but also—for the first time—in traditionally low-inequality countries, such as Germany, Denmark, and Sweden (and other Nordic countries), where inequality grew more than anywhere else in the 2000s.

Rising income inequality creates economic, social and political challenges.

Are redistributive strategies based on governments transfers the right remedy? Experience says no. They are neither effective nor financially sustainable.

Pre-distribution policies could be a new interesting approach. Investing in the human capital is the strategic key. In his paper on innovation and inequality Phelps expresses the view that "there is no question that effective initiatives can be taken to address particular inequalities. Subsidies for employers to hire low-wage workers is one initiative that could be taken to address a particularly serious inequality. But there is no way to restore the sense of equality that prevailed as late as the 1960s without remedying the ills that caused inequalities to widen: the narrowing of high innovation to a handful of industries and the consequent slowing of economic growth to a snail's pace".

J. Stiglitz argued in his recent book "The price of inequality" that structural changes in inequality played a significant role in our present crises. More inequality leads to lower aggregate demand which then leads to even more inequality.

Stiglitz said that this dynamic is the result of the wealthiest 1 % having a much higher savings rate than the middle class, which tends to spend most of what it earns. The drop in aggregate demand causes then hits to the middle class even harder, leading to a further drop in demand that harms the middle class more than the top 1 %.

Much of the growth in the share of income controlled by the wealthiest 1 % has come from inefficient and predatory activity that takes slices of the economic pie rather than creating more for everyone. Economists call this behavior "rent seeking." Stamping out this type of economic activity would benefit the rest of society greatly, while also lowering inequality.

The European Commission presented in 2012 an assessment of the economic impact of ageing in EU supporting the idea that fiscal challenges are more and more coming from both a higher share of the total population in older age and a decline in the share of the population that is economically active.

Nevertheless employment rates and levels are projected to continue rising for at least a decade. This fact will temporary offset the decline in the size of the working-age populations, and will provide a window of opportunity to undertake necessary reform measures. Secondly, the projections underpin the validity of the approach adopted by the EU in the Lisbon strategy, including the need to invest in human capital formation.

The economic impact of ageing population has several different features.

1. If individual's productivity declines with age then a rising share of older workers could reduce overall productivity.
2. Ageing has an impact on saving behavior. Elderly tend to consume less than they might and tend to save as a precautionary measure.
3. Ageing could hamper innovation.
4. The increase in age related expenditure is not only a budgetary problem but also a crucial economic issue. Raising taxes on workers to finance pensions could reduce the total amount of physical capital that can be accumulated.

The general conclusion that can be drawn is that structural factors are the prevailing features of the crisis. In this contest austerity is a not working strategy. Internal devaluation, lower wages are not the right answer.

If internal devaluation were the solution, the gold standard would not have been a problem in the Great Depression (J. Stiglitz). Europe's talent and resources are the same today as they were before the crisis began. What is needed are industrial policies, investment in European infrastructures that could promote exports and productivity in Europe and structural reforms mainly of the Eurozone's institutional arrangements.

Restoring Europe's Luster

Indermit Gill and Martin Raiser

Abstract What has Europe accomplished that other parts of the world could not? Which aspects of its economic model are unsustainable? Which changes are needed now, and which can wait? These are the questions that this paper asks. The short answers: Europe has achieved economic growth and convergence that is unprecedented. Most countries in Europe are doing well in trade and finance, many in enterprise and innovation, but far fewer are doing well in labor and government. So Europe needs many changes to make its governments and labor markets work better, fewer to foster innovation and productivity growth in enterprises, and fewer still to reform finance and trade. These deficiencies are rooted in how some activities are organized and they will need to be reorganized. Stalled productivity, declining populations, and growing fiscal imbalances have made some changes urgent. But in addressing these shortcomings, Europeans should not forget the successes of their growth model. By fostering a regional economic integration unique in both depth and scope, Europe has become a "convergence machine." By engineering an entrepreneurial dynamism in the countries that balanced market forces and social responsibility, it has made "brand Europe" globally valued. And by allowing a balance between life and work, it made Europe the world's "lifestyle superpower." Europeans now have to do three progressively tougher tasks: restart the convergence machine, rebuild Europe's global brand, and recalibrate the balance between work and leisure to make their lifestyles affordable.

I. Gill (✉)
Development Economics, The World Bank, Washington, DC, USA
e-mail: igill@worldbank.org

M. Raiser
Europe and Central Asia Region, The World Bank, Washington, DC, USA
e-mail: mraiser@worldbank.org

L. Paganetto (ed.), *Wealth, Income Inequalities, and Demography*,
DOI 10.1007/978-3-319-05909-9_2,

1 Introduction

Fifty years ago, the *American Economic Review* published a short article titled "The Golden Rule of Accumulation". In it, Edmund Phelps, an American economist, proposed a simple rule for a nation's wealth to grow and provide the highest standard of living for its citizens—present and future (Phelps 1961). The rule essentially specified how much people had to work, save, and invest today so that future generations could be at least as well off as they were. The paper used the insights of economists from around the world, including France, Germany, Hungary, the Netherlands, and the United Kingdom.[1] All were to have distinguished careers, and some would get the Nobel Prize. In 2006, the Nobel Committee awarded the prize to Phelps for "his analysis of intertemporal tradeoffs in macroeconomic policy."

Many economists still consider the golden rule the most basic proposition of optimum growth theory. It is the inspiration for the title of this report, and forms the roots of its policy prescriptions. Following the golden rule means that today's Europeans work and consume just so much that future generations neither resent them for consuming too much, nor pity them for consuming too little. Keeping to the rule is perhaps the most telling sign of a country's—or a continent's—economic maturity.

Europe's growth is already different from other economies' in two aspects, reflecting its cultural and demographic maturity. Perhaps more than others around the world, the citizens of Europe want economic growth to be smarter, kinder, and cleaner, and they are willing to accept less for "better" growth. The single word that summarizes these ideals might be "golden."

Europe's growth will have to be golden in yet another sense. Economic prosperity has brought to Europeans the gift of longer lives, and the continent's population has aged a lot over the last five decades. Over the next five, it will age even more: by 2060, almost a third of Europeans will be older than 65 years. Europe will have to rebuild its structures to make fuller use of the energies and experience of its more mature populations—people in their golden years.

These desires and developments already make the European growth model distinct. Keeping to the discipline of the golden rule would make it distinguished. This report shows how Europeans have organized the six principal economic activities—trade, finance, enterprise, innovation, labor, and government—in unique ways. But policies in parts of Europe do not recognize the imperatives of demographic maturity and clash with growth's golden rule. Making growth across the continent conform both to Europe's ideals and to the iron laws of economics will require difficult decisions. This paper summaries a report that was written to inform them. Its findings: the changes needed to make trade and finance will not be as hard as those to improve enterprise and innovation; these in turn are not as arduous and

[1]Among the economists were Maurice Allais, Tjalling Koopmans, Christian von Weisacker, Joan Robinson, John von Neumann, Robert Solow, and Trevor Swan.

urgent as the changes needed to restructure work and government. Its message: the remedies are not out of reach for a part of the world that has proven itself both intrepid and inclusive.[2]

2 A Distinctive Model

It is common these days to hear Europeans calling for a "new growth model." The public debt crisis has shaken confidence not just in the euro but in Europe. Aging Europeans are being squeezed between innovative Americans and efficient Asians, it is said. With debt and demographics weighing down European economies, the argument runs that they will not grow much unless they discover radically new ways.

The end of complacency among Europeans is good, because developments in and outside the continent have made changes necessary. But loss of confidence could be dangerous. The danger is that in rushing to restructure and restart growth, Europe may throw out the attractive attributes of its development model with the weak ones. In fact, the European growth model has many strong points and enviable accomplishments.

Between 1950 and 1973, Western European incomes converged quickly towards those in the United States. Then, until the early 1990s, the incomes of more than 100 million people in the poorer southern periphery—Greece, southern Italy, Portugal, and Spain—grew closer to those in advanced Europe. With the first association agreements with Hungary and Poland in 1994, another 100 million people in Central and Eastern Europe were absorbed into the European Union, and their incomes increased quickly. Another 100 million in the candidate countries in Southeastern Europe are already benefiting from the same aspirations and similar institutions that have helped almost half a billion people achieve the highest standards of living on the planet. If European integration continues, the 75 million people in the eastern partnership will profit in ways that are similar in scope and speed.

It is no exaggeration to say that Europe invented a "convergence machine," taking in poor countries and helping them become high-income economies. Over the last four decades, the countries in Europe experienced a convergence in consumption levels that is unmatched (Fig. 1). Annual per capita consumption in the poorer parts of Europe grew by 4 % while in the wealthier countries it increased at a still-impressive 2 %. The rest of the world—apart from East Asia—has seen little or no convergence. That is why the European model was so attractive. That is why European growth is distinct.

---

[2]The report covers 45 countries: the 27 member states of the European Union, 4 countries in the European Free Trade Association (Iceland, Liechtenstein, Norway, and Switzerland), 8 candidate and potential candidate countries (Albania, Bosnia and Herzegovina, Croatia, Kosovo, the former Yugoslav Republic of Macedonia, Montenegro, Serbia, and Turkey), and six eastern partnership countries (Armenia, Azerbaijan, Belarus, Georgia, Moldova, and Ukraine).

Fig. 1 In Europe, a rapid convergence in living standards—not much elsewhere (growth of consumption per capita between 1970 and 2009, by level of consumption in 1970). *Source*: World Bank staff calculations based on Heston et al. (2011)

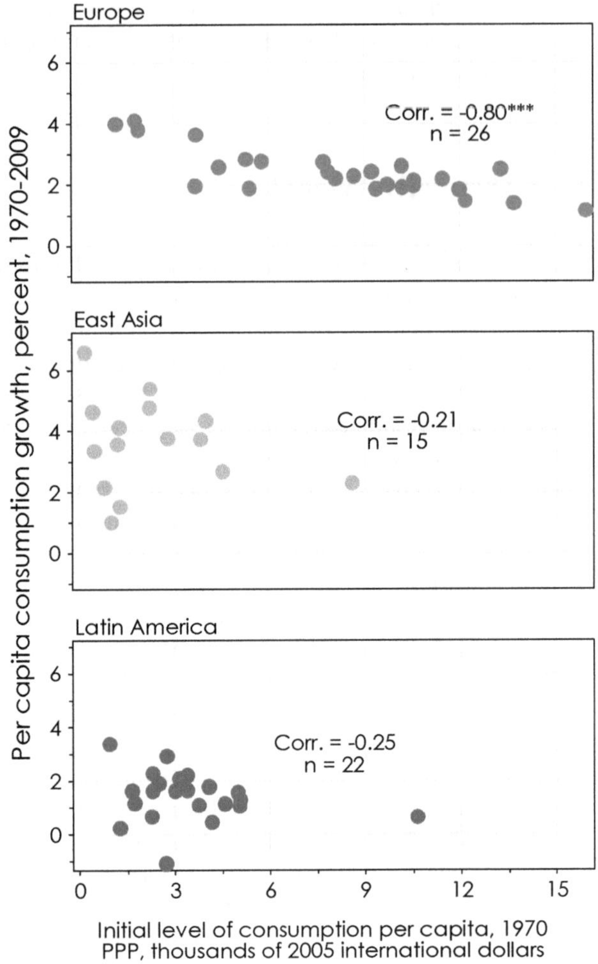

Given Europe's diversity, it is not easy to identify a single "European growth model." There are big differences in how Italy and Ireland regulate work and enterprise, and how Greece and Germany balance fiscal policies and social objectives. There are big differences in what Spain and Sweden export, and how they regulate commerce. There are differences in how Portugal and Poland have regulated their banks, and not just because one of them shares a common currency while the other has one of its own. And there are differences in how Finland and France provide government services such as education and health.

But these differences in specifics do not rule out the existence of common approach to economic growth and social progress. This approach consists of policies and institutions that govern trade and finance, enterprise and innovation, and work and government that have common elements. Together, these elements define an economic and social model distinctly European.

These elements have been associated with Europe's biggest successes since World War II: unprecedented regional integration, global economic power, and the attainment of the highest quality of life in human history.

- ***Trade, finance, and unprecedented regional integration***: Europe's rich and poorer economies are more integrated through trade in goods and services than in any other part of the world, resulting in quicker convergence in incomes and living standards. Private capital in all its forms—foreign direct investment (FDI), financial FDI, and portfolio funds—has flowed from richer to poorer countries, and from low- to high-growth economies. Trade and finance—facilitated by the single market instituted by the European Union and its forebears—have fueled convergence in incomes and living standards.
- ***Enterprise, innovation, and global economic influence***: Private enterprises are held accountable for profits by shareholders, but are also more socially and environmentally responsible than companies in most other parts of the world. Research and development and tertiary education, recognized around the globe for their economic spillovers, are seen as a responsibility not just of firms but also the state. Enterprise and innovation—aided by deep and comprehensive regional economic integration—enable Europe to account for about a third of world gross domestic product (GDP) with less than one-tenth of its population.
- ***Labor, government, and high living standards***: Workers in Europe are accorded strong protection against abuse by employers, and have unprecedented income security after job loss and in old age. European governments are the most decentralized and representative of local interests and Europe has developed the most effective institutions for regional coordination in human history. Europe's model of labor and government—facilitated by the growing consensus for continental cohesion and made affordable by its economic heft—has made the European lifestyle admired and envied around the world.

What has Europe accomplished that other parts of the world could not? Which aspects of the model are no longer sustainable, either because of unanticipated changes in Europe and elsewhere or because some European countries have transformed themselves too fast? Which changes are needed now, and which can wait? These are the questions that this paper asks.

The short answers: Europe has achieved remarkable economic growth and convergence that is unprecedented (Table 1). Most countries in Europe are doing well in trade and finance, many are doing well in enterprise and innovation, but far fewer are doing well in labor and government. So Europe needs many changes to make its governments and labor markets work better, somewhat fewer to foster innovation and productivity growth in enterprises, and fewer still to reform finance and trade. Stalled productivity, declining populations, and growing fiscal imbalances have made some of these changes urgent. These deficiencies are rooted in how some activities have been organized—and they will need to be reorganized.

But in addressing these shortcomings, Europeans should not forget the singular successes of their growth model. By fostering a regional economic integration

Table 1 Relentless growth in the United States, revival in Asia, and a postwar miracle in Europe (average annual compound growth rates, 1820–2008, US$ 1990 Geary–Khamis PPP estimates)

Year	Western Europe	Southern Europe	Eastern Europe	Former Soviet Union	United States	Japan	East Asia	Latin America
1820–1870	1.0	0.6	0.6	0.6	1.3	0.2	−0.1	0.0
1870–1913	1.3	1.0	1.4	1.0	1.8	1.4	0.8	1.8
1913–1950	0.8	0.4	0.6	1.7	1.6	0.9	−0.2	1.4
1950–1973	3.8	4.5	3.6	3.2	2.3	7.7	2.3	2.5
1973–1994	1.7	1.9	−0.2	−1.6	1.7	2.5	0.3	0.9
1994–2008	1.6	2.7	4.0	4.2	1.7	1.0	3.9	1.6

Note: Regional aggregates are population weighted. See Spotlight One for details
Source: Maddison (1996) and Groningen Growth and Development Centre and The Conference Board (2011) *Total Economy Database*

unique in both depth and scope, Europe has become a "convergence machine"—taking in poorer countries and helping turn them into high-income economies. By engineering entrepreneurial dynamism in the countries that balanced market forces and social responsibility, it has made the European brand recognized around the world. And by allowing a balance between life and work, it made Europe the world's "lifestyle superpower". To continue the progress of the last five decades, Europeans now have to do three progressively tougher tasks: restart the convergence machine, rebuild its global brand, and recalibrate the balance between work and leisure to make their lifestyles affordable.

3 The Convergence Machine

An increasingly vigorous flow of goods, services, and finance over the last five decades has fueled European growth. Europe's economies are the most open in the world. Before the global crisis of 2008–2009, half of the world's approximately $15 trillion trade in goods and services involved Europe (Fig. 2). Two-thirds of it was among the 45 countries discussed in this report. Financial flows have been equally vigorous. In 2007, for example, annual FDI in Europe exceeded $1 trillion. Big and growing trade and financial links facilitated by the single market form the core of the European convergence machine.

3.1 Increasingly Sophisticated Trade

During the last two decades, the new member states of the European Union have done especially well at taking advantage of the opportunities offered to them, integrating westward by trading goods and modern business services. During the last

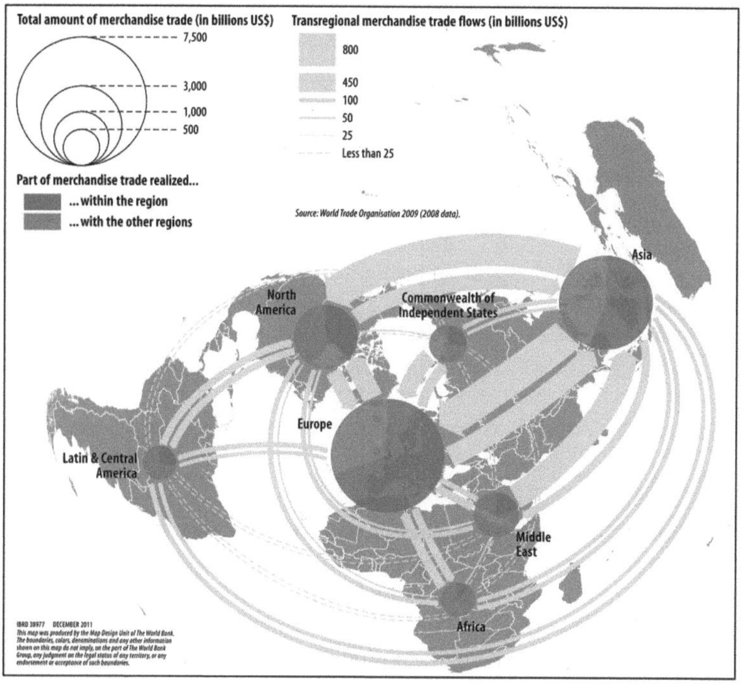

Fig. 2 Almost half of the global goods trade involves Europe (merchandise trade in 2008, US$ billion). *Source*: World Bank staff, based on WTO (2009)

decade, the candidate countries of Southeastern Europe have been doing it through trade in merchandise and more traditional services such as travel and transport. This has helped enterprises in Western Europe too. With FDI and offshoring, enterprises in Western Europe such as Fiat, Renault, and Volkswagen have made themselves and eastern enterprises like Yugo, Dacia, and Škoda more efficient and sophisticated. Simpler tasks are being given to countries outside Europe; advanced Europe is getting emerging Europe to do more difficult things, and both regions are benefiting. Countries in the European Union's eastern partnership such as Georgia and Ukraine have also gained.

The goods trade between advanced and emerging Europe has grown rapidly since the mid-1990s—when the European Union signed its first association agreements with Hungary and Poland—and this does not appear to be injuring trade with other parts of the world. Europe does a brisk goods trade with North America, Asia, the former Soviet Union, and Africa (see Fig. 2). But trade within the region has grown much more sophisticated over the last decade, aiding quick convergence in productive capacity and living standards. It is helping to create a bigger and stronger economic union between the European Free Trade Association (EFTA), the EU15, the new member states, the EU candidate countries, and even the eastern partnership economies.

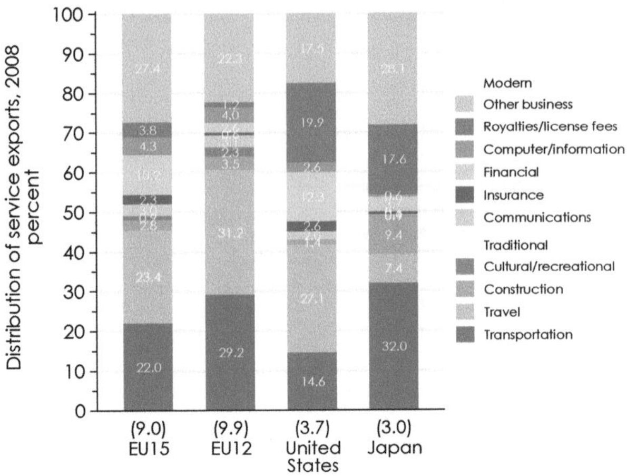

Fig. 3 More trade in services in Europe, but apparently in more traditional services (service exports in the European Union, United States and Japan, 2008). *Note*: The *numbers in parentheses* refer to the sum of traditional and modern service exports as a percentage of GDP. *Source*: World Bank staff calculations, based on IMF *Balance of Payment Statistics Yearbook*

Factory Europe may not be expanding as fast as Factory Asia, but it has become smarter. With economic recovery and better trade facilities—especially information and communications infrastructure in the European Union's new member states and the candidate countries—regional goods trade could double over the next decade.

The trade in modern—especially digital—services in Europe is increasing too, but not fast enough for many Europeans. The benchmark for merchandise trade is East Asia, a developing region, but the European Union gauges the single market for services against the United States, a developed country. Trading services is not easy: it often requires movement of people across borders, ease in establishing a local presence, and harmonious home–host regulations. Given all this, Europe's trade in services does not seem stunted (Fig. 3). But progress is mixed: travel and financial services have done well but transport and other business services—especially those involving new technologies and the Internet—have not. With reforms that make adopting newer technologies easier, better regulations, and greater mobility of workers, Europe's trade in services could triple in size over the next decade. More important, though, productivity in the general services sector—which is about 70 % of the activity in Europe—would increase.

The opportunity that Europe might really be missing involves regional trade in agriculture. The European Union pays for its agricultural trade policies not just with the roughly €50 billion a year the European Commission spends on agriculture and rural development and their large indirect efficiency costs, but also through missed opportunities for closer economic integration with eastern partnership countries. In Georgia and Ukraine, a third of all workers still depend on agriculture for a living. Allowing better access to European farm markets would aid their development, win friends, and influence policies in the countries of the eastern partnership.

Despite these weaknesses, the overall assessment of European trade is positive. In 2009, Europe's merchandise trade was worth about $4.5 trillion, more than East Asia's and North America's combined. Its trade in services was worth $2.25 trillion,

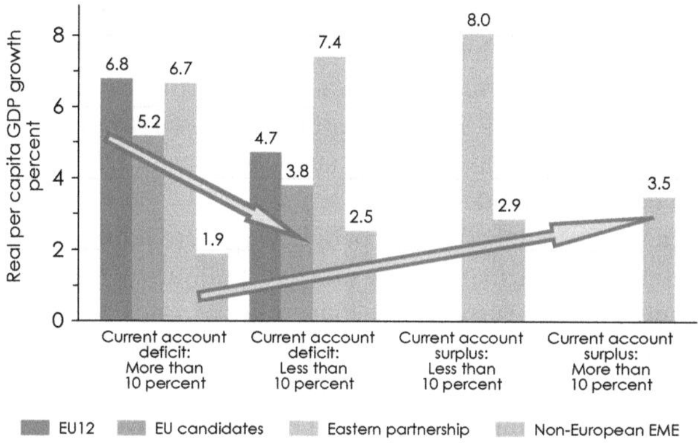

Fig. 4 In Europe, foreign capital has boosted growth in emerging economies (current account deficits and per capita growth, by groups of countries). *Note*: Average growth rates calculated using three 4-year periods in 1997–2008. *Source*: World Bank staff calculations based on IMF *World Economic Outlook*

more than the rest of the world combined. Trade is the mainstay of the European economic model, and its most attractive attribute.

3.2 *Finance That Flows Downhill*

Financial integration is the second part of the convergence machine. Finance has served Europe well. This may come as a surprise to those who blame the current crisis in the Eurozone on banks that lent money to spendthrift governments. But European finance has a desirable attribute: capital of all types flows from richer to poorer countries, from low- to high-growth countries. In the rest of the world, larger capital inflows are more likely to mean slower growth. Financial FDI—big investments by Austrian, French, Italian, and Swedish banks in Central and Eastern Europe—is a unique feature of Europe. In the east, it has helped.

Figure 4 shows the relationship between economic growth and current account deficits in the new member states of the European Union, its candidates, the eastern partnership countries, and other emerging economies. An upward sloping line means that countries that run smaller deficits or larger external account surpluses grow faster. In other words, a country grows faster if it lends rather than borrows abroad. And for emerging economies outside Europe, this is indeed what we see: capital flows from poorer, high-growth countries to richer, low-growth countries (upward-sloping arrow). Call this the "China syndrome."

In Europe, capital behaves the way it should: it flows from richer to poorer economies, and countries receiving more capital grow faster. The laws of economics have held in Europe. They hold more firmly the more institutionally integrated the economies have become with Western Europe—by membership in the European

Union or by signaling the intention to join. Belarus and Ukraine, for example, have done neither, and they look a lot like emerging market economies outside Europe, growing faster when they have external account surpluses (capital outflows) or smaller current account deficits. A big part of these capital flows in eastern Europe is the sizeable FDI by foreign banks, making such “financial FDI” a distinctive feature of the European economic model.

In 2008, when the financial crisis hit, people who were familiar with earlier crises in Asia and Latin America expected a massive pullout by western banks. It did not happen: foreign banks stayed, and loan rollover rates were close to 100 %, much higher than in previous crises. Of course, during the preceding boom some governments, enterprises, banks, and households abused the opportunities provided by this model of financial integration, but the benefits have been greater than the excesses. And today, as western banks face pressures to offset losses in southern Europe, they may have to sell their profitable businesses in Eastern Europe. But the needed reforms will stay the same: better management of public finance during booms in both advanced and emerging Europe, and more adept regulatory structures to crisis-proof private finance. With these improvements, finance will be an even more beneficial feature of the European economic model. To grow at high and steady rates, economies in emerging Europe have not had to “become Asian.” Nor should they have to now.

3.3 Restarting the Convergence Machine

In the early 2000s, an important debate took place. For two decades, economists had been puzzled by the finding that a country was able to invest only as much as what it could itself save. In theory, capital flows should allow savers in wealthier, or low-growth, countries to finance investment in poorer, or high-growth, economies. They would get a higher return on their money, and these financial flows would allow the people in developing nations to save less and consume more, and invest more and grow faster. Unfortunately, it did not seem to happen; instead, there was a strong correlation between saving and investment across countries (Feldstein and Horioka 1980). But in the European Union between 1992 and 2001, especially the Eurozone, research was showing that something had changed. Greece and Portugal had run large current account deficits financed by foreign capital inflows; their savings had fallen, investment had increased, and their economies had grown (Blanchard and Giavazzi 2002). The question was whether policymakers—national governments, the European Union, and the European Central Bank—should welcome these growing imbalances, or worry about them.

With the benefit of hindsight the answer is, of course, both. The capital inflows were the result of trade and financial integration, and they were supposed to make Greece and Portugal more productive and richer economies. And until about 2001, they did. But from 2002 to 2008, labor productivity in these countries actually fell. In others, after a while, the sheer volume of flows meant that some inflows replaced domestic saving, but did not fund productive investment. Obviously, the borrowed money had not been used well. It had flowed in on the belief that Greek and Portuguese debts would be serviced or repaid. By 2009, it was clear that this was going to be difficult.

In the new member states, the same story was being played out, but with many more happy endings than sad. In countries such as the Czech Republic and Poland, foreign savings flowed into productive uses, and both Western European savers and Eastern European investors benefited. In some others, ever larger flows began to finance consumption, sometimes by the government but more often by households. In these countries, economic growth went into reverse during the global financial crisis.

Restarting the convergence machine will not be difficult. The single market for services is becoming more efficient, and national governments can accelerate the process by fully implementing the European Union's Services Directive. For many services, measures to increase mobility of labor among countries will help greatly. Countries in Central and Eastern Europe will have to continue easing the bottlenecks in transport and communication infrastructure and modern services, so that trade in manufactures can facilitate the production networks that have been growing in size and sophistication, especially in the European Union's new member states and candidate countries. The European Union can also help millions of people in the eastern partnership countries—whose combined GDP is less than $0.5 trillion—by giving better access to its $1 trillion market for food and other farm products.

A lot of this is happening. It is the finance, the fuel for the machine, which needs more attention. Europe's convergence machine needs a better regulator of financial flows. Finance flows in the right direction in Europe—proof positive of the soundness of the system. But the flows are erratic, flooding Europe's less advanced economies when finance is plentiful, and starving them of finance when savers and investors in advanced countries become skittish. Financial flows could be made steadier through a combination of conservative fiscal policies and prudential regulations, so that they do not suddenly stop when growth slows. Canada, Czech Republic, Croatia, and Poland showed what can be done during good times, and Sweden and South Korea have shown ways to quickly get firms and households out from under a debt overhang when boom-time finance fuel excesses and cause busts (Iwulska 2011).

4 "Europe": A Global Brand

As convergence has slowed and even gone into reverse in parts of Europe, the entire region is getting a bad press. Europe's best days are behind it, it is now said. High unemployment among young people, stagnant worker productivity, unsustainable public finances, and archaic social protection and innovation systems that are unsuited for a globalized economy are all presented as symptoms of economic decay. But the heart of an economy is neither labor nor government—it is enterprise. Since the mid-1990s, during a period when Asia had a huge financial crisis and

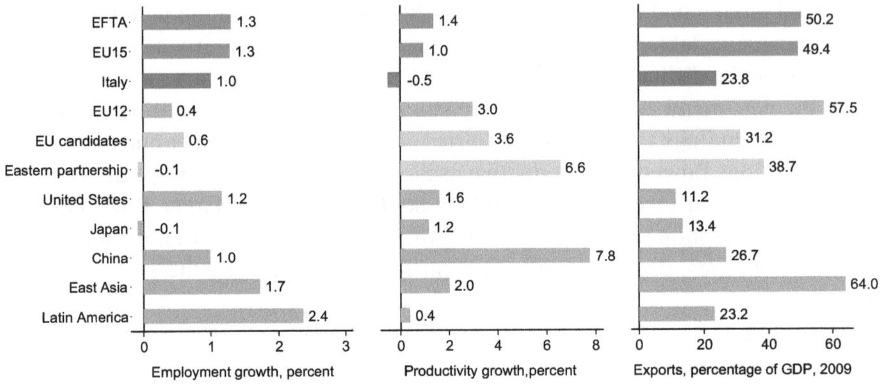

Fig. 5 European enterprises have delivered jobs, productivity, and exports (performance of European sub-regions and benchmark countries, 1995–2009). *Note*: Growth rates in employment and productivity are compound annual growth rates. Average values by group are shown. China and Japan are also included in the calculation of East Asia regional average. *Source*: World Bank staff calculations, based on World Bank (2011) and ILO (2011)

bigger recovery, and the United States had a spectacular technology boom and a massive financial crisis, European enterprise has quietly flourished.

This is no mean achievement, because Europe expects much from its enterprises. Their shareholders expect them to add value and turn a profit, workers expect them to create jobs, and governments want them to bring in export earnings. Remarkably, over the last decade and a half, European enterprises have delivered all three. Between 1995 and 2009, job growth in advanced Europe outstripped that in the United States. The new member states of the European Union and the candidate countries engineered productivity increases that outstripped those in East Asia and Latin America. Exports of goods and services in advanced and emerging Europe rose faster than output, and exceeded the growth rates even of the heralded BRIC economies (Fig. 5). German and Swedish manufactures, produce from France and the Netherlands, and U.K. and Italian banks have global reach and reputation. Czech engineering, Estonian information technology, and Turkish construction companies are quickly acquiring them. These are not the signs of a region in decay.

With Asian enterprises becoming more active globally, the next few decades might well require European enterprises to make changes in how and where they do business. For now, the numbers show that in aggregate, European enterprise has been a reliable component of the economic model.

4.1 Southern Enterprise Falters

But not all is well. Employment growth in the EU12 could have been quicker, productivity growth in the EU15 should have been faster, and EU candidate and

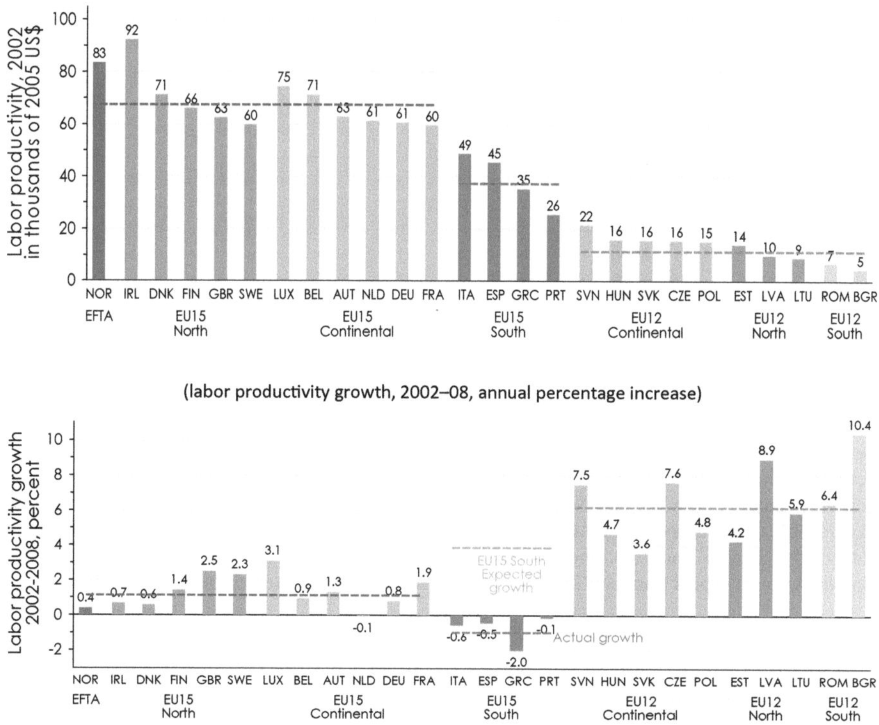

Fig. 6 Much of Europe is becoming more productive, but the south has fallen behind (productivity levels in 2002, thousands of 2005 dollars). *Note*: For Belgium, Greece, and Norway, productivity levels refer to 2003 (*top panel*). In the *bottom panel*, the period considered varies: Belgium and Norway (2003–2008), Greece (2003–2007), and Czech Republic, France, Latvia, Romania, and the United Kingdom (2002–2007). The *three lines* in each panel show average values for countries covered by each line. Expected growth for EU15 South is obtained by computing gaps in productivity levels between EU15 South and each of the other two groups and then applying these shares to the difference in growth between the first (that is, EFTA, EU15 North, and EU15 Continental) and the third (EU12) groups. *Source*: World Bank staff calculations, based on Eurostat structural business statistics

eastern partnership countries should raise exports to levels seen in the rest of Europe (see top six bars in Fig. 5). Perhaps most worrisome are the productivity patterns since 2002, which show that parts of Europe have been faltering (Fig. 6). Northern countries such as Finland, Sweden, and the United Kingdom—and later the Baltic economies—have done well, and continental economies such as Austria, France, Luxembourg, and Germany—and later the Czech Republic, Poland, and others—have been doing well too. But Southern Europe—Greece, Italy, Portugal, and Spain—have not done well. From 2002 to 2008, they created jobs, but mainly in cyclical activities like construction or in less productive enterprises (like micro and family firms). And the productivity of their workers has been falling.

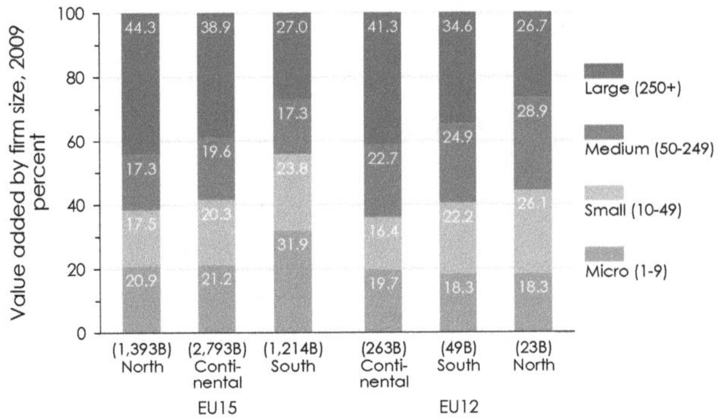

Fig. 7 Smaller firms contribute half of value added in the EU15 South, but just a third elsewhere (contributions to value added by size of enterprises, 2009). *Note*: The *numbers in parentheses* are the total value added expressed in billions of constant 2005 U.S. dollars. The EU15 comprises Denmark, Finland, Ireland, Sweden, and the United Kingdom (*North*); Austria, Belgium, France, Germany, Luxembourg and the Netherlands (*Continental*); and Greece, Italy, Portugal, and Spain (*South*). EU12 comprises Estonia, Latvia, and Lithuania (*North*); Czech Republic, Hungary, Poland, the Slovak Republic, and Slovenia (*Continental*); and Bulgaria, Cyprus, and Romania (*South*). *Source*: World Bank staff calculations, based on Eurostat structural business statistics

A premature adoption of the euro by southern economies is sometimes blamed for this reversal of fortune. Others say that letting the formerly communist countries into the European Union so soon did not give the south enough time to become competitive. But perhaps the most likely explanation is that of all the economies in Europe, the entrepreneurial structures of Greece, Italy, Portugal, and Spain were least suited for the wider European economy. For one thing, a sizable chunk of net output in southern economies was generated in small enterprises—almost a third of it in tiny enterprises (with fewer than ten workers; Fig. 7). This is not an entrepreneurial profile suited for a big market. Unsurprisingly, with the expansion of the single market in the 2000s, foreign capital from the richer economies of Continental Europe quickly changed direction, going east instead of south as it had done in the 1990s (Fig. 8).

Did the south need more time to adjust, or did it squander opportunities? The latter seems more plausible. Ireland has shown that EU institutions and resources can be translated quickly into competitiveness. The Baltic economies are now doing the same. The chief culprits for the south's poor performance were high taxes and too many regulations, often poorly administered. While these mattered less when its eastern neighbors, China, and India suffered the least business-friendly systems in the world, they are now crippling southern enterprise (Fig. 9).

But there are reasons to be optimistic. The sovereign debt crisis has led to a resumption of regulatory reform in these countries, and the experience of countries such as Latvia and Lithuania shows that the necessary improvements can be done over years, not decades. And they need to be done quickly. From 2003 to 2006, Europeans who felt that globalization was an opportunity for their enterprises fell

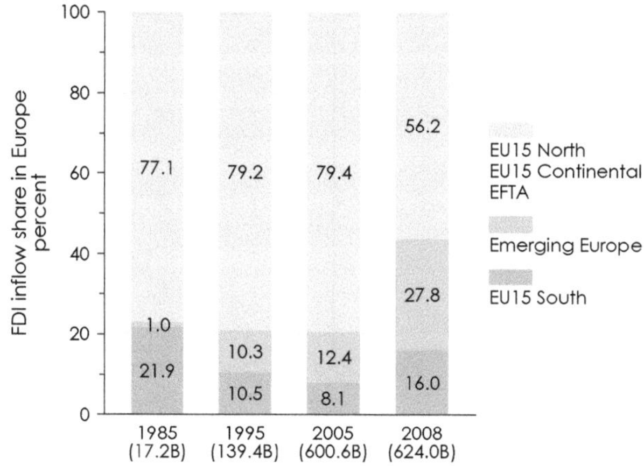

Fig. 8 Western European investors have been looking east, not south (foreign direct investment inflows in Europe, 1985, 1995, 2005 and 2008). *Note*: The *numbers in parenthesis* are the amount of inflows expressed in billions of US dollars. *Source*: World Bank staff calculations based on UNCTAD (2010)

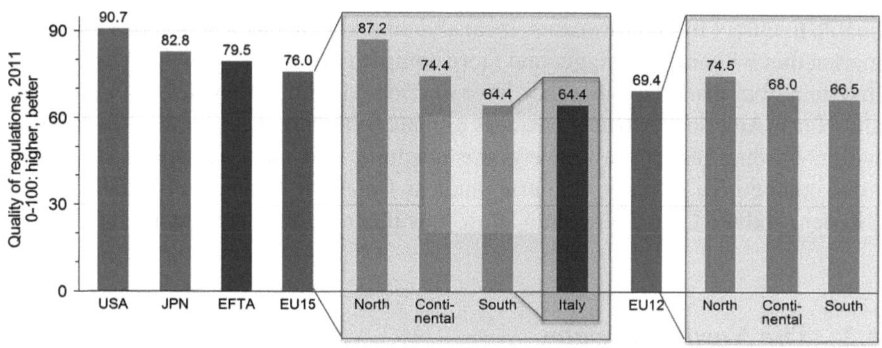

Fig. 9 Southern Europe must make it easier to do business (principal components index of the ease of doing business in 2011, scaled from 0 [poor] to 100 [excellent]). *Note*: Averages computed using principal component analysis. EFTA here comprises Iceland, Norway, and Switzerland. The EU15 comprises Denmark, Finland, Ireland, Sweden, and the United Kingdom (*North*); Austria, Belgium, France, Germany, Luxembourg, and the Netherlands (*Continental*); and Greece, Italy, Portugal, and Spain (*South*). EU12 comprises Estonia, Latvia, and Lithuania (*North*); Czech Republic, Hungary, Poland, the Slovak Republic, and Slovenia (*Continental*); and Bulgaria, Cyprus, and Romania (*South*). *Source*: World Bank staff calculations, based on *Doing Business* 2012

from 56 to 37 %. By 2006, the share of people who felt it was a threat to European enterprises and employment was almost half. The Danes, Swedes, Dutch, and Estonians were the most positively disposed to globalization; the French, Greeks, Belgians, and Cypriots the least (Eurobarometer 2006). Figure 9 helps show why.

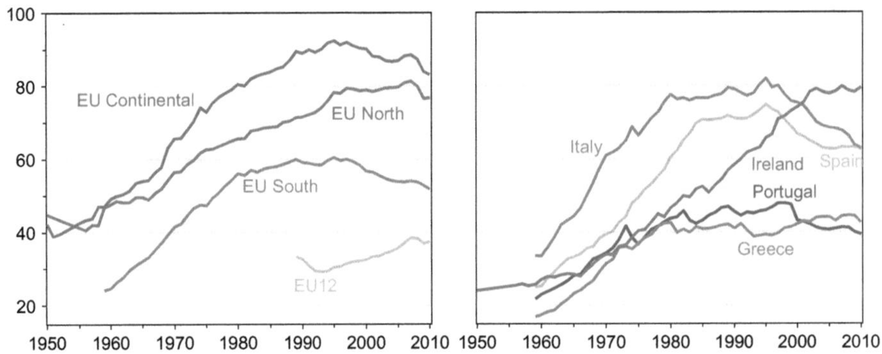

Fig. 10 Productivity growth in Europe's leading economies has slowed down since the mid-1990s (EU15 labor productivity, indexed to the United States and Japan). *Source*: World Bank staff calculations, based on the Organisation for Economic Co-operation and Development

Europe will get even more from its enterprises if it made doing business easier. Southern Europe has to do this now, Central and Eastern Europe will have to do it soon. Otherwise, enterprises will remain small and unproductive—increasingly unable to attract foreign investors, incapable of taking advantage of a pan-European market that will only get bigger and more competitive, and progressively uncompetitive in global markets where they have to contend with enterprises from East Asia and North America. A better business climate will stem the growth of imbalances within Europe, restart the convergence machine, and make European enterprises more competitive globally. Countries such as Denmark, Germany, Finland, Ireland, Sweden, and the United Kingdom show how it can be done (Iwulska 2011).

4.2 The North Innovates

But making it easier to do business will not be enough on its own. When productivity gaps were growing within Europe, the gap between the advanced economies of Europe and the United States started to widen after almost disappearing in the mid-1990s. Indeed, the 2000s were a decade of declining productivity in the EU15 relative to both the United States and Japan, the world's next two largest economies after the European Union during that time (Fig. 10). Between 1995 and 2009, labor productivity in the United States grew at 1.6 % annually, in Japan at 1.2 %, and in the EU15 at just 1 % (see Fig. 5).

Reassuringly, productivity in northern Europe grew at 1.7 % per year during the same period. What has the north done to encourage enterprise and innovation? Much of its success has come from creating a good climate for doing business. All the northern economies are in the top 15 countries of 183 in the World Bank's *Doing Business* rankings; at 14, Sweden is the lowest ranked among them. All the countries have given their enterprises considerable economic freedom. Their governments are doing more. They have speeded up innovation by helping them download the "killer applications" that have made the United States the global leader in technology: better incentives for enterprise-sponsored research and development (R&D), public funding mechanisms and intellectual property regimes to foster profitable relations between universities and firms, and a steady supply of workers with tertiary education. Tellingly, Europe's innovation leaders perform especially well in areas where Europe as a whole lags the United States the most. These features make them global leaders; combining them with generous government spending on R&D and public education systems makes their innovation systems distinctively European.

For Europe's larger continental economies that have reached or exceeded U.S. standards in physical, financial, and human capital, R&D and other innovation deficits are likely to be growth inhibitors. In dynamic Eastern Europe, countries need not invest much more in R&D and the production of knowledge. But they must still innovate through osmosis: they have considerable scope for the quick adoption of existing technologies, using FDI and trade links as conduits. The south is becoming slower in importing new technologies: FDI inflows and outflows have been falling since the economies in emerging Europe integrated with Continental and Northern Europe. For these increasingly service-oriented economies, reform of domestic regulations—not more R&D spending—may be the best way to speed up innovation.

What has been more perplexing is Europe's generally poor performance in the most technology-intensive sectors—the Internet, biotechnology, computer software, health care equipment, and semiconductors. Put another way, the United States, the Republic of Korea, and Taiwan, China, have been doing well in sectors that are huge now but barely existed in 1975. Europe has been doing better in the more established sectors, especially industrial machinery, electrical equipment, telecommunications, aerospace, automobiles, and personal goods. The United States has Amazon, Amgen, Apple, Google, Intel, and Microsoft; Europe has Airbus, Mercedes, Nokia, and Volkswagen.

Europe's young leading innovators (called "Yollies" for short) are as R&D intensive as those in the United States. Europe just has a lot fewer Yollies. As a result, while more than a third of U.S. R&D spending is by Yollies, it is less than one-fifteenth in Europe. The United States focuses its R&D efforts on innovation-based growth sectors (Fig. 11). Europe specializes in sectors with medium R&D intensity. Japan is showing other East Asian countries how productivity growth can be maintained in established industries such as automobiles and electronics, and Germany may be doing the same. But for the European economy as a whole, with its size and diversity, productivity growth will likely come from doing what Japan is has done and emulating the American innovation system. To do either, the common market will have to become more of a single economy.

All European countries should have the friendly business climate that Denmark, Ireland, and Norway have. It is not a coincidence that the only large European economies that rival the United States and Japan in innovation are Germany and

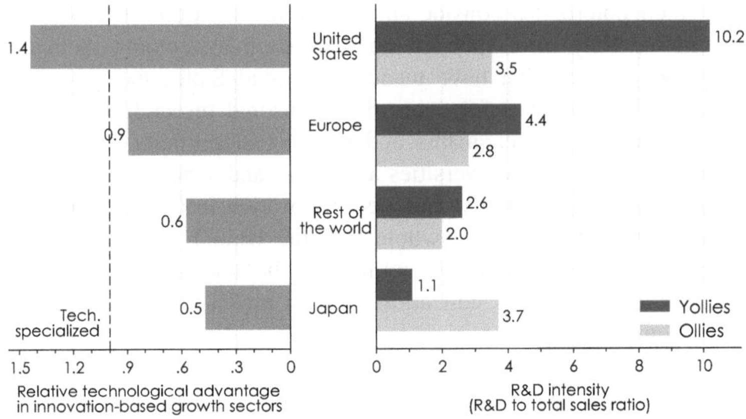

Fig. 11 The United States specializes in younger, more R&D intensive products (relative technological advantage and R&D efforts by young and old innovation leaders in the United States, Europe and the rest of the world). *Note*: R&D intensity is measured as the ratio of R&D spending to total sales, for firms established after 1975 (young leading innovators or "Yollies") or before 1975 ("Ollies"). The relative technological advantage is calculated as the share of each region or country (say Europe) in the R&D of a particular sector (say the Internet) relative to the share of Europe in world R&D; values greater than one indicate the region is technology specialized in the sector. *Source*: Bruegel and World Bank staff calculations based on IPTS R&D Scoreboard

the United Kingdom, which were both ranked in the top 20 countries for ease of doing business in 2011. Many more European countries should have the universities that the United States and Japan have where the share of people ages 30–34 who have completed college is about 55 %: today, only Ireland, Denmark, Norway, Luxembourg, and Finland exceed 45 %. More countries will have to improve their business–science links to rival those in the United States and Japan; currently, only Switzerland and Scandinavia do as well.

4.3 Burnishing the Brand

Perhaps the simplest way to assess how innovative a country is to see how much more productive its enterprises are becoming every year—that is, how much better they are in buying, producing, and selling. During the last decade, two things have happened that should worry Europe's entrepreneurs and policymakers. The first is that since the mid-1990s, labor productivity in Europe's advanced economies has been falling relative to the United States (and Japan). The second is that productivity in Southern Europe has been falling compared both to the advanced countries in Western Europe and the less well-off countries in emerging Europe. How can these gaps be closed?

It depends on the gap. For reducing that between the south and the north, the most important steps involve improving the business climate. Countries in the EU12 South—notably Bulgaria—and Georgia have been showing that this can be done even in poorer parts of Europe. For closing the transatlantic productivity gap, even more is necessary. Leading European economies such as Switzerland, Sweden, Finland, Denmark, and Germany are showing the way. Following their example would mean giving up the fixation on public R&D spending targets, and focusing instead on improving competition among enterprises, increasing private funding of universities, changing the way research funding is provided so that it strengthens business-university linkages, and making the common market work for services.

There are reasons to be optimistic. During the last two decades, countries in EFTA—Iceland, Norway, and Switzerland principally—have actually done better than the United States. Northern parts of the EU15—especially Denmark, Finland, Ireland, and Sweden—have also been doing well. The trouble is that their economies add up to less than $1.5 trillion in purchasing power terms, roughly the GDP of Spain or Texas and just a tenth of the European Union's economy. If the rest of Europe could take fuller advantage of these countries' dynamism—by learning from them or leaning on them—Europe's innovation goals might quickly be reached.

Chapters "Institutional Creativity for Happy High-Income Societies: Can Basic Income-Based Reforms Help to Build Them?" and "Crisis in the Eurozone: Some Popular Fallacies and a Few Unpleasant Remarks" make it clear that building a global brand is more difficult than just restarting convergence. To stay competitive on world markets, Europe will have to make trade even more vigorous and finance more durable so that the region eventually becomes a single economy. To help redress the continent's growing productivity gaps, governments in Southern Europe have to quickly improve the climate for doing business. The more dynamic countries in Eastern Europe will have to do all this and invest in infrastructure. To close the growing transatlantic productivity divide, continental countries must give their enterprises more economic freedom. Enterprises in the northern and EFTA economies—already among the world's most innovative—will need fuller access to markets in the rest of Europe. Europe will have to become the top destination for those seeking higher education and an opportunity to become entrepreneurs. Only then can European enterprises be globally competitive, and Europe the place of choice of entrepreneurs from around the world.

5 The Lifestyle Superpower

In 2008, Europe was already the place of choice for tourists: of the busiest 20 international tourist destinations, more than half were in Europe. The United States had the might and China the momentum, but Europeans had the highest standard of living. Millions of people from around the world visited Europe to see and

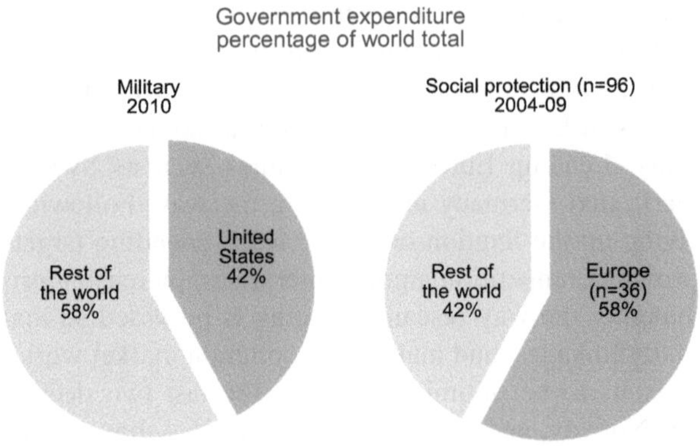

Fig. 12 Outspending the rest of the world (general government spending on defense [United States] and social protection [Europe], 2004–2009, share of total world spending). *Notes*: For social protection spending, due to the data availability, averages over 2004–2009 by country are used. *n* is the number of countries included in the calculations. Data cover general government but, if unavailable, refer to central government only. *Sources*: World Bank staff calculations, based on Stockholm International Peace Research Institute (2011), IMF *Government Finance Statistics*, World Bank *World Development Indicators*, and Weigand and Grosh (2008)

experience it first hand. With average incomes still a quarter short of those in the United States, Europe had become the "lifestyle superpower" that Prime Minister Kiichi Miyazawa of Japan had promised to make his country in the 1990s.

Superpowers tend to spend a lot to protect their interests and project influence. To remain the political superpower, the United States spends almost as much on defense as the next 15 countries do together. To keep its status as the lifestyle superpower, Europe spends more on social protection than the rest of the world combined (Fig. 12).

5.1 The Decline of Work

The hallmark of the European economic model is perhaps the balance between work and life. With prosperity, Americans buy more goods and services, Europeans more leisure. In the 1950s, Western Europeans worked the equivalent of almost a month more than Americans. By the 1970s, they worked about the same amount. Today, Americans work a month a year more than Dutch, French, Germans, and Swedes, and work notably longer than the less well-off Greeks, Hungarians, Poles, and Spaniards.

Europeans have also cut the years they work during their (ever-lengthening) lives. Today, men in France, Hungary, Poland, and Turkey effectively retire more than 8 years earlier than in the mid-1960s. The average European can also expect to live 4 years longer. By 2007, Frenchmen expected to draw pensions for 15 more years

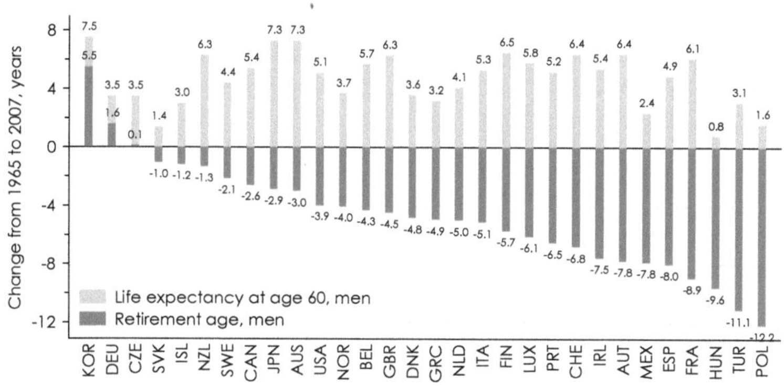

Fig. 13 Europe's pension systems have to support people for many more years (changes in life expectancy at 60 and effective retirement age, 1965–2007). *Source*: OECD Health Data

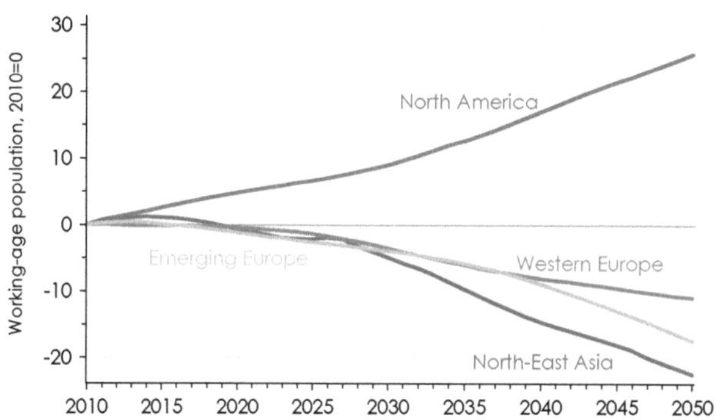

Fig. 14 Europe's labor force will shrink, while North America's will grow by a quarter (projected change in working-age population, percent, 2010–2050). *Source*: United Nations population projections

than in 1965, and Austrian, Polish, Spanish, Swiss, and Turkish men more than a dozen. In Organisation for Economic Co-operation and Development countries, only Korean, German, and Czech men work more years today than they did 50 years ago (Fig. 13).

American, Australian, and Canadian men also retire about 4 years sooner than they used to. But their countries have more favorable demographics than the typical European country (Fig. 14). On current immigration and work participation trends, the 45 countries covered by this report will lose about 50 million workers over the next five decades, and have a workforce of about 275 million by 2060. In the 2030s alone, the labor force will fall by 15 million people. The decline will be most severe for the EU (countries such as France which have high fertility rates today do better), but candidate and neighborhood countries will also lose workers. The exception is Turkey, where the labor force is projected to increase until 2060.

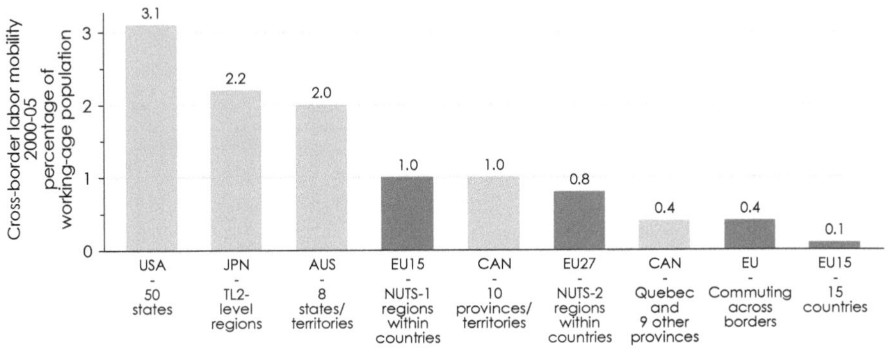

Fig. 15 Europeans are less mobile, even within their own countries (labor mobility, share of working age population that has moved, 2000–2005). *Source*: US Census Current Population Survey, Eurostat, Statistics Canada, and OECD (2005)

Only with radical changes can Europe counteract the shrinking of its labor force. If participation rates in all countries were to converge with those seen in Northern Europe, or if the retirement age were to increase by 10 years across the board, the European labor force would increase marginally over the next 50 years. If female labor force participation converged with men's, the labor force would still decrease by 5 %. But none of these changes would completely offset the loss of young workers. For that, Europe will need to integrate Turks into the European labor market and attract talented young workers from around the world. In one plausible scenario, Turkey could contribute 40 % of the gains in the European labor force, and almost all of the increase in young workers.

Fixing the European labor market will require a lot: increasing the competition for jobs, improving labor mobility within Europe, fixing how work and welfare interact, and rethinking immigration policies. These changes will not happen without a new social consensus, which has yet to be built.

Perhaps the best way to start is to accelerate internal labor mobility in Europe, especially in the European Union. Mobility in the European Union is the lowest in the developed world (Fig. 15), for three reasons that policy makers can influence: wages rarely signal labor shortages and surpluses quickly, housing markets do not function well, and a Europe-wide social safety net is lacking. To create a single market for labor in Europe, there will have to be changes in how wages are set and how national safety nets are stitched together to cushion the shocks that come with mobility and migration. To make the single market work better, making labor more mobile should be a priority for all Europe's countries. For the countries that share the common currency, it is a prerequisite (Box 1).

Then, Europe has to make changes in how work is regulated and social security provided. Many countries in Western Europe had started to reverse the decline in work participation during the late 1990s and early 2000s; many in Central, Eastern, and Southern Europe now must do the same. The main attribute of the European economic model that needs to be reassessed is employment protection legislation, which is lowering participation and reducing employment in many countries. In countries such as Spain, it may be responsible for youth unemployment rates as high as 40 %. Paradoxically, Europe has impending shortages of young workers and high joblessness among its youth.

Denmark and Germany have shown how this can be remedied (Iwulska 2011). Other countries like Croatia, Moldova, Poland, Romania, and Turkey may have to learn quickly and carefully implement the lessons. The countries in emerging Europe will also have to decide—based on their cultural and political antecedents—whether to move toward greater job security and join countries such as Belgium and France, or toward greater flexibility and become more like the North Americans and East Asians. To have both as in Denmark, they will have to consider the greater fiscal costs of "flexicurity." At the moment, most countries have neither.

While all this is being done, Europe's policymakers could get people to appreciate the need for a new approach to immigration. Europe needs an immigration policy that is more selfish—driven by economic need instead of purely humanitarian concerns. Today the debate is about how to best manage migration from North Africa. Tomorrow's debate should be about the policies and practices that will make Europe a global magnet for talent. Countries like Sweden and the United Kingdom have been doing this, but not quite as effectively as Canada and the United States (Iwulska 2011).

Box 1: The Unmet Precondition of the Common Currency—Labor Mobility The September 1961 volume of the *American Economic Review* might well be the most influential issue of an economic journal ever. A dozen or so pages after the article on optimum growth paths by Phelps is a short communication from Robert Mundell that outlines a theory of "optimum currency areas." In it are the conditions that the countries in a monetary union had to have—or quickly institute—to share a single currency profitably. In practical terms, it meant ensuring that the single currency should not lead to persistently high unemployment rates in some parts of the monetary union, nor to unacceptably high rates of inflation in others. In 1999, Mundell was awarded the Nobel Prize for "his analysis of monetary and fiscal policy under different exchange rate regimes and his analysis of optimum currency areas."

The conditions for a successful monetary union identified in the 1961 article can be distilled to mobility of labor and capital among the member states. To understand why, imagine a fall in economic activity in one part of the union (say the south) and a rise in another (say the north). This would cause unemployment to rise in the south, and inflationary pressures and balance-of-payments surpluses to increase in the north. If the central

(continued)

Box 1 (continued)

bank increases the money supply, it might help the south but would aggravate inflation in the north. If it does not, high unemployment in the south would cause suffering. But if capital and labor were quick to move within the monetary union, the dilemma would disappear.

For a practical application of his ideas, Mundell chose Western Europe, presaging today's debates about the euro. "In Western Europe the creation of the Common Market is regarded by many as an important step toward eventual political union, and the subject of a common currency ... has been much discussed. One can cite the well-known position of J. E. Meade, who argues that the conditions for a common currency in Western Europe do not exist, and that, especially because of the lack of labor mobility, a system of flexible exchange rates would be more effective in promoting balance-of-payments equilibrium and internal stability; and the apparently opposite view of Tibor Scitovsky who favors a common currency because he believes that it would induce a greater degree of capital mobility, but further adds that steps must be taken to make labor more mobile and to facilitate supranational employment policies."

The introduction of the euro undoubtedly increased capital mobility in the Eurozone; one can reasonably expect a single currency to greatly facilitate financial integration. The single currency undoubtedly also facilitated the exchange of goods. But a single currency cannot by itself increase people's mobility. This requires states to harmonize labor regulations, education and training arrangements, and social security and welfare systems. Growing goods trade in the Eurozone may reduce the need for labor mobility, but trade in services—now three-quarters of Western Europe's output—itself often requires movement of people. So does keeping manageable unemployment differences among countries.

In the decade before the global financial crisis, European economic integration showed impressive progress. But for many countries, the progress was unbalanced (see below figure) —more rapid in financial areas (interest rates and inflation) than in real sectors (trade and incomes). It was more balanced for the eastern partnership countries and the new member states. Poland, for example, became more integrated in financial and real terms. The EU candidate countries (represented here by Croatia and Turkey) experienced just financial integration. But while integrating in monetary and financial aspects, Greece became less integrated within the EU15 in real terms.

(continued)

Box 1 (continued)

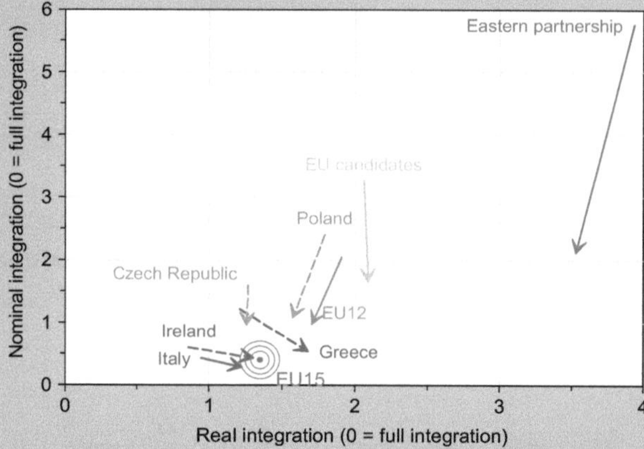

More monetary and financial than real integration in Europe during the last decade (*arrows* begin in 1997 and end in 2008; the origin indicates complete nominal and real integration). *Note*: The figure shows the extent of economic integration, using the theory of optimum currency areas (Mundell 1961). The vertical axis combines in one index of dissimilarity three indicators of nominal integration—volatility of exchange rates, convergence in inflation rates, and convergence in interest rates. The horizontal axis does the same with three indicators of real integration—extent of synchronization in business cycles measured by indexes of industrial production, trade integration, and per capita income. The origin in the figure represents perfect economic integration, and the *arrows* show the integration path of each country or group of countries in 1997–2008. EU candidates are represented by Croatia and Turkey; the eastern partnership countries by Armenia, Azerbaijan, Belarus, Georgia, Moldova, and Ukraine; and the EU's new member states by Bulgaria, the Czech Republic, Estonia, Hungary, Latvia, Lithuania, Poland, Romania, the Slovak Republic, and Slovenia. *Source*: Sugawara and Zalduendo (2010)

Labor mobility in Europe is the lowest in the developed world. Mundell's communication 50 years ago suggests that this will be a serious problem for the Eurozone. Increasing labor mobility may be a privilege in Europe, but it is a prerequisite in the Eurozone. Countries that integrate their labor markets will be able to share a single currency profitably. Others will have to deal with stressful tradeoffs between inflation and unemployment.

Source: Mundell (1961) and Sugawara and Zalduendo (2010).

5.2 *The Precipitate Promise of Social Protection*

Europe will have to make big changes in how it organizes labor and government. The reasons are becoming ever more obvious: the labor force is shrinking, societies are aging, social security is already a large part of government spending, and fiscal deficits and public debt are often already onerous.

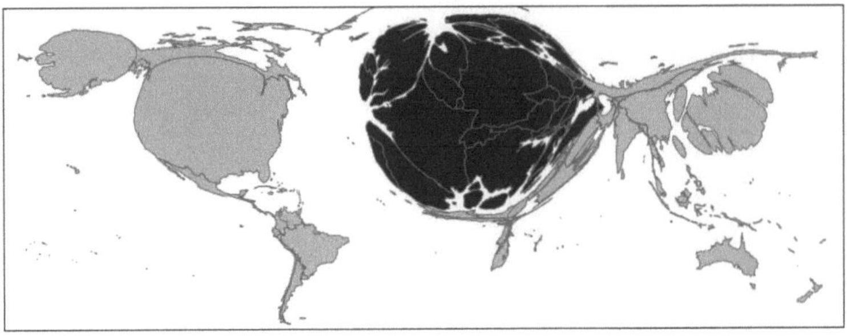

Fig. 16 Governments in Europe are big (the world resized by government spending in dollars, 2009). *Source*: World Bank staff, using IMF *Government Financial Statistics*

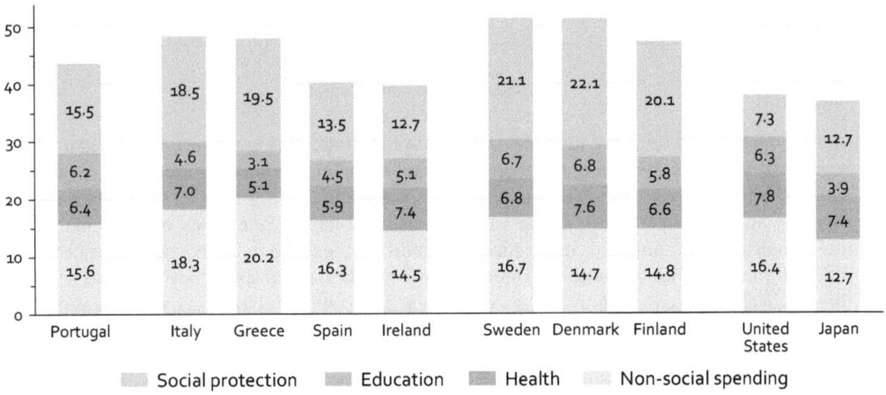

Fig. 17 Social protection explains the difference in government size between Europe and its peers (government spending, share of GDP, 2007–2008). *Note*: "Social protection" includes benefits related to sickness and disability, old age, survivors, family and children, unemployment, and housing. *Source*: IMF *Government Finance Statistics*

In dealing with government spending, deficits, and debt, it is sensible to start by asking whether European governments are too big (that is, they spend too much). They are obviously bigger than their peers. In the EU15, governments spent 50 % of GDP in 2009; in much of the rest of Europe, this share was about 45 %—versus less than 40 % in the United States and Japan, 33 % in Latin America, and about 25 % in emerging East Asia. A map of the world resized to reflect government spending instead of land area shows how Europe might look to outsiders (Fig. 16).

Governments in Europe spend about 10 % of GDP more than their peers elsewhere, largely for social protection (Fig. 17). Countries in Western Europe spend 9 % of GDP more on social transfers and about 10 % of GDP more on public spending overall than the United States, Canada, Australia, and Japan.

There are good—and not so good—reasons for having bigger governments. If governments are good at supplying essential social services, and if European society wants to redistribute more to protect the welfare of the elderly, infirm or unfortunate, they should provide these amenities. If European populations are older and social security systems have to be bigger, that may be another good reason for high-spending governments. European societies have been more redistributive and to good effect—look at the impressive declines in poverty in Western Europe since World War II and in Eastern Europe since the end of the Cold War.

But social services, social welfare, and social security have to be financed by taxes, and tax rates in Europe are the highest in the world. For example, the tax wedge in the Republic of Korea—the amount that Korean employers pay besides wages when hiring workers—is about a third of what Belgian enterprises pay, under half in many countries in Europe, and close to half in Greece and Turkey. So the more pertinent question is: has big government become a drag on growth in Europe? It appears it has. Over the last 15 years, a 10 percentage point increase in initial government spending in Europe has lowered annual growth by 0.6–0.9 percentage points. Countries with government spending-to-GDP ratios above 40 % grow by 2 percentage points of GDP less than those with lower ratios.

Of course, size is not the only feature that matters. What government does and how it finances its activities is as important. European governments regulate the largest economic area in the world; encourage a vigorous exchange of goods, services, and capital; promote voice and accountability; provide or enable the provision of public goods; and redistribute wealth. Bigger governments are often better at doing these things, especially when social trust ensures that everybody plays by the same rules. As countries like Sweden show, such big governments can go together with thriving, dynamic economies.

Yet Europe's governments will have to become more efficient. Fortunately they have wide scope for savings while adhering to the continent's principles. (For example, although government spending has done well in improving health outcomes, it has done less well in public education.) Studies point to three sources of general inefficiencies: inability to adjust spending patterns to shifting demographic trends, weak incentives for local costs savings, and attempts to improve equity without proper evaluation of policy outcomes. But cost pressures in health could turn out to be greater than for pensions, because European countries have been doing more to reform public pensions than long-term health care, and because health costs have been rising sharply with incomes and advances in technology.

Underlining the fact that social protection is a weight in European governments' spending, Europe's states are not big spenders on either health or education. The variation among countries stems from a difference in spending on pensions and social assistance. Europe's countries also differ in the way they tax these benefits; northern European countries tax the social security benefits of people with high incomes more than others in Europe. After taxes are considered, the southern periphery is the biggest social spender in Western Europe. But the reason why Europe spends more than its peers on public pensions is the same in the north, center and south. This is not because Europe has the oldest population (Japan's is much older) nor because of higher pension benefits (annual subsidies per pensioner are about the same in Greece as in Japan). It spends more because of easier and earlier eligibility for pensions (Fig. 18).

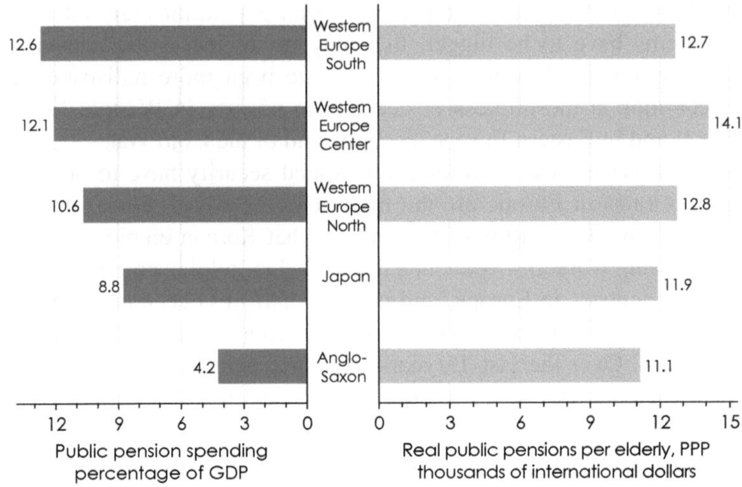

Fig. 18 Small differences in annual pensions per beneficiary, big in overall public pension spending (public pension spending in 2007). *Note*: Median values by group are shown. *Source*: Eurostat; Organisation for Economic Co-operation and Development

Fiscal consolidation should be a top policy priority in Europe during the next decade. Fiscal pressures are high for five reasons: fiscal deficits and public debt increased sharply during the crisis; postcrisis growth might be weaker; rapid aging is adding to fiscal pressures; fiscal policy has to be put on a stable footing before the next crisis; and markets are paying more attention to fiscal vulnerabilities. There are differences among countries in the different parts of Europe, but only in the degree to which governments have to reduce public spending.

Western Europe has to improve its primary balance—adjusted for the business cycle—by about 6 % of GDP during this decade to reduce public debt to 60 % of GDP by 2030 (Fig. 19). Among the countries of Western Europe, the need for consolidating public spending is greatest in the south and lowest in the north. Among Europe's emerging economies, with a lower public debt target of 40 % of GDP, the adjustment needs are about 5 % of GDP. They are lowest in the European Union's new member states. Bigger adjustments will needed in candidate countries and the economies of the eastern partnership, because many of them have not seriously started reforming their social protection systems—pensions and survivor benefits, unemployment insurance and social assistance.

Public expenses related to aging include the ever-increasing costs of providing long-term health care. Unless there are comprehensive reforms to pensions and long term health care, these costs could add more than 3 % of GDP to the governments' fiscal imbalance during the next two decades. Governments in Europe that spend more than 10 % of GDP on such benefits may be risking underinvestment in activities that help economic growth—education, infrastructure, and innovation.

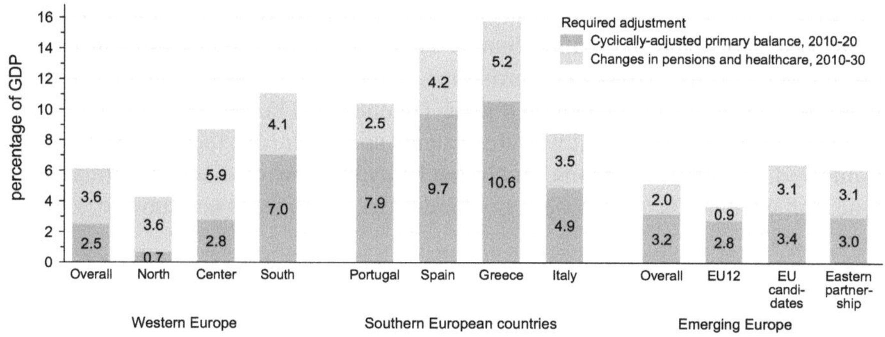

Fig. 19 Western Europe has to reduce fiscal deficits by 6 % of GDP, emerging Europe by less (illustrative fiscal adjustment needs, 2010–2030). *Note*: The fiscal impacts of aging on pensions and health care systems are missing for EU candidate and eastern partnership countries. For this exercise, the sum of adjustment in health care spending is assumed to be the same as for the new member states. The adjustment in pension related spending is assumed to be the same as that for southern Europe. *Sources*: IMF, Institute of Structural Research (Poland), and World Bank

Countries such as Serbia and Ukraine which already spend 15 % or more on social security alone may be jeopardizing the welfare of generations.

5.3 Recalibrating the Work–Life Balance

The European model of work provides income security more than any other, and some countries such as Austria, Denmark, Ireland, and Switzerland have adapted it to combine security with flexibility in hiring and firing to foster both efficiency and equity in labor market outcomes. But for much of Europe, the imbalances between work and life need to be mitigated, as do the fiscal imbalances that have emerged as a result of public spending to protect societies from the rougher facets of private enterprise.

Since the mid-1980s, a billion Asian workers have entered the global marketplace. Over the same period, Europeans have been working fewer hours per week, fewer weeks per year, and fewer years over their lifetimes. It is worrisome that their productivity is not increasing as quickly as it should. In Europe's south, for example, productivity growth during the last decade fell by 1 % each year, when—given its productivity levels relative to continental and northern Europe—it should have increased by about 4 % annually. It is also worrisome that in many parts of Europe, taxes bring in less than what governments spend. France, for example, has not had a fiscal surplus since the 1970s, Greece expected a budget deficit of about 10 % of GDP in 2011 and Hungary, Serbia, Ukraine, and many others have been struggling unsuccessfully to contain budgetary imbalances.

This will have to change. The reform of pensions and disability allowances will have to be the highest priority now, with costs of long term health care soon becoming a pressing problem. Europe already spends twice as much on social security as Japan and the United States. There are some countries in Europe that are showing how to address these problems. Some such as Sweden are well-known; others like Iceland could be studied more (Iwulska 2011). European societies will also have to modernize social welfare systems so that the disincentives to work are minimized. Denmark, Germany, and Ireland may be showing others how this can be done. But what needs to be done is not hard to see: Europeans will have to work for more years.

6 From Distinct to Distinguished

In 2007 *An East Asian Renaissance*, a report by the World Bank, introduced the notion of the "middle income trap" (Gill and Kharas 2007). It was about why countries seem to easily grow from low per capita income levels to middle income, but find it difficult to become and remain high income economies. Later research identified about two dozen countries that have grown from middle-income to high income since 1987. Some had discovered oil, like Oman and Trinidad and Tobago. But this can hardly be a development model for others to emulate, because it is a matter more of providence than policy. Some like Hong Kong SAR, China, Singapore, and the Republic of Korea had translated peace into prosperity through aggressive export-led strategies which involved working and saving a lot and sometimes postponing political liberties for later. They had to be aggressive, like tigers, looking out only for themselves.

But of the countries that have grown quickly from middle income to high income, half—Croatia, Cyprus, Czech Republic, Estonia, Greece, Hungary, Latvia, Malta, Poland, Portugal, the Slovak Republic, and Slovenia—are in Europe. If you can be a part of the formidable European convergence machine, you do not need to be extraordinarily fortunate to become prosperous nor—like the East Asian Tigers—do you have to be ferocious. You just have to be disciplined.

The inability of this convergence machine to continue to deliver rapid growth and improved quality of life in the advanced economies of Western Europe has been recognized for some time. Europe's policymakers have put together protocols and commitments to encourage innovation and dynamism. Policies that were a core component of Europe's post-war growth model—or those that evolved from it—are not giving European economies enough flexibility take advantage of new technologies that have led to high productivity growth in Asia and North America during the last 15 years. It is not that European product market regulation and employment protection have become more stringent over time, they just became more costly.

The Western European model that so effectively enabled catch up has created "afterglow" institutions that are hindering growth in a different era—an era of greater competition abroad and big demographic shifts at home. These institutions now need updating. In the states aspiring to become part of the machine, notably

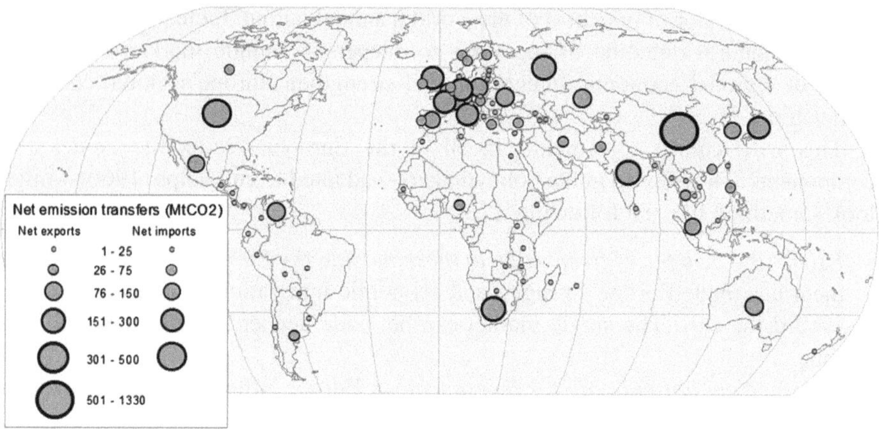

Fig. 20 Letting others do the dirty work (net CO_2 emission transfers [territorial minus consumption emissions], 2008). *Note*: $MtCO_2$ = million tons of carbon dioxide. *Source*: Gill and Raiser, (2012)

the candidates, potential candidates, and the Eastern Neighborhood, the afterglow structures will probably not preclude the benefits that come from greater economic union. In the new member states too, they may not yet prevent productivity gains if their ties with advanced Europe become stronger and sophisticated. In the western economies, the structures must quickly be made more flexible. Convergence to a rigid core may soon become unappealing.

The European Union has a growth strategy, *Europe 2020*, which recognizes this imperative. Not all of the 45 countries covered here are in the European Union, but most share the aspirations of *Europe 2020*: economic development that is smart, sustainable, and inclusive. Europe's way of life—and its growth ambitions—put a premium on combining economic dynamism with environmental sustainability and social cohesion.

Europe's economic model is already more environment-friendly than most. It has made production cleaner than any other part of the world except Japan, and will become the lowest per capita emitter of carbon dioxide by 2020. But it is still the largest importer of emissions (embedded in imported products—Fig. 20), polluting not as much through production as by proxy. Europeans will need to do more on the consumption side to be considered truly green. It is testament to European ideals that Europe is willing to pay the most to avert global warming while it is likely to be damaged least. There is reason to believe that Europe's economic model can become greener without unduly sacrificing growth: Germany, France, and Sweden may already be showing the way.

Social cohesion is the cornerstone of Europe's economic model, but this aspiration must be implemented in ways consistent with sound economic principles. It can be, because Europe has three priceless assets: the European Union's Single Market, a momentum for regional integration, and the global influence that comes from being the generator of one third of the world's annual output. Inclusive development can be a natural outcome of measures to deepen the single market, expand the scope of regional economic integration and strengthen Europe's global economic leadership.

This will require adjustments in all of the European economic model's six components. The rules to guide policymakers—adapted from Phelps (1966)—might look something like the following:

- *Extend the benefits of freer trade to those outside the European Union.* Enlargement has made Europe stronger, and economic integration should be continued toward the east. The single market can be made deeper and wider at the same time.
- *Borrow from abroad only for investment.* In Europe, where foreign finance has been used for private investment, it has fueled growth and convergence. But relying on foreign capital to finance consumption makes economies everywhere more vulnerable than dynamic.
- *Provide enterprises with the freedom to start up, grow, and shut down.* Efficient regulation of enterprise trusts but verifies, makes compliance easy but punishes violation, and assesses risks and concentrates resources where risks are highest.
- *Use public money to catalyze private innovation, not substitute for it.* Effective innovation policy sets the table for innovators to thrive by supporting inventions, mobilizing finance, and bringing the power of choice and the resources of business into Europe's universities.
- *Design labor laws to treat insiders and outsiders more equally.* Regulations should not favor either those who have jobs or those who are looking for work. Seeing labor as a fixed lump to be divided among workers leads to poor rules for regulating work.
- *Consider government debt mainly as a way to finance public investment.* With high debt levels and modest growth prospects, public finance should be premised on the expectation that future generations will not be much wealthier than today's.

European economies do not have to become North American or East Asian to keep to these rules. But Europe might learn a few lessons from them. From North Americans, Europe could learn that economic liberty and social security have to be balanced with care: nations that sacrifice too much economic freedom for social security can end up with neither, impairing both enterprise and government. To get this balance wrong could mean giving up Europe's way of life and its place in the world. From the Japanese, Koreans, and Chinese, Europe might learn that while the gifts of prosperity and longevity arrive together, they have to be unbundled: being wealthier means that Europeans do not have to work as hard as before, but living longer means having to work more years, not fewer. To do otherwise unjustly burdens future generations, and violates growth's golden rule.

Europeans can of course learn easiest and most from their own experiences. The countries in Europe that have instituted policies that manifest both cultural maturity and economic discipline have shown how a distinct growth model can be made distinguished.

Appendix: 30 Questions, 30 Answers

Questions	→	Answers
Chapter 1		
• What makes the European economic model unique?	→	The principal components of Europe's growth model—trade, finance, enterprise, innovation, labor, and government—are organized in unique ways.
• Have changes in Europe and the rest of the world made a new economic model necessary?	→	Sluggish productivity growth, a declining workforce, and growing fiscal imbalances have revealed weaknesses of the European economic model, and the entry of a billion Asian workers into the global market is adding to the stress.
• Which parts of the European model should be preserved, and which changed?	→	Many changes are needed in how governments and labor markets are organized. Fewer changes are needed to foster innovation, productivity growth, and job creation by enterprises, and fewer still to improve finance and trade in Europe.
Chapter 2		
• Is "Factory Europe" as dynamic as "Factory Asia"?	→	Factory Asia is growing faster, but goods trade in Europe is more sophisticated.
• Is the single market for services underachieving compared with the United States?	→	The single market is working quite well for traditional services such as travel and transport, but it is underperforming in modern services such as insurance, information technology, and other business services.
• Is the common agricultural policy compromising	→	The European Union's agricultural policies hobble the extension of the single market to its neighbors,

(continued)

Questions	→	Answers
Europe's global leadership?		and Europe is missing an opportunity to improve the lives of 75 million people in the eastern partnership countries.
Chapter 3		
• Why is finance in emerging Europe different from other regions?	→	The prospect of membership in the European Union exerts a powerful policy and institutional pull, making Europe unique and strengthening the link between foreign savings and economic growth.
• How did some European economies benefit more from international financial flows than others?	→	European economies that managed to "boom-proof" public finances and "crisis-proof" private financing without resorting to the costly self-insurance seen in Asia benefited from foreign financial flows.
• Is there evidence of a "debt overhang" in emerging Europe that reduces growth and justifies government intervention?	→	In emerging Europe, treasuries, enterprises, and households do not face a debt overhang, but in the Eurozone's periphery this problem is acute, posing a danger for banks everywhere.
Chapter 4		
• What does Europe expect from its enterprises?	→	Workers expect enterprises in Europe to create jobs, shareholders to generate value added, and governments to bring in sizable export earnings.

(continued)

Questions	→	Answers
•How have European firms done in an enlarged Europe?	→	In most parts of Europe, firms have taken advantage of greater regional integration to decentralize production, attract foreign investment, and expand the markets for their products.
• Why did some parts of Europe do better than others?	→	In Western and Eastern Europe, industrial structures were better suited for a single market; Southern European enterprises have been slower to offshore activities and to attract foreign investors.
• Which government policies help enterprises do better?	→	In advanced European economies, many governments have to streamline regulations to make doing business easier; in emerging Europe, most have to improve infrastructure and credit as well.
Chapter 5		
• How much does Europe's innovation deficit matter?	→	Europe's innovation deficit matters most for the EU15, and so it also matters for the economies of emerging Europe because they are closely integrated.
• Why does Europe do less R&D than the United States, Japan, and the Republic of Korea?	→	European enterprises do less R&D than their American firms because they tend to be in sectors that are not as innovation-oriented.
• What are the special attributes of a successful European innovation system?	→	The most innovative European economies such as Switzerland spend a lot on R&D, but also share key attributes with the United States—tight business–university links, good management skills, and top universities.

(continued)

Questions	→	Answers
• What should European governments do to increase innovation?	→	Measures to fully integrate the single market for services will provide the scale, more privately funded universities will supply the skills, and regulations that foster competition will create the incentives for European enterprises to innovate.
Chapter 6		
• Is there a European work model?	→	European economies generally have more stringent employment protection and more generous social benefits than their peers in North America and East Asia.
• Given demographic changes, how can Europe achieve a stable and more productive workforce?	→	Increased participation can help stem the decline of the workforce, but more competition for jobs, greater mobility within Europe, and measures to attract global talent will still be necessary.
• Are employment and social protection practices inhibiting labor participation and efficiency?	→	Employment protection gives too much power to those with jobs while banishing others to the fringes of the labor market, and generous social benefits weaken the incentives to work.
• Is Europe taking full advantage of the benefits associated with internal labor mobility?	→	Migration among and within countries in Europe is still low, and even intra-EU migration falls short of the European Union's aspiration of a fully integrated labor market.

(continued)

Questions	→	Answers
• How can Europe become a global magnet for talent?	→	Europe needs an approach to global talent with policies that link immigration to labor markets, and a business climate that rewards skills and entrepreneurship.
Chapter 7		
• Are governments in Europe bigger than elsewhere?	→	Governments in Europe spend about 10 % of GDP more than their peers, and this is almost entirely because they spend more on social protection.
• Is big government a drag on growth in Europe?	→	Controlling for other differences, European economies with government spending greater than 40 % of GDP have had much lower growth rates during the last 15 years.
• If big government impedes growth, how do countries such as Sweden do so well?	→	Countries like Sweden have big governments, but they deliver high-quality social services, make it easy for citizens and enterprises to comply with taxes and regulations, and have high levels of social trust.
• How can governments be made more efficient?	→	Countries where government works have made their bureaucracies leaner, fiscal institutions more reliable, public services competitive, tax administration effective, and citizens more empowered.
• Should fiscal consolidation be a top policy priority in Europe?	→	To respond to market pressures and aging populations, almost every country in Europe must make big fiscal adjustments to reduce public debt to precrisis levels.
Chapter 8		
• How can Europe make the single	→	Greater labor mobility and more uniform national regulations for modern business services are

(continued)

Questions	→	Answers
market more efficient?		making the single market more efficient.
• How can Europe maintain the momentum for regional economic integration?	→	Sustaining economic integration requires making the single market efficient, crisis-proofing financial flows, and facilitating production networks through improved public services in emerging Europe.
• What is needed to maintain Europe's global leadership?	→	To remain a global economic leader, Europe has to sustain regional integration, reduce public debt, reform social security, revamp employment protection laws, and institute policies to attract talent from around the world.

Source: Gill and Raiser (2012)

References

Blanchard O, Giavazzi F (2002) Current account deficits in the Euro area: the end of the Feldstein Horioka puzzle? Brookings Papers on Economic Activity, Economic Studies Program, The Brookings Institution, vol 33(2), pp 147–210

Eurobarometer (2006) The future of Europe. http://ec.europa.eu/public_opinion. Accessed 25 Dec 2011

Feldstein M, Horioka C (1980) Domestic saving and international capital flows. Econ J 90(358):314–329

Gill I, Kharas H (2007) An East Asian renaissance: ideas for economic growth. The World Bank, Washington, DC

Gill I, Raiser M (2012) Golden growth: restoring the lustre of the European economic model. World Bank, Washington, DC. www.worldbank.org/goldengrowth

Groningen Growth and Development Centre and The Conference Board (2011) Total economy database. www.conference-board.org/data/economydatabase/

Heston A, Summers R, Aten B (2011) Penn World Table Version 7.0. University of Pennsylvania, Philadelphia. http://pwt.econ.upenn.edu. Accessed 14 July 2011

ILO (International Labour Organization) (2011) Key indicators of the labour market. www.ilo.org/kilm. Accessed 27 Sept 2011

Iwulska A (2011) European and global policy benchmarks, briefs prepared for Gill and Raiser (2012). Avaiable at www.worldbank.org/goldengrowth

Maddison A (1996) Macroeconomic accounts for European countries. In: van Ark B, Crafts N (eds) Quantitative aspects of post-war European economic growth. Cambridge University Press, Cambridge, UK

Mundell RA (1961) A theory of optimum currency areas. Am Econ Rev 51(4):657–665

OECD Employment Outlook 2005, Paris: OECD

Phelps ES (1961) The golden rule of accumulation: a fable for Growthmen. Am Econ Rev 51(4):638–643
Phelps ES (1966) Golden rules of economic growth: studies of efficient and optimal investment. W.W. Norton, New York
Sugawara N, Zalduendo J (2010) How much economic integration is there in Europe? World Bank, Office of the Chief Economist, Europe and Central Asia Region, Washington, DC
United Nations Conference on Trade and Development (2010). World Investment Report 2010: investing in a low-carbon economy. United Nations, New York. www.unctad.org/Templates/WebFlyer.asp?intItemID=5539&lang=1. Accessed 8 Aug 2011
Weigand C, Grosh M (2008) Levels and patterns of safety net spending in developing and transition countries. Social Protection Discussion Paper 0817. World Bank, Washington, DC
World Bank (2011) World development indicators. http://data.worldbank.org/data-catalog/world-development-indicators. Accessed 31 Oct 2011
WTO (World Trade Organization) (2009) International Trade Statistics 2009. Geneva: WTO

Russian Federation: National and Regional Trends in Regulatory Burden and Corruption

Gregory Kisunko and Stephen Knack

Abstract The chapter assesses trends over time in corruption and the regulatory burden in Russia, and draws comparisons with the regional averages for Eastern Europe and Central Asia region as a whole. For the first time, this BEEPS also permits comparisons across 37 Russian regions—from Moscow to Primorsky Kray and from Kaliningrad to Rostov Oblast—accounting for the majority of economic activity, value-added and population in the country. We also identify regions where private sector development confronts the most serious challenges, and regions where problems are much less severe. The chapter concludes that while Russia has made significant progress in reforming its institutions, in the longer run, sustained growth that is more balanced—both geographically and across a more diverse set of sectors—will likely require thoroughgoing improvement in Russia's regulatory climate for private investment and enterprise.

1 Executive Summary

A broad range of evidence from other Bank and external sources shows that overly burdensome regulation and corruption are significant impediments to firm entry, productivity and growth. This policy note uses results of the fifth round of the Business Environment and Enterprise Performance Survey (BEEPS) to assess levels and trends in administrative burden and corruption facing Russian private

---

G. Kisunko (✉)
Europe and Central Asia Region, The World Bank, Washington, DC, USA
e-mail: gkisunko@worldbank.org

S. Knack
Development Research/Public Sector Governance, The World Bank, Washington, DC, USA
e-mail: sknack@worldbank.org

L. Paganetto (ed.), *Wealth, Income Inequalities, and Demography*,
DOI 10.1007/978-3-319-05909-9_3,

businesses. The intended audiences of this note are policymakers, policy analysts in the NGO and academic communities, and representatives of the private sector.

This 2011 survey, for the first time, was designed to be representative not only at the national level but also at the regional level, allowing comparisons across 37 Russian regions—from Moscow to Primorsky Kray and from Kaliningrad to Rostov Oblast—accounting for the majority of economic activity, value-added and population in the country.

This report assesses trends at the country level, and draws comparisons with the ECA region as a whole. It also identifies regions where the private sector confronts the most serious challenges, and regions where problems are much less severe, that may suggest the way for other regions to lighten the burden of regulation on firms and reduce corruption. Cross-regional variation in corruption and regulatory burden in Russia is a potentially important factor in explaining differential performance in private sector development, income levels and growth rates.

Two major policy implications emerge from the data analysis:

- Greater transparency and government dissemination of information can strengthen accountability and improve the business climate. Regional government procurement systems that are more transparent are associated with a lower average "kickback tax" firms report paying to officials. Perceptions of state capture and frequency of administrative bribery are lower in regions with higher newspaper circulation.
- Streamlining regulation can reduce some aspects of regulatory burden experienced by firms. Interacting with officials in more regulatory areas, and being subject to more tax inspections and meetings is associated with more frequent complaints about tax administration, licensing and permits, and a higher incidence of bribe paying. More intensive research is required however to gain greater clarity regarding which reforms will have the largest effects on firm entry and operations, or whether their effects are additive or redundant. Established firms may work strategically with officials to impede potential competitors effectively through only one or two administrative barriers.

Since the previous round of the BEEPS conducted in 2008, Russia has made significant progress in addressing the *administrative burden imposed on firms* by regulations, tax and court administration, etc. Overall, trends in the administrative burden are favorable, as measured by the BEEPS:

- The average "time tax" is significantly lower in 2011 with 17 % of senior management time spent on dealing with regulations, compared to 22 % in 2008.[1]
- Among the various regulatory and administrative sub-sectors, licensing, courts and tax administration are the areas where perceptions have improved the most (Fig. 1).

[1]All reported differences between the 2008 and 2011 estimates for the various measures are statistically significant at the 10 % level or better, unless indicated otherwise.

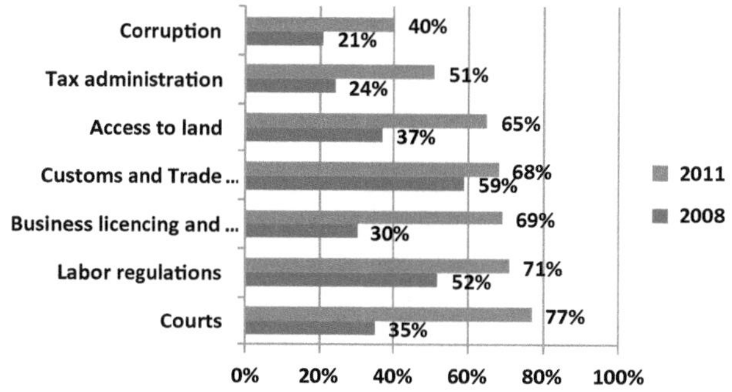

Fig. 1 Regulatory obstacles to doing business (percentage of respondents indicating issue is NO obstacle)

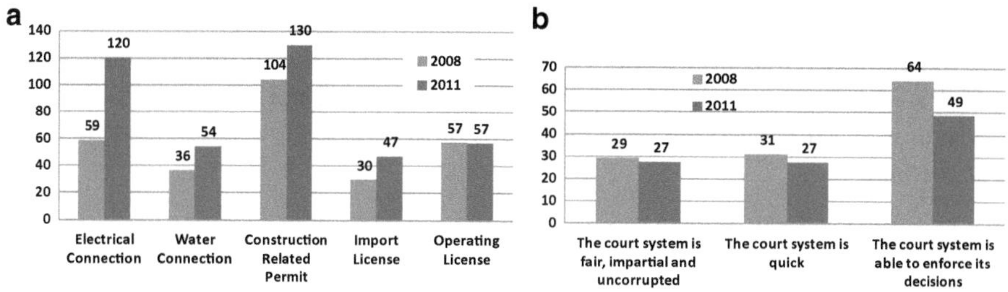

Fig. 2 (**a**) Average time needed to obtain selected permits and licenses, 2008 and 2011 (days). (**b**) Perception of courts (percentage of respondents stating that they tend to agree or strongly agree with a statement)

While respondents see these areas as less problematic than before, the survey results also suggest areas for further improvements (Fig. 2a, b):

- Evidence regarding licensing, permits and utility connections suggests that while fewer firms cite licensing and permits as an obstacle to their business, in some cases (e.g., new electrical connection) they have to endure longer average waiting times in 2011 than in 2008.[2]
- Similarly, fewer firms report that courts are an obstacle, but the reasons for this trend are unclear. Firms in 2011 are less likely to agree that court decisions will be reliably enforced, perhaps partly explaining why fewer firms report having used courts.

Corruption was ranked by firms in the 2008 BEEPS as the third most serious problem doing business in Russia. In 2011, corruption moved up to second on the list of most frequently-cited problems, moving ahead of "inadequately educated

[2]The differences in water connection, construction permits, import and operating licenses are not statistically significant.

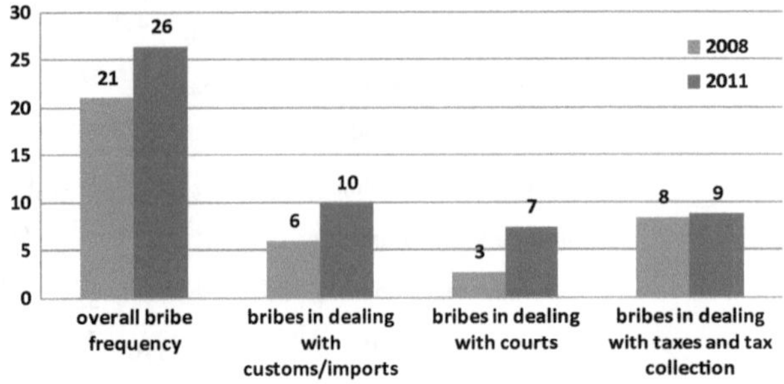

Fig. 3 Unofficial payments to "get things done", 2008 and 2011 (percentage of respondents reported payments are needed at least frequently)

workforce" and behind only "tax rates." This does not necessarily mean corruption worsened. In fact, fewer firms cited corruption as a major or very severe problem in 2011 (33.5 %) than in 2008 (50 %). Rather, the improvements in areas other than taming corruption were even larger. Further complicating interpretations of the trends in this question is that corruption can take many forms. Fortunately, the BEEPS includes more detailed questions on some (but not all) specific forms of corruption as experienced or perceived by business firms, allowing for more nuanced conclusions.

- A summary "Graft Index" representing the share of all interactions between firms and public officials in which a bribe was expected has also improved. In 2008 the index value was 0.18, i.e. every fifth transaction would involve a bribe; in 2011 Russia's value improved to 0.081 (one in 12 transactions involves a bribe). By comparison, the ECA average in 2008 was 0.15, but in ten Eastern European countries the ratio was 1 in 20 or less.
- The "bribe tax" or percentage of annual sales spent on bribe payments has also decreased from 1.7 % of sales (above the ECA average of 1.0 %) to 0.9 % of sales in 2011.[3]
- Among firms reporting payments, however, bribes as a percentage of sales increased from 4.5 % of sales in 2008 to 7.3 % in 2011. Payment of bribes thus became more concentrated over time: fewer firms report paying them, but those that do pay more.
- Bribe requests were slightly more frequent in 2011 relative to 2008 for obtaining electrical and water connections, operating and import licenses,[4] but downward trends are observed for construction permits, and meetings with tax officials.
- A more general question about bribe frequency shows that a somewhat greater share of firms in 2011, compared to 2008, indicates that bribes are frequently (or always) necessary (Fig. 3).[5]

[3]Marginally statistically significant ($P = 0.120$).

[4]None of these changes were statistically significant.

[5]The differences in overall bribe frequency and bribes in dealing with customs/imports are not statistically significant.

Fig. 4 Private payments/gifts to public officials to gain advantages have NO impact (percentage of respondents)

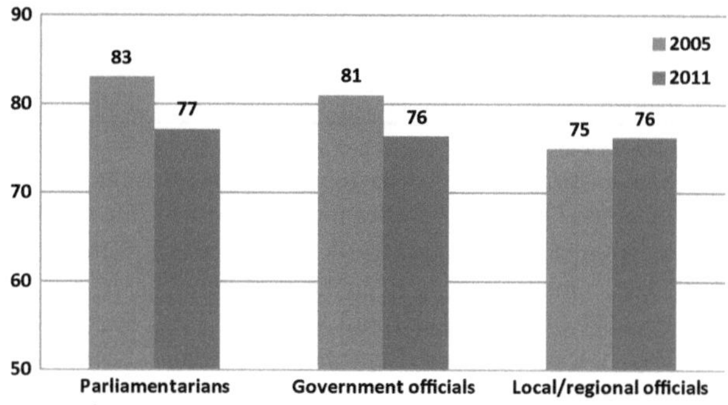

Administrative corruption is not necessarily the most damaging form of graft for economic growth and private sector development. The 2011 BEEPS marked the return of several questions on "*state capture*"[6] that were included in the 1999, 2002 and 2005 BEEPS, but dropped from the 2008 survey.

The perceived impact of state capture increased between 2005 and 2011. As shown in Fig. 4, the percentage of firms claiming that these practices had no impact on their business declined, by 6 and 5 percentage points for officials holding federal-level elected and executive offices, respectively, but remained almost unchanged—increasing by 1 percentage point—for local and regional officials. Viewing responses from the other end of the scale, the adverse trend appears more serious. The percentage of firms claiming a major or decisive impact doubled for the latter category of official and tripled for the former two.

The BEEPS questions on administrative bribe-paying and state capture are intended to measure the experiences and perceptions of firms on aspects of government corruption that affect them directly. An alternative source, the World Economic Forum (WEF) surveys, complements the BEEPS by its inclusion of survey questions on other aspects of corruption. The WEF's indicators on corrupt diversion of public funds for private use, and on financial honesty of public officials, have shown a deteriorating trend in the last several years, and its state capture indicators corroborate the worsening trend exhibited in the BEEPS.

Results show that the business environment differs significantly across the *37 regions* included in the BEEPS. The region in which firms are located turns out to have stronger implications for the degree of corruption and the regulatory burden they confront than other firm characteristics such as firm size age, ownership, main activity, and product or service accounting for the largest proportion of sales.

[6]The term "state capture" refers to "the actions of individuals, groups or firms both in the public and private sector to influence the formation of laws, regulations, decrees and other government policies to their own advantage as a result of the illicit and non-transparent provision of private benefits to public officials" (World Bank 2000).

Table 1 Composite indexes of regional performance—regions in the top and bottom quintiles

	Administrative burden index	Administrative corruption index	Graft index	State capture index
Top performers				
1	Smolensk Oblast	Stavropol Kray	Smolensk Oblast	Khabarovsk Kray
2	Belgorod Oblast	Ulyanovsk Oblast	Novosibirsk Oblast	Kursk Oblast
3	Stavropol Kray	Lipetsk Oblast	Saint Petersburg	Ulyanovsk Oblast
4	Irkutsk Oblast	Republic of Mordovia	Moscow City	Republic of Mordovia
5	Republic of Mordovia	Tomsk Oblast	Primorsky Kray	Omsk Oblast
6	Rep. of Bashkortostan	Republic of Tatarstan	Leningrad Oblast	Tomsk Oblast
7	Tomsk Oblast	Rep. Sakha (Yakutia)	Chelyabinsk Oblast	Voronezh Oblast
Poor performers				
31	Volgograd Oblast	Moscow City	Samara Oblast	Kaluga Oblast
32	Kaliningrad Oblast	Krasnodar Kray	Yaroslavl Oblast	Belgorod Oblast
33	Saint Petersburg	Irkutsk Oblast	Perm Kray	Tver Oblast
34	Krasnodar Kray	Chelyabinsk Oblast	N. Novgorod Oblast	Krasnodar Kray
35	Samara Oblast	Rostov Oblast	Krasnodar Kray	Rostov Oblast
36	Leningrad Oblast	Tver Oblast	Rep. Bashkortostan	Irkutsk Oblast
37	Rostov Oblast	Primorsky Kray	Voronezh Oblast	Primorsky Kray

Although regions differ significantly from each other, the same regions that rank at or near the top on some indicators—perhaps surprisingly—rank at or near the bottom on others. For example, Smolensk Oblast ranks best on waiting time for electrical connections, with an average of only 8 days, while waiting time for Primorsky Kray is 730 days, nearly double the time for any other region. On the other hand, Primorsky Kray has the shortest average wait for water connections, at only one day, while Smolensk Oblast was in second place at 1.8 days average wait.

In order to summarize various aspects of business-government interactions, a statistically reliable composite index of Administrative Burden was constructed from questions pertaining to seven potential obstacles to firm operations and growth. The top five regions having the lowest values of this index are: Smolensk, Belgorod, Stavropol, and Irkutsk Oblasts and Republic of Mordovia. The bottom five regions are (starting with the worst): Rostov, Leningrad, and Samara Oblast, Krasnodar Kray, and St. Petersburg City (Table 1).

While regional patterns of firm behavior show highly significant variation, results of the regional BEEPS confirmed several important propositions:

- Excessive red tape can provide public officials with more opportunities to deliberately slow down processing to increase the incentives for firms to pay bribes. The BEEPS data are consistent with this idea: regions with more burdensome regulation exhibit a higher incidence of corruption.
- The need to pay bribes and the administrative procedures they are intended to circumvent both constitute significant obstacles from the standpoint of firms. Regions where firms report tax administration as a more serious obstacle also tend to be regions where firms report a higher number of meetings with tax

officials, and a greater need to pay bribes in connection with paying taxes. Moreover, firms reporting a higher "bribe tax" also tend to report a higher "time tax".

- Firms that report interacting with officials in more "sub-sectors"—tax, utility connections, operating licensing, etc.—tend to report a higher "time tax," higher perceptions of bribe frequency, a higher "bribe tax," and more frequently cite licensing and permits as an obstacle. Moreover, they also report paying bribes in a greater *proportion* of these interactions (as measured by the Graft Index), not merely in a larger absolute number of them.
- The earlier BEEPS showed that two types of corruption—administrative and state capture—were positively correlated among countries in the ECA region, although the relationship was only modest in strength. In Russia, the relationship between state capture and administrative corruption appears to be strong—bribe frequency is strongly correlated with state capture.

There are several implications for regulatory and anti-corruption policies that emerge from the analyses:

- Less onerous regulatory requirements are associated with a lower average "time tax", shorter wait times to obtain an operating license, fewer firms citing licensing and permits as an obstacle to their operations, and lowered bribe expectations (as measured by the Graft Index).
- Contrary to common findings in the cross-country literature, corruption and regulatory burden at the regional level in Russia are not worse in poorer regions (as measured by per capita gross regional product), or in regions more dependent on natural resource extraction.
- Contrary to some other sources, corruption and regulatory burden are not worse in southern than in northern regions.
- Voting participation and freedom of information practices in the regions are unrelated to corruption and regulatory burden, but some types of corruption are less severe in regions with higher newspaper circulation.
- Bribe-paying to obtain government contracts is less frequent in regions with more transparency in regional-government procurement systems.

The analyses in this report do not exhaust all of the rich data available on the Russian regions from government and other sources; nor do they provide thorough tests of all of the various fiscal and political economy hypotheses that can be derived from the literature. This report nevertheless provides a description of selected BEEPS indicators, and illustrative examples of how the data can be used to investigate why the business climate varies so much across regions. In conjunction with the accompanying BEEPS-at-a-Glance report for Russia, the report can facilitate independent interpretations, and complementary and more in-depth analyses, by researchers in government, civil society and academia.

2 Introduction

Using data from BEEPS and other Enterprise Surveys, studies have shown that firm entry, growth and productivity are impeded by corruption and overly burdensome regulation.[7] Most of these studies have been based on cross-country data (e.g. Barseghyan 2008), or country-specific studies of firms in China (e.g. Cai et al. 2011; Cull and Xu 2005), Mexico (Bruhn 2011) and other nations. Other studies, however, are specific to Russia (e.g. Yakovlev and Zhuravskaya 2007). Cross-regional variation in corruption and regulatory burden in Russia are potentially important factors in explaining differential performance in private sector development, income levels and growth rates.

This report assesses trends over time in corruption and the regulatory burden in Russia, draws comparisons with the ECA region as a whole, and for the first time uses BEEPS to make comparisons across 37 Russian regions that represent the majority of economic activity and value-added produced in the country.[8] The intended audiences of this note are policymakers and policy analysts in the NGO and academic communities who are interested in regulatory reform, corruption, and related aspects of the business environment in Russia.

Box 1: Useful definitions regulatory (or administrative) burden refers to the administrative costs incurred by firms in dealing with government regulation of business. Use of the term "burden" should not be taken to imply that the optimal amount of regulations is zero, but reflects instead the fact that costs of complying with regulations (in senior managers' time, fees and bribes) remain unnecessarily high for transitional countries overall, for example in comparison with OECD countries.

State capture refers to the actions of individuals, groups, or firms both in the public and private sectors to influence the formation of laws, regulations, decrees, and other government policies to their own advantage as a result of the illicit and non-transparent provision of private benefits to public officials. All forms of state capture are directed toward extracting rents through distorting the basic legal and regulatory framework with potentially enormous losses for the society at large. They thrive where economic power is highly concentrated, countervailing social interests are weak, and the formal channels of political influence and interest intermediation are underdeveloped.

(continued)

[7]Djankov (2009) provides a useful review of the literature on the effects of regulatory barriers to starting new businesses.

[8]The list of 37 regions with accompanying variables is shown in Table 2, Appendix 1 and Table 6, Appendix 2.

Box 1 (continued)

While state capture encodes advantages for particular individuals or groups in the basic legal or regulatory framework, **administrative corruption** refers to the intentional imposition of distortions in the prescribed implementation of existing laws, rules, and regulations to provide advantages to either state or non-state actors as a result of the illicit and non-transparent provision of private gains to public officials. The classic example of administrative corruption is that of business owners forced to pay bribes to a seemingly endless stream of official inspectors to overlook minor (or possibly major) infractions of existing regulations, or "grease payments" to gain licenses, to win public procurement contracts, etc. Finally, state officials can simply misdirect public funds under their control for their own or their family's direct financial benefit.

Sources: World Bank (2000, 2011).

Section 3 of this report discusses trends at the national level in regulatory burden and corruption in Russia, comparing findings from the new 2011 BEEPS to results from the 2008 survey, and for state capture questions from the 2005 survey. Most indicators show improvement over time, but there are a few exceptions, including the "state capture" questions that returned to the 2011 survey after being omitted in 2008.

Box 2: The Russia 2012 Business Environment and Enterprise Performance Survey Data Set The Russian Regional Business Environment and Enterprise Performance Survey (RRS) was conducted between August 2011 and June 2012 as part of the fifth round of the Business Environment and Enterprise Performance Survey (BEEPS), a joint initiative of the World Bank Group (WB) and the European Bank for Reconstruction and Development (EBRD). The main objective of the survey was to gain an understanding of firms' perception of the environment in which they operate. The survey was until now administered four times at an interval of approximately 3 years with samples representative at country level. This RRS is the first BEEPS survey that provides representative though small samples for 37 separate regions of the country. A total of 4,223 firms were interviewed.

The sample for Russia was selected using stratified random sampling. Three levels of stratification were used: industry, establishment size, and region:

(continued)

Box 2 (continued)

1. Industry stratification split the universe into eight manufacturing industries (food, wood and furniture, chemicals and plastics and rubber, non-metallic mineral products, fabricated metal products, machinery and equipment, electronics and precision instruments, and other manufacturing), and seven service industries (construction, wholesale, retail, hotels and restaurants, supporting transport activities, IT, and other services).
2. Size stratification defined small (5–19 employees), medium (20–99 employees), and large (more than 99 employees), where the number of employees was defined on the basis of reported permanent full-time workers.
3. Regional stratification was defined in 37 regions (city and the surrounding business area) throughout Russia.

The sampling methodology was the same that was used for BEEPS IV and therefore allows for a direct comparison of country level results for 2008 and 2011. The 2008 BEEPS questionnaire and sampling methodology were significantly modified from previous rounds to enhance comparability of BEEPS and enterprise surveys in other regions. For that reason country level comparisons with earlier periods are avoided, except for "state capture" questions that were a part of the 2005 survey, but omitted in the 2008 round.

Great efforts were made to obtain the best source for regional sampling frames. In the majority of 37 sampled regions the survey yielded approximately 120 interviews per region. Where needed adjustments were made to correct for the presence of ineligible units within regional sampling frames. These adjustments and other implementation-specific challenges are reflected in and addressed through the sampling weights computation. All estimates, if not specified otherwise, are weighted.

Source: The detailed sampling methodology and the survey questionnaire can be found at http://www.enterprisesurveys.org/documents/Implementation_note.pdf.

More importantly, the 2011 BEEPS is the first one designed to be representative both at the national and regional levels. Section 4 discusses regional-level differences in regulatory burden and corruption. There are significant differences across Russian regions in per capita income, and lagging regions (particularly those that are not rich in natural resources) are unlikely to catch up without major improvements in the business climate. As shown in this report, there is enormous variation among regional-level means for most of the indicators. There are no strong and consistent patterns that can justify constructing a single overall index of business climate for the regions. However, it is possible to point to several specific regions that tend to rank high, and others that rank low, on many indicators.

The high degree of regional variation not only identifies where private sector development confronts the most serious challenges. It also identifies regions where problems are much less severe, that can potentially point the way for other regions to reduce corruption and lighten the burden of regulation on firms. However, this report makes only limited progress in identifying policy differences or other underlying factors that explain why corruption and regulatory burden are much less severe in some regions than in others. For this reason, policy implications (discussed in Sect. 5) must remain somewhat tentative and conjectural.

This paper is accompanied by the BEEPS-at-a-Glance report for Russia—a compendium of graphical illustrations of various aspects of business environment measured by BEEPS in 2008 and 2011. The dataset and questionnaire are publicly available,[9] and cover many more topics than can be addressed in this paper. Interested parties can conduct their own complementary analyses on regulatory, corruption-related or other issues.

3 National Trends

3.1 Administrative Burden

Regulations and red tape are commonly considered to be a major problem for starting and operating private sector businesses in Russia. Overall, the BEEPS indicates progress in this area between 2008 and 2011.

In the 2008 BEEPS, firms reported that 22 % of the total time of their senior management on average was spent on "dealing with requirements imposed by government regulations." This figure represented a large increase for Russia from the 2005 BEEPS, and was nearly double the 12 % average for ECA overall. In 2011, the average "time tax" for Russian firms declined to 17 %. The share of firms reporting that no time was required to deal with regulations increased from 9 to 17 % (see Fig. 5). Among those firms reporting some time was required, the average fell from 25 to 21 %.[10] This summary indicator of administrative burden on firms thus shows substantial improvement over the 3-year interval.

Fewer firms in 2011 also cite business licensing and permits as an obstacle to their current operations. In 2008, 30 % indicated licensing and permits was not a problem, well under the ECA average of 45 %. The situation improved even further—69 % of respondents indicated that licensing and permits was not a problem in 2011 (see Appendix 1, Fig. 22).

Despite the reduction in complaints regarding licensing and permits as an obstacle, several other BEEPS questions indicate that the average waiting time between application and receipt of licenses and permits or utility connections

---

[9] http://www.enterprisesurveys.org.

[10] This difference is not statistically significant.

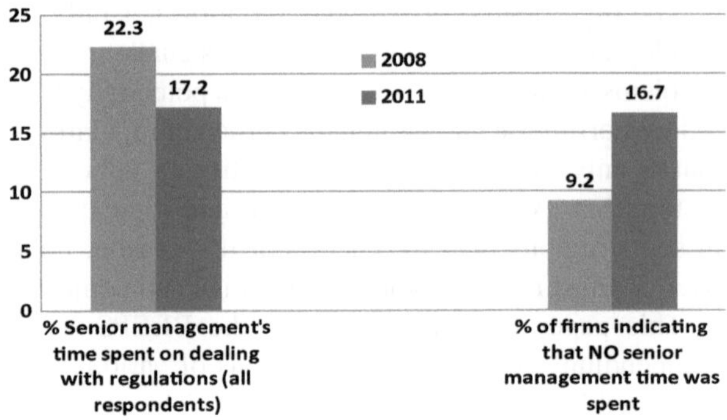

Fig. 5 Percentage of senior management time spent on dealing with regulations

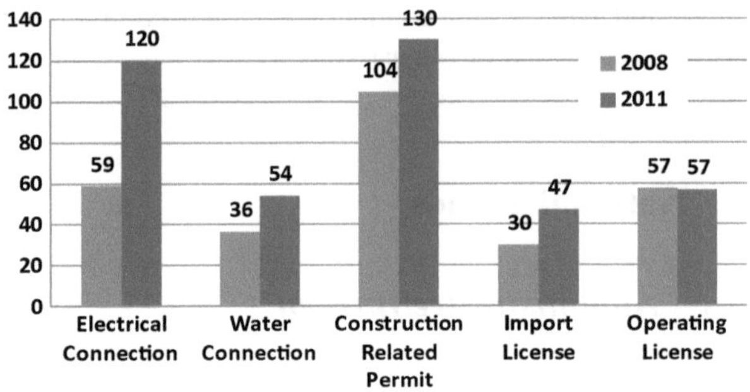

Fig. 6 Average time needed to obtain selected permits and licenses, 2008 and 2011 (days)

increased somewhat between 2008 and 2011, most notably for electrical connections (see Fig. 6).[11]

Fewer firms in 2011 cite tax administration as an obstacle to their current operations. In 2008, 24 % indicated tax administration was not a problem, below the ECA average of 33 %. The figure for Russia more than doubled to 51 % in 2011 (see Fig. 22 in Appendix 1).

The BEEPS includes a question about the number of times either the firm was inspected by tax officials, or its managers were required to meet with them. Trends over time in responses to this question are consistent with improvement in the number of firms citing tax administration as an obstacle. In 2008, 63 % of firms reported they were subject to at least one such meeting or inspection, slightly higher than the 58 % average for ECA. In 2011, as shown in Fig. 7a, only 49 % of Russian firms were required to meet with or be inspected by tax officials. Figure 7b shows that among firms required to deal with tax officials, the average number of meetings or inspections declined, from 3.2 in 2008 to 2.6 in 2011.[12] In comparison, the ECA average for 2008 was slightly higher, at 3.4.

[11] None of the differences in Fig. 2 are statistically significant, except for "Electrical Connection."

[12] This difference is not statistically significant.

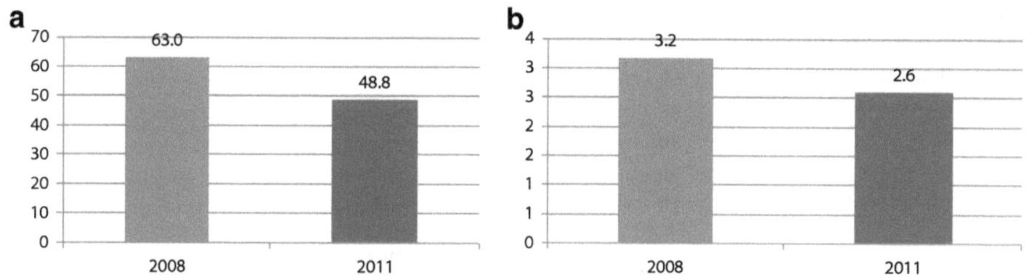

Fig. 7 (**a**) Percentage of firms inspected by tax officials (last year). (**b**) Average number of visits and inspections by tax officials (last year)

The share of firms citing labor regulations, and customs and trade regulations, as obstacles to their business operations also declined, but only slightly, between 2008 and 2011. On both of these indicators Russia's values were very close to the ECA average in 2008 (see Appendix 1, Fig. 22).

Perceptions of courts also improved between 2008 and 2011. In 2008, 21 % of firms viewed the courts as a major or severe obstacle; compared to only 7 % in 2011 (see Appendix 1, Fig. 23). Fewer firms also report having been to court in the last 3 years, either as a plaintiff or defendant, in 2011 (32 %) than in 2008 (43 %). However, court usage in both years was higher than the ECA average of only 27 % for 2008.

Three additional BEEPS questions inquire about the quality of courts. As shown in Fig. 8, there is little change between 2008 and 2011 in the share of firms that agree courts are "quick" or "fair, impartial and uncorrupted." There is a substantial decline however in the share of firms agreeing that "the court system is able to enforce its decisions."[13] This decline appears to be inconsistent with the fact that fewer firms consider courts a major obstacle to business operations in 2011 than in 2008. However, both trends may be related in part to the lower usage of courts that firms also report. Firms may avoid courts because of low confidence in their ability to enforce decisions, and may complain less about them as an obstacle if they have not had as much recent experience with them.

Overall, trends in the administrative burden imposed on Russian firms by regulations, tax and court administration are favorable, as measured by the BEEPS:

1. The average "time tax" is significantly lower in 2011 than in 2008.
2. Among the various regulatory and administrative sub-sectors, licensing, courts and tax administration are the areas where perceptions of positive trends—measured by the share of firms stating that these are not an obstacle—are most unambiguous.

---

[13]Changes in perceptions of enforcement are statistically significant, but not changes in perceptions that courts are "quick" or fair and impartial.

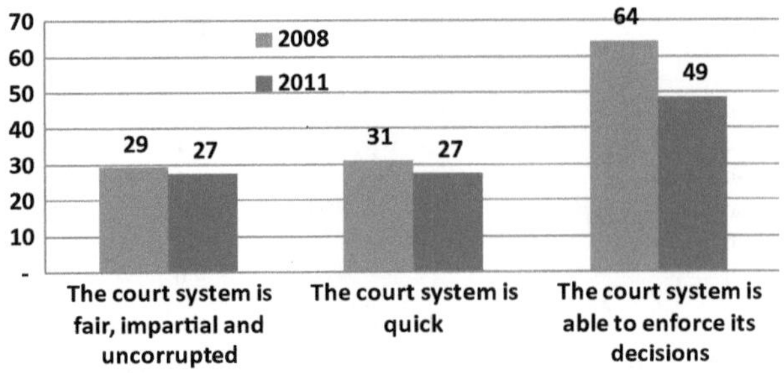

Fig. 8 Perception of courts (percentage of respondents stating that they tend to agree or strongly agree with a statement

3. Evidence regarding licensing, permits and utility connections is somewhat mixed: firms report longer average waiting times in 2011 for electrical connections, but fewer of them cite licensing and permits as an obstacle to their business operations.
4. Similarly, fewer firms report that courts are an obstacle, but the reason for this trend is unclear. Firms in 2011 are less likely to agree that court decisions will be reliably enforced, perhaps partly explaining why fewer firms report having used them.

3.2 *Corruption*

Corruption was ranked by firms in the 2008 BEEPS as the third most serious problem for doing business in Russia, from a list of 16 potential problem areas. In this respect Russia was typical for the ECA region. Six other countries also ranked corruption 3rd, 10 ranked it higher (1st or 2nd), and 12 others ranked it lower (anywhere between 4th and 13th).

In 2011, corruption moved up to second on the list of most frequently-cited problems, moving ahead of "inadequately educated workforce" and behind only "tax rates." This does not necessarily mean corruption worsened. In fact, fewer firms cited corruption as a major or very severe problem in 2011 (33.5 %) than in 2008 (50 %). Rather, the improvements in most other areas were even larger. For example, 57 % of firms cited an inadequately educated workforce as a major or very severe problem in 2008, compared to only 26 % in 2011 (see Appendix 1, Fig. 23). Firms in 2008 were more pessimistic about most of the possible problem areas on the list, not only compared to 2011 but also relative to the 2005 BEEPS. A possible explanation is that the 2005 and 2011 BEEPS were both administered during periods of healthy economic growth; in contrast the 2008 BEEPS was administered during the sharp but brief recession of late 2008 and 2009. When the economy—and thus firms' revenues and profits—is expanding, managers of firms may be more optimistic and cite fewer problems. General economic conditions are obviously not the only factor affecting responses to these questions—not all of them move up or down together

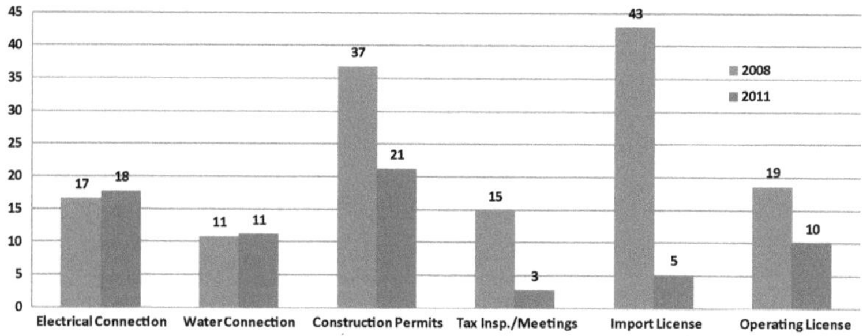

Fig. 9 Percentage of respondents stated that an informal payment was expected or requested when obtaining a specific permit, license or utility connection, 2008 and 2011

over time—but may be important enough that they complicate efforts at identifying real trends.

Further complicating interpretations of the corruption-as-obstacle question is that corruption can take many forms, and it is not obvious which ones firm managers have in mind in responding to the question. Fortunately, some (but not all) specific forms of corruption as experienced or perceived by business firms are covered by other BEEPS questions, particularly for various aspects of administrative corruption.

3.2.1 Administrative Corruption

Questions on administrative corruption in the BEEPS present a mixed picture. Some questions inquire more directly about the firm's own experiences. Other more indirect questions ask about how likely or common it is for similar firms to pay bribes to accomplish certain purposes. The more direct questions mostly show an improving trend, while the indirect questions mostly exhibit a worsening trend.

The BEEPS includes six questions of the direct-experience form, pertaining to utility connections, licenses and permits, and tax administration. Firms that indicate they engaged in the relevant transaction with public officials (e.g. applied for an electrical connection, or were visited by tax officials) were asked whether or not "an informal gift or payment" was "expected or requested." As shown in Fig. 9, bribe requests were slightly more frequent in 2011 than in 2008 for obtaining electrical and water connections, but strong downward trends are observed for construction permits and meetings with tax officials.[14]

A summary index of the "incidence of graft" can be constructed from those six indicators, following the method of Gonzalez et al. (2007). The index is constructed by (1) summing all instances in which firms report a gift or extra payment was

[14]The differences for bribes expected for electrical connection, water connection, import and operating licenses are not statistically significant.

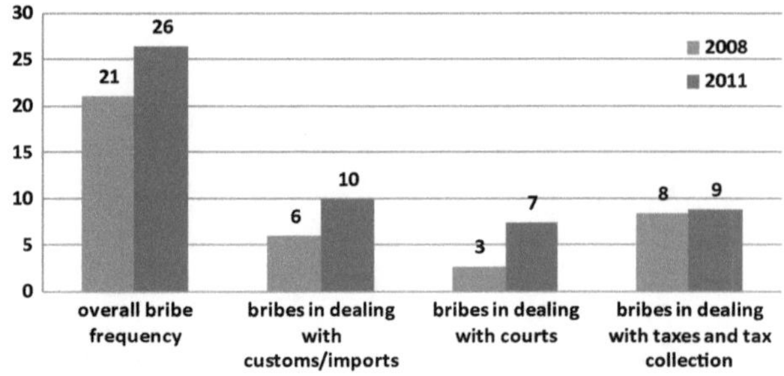

Fig. 10 Unofficial payments to "get things done", 2008 and 2011 (percentage of respondents reported payments are needed at least frequently)

expected (varying from 0 to a maximum of 6 for each firm), (2) summing all of the relevant transactions reported by all firms (again varying from 0 to 6 for each firm), and (3) taking the ratio of (1) to (2). This "Graft Index" therefore represents an estimate of the share of all six areas of interactions between firms and public officials in which a bribe was expected. In the 2008 BEEPS, Russia's Graft Index was 0.18, above the values for most ECA countries with the exception of the Central Asian republics. In 2011, Russia's value improved to 0.08, about half the ECA average of 0.15 in 2008. Despite the improvement, it is still striking that about 1 in 12 transactions involves bribe expectations or requests. By comparison, in ten ECA countries in 2008 (all in Eastern Europe) the ratio was 1 in 20 or less, including about 1 in 60 in Slovenia and less than 1 in 100 in Hungary.

A more general and less direct "Bribe Frequency" question in the BEEPS asks respondents whether the following statement is "always, usually, frequently, sometimes, seldom, or never true":

> It is common for firms in my line of business to have to pay some irregular "additional payments or gifts" to get things done with regard to customs, taxes, licenses, regulations, services, etc.

Figure 5 shows that in the 2008 survey, 21 % of Russian firms indicated that bribes were frequently, usually or always needed, higher than the ECA average of 13 %. In the 2011 BEEPS, the figure for Russia increased to 26 % (Fig. 10).

Three similar questions ask about how often extra payments would be needed for "establishments like this one" in dealing more specifically with "customs/imports," "courts," and "taxes and tax collection." In each of these three areas, a somewhat greater share of firms in 2011, compared to 2008, indicates that bribes are frequently (or always) necessary.[15]

The conflicting trend in the more direct and indirect questions on frequency of administrative bribery present something of a paradox. The more indirect questions regarding what tends to happen "for firms in my line of business" or for "establishments like this one" may elicit more candid answers than direct questions.

[15] The differences in overall bribe frequency, bribes in dealing with customs, and in dealing with taxes are not significant. Only the difference in bribe frequency in dealing with courts is statistically significant.

Some firms may be reticent to tell surveyors that a bribe was expected in one of its particular interactions with a public official. On the other hand, the more indirect questions may be more subject to the possibility of inaccurate perceptions of other firms' experiences, based on second-hand information or media reports. Both types of questions have their virtues and drawbacks, so it is difficult to conclude with much confidence that administrative corruption overall has either risen or fallen since 2008.

Another administrative corruption question in the BEEPS concerns the amount paid in bribes, or "bribe tax":

> It is said that establishments are sometimes required to make gifts or informal payments to public officials to "get things done" with regard to customs, taxes, licenses, regulations, services, etc. On average, what percentage of total annual sales, or estimated total annual value, do establishments like this one pay in informal payments or gifts to public officials for this purpose?

For firms responding in terms of value in currency units, information on annual sales from another survey question is used to convert responses to bribe payments as a percentage of sales.[16] In 2008, 29 % of Russian firms indicated they had made informal payments or gifts (i.e. a % greater than 0), compared to the ECA average of only 17 %. In 2011, only 13 % of Russian firms reported positive payments. Averaged over all firms, the "bribe tax" in 2008 was 1.7 % of sales, above the ECA average of 1.0 %. In 2011, the average "bribe tax" for Russia declined to 0.9 % of sales.[17] These findings are consistent with the declining trend in administrative corruption reflected in the more direct experiential questions in the survey, discussed above.

Among those firms reporting positive payments, however, bribes as a percentage of sales increased from 4.5 % of sales in 2008 to 7.3 % in 2011. Payment of bribes thus became more concentrated over time: fewer firms report paying them, but those that do pay more.

Public procurement is one final category of firms' interactions with public officials covered by the BEEPS. This type of interaction is considered separately from the others, because it applies only to a subset of firms that seek to obtain government contracts. In contrast, all firms are subject to taxes and licensing requirements, and nearly all must obtain utility connections.

In 2008, 36 % of Russian firms reported that they secured or attempted to secure a government contract over the last year, far exceeding the ECA average of only 19 %. In 2011, only 27 % of Russian firms reported obtaining or seeking to obtain a government contract (Fig. 11a).

---

[16]The estimated "bribe tax" is much higher on average for firms that respond to the question directly in terms of a percentage, compared to those answering in terms of currency units. Responses in percentage units may well be biased upward, but any such bias should not affect comparisons from 2008 to 2011.

[17]This difference is only marginally significant ($p = 0.120$).

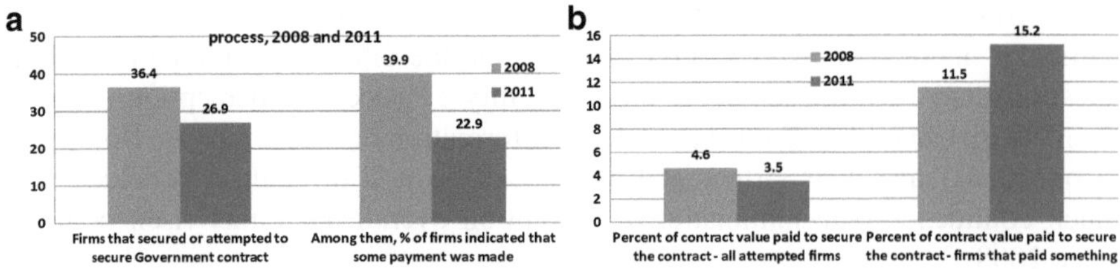

Fig. 11 (**a**) Percentage of firms that attempted to secure government contract and those among them that indicated that a unofficial payment was made in the process, 2008 and 2011. (**b**) Percentage of government contract value paid to secure such contract, 2008 and 2011

Firms that sought to obtain a contract were asked a follow-up question regarding "kick-backs":

> When establishments like this one do business with the government, what percent of the contract value would be typically paid in informal payments or gifts to secure the contract?

In 2008, 40 % of Russian firms that were asked this question reported that some payment would typically be needed. However, the corresponding figure for 2011 was only 23 %. The average "kickback tax" for all firms responding (including the 0 % responses) was 4.6 % in 2008, more than double the ECA average of 2.1 %. For 2011, the average payment was 3.5 % of the contract value.[18] Among only those firms indicating that some payment was required (i.e. with the 0 % responses dropped), however, the average payment rose from 11.5 % of contract value in 2008 to 15 % in 2011 (Fig. 11b).[19]

3.2.2 State Capture

Administrative corruption is not necessarily the most damaging form of graft for economic growth and private sector development. The 2011 BEEPS witnessed the return of several questions on "state capture" that were included in the 1999, 2002 and 2005 BEEPS, but dropped from the 2008 survey. Trends in state capture between 2005 and 2011 in Russia are unfavorable.

The term "state capture" refers to "the actions of individuals, groups or firms both in the public and private sector *to influence the formation* of laws, regulations, decrees and other government policies to their own advantage as a result of the illicit and non-transparent provision of private benefits to public officials" (World Bank 2000). While administrative corruption distorts the implementation of laws and regulations, state capture distorts their content to favor certain firms or officials.

[18]The difference is not statistically significant.

[19]The difference is only statistically significant for firms that paid something; it is not significant for all firms attempting to obtain a contract.

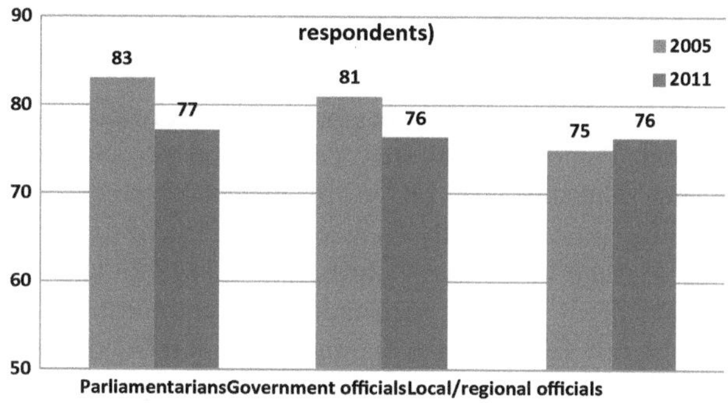

Fig. 12 Private payments/gifts to public officials to gain advantages have NO impact (percentage of respondents)

More generally, the term state capture is sometimes applied to cases where high-level government officials "capture" profitable private firms, allocating their assets or top management positions to political allies. "Crony capitalism" is a useful term that covers any system in which boundaries between the private and public sectors are blurred, whether due to private firms "capturing" the state or to state officials "capturing" private firms. The key distinction is not "who captures whom" but that "the concept of a conflict between public duties and private interests is either poorly understood or inadequately respected" (World Bank 2000, p. 9).

The first *Anti-Corruption in Transition* report (World Bank 2000), using data from the 1999 BEEPS, found only a modest correlation across ECA countries between a state capture index and another index of administrative corruption. Russia ranked near the median country in ECA on administrative corruption, but problems of state capture were more severe than in most ECA countries, according to the 1999 BEEPS.

The 2011 BEEPS included the following three "state capture" questions for which comparisons can be made with 2005:

> It is often said that firms make unofficial payments/gifts, private payments or other benefits to public officials to gain advantages in the drafting of laws, decrees, regulations, and other binding government decisions. To what extent have the following practices had a direct impact on your business? (No impact, minor impact, moderate impact, major impact, decisive impact)
>
> a. Private payments/gifts or other benefits to Parliamentarians to affect their votes.
> b. Private payments/gifts or other benefits to Government officials to affect the content of government decrees.
> c. Private payments/gifts or other benefits to local or regional government officials to affect their votes or content of government decrees.

The perceived impact of state capture, as measured by each of these three questions, increased between 2005 and 2011. As shown in Fig. 12, the percentage of firms claiming no impact of these practices declined, by 6 and 5 percentage points for questions (a) and (b), respectively, but remained almost unchanged—increasing by 1 point—for question (c). Viewing responses from the other end of the scale, the adverse trend appears more serious. The percentage of firms claiming a major or decisive impact doubled for question (c) and tripled for questions (a) and (b).

3.3 Summary

Overall, trends in regulatory burden and corruption as measured by the BEEPS are mixed. Perceptions of state capture and perceived frequency of bribe-paying by firms "like this one" or "in my line of business" have increased in recent years. Waiting time for utility connections and permits has increased. On the other hand, the average "time tax," "bribe tax," and "kickback tax" have all declined. The incidence of graft, as measured by direct questions about firms' experiences with public officials, has also declined. The number of tax inspections and meetings has declined, and perceptions that tax administration, business licensing and permits, and corruption are serious obstacles to business operations have all improved. The subsequent section examines evidence from other sources that complement—and potentially corroborate or conflict with—evidence from the BEEPS.

3.4 Other Sources

The World Bank's *Doing Business* (DB) indicators address some of the same regulatory issues as are measured in the BEEPS. The DB methodology is quite different, however. First, it does not attempt to ascertain what actual firms have experienced. Rather, it identifies the procedures that are officially required to accomplish a task, and estimates the minimum time and costs necessary "under normal circumstances" (e.g. it assumes procedures cannot be bypassed and processing time cannot be reduced by paying a bribe). Second, because official requirements can vary based on firm characteristics (location, size, ownership, etc.), it measures them for a hypothetical firm that fits a particular set of assumptions. Among other assumptions, most DB indicators assume the firm is located in the country's largest city, is 100 % domestically owned, and does not engage in foreign trade. The relevance of the DB indicators will therefore vary by country: they will be most relevant for small countries with centralized governments and a large share of its firms operating in the largest city (Singapore is an extreme example). In large, decentralized countries such as Russia, the U.S. or India, the indicator values may strictly apply to only a small fraction of firms. Nevertheless, trends in DB indicators may provide a rough measure of trends in the regulatory environment in a country more widely.

The declining number of firms in the BEEPS that cite tax administration as an obstacle is consistent with changes over time in the "Paying Taxes" indicators for Russia in DB. In 2008, according to DB, ten different tax payments were required, and filing the forms was estimated to take 448 hours. In 2011, only nine payments requiring 290 hours were required. However, caution must be exercised in attributing firms' improved perceptions of tax administration as measured in BEEPS to any reduction in time required to file taxes as measured by DB. As mentioned above, the DB estimates apply only to firms with a specified set of characteristics (including being based in the country's largest city), and no details are provided by

DB regarding what reforms might have accounted for the improvements in Russia (Moscow, specifically) between 2008 and 2011.

The increased waiting time for construction permits as measured in BEEPS conflicts with an opposite trend in official requirements, as measured by DB. According to DB, the time required to obtain construction permits fell from 623 to 423 days in 2011, when "Russia eased construction permitting by implementing a single window for all procedures related to land use."[20] However, the actual average waiting time as measured by BEEPS increased from 104 days in 2008 to 130 days in 2011. Note that the two sources are not measuring the same thing—even ignoring the caveats regarding the DB methodology mentioned above. The BEEPS question asks about one important step in the process: waiting time once the application was made. The DB indicator covers additional steps. This provides one more illustration as to why evidence from the BEEPS and DB may appear to conflict, even if they are both accurately measuring what they attempt to measure.

The cost of obtaining construction permits, as measured by DB, fell by more than 90 % from 2008 to 2011. This improvement is consistent with the fact that fewer firms in BEEPS regarded business licensing and permits as a major obstacle in 2011 compared to 2008, although many other factors undoubtedly contribute to the latter trend.

Russia's DB indicators exhibit little or no change during the 2008 to 2011 period in several other regulatory areas covered by BEEPS. These include the DB categories "Starting a Business," "Registering Property," "Getting Electricity," "Trading Across Borders" and "Enforcing Contracts."

An important caveat is that the cross-country DB database applies only to the largest city in each country—Moscow, in the case of Russia—and rules may vary substantially across cities and regions within a country. In several countries, including Russia, sub-national studies have been conducted. The Russia study covers only the 4 areas of regulation, out of 11 total DB topics, where sub-national governments have substantial responsibility and exhibit meaningful variation in the data (World Bank 2012, p. 7). Moscow ranks at or near the bottom among the 30 municipalities covered in the sub-national Russia DB study, so Russia's relatively low ranking in the cross-country DB does not accurately reflect the rules facing firms in most parts of the country. Moreover, the sub-national study documents reforms in these four areas in many Russian municipalities implemented in recent years, even when no reforms were implemented in Moscow.

The World Economic Forum's annual "Executive Opinion Survey" (EOS) conducted in Russia and about 140 other countries, is another useful source that includes numerous questions pertaining to regulatory burden and corruption. Although survey respondents are firm managers, the sample of firms is not designed to be nationally representative as with the BEEPS. Instead, the goal is to identify respondents who are relatively well-informed about Russia in cross-national perspective. The resulting sample over-represents firms that are larger, trade across

---

[20]See http://www.doingbusiness.org/reforms/overview/economy/russia.

borders, and have some foreign ownership. For many countries, the sample is small (well under 100 for some), but for Russia the sample in most years is between 350 and 600.

One EOS question asks whether complying with government's regulatory requirements are "burdensome," on a scale of 1 to 7, where higher ratings reflect perceptions of a lower burden. The average score for Russia has fluctuated slightly in recent years, but is higher (i.e. better) in the most recent survey than in any prior year. A separate question on efficiency of customs exhibits some year-to-year variation but no evidence of a trend.

Questions pertaining to state capture show a worsening trend in recent years, consistent with the BEEPS indicators. One difference however is that BEEPS data on perceptions of state capture as a problem are available only for 2005 and 2011, not for the intervening years. The annual data in the EOS show a favorable trend between 2005 and 2008, followed by steady deterioration between 2008 and 2011. The EOS question most similar to the BEEPS questions asks whether the respondent's firm is adversely affected by illegal payments influencing policies, laws and regulations. A second relevant question asks about whether "well-connected" firms receive favorable treatment when public officials make decisions on policies and government contracts. Both of these questions show a similar worsening trend in the last several surveys conducted by the WEF in Russia. Another question indicates declining trust in the financial honesty of politicians over the last few years, partially negating a sizeable jump that occurred between 2008 and 2009. Perceptions that corrupt diversion of public funds for private use have also increased every year beginning in 2007.

Transparency International (TI) and the Worldwide Governance Indicators (WGI) both publish composite indexes of corruption, based on numerous "expert" (e.g. from the EIU) and survey (e.g. the WEF) sources. These indexes mix administrative corruption, state capture and other forms of graft, so they reflect a very broad definition of corruption. Moreover, the methodology of these indexes is designed primarily to compare countries to each other at a point in time, rather than to measure progress over time for a given country. Nevertheless, they can be a useful tool for assessing whether corruption perceptions in a country are improving over time *relative to other countries*. Russia's most recent TI "Corruption Perceptions Index" rating (published in 2011 but reflecting a mix of sources from the years 2009 through 2011) of 2.4 represents its highest rating in the last 5 years. The WGI "Control of Corruption" index (constructed using the same sources as TI, plus a few additional ones) exhibits a similar trend: following a steady decline from 2003 to 2009, Russia's rating improved slightly in 2010 and then again in 2011.

The WGI also provides a composite index of "Regulatory Quality." Higher scores reflect a lower regulatory burden. Russia ranks much higher on this index (at about the 40th percentile among all countries) than on WGI's corruption index (10th or 15th percentile), but its rating has changed very little since 2006.

4 Regional Comparisons

The 2012 Russia survey is the first BEEPS designed to be representative at sub-national levels within a country. In most of the 37 regions included in the survey, about 120 firms are represented.

Results show that the business environment differs significantly across regions. The region in which firms are located turns out to have fairly strong implications for the degree of corruption and the regulatory burden they confront. For example, a full set of regional dummy variables statistically accounts for 12 % of the variation in firms' reported "time tax." In contrast, only 6 % of the variation can be explained collectively by many other firm characteristics: firm size (measured by number of employees and revenue), age, ownership (private, foreign and public), industry, and product or service accounting for the largest proportion of sales. Similarly, about 20 % of the variation in firms' perceptions of "state capture" can be statistically explained by their location (i.e. by regional dummy variables), compared to only about 6 % for size, age, ownership, industry and main product or service.[21]

The large regional variation in these and other BEEPS indicators is shown in Table 2 in Appendix 1 and Table 6 in Appendix 2. For the 37 regions included in the BEEPS, this table presents averages for selected administrative burden and corruption indicators. For example, the "time tax" indicator exemplifies the dramatic variation across regions—the mean "time tax" varies from 1 % for Primorsky Kray to 49 % for Stavropol Kray. Moscow is in the middle of the distribution, at 19 %.

4.1 Administrative Burden

Although regions differ significantly from each other, the same regions that rank at or near the top on some indicators—perhaps surprisingly—rank at or near the bottom on others. The average number of meetings with tax officials ranges from 1.3 for Smolensk to 5.3 for Ulyanovsk Oblast. Stavropol Kray ranks 5th best, with an average of 1.8 per firm, despite having the highest average "time tax."

Smolensk Oblast also ranks best on waiting time for electrical connections, with an average of only 8 days. Average waiting time is longest for Primorsky Kray, at 730 days, nearly double the time for any other region. On the other hand, Primorsky Kray has the shortest average wait for water connections, at only one day. Smolensk Oblast ranks 2nd-best at 1.8 days, while the 315-day wait for St. Petersburg is more than double the waiting time in any other region.

[21] Analysis of cross-country results of earlier rounds of BEEPS have also shown that country dummies account for more significant portions of variation than special attributes of individual firms in the sample.

Firms in Murmansk Oblast report an average wait of only 15 days for construction permits, compared to a high of 515 days for Yaroslavl Oblast Smolensk Oblast and Moscow rank 2nd- and 3rd-best, at 30 days. Waiting time for operating licenses averages only 8 days in Kirov Oblast, but 82 days in Perm Oblast. Stavropol Kray (22 days) and Smolensk Oblast (28) rank 2nd- and 3rd-best.

When multiple indicators are available to measure performance on a broad underlying concept such as administrative burden and red tape, it is common to construct a single summary index. For example, the *Doing Business* project publishes an overall index of "Ease of Doing Business" constructed from all of its sub-indicators. If correlations among the indicators are low, however, index reliability will be low and a single measure may obscure more than it reveals. In the 2011 Russia BEEPS, the region-level correlation between waiting times for electrical and water connections is only 0.19, and the correlation between waiting times for operating licenses and construction permits is only 0.12. A composite index of these BEEPS wait-time indicators would rank Smolensk Oblast at the top, which accurately summarizes the fact that Smolensk Oblast ranks very high on a range of relevant indicators. Primorsky Kray would rank near the middle, however, which would unhelpfully obscure the fact that it performs very well on some indicators (and could even serve as a model for other regions) and very poorly on some others (so may benefit from looking to Smolensk Oblast and other regions as models for reform efforts).

A more statistically reliable composite index for purposes of ranking regions can be constructed from a different set of BEEPS questions, pertaining to various potential obstacles to firm operations and growth. Questions are of the general form "to what degree is [e.g.] business licensing and permits an obstacle to the current operations" of the firm (see Appendix 2 for more details). Seven questions were selected, each measuring some aspect of regulatory burden:

- business licensing and permits;
- tax administration;
- customs and trade regulations;
- access to land;
- labor regulations;
- courts;
- corruption.

Courts are included because they are often used as mechanisms for enforcing or appealing regulatory decisions. Corruption is included because regulations are sometimes formulated or applied by public officials in ways designed to extract bribes, and because firms sometimes offer bribes or "gifts" to influence the content or enforcement of regulation.

An "Administrative Obstacles" index was constructed as the simple average of these seven indicators. The index has a very high reliability coefficient of 0.90, and the average inter-item correlation among the seven questions is 0.55.[22]

Table 6 in Appendix 2 shows the full regional rankings on this index. The top five regions in order are: Smolensk, Belgorod, Stavropol, and Irkutsk Oblasts and Republic of Mordovia. The bottom five regions are (starting with the worst): Rostov, Leningrad, and Samara Oblast, Krasnodar Kray, and St. Petersburg City.

4.2 Corruption

Smolensk Oblast easily ranks as the region where corruption is perceived least often as an obstacle to operating a business. Its mean on a 0–4 scale (with 0 indicating no obstacle, and 4 indicating "very severe" obstacle) is only 0.2. Irkutsk Oblast and Kirov Oblast rank 2nd and 3rd at 0.8, while corruption is most perceived as a problem for firms in St. Petersburg (2.3),[23] closely followed by Leningrad Oblast, Moscow and Rostov Oblast.

Regions where corruption is perceived as a more serious obstacle also tend to be the ones where higher "bribe taxes" are reported (correlation = 0.42) and where firms indicate that "irregular payments" are frequently needed "to get things done with regard to customs, taxes, licenses, regulations, etc." (correlation = 0.41). The survey question on whether corruption is an obstacle to the firm's operations does not provide a definition for corruption, so it is not obvious whether firms harmed by corruption perceive administrative corruption or state capture as the bigger problem. To answer this question, firm-level responses to the corruption-as-obstacle question were regressed on a number of firm and regional characteristics, including responses to the more specific survey questions on state capture and administrative bribery. These tests provide a strong indication that administrative bribery is the main corruption-related obstacle that enterprise managers have in mind when responding to the question. Responses to the "bribe frequency" and state capture questions are both significant predictors of the degree to which whether firms perceive corruption as an obstacle, but the former question is a far more powerful predictor than the latter (see Appendix 3, regression 4.2). Similarly, the Graft index—reflecting firms' recent experiences with administrative bribery—is also a far more powerful predictor of whether firms cite corruption as an obstacle than are firms' perceptions of state capture.

Table 6 of Appendix 2 shows how the regions rank on two indexes constructed from BEEPS questions pertaining to administrative corruption. One is the Graft

---

[22]The reliability coefficient increases with the number of items in an index and with the average inter-item correlation.

[23]In other words, corruption is more than a moderate obstacle to firm operations and growth in this region.

Index, defined above as the share of firms' reported interactions with officials in which they report needing to pay a bribe. A second index, the "Administrative Corruption Index," is constructed from responses to the "bribe frequency" question as well as three similar questions that ask more specifically about whether it is common for "establishments like this one" to pay bribes in dealing with customs, courts and taxes.

Stavropol Kray ranks at the top on this Administrative Corruption Index, followed by Ulyanovsk Oblast, Lipetsk Oblast and the Republic of Mordovia (where 1 indicates bribes are "never" needed and 7 indicates "always"). Smolensk Oblast ranks 8th-best among the 37 regions at 1.9. Primorsky Kray (3.1) ranks at the bottom, just above Tver Oblast, Rostov Oblast, and Chelyabinsk Oblast.

Rankings on the Graft Index look quite different, despite the fact that both indexes pertain to administrative bribery. The difference between them is that one is based on questions about the firm's reported *experiences* related to a set of specified transactions, while the other is based on questions about respondents' *perceptions*, namely what they *think* happens with similar firms, for a similar (but not identical) set of specified interactions.

These subtle distinctions in how questions are asked have surprisingly large implications for firms' responses: correlations between the two types of indicators turn out to be extremely low. None of the top-ranked regions on the Administrative Corruption Index appears among those highly-ranked on the Graft Index. Smolensk Oblast is the top-ranked region on the Graft Index, followed by Novosibirsk Oblast, St. Petersburg, Moscow City, and Primorsky Kray. The regions at the bottom of the list are also entirely different. Voronezh Oblast, the Republic of Bashkortostan, and Krasnodar Kray are the regions ranked worst on the Graft Index.

The policy implications of perceptions questions vs. experiential questions may also differ. For example, perceptions of corruption in two jurisdictions with the same incidence of actual corruption may differ, if there are more effective channels of communication in one jurisdiction than in the other. Freedom of information laws and a more independent and competitive media can worsen perceptions of corruption (e.g. Costa 2012).

Region-level correlations among the three state capture indicators are extremely high, ranging from 0.94 to 0.98. Table 6 of Appendix 2 shows how the regions rank on a State Capture index, constructed as the mean of these three indicators. Khaborovsk Kray, Kursk Oblast, and Ulyanovsk Oblast are the top-ranking three regions on this index. All three of them rank in the middle among regions on the "Administrative Obstacles" index. The Republic of Mordovia is the only region ranking in the top 5 on both the State Capture index (4th) and on the Administrative Obstacles index (5th). It is also one of only two regions (along with Ulyanovsk Oblast) to rank in the top 5 on both State Capture and Administrative Corruption. Despite its top ranking among the 37 regions on both the Administrative Obstacles Index and Graft Index, Smolensk Oblast ranks only 20th-best on the State Capture index.

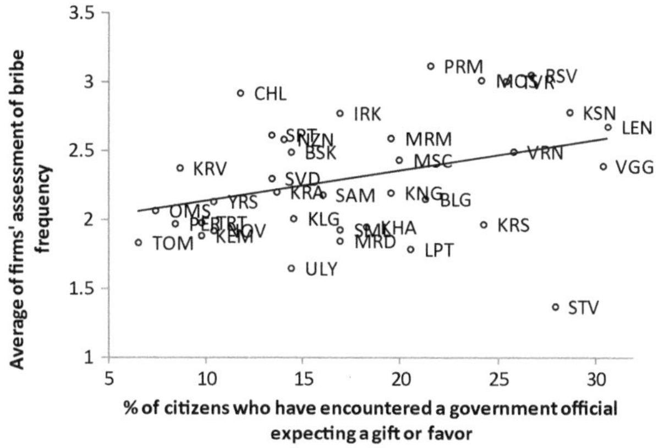

Fig. 13 Perception of corruption by firms and households

Primorsky Kray and Irkutsk Oblast (ranked only 36th on the State Capture index, but 4th on the Administrative Obstacles index) are ranked in the top 5 on one of the four indexes in Table 6 of Appendix 2, but in the bottom 5 on another index. Only one region, Krasnodar Kray, is ranked in the bottom 5 on all four indexes. Rostov Oblast is ranked among the bottom 3 on three of the four indexes. Although the three state capture indicators are strongly correlated (at about 0.70) across regions with the "bribe frequency" indicator, they are only weakly correlated with the corruption-as-obstacle indicator and with responses to the "bribe tax" question. Moreover, questions on direct experience with bribe paying (in connection with taxes, permits, and utility connections) are weakly correlated with most other corruption indicators at the regional level.

Public opinion surveys in Russia, designed to be representative at the regional level, have included some corruption-related questions. There is some congruence between firms' experiences and perceptions in the BEEPS, and citizens' experiences and perceptions in these household opinion surveys. For example, a 2011 Public Opinion Foundation (FOM) survey asked whether or not a public official has requested an "unofficial payment" or favor from them in the last 1 or 2 years. Among regions represented in the BEEPS, the percentage of citizen respondents who had been asked for a bribe ranged from a low of 6 % in Tomsk to a high of 31 % in St. Petersburg. Responses in this survey were positively correlated at the regional level with several BEEPS indicators. Figure 13[24] shows the relationship (correlation = 0.35) between this FOM question and firms' reports of "bribe frequency," i.e. whether or not it is frequently necessary for similar firms to make unofficial payments "to get things done." The FOM indicator is also positively correlated (at 0.35) with firms' perceptions of the impact on their businesses of state capture at the local and regional level.

[24] Abbreviation of region names is given in Appendix 2, Table 6.

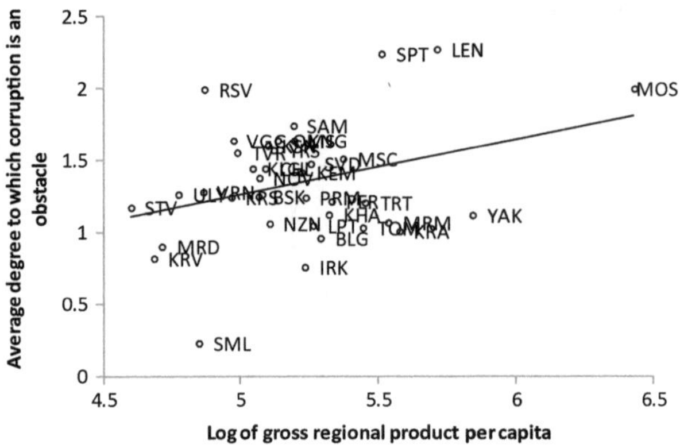

Fig. 14 GRP and perception of corruption as an obstacle

4.3 *Why Do Regions Differ?*

Although regulatory burden and corruption challenges confronting firms can be predicted to a significant degree from their location, it is not easy to identify *why* regions matter. Regions differ with respect to historical influences, income levels, dependence on natural resources, and in regulatory and anti-corruption policies. These differences potentially account for why firms in different regions report greater or lesser problems related to red tape and corruption. It turns out to be difficult however to empirically establish significant linkages between regional characteristics and measures of regulatory burden and corruption.

Cross-country studies on corruption, including those using cross-country BEEPS results, often find positive correlations with per capita income (e.g. Treisman 2007) and other measures of socioeconomic development. Dininio and Orttung (2005) analyze 40 Russian regions, and show that higher gross regional product (GRP) per capita is associated with lower administrative corruption, as measured by surveys of experiences of citizens and entrepreneurs. Their survey data were collected in 2002 (by Transparency International and the INDEM Foundation), and only 27 of their 40 regions are represented in the 37-region BEEPS survey. Most regional-level indicators of regulatory burden and corruption in the BEEPS are not significantly correlated with per capita GRP. In the few cases where a significant relationship is found, the correlation is actually positive. Figure 14 shows regional values for GRP per capita in the X axis, and regional means for the BEEPS corruption-as-an-obstacle question on the Y axis. The positive relation shown by the least-squares line in the figure appears to be sensitive to the case of Moscow, a rather extreme outlier on GRP per capita. When Moscow is dropped, the relationship remains positive but is weaker and not statistically significant.

Dininio and Orttung (2005) also find that citizens and firms report experiencing more corruption in regions with larger government, as measured by the number of bureaucrats. Controlling for regional population and other variables, however, there is no significant relationship in the BEEPS data between the number of regional civil servants (or the civil servant wage bill) on the one hand, and indicators of corruption and regulatory burden on the other. Region size itself appears to matter for some forms of corruption: in more populous regions, other things equal, the bribe tax and Graft index tend to be higher, and firms are more likely to report that corruption is an obstacle (see Appendix 3).

Some cross-country studies have also found a positive relation between corruption and dependence on natural resource revenues. In their study of 40 Russian regions, however, Dininio and Orttung (2005) are unable to detect any significant link between resource dependence and administrative corruption. Chirkova and Bowser (2005) observed from the same TI/INDEM survey data that—counter to conventional wisdom—corruption was lower in the natural-resource-rich regions such as Tyumen Oblast and Bashkortostan. The BEEPS data produce similar results: natural resource extraction as a share of GRP tends to be weakly related to most measures of corruption and regulatory burden from the BEEPS. Controlling statistically for other regional- and firm-level factors in multiple regression analyses, firms located in more resource-dependent regions are actually significantly *less* likely to report that corruption is an obstacle, or that irregular payments are often required to get things done ("bribe frequency"), or that state capture has an impact on their firms (see Appendix 3 for full regression results).

In reporting on the TI/INDEM survey findings, Dininio and Orttung (2005) and Chirkova and Bowser (2005) conclude that corruption tends to be more severe in southern regions such as Rostov Oblast than in northern regions such as Karelia and Yaroslavl Oblast. In contrast, most of the BEEPS indicators on corruption and regulatory burden exhibit no discernible geographic pattern for the Administrative Obstacles index. Controlling for other region and firm characteristics in multiple regression analyses (see Appendix 3), latitude is insignificant in most cases; for the Graft index and the bribe tax, corruption tends to be significantly *worse* in the northern regions (i.e. latitude has a significant and positive coefficient), counter to expectations.

Regional policies potentially affect the level of certain aspects of corruption as experienced by firms. Transparency of information on public procurement is one such area. Balsevich et al. (2011) examined how well 83 regional public procurement web sites complied in 2007 with the recently-passed Federal Law on Public Procurement. Their overall Transparency Index was constructed from four sub-indicators, on Current Procurements, Completed Procurements, Search functions, and Additional Features (including feedback mechanisms and availability of summary statistics on regional procurement).

A natural hypothesis is that in regions with greater transparency in public procurement, the average "kickback tax" to obtain government contracts reported by firms in the BEEPS would be lower. Controlling for per capita GRP and region population, this hypothesis is supported in a multiple regression analysis. The relationship is significant at the 0.05 level for the overall Transparency Index and at the 0.01 level if the Completed Procurements indicator is used instead.

Figure 15 shows the partial relationship between transparency in Completed Procurements and the mean "extra payments" needed to secure a contract as a share

Fig. 15 Transparency and corruption in procurement

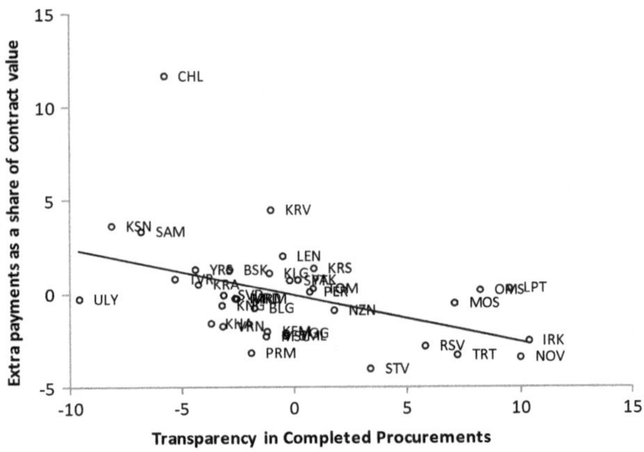

of contract value, controlling for population and per capita GRP (see Appendix 3, regression 6.6 for details). Chelyabinsk is an outlier in the regression, with relatively low transparency and extremely high "extra payments." It is an industrial region with a high level of military production, which may have something to do with its relatively low level of transparency in government procurement. If Chelyabinsk is dropped from the regression, the slope of the regression line declines from −0.27 to −0.20, but statistical significance of the relationship actually strengthens.[25]

Regions also differ with respect to freedom of information (FOI) policies. Transparency International Russia recently classified all regions into one of three categories: those with effective FOI laws, those with effective FOI decrees, and those with neither.[26] These three categories of regions do not differ significantly on average. However, on the BEEPS indicators of regulatory burden and corruption (e.g. see Table 12 in Appendix 3).

Dininio and Orttung (2005) tested two additional proxy "measures for getting at political and civil aspects of accountability" (p. 504). Neither of these measures—voting turnout rates and an index of media freedoms in the region—were significant predictors of regional corruption rates in their study. Voting turnout (using more recent data) is also unrelated to the BEEPS corruption indicators, in regional-level analyses.

Nevertheless, there are some evidence that better-informed voters and users of government services can be effective in limiting corruption. Other things equal, state capture and bribe frequency is lower in regions with higher per capita newspaper circulation (see Appendix 3, Table 12, regressions 5.2 and 5.6).

---

[25]Regions, not firms, are the unit of analysis in these regressions. Table 13 in Appendix 3 demonstrates that the relationships described here also hold in firm-level analyses that control for a large number of firm and region characteristics.

[26]http://transparency.org.ru/en/news/russia-celebrates-the-10th-anniversary-of-international-right-to-know-day.

Fig. 16 Correlation of DB and licensing as an obstacle indexes

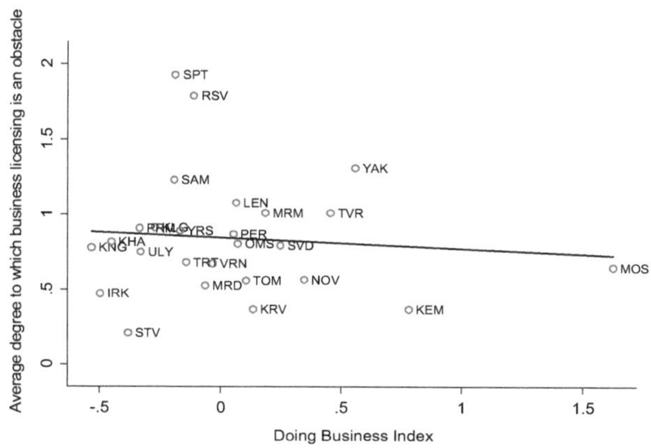

Regional policies with respect to regulation also potentially affect firms' experiences and perceptions of regulatory burden and corruption. The recent regional-level *Doing Business* (DB) study for Russia (World Bank 2012) covered four topics: Starting a Business, Getting Electricity, Dealing with Construction Permits, and Registering Property. The BEEPS also includes questions directly pertaining to the first three of these issues. Controlling for other variables, firms report a shorter waiting time for obtaining an operating license in regions where DB indicates that the process can be completed in fewer days (Appendix 3, Table 9, regression 2.5). More often than not, unfortunately, DB indicators are able to explain very little, if any, of the variation in regulatory burden as reported by firms in the BEEPS.

An overall "Doing Business" index can be constructed as an equal-weighted average of 4 DB sub-indexes, each in turn reflecting an equal-weighted average of the several indicators under each of the four topics covered by the Russian regional DB study. Higher values of the index reflect more procedures, longer waiting times and higher costs. This index, however, is not significantly related to the "time tax" reported by firms (see Appendix 3, Table 8, regression 1.2), or firms' perceptions of licensing and permits as an obstacle (Appendix 3, Table 10, regression 3.2).

Figure 16, above portrays the regional average of this licensing-as-an-obstacle indicator on the Y axis, and number of days required to obtain an operating license as measured by DB on the X axis. As shown by the super-imposed least-squares line, there is a weak negative (i.e. counterintuitive) relation between them. The absence of any strong positive relationship in this figure does not imply that waiting time for licenses is not a problem for firms.

The BEEPS includes a question on firms' actual experiences with waiting time for operating licenses. As shown in Fig. 17, regions with higher average wait times tend to be the same regions where firms are most likely to report that licenses and

Fig. 17 Time and difficulty of obtaining a license

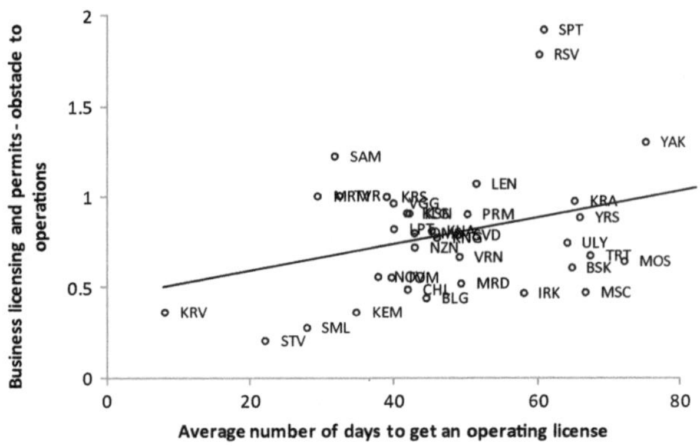

permits are an obstacle to them.[27] Firms within a given region report widely varying waiting times, not only diverging from each other but also from the waiting time estimated for a hypothetical "typical" firm in the DB study.

The number of *days* required to obtain an electrical connection as measured by DB is uncorrelated with BEEPS indicators on (1) waiting time for an electrical connection, and (2) perceptions of electricity as an obstacle to business operation. The number of *procedures* required to obtain an electrical connection as measured by DB is uncorrelated with the BEEPS indicator on waiting time for an electrical connection, but paradoxically is *inversely* correlated with perceptions of electricity as an obstacle to business operation.

At the cross-country level, an overall Ease of Doing Business index (constructed from more topics than the four available in the Russia study) is strongly correlated with TI's Corruption Perceptions Index: where rules impede business less, corruption is lower.[28] At the cross-regional level in Russia, there are good reasons to expect a more modest link between them. First, there is much less variation among Russian regions than across countries in the DB data, especially in the indicators on Starting a Business and Registering Property. Second, the strong cross-country relationship is likely to be biased upward by omitted variables—e.g. cultural, historical and institutional differences—that are correlated with regulation and corruption. In analyzing a single country, many such factors are effectively held constant, limiting the potential for spurious correlation. The overall DB index turns out to be only weakly related to most corruption indicators in the BEEPS. One exception is the Graft index (see Appendix 3, Table 13, regression 6.2). Firms located in regions that DB ranks as having more onerous rules are more likely to report having paid bribes in their dealings with public officials. Looking separately at the components of the

[27] This relation also holds when controlling for numerous other variables, as shown in regression 3.4 of Appendix 2.

[28] See chart accompanying "Doing Business 2013: Getting Better," *The Economist*, October 27, 2012.

DB index, it turns out that the sub-index on Getting Electricity is driving this result. The other three sub-indexes are unrelated to the likelihood of paying bribes.

A third possible explanation for many of the modest regional-level correlations described in this note is that special interests wishing to block entry or disadvantage new competitors may focus on a single area. They may sometimes be able to create high costs for competitors—and preserve rents for themselves—through imposing lengthy delays or high fees or bribes in only one or two important administrative transactions. Imposing additional costs in other transactions may be largely redundant, and entail more costs to the rent-seeking coalitions. These particular transactions or regulatory areas may be different in different regions. If so, the same regions performing poorly on one area (for example tax administration) would not necessarily be expected to perform poorly in another (for example operating licenses). From this perspective, bureaucratic capacity is not the key factor affecting regulatory burden and corruption in the regions. In contrast, the higher cross-country correlations generally observed among these indicators is more likely to reflect variations in bureaucratic capacity, as countries vary far more in administrative traditions and income than do the Russian regions.

4.4 *Regulatory Burden, Administrative Corruption and State Capture*

It is often argued that excessive regulation can encourage corruption. For example, if firms are required to fill out numerous forms, to visit multiple offices, and to pay numerous and large fees to set up a new business, public officials may be tempted to accept—and even solicit—extra "unofficial payments" or "gifts" to speed up the process. Excessive red tape can provide public officials with more opportunities to deliberately slow down processing, or even to "misplace" an application, to increase the incentives for firms to pay bribes. For these reasons, regions with more burdensome regulation can be expected to exhibit a higher incidence of corruption. The BEEPS data confirms this proposition.

Figure 18 supports this view. It plots the regional-level means of "bribe frequency" (on how often it is necessary to make unofficial payments "to get things done") on the X axis, and the regional means of the question on licensing and permits as an obstacle on the Y axis.

The need to pay bribes and the administrative procedures they are intended to circumvent both constitute significant obstacles from the standpoint of firms.

Figures 19 and 20 respectively show that regions where firms report tax administration as a more serious obstacle also tend to be regions where firms report a higher number of meetings with tax officials (Fig. 19), and a greater need to pay bribes in connection with paying taxes (Fig. 20). Moreover, firms reporting a higher "bribe tax" also tend to report a higher "time tax" (see Appendix 3, Table 13, regression 6.4). The fact that bribery and red tape tend to be observed together does

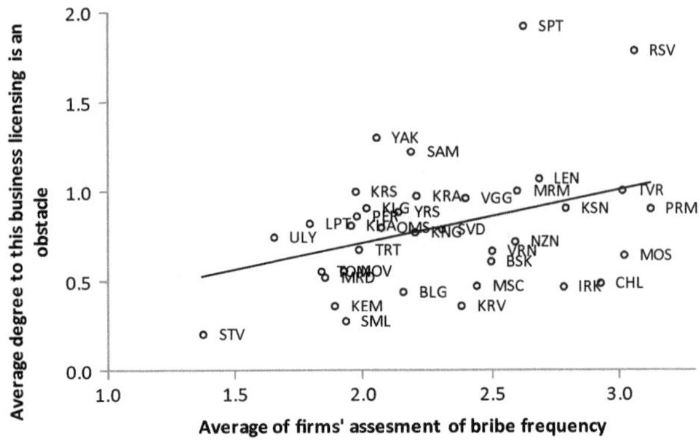

Fig. 18 Degree of difficulty in obtaining a license and bribe frequency

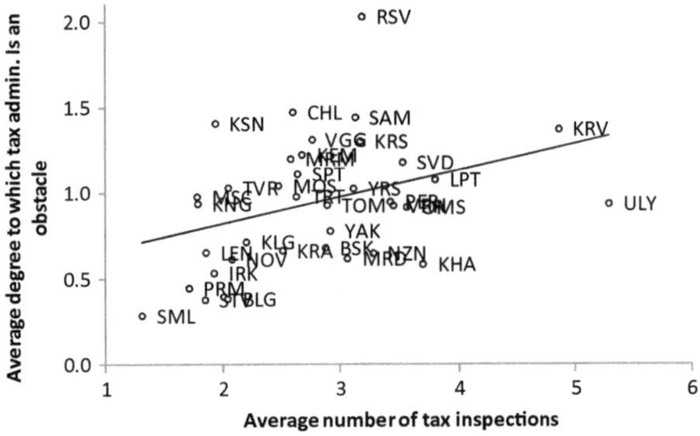

Fig. 19 Tax administration as an obstacle in relation to the number of tax inspections

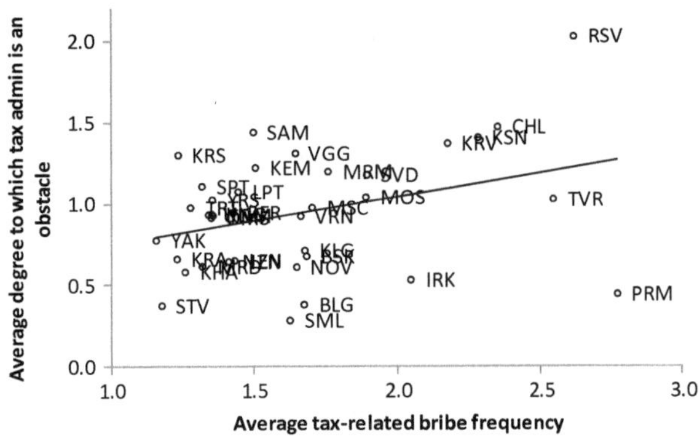

Fig. 20 Relation of bribe frequency and obstacles in tax administration

not necessarily mean that paying a bribe is never an effective strategy to "get things done" from the standpoint of an individual firm. It is consistent however with the view that an excessive regulatory burden is imposed in many cases as a deliberate strategy to extract rents from firms.

Firms that report interacting with officials in more of the six "sub-sectors" measured in the Graft Index (tax, utility applications, operating licensing, etc.)

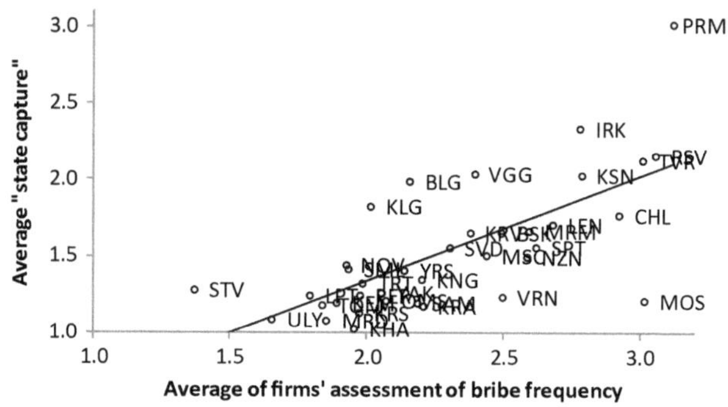

Fig. 21 Bribe frequency and state capture at the local level

tend to report a higher "time tax," greater perceptions of bribe frequency, a higher "bribe tax," and more frequently cite licensing and permits as an obstacle to their operations (see Appendix 3 regressions). Moreover, they also report paying bribes in a greater *proportion* of these interactions—as measured by the Graft Index—not merely in a larger absolute number of them. These results are consistent with the common anti-corruption policy prescription of instituting reforms that limit the number of opportunities for officials to solicit bribes.

The first World Bank (2000) report based on BEEPS data, using the 1999 surveys, introduced a corruption typology that distinguished between "administrative corruption" and "state capture." In general, the two types were empirically correlated among countries in the ECA region: some countries such as Slovenia and Estonia ranked well on both, while others such as Azerbaijan and Ukraine ranked poorly on both. However, the positive relationship was sufficiently modest in strength that several countries ranked highly on one concept but were ranked low on the other. For example, Croatia ranked best on administrative corruption in the region, but ranked worse than the majority of countries on "state capture."

In the Russia regional BEEPS, the relationship between state capture and administrative corruption appears to be stronger. Figure 21 depicts "bribe frequency" (necessity of paying bribes "to get things done") on the X axis, with the "state capture" question pertaining to regional and local officials on the Y axis. (Results are very similar using either of the other two state capture questions.) There are very few outliers. Only Moscow stands out as a region ranking very well on one type (capture) and poorly on the other type (administrative corruption).

4.5 *Why Do Firms Differ Within Regions?*

As stated above, location matters more than firm-level characteristics for regulatory burden and corruption perceptions and experiences. However, it is worth noting briefly some of the significant firm-level factors identified in the regression analyses in Appendix 3.[29]

Older firms, in particular those formed prior to the transition, are arguably more likely to have established connections with government officials, and to be treated more favorably in the formulation and implementation of regulatory policies. Age of firms turned out not to matter, however, for firms' perceptions and experiences of corruption and regulatory burden. The regressions reported in Appendix 3 include, instead of a continuous measure of firm age, a dummy variable for firms established prior to the transition (only 5.2 % of the sample). This proxy for established connections with government officials also proved insignificant in every test.

Several studies have shown that membership in business associations can help Russian firms influence policies or contest predation by government officials, although sometimes by imposing costs on the rest of society (Pyle 2011; Pyle and Solanko 2013). The BEEPS questionnaire unfortunately does not ascertain membership in business associations, so it is an omitted variable in the context of the analyses reported in Appendix 3.

Larger firms—as measured by number of employees (or revenues)—report a higher average "time tax," more tax meetings, longer waits for operating licenses, and greater perceptions of bribe frequency. However, they do not have a higher incidence of bribe paying as measured by the Graft Index; moreover, they do not perceive more state capture, nor are they more likely to report that corruption is a serious obstacle. This may be attributable to the lower "bribe tax" they report paying. Consistent with other studies, as summarized in Kaufmann et al. (2008), bribe paying in the BEEPS acts as a regressive tax, with smaller firms paying a larger share of firm revenues.

Exporting firms (9.6 % of the sample) report both a higher incidence of bribe paying (as measured by the Graft Index), and heightened perceptions of corruption (as measured by the "bribe frequency" question). They are more likely than non-exporting firms to report that corruption (but not licensing and permits) is an obstacle to doing business.

Retail firms (11 % of the sample) are more likely than other firms to cite licensing and permits as an obstacle, but paradoxically they report lower average waits for operating licenses. One possibility is that they pay bribes to shorten waiting times; however, they also report a smaller average "bribe tax."

Several studies have concluded based on evidence from household surveys, firm surveys, and lab experiments that women tend to be less corrupt than men, in terms of demanding or complying with demands for bribes (e.g. Rivas 2012; Swamy et al. 2001). The top manager is female in 20 % of the BEEPS sample. Controlling for other factors, female-managed firms pay lower bribes, as measured by the "bribe tax" and "kickback tax" paid to obtain government contracts. They are less likely to

---

[29] All results reported below are significant at the 0.10 levels or better, and most are significant at the 0.05 level. These are all "partial" effects, meaning the estimated effect holding all other variables in the analysis constant.

perceive state capture as a problem for their firm, and less likely to cite corruption more generally as an obstacle to firm operations. Female-managed firms report a "time tax" averaging 2 percentage points higher than other firms, however, despite a lower average wait (by about 10 days) for an operating license.

Firms with a higher share of foreign ownership report more tax meetings, but less state capture, and no difference from other firms in experience or perceptions of administrative corruption. The foreign ownership share averages only 2 % in the sample. Among the 120 firms reporting some foreign ownership (about 3 % of the sample), foreign ownership averages 68 %.

Unsurprisingly, government-owned firms are less likely to cite corruption as an obstacle to their operations. More surprisingly, they do not differ significantly from other firms with respect to most indicators of corruption and regulatory burden. This may be due in part to lack of sufficient variation in the data. Government ownership averages only 0.5 % in the sample. Only 38 firms (less than 1 %) report some government ownership, and among those 38, government ownership averages 50 %.

5 Conclusions

A broad range of evidence shows that overly burdensome regulation and corruption are significant impediments to firm entry, productivity and growth. Although in terms of per capita income, Russia is gradually converging toward the levels of OECD countries, growth rates fall short of those experienced by most other BRICs and large middle-income comparator countries. Moreover, growth has been driven primarily by revenues from commodity producers, and is disproportionately concentrated in resource-rich regions and a few large cities. In the longer run, sustained growth that is more balanced, both geographically and across a more diverse set of sectors, will likely require thoroughgoing improvement in Russia's regulatory climate for private investment and enterprise (World Economic Forum 2011; Desai 2008).

This report assesses trends over time in corruption and the regulatory burden in Russia, draws comparisons with the ECA region as a whole, and for the first time using BEEPS data is able to make comparisons across 37 Russian regions. Most of the available indicators show improvement over time, between the 2008 BEEPS and the 2011 surveys at the country level. For example, senior managers' time spent on dealing with regulation (the "time tax") declined from an average of about 22 % in 2008 to 17 % in 2011. In dealing with administrative requirements such as obtaining licenses or dealing with tax officials, fewer firms report that "gifts" or irregular payments were expected by officials: a Graft Index, reflecting the proportion of such interaction where a bribe was expected, improved from 0.18 in 2008 to 0.08 in the 2011 BEEPS. Far fewer firms in 2011 than in 2008 reported that licensing and permits, or courts, or tax administration or corruption were significant obstacles to their operations.

There are several important exceptions to this favorable trend, however. Firms report somewhat longer delays in obtaining licenses, permits and utility connections in 2011 than in 2008. Most notably, perceptions of the extent of "state capture" show worrisome deterioration in the 2011 survey, relative to results from 2005, when these questions were last included in the survey.

Cross-regional variation in corruption and regulatory burden in Russia is a potentially important factor in explaining differential performance in private sector development, income levels and growth rates. The 2011 Russia BEEPS for the first time is able to demonstrate substantial regional-level differences in regulatory burden and corruption. Location—i.e. knowing what region a firm is located in—turns out to be a much more powerful predictor of the "time tax," bribe expectations, etc. that firms face than knowing the firm's size, industry, major products, and age.

Regional variation captured by the BEEPS, and summarized by a set of indexes in Appendix 2, Table 6, not only identifies regions (such as Rostov Oblast and Krasnodar Kray) where private sector development confronts the most serious challenges. It also identifies regions (such as Smolensk Oblast and the Republic of Mordovia) where problems are much less severe, that can potentially point the way for other regions to reduce corruption and lighten the burden of regulation on firms.

Few if any regions rank uniformly well or poorly across all BEEPS indicators, however. For example, St. Petersburg and Primorsky Kray rank very highly on the Graft Index, despite ranking poorly on the other indexes in Appendix 1.

This report provides exploratory analyses of what policy differences or other regional characteristics may underlie these sizeable variations in corruption and regulatory burden across the 37 regions represented in the survey. Several policy messages receive at least some support from the data analysis. Transparency in regional government procurement systems is associated with a lower average "kickback tax" firms report paying to officials. The importance of transparency and information for improved public sector accountability is also demonstrated by the fact that perceptions of state capture and frequency of administrative bribery are lower in regions with higher newspaper circulation (controlling for regional income and other factors). However, freedom of information laws and decrees—using a classification developed by TI Russia—appear to be unrelated to the incidence of corruption and the administrative burden of regulation.

Less onerous regulatory requirements, as measured by one or more of the indicators in the Russia sub-national "Doing Business" study, are associated with a lower average "time tax," shorter wait times to obtain an operating license, fewer firms citing licensing and permits as an obstacle to their operations, and lowered bribe expectations (as measured by the Graft Index). In many other cases, however, Doing Business indicators prove to be unrelated to anticipated outcomes; e.g. more firms perceive electricity as an obstacle to their operations in regions where fewer procedures are required to obtain an electrical connection, as measured by DB. Reforms intended to improve rankings in the Doing Business study can lead to improved outcomes, particularly if they are not narrowly tailored merely to target the indicator, but represent real improvements in the business environment for all firms in a region. However, even in the top-ranked regions on the Doing Business indicators, there is wide variation in "time tax," waiting times, reports of Graft, and other indicators. Expectations of the likely impact of regulatory reforms captured by the Doing Business indicators should not be exaggerated.[30]

There is a plethora of data available on the Russian regions from government and other sources, and it is beyond the scope of this report to provide rigorous tests of all possible determinants of differences in the business climate across regions, including fiscal and political economy explanations.[31] This report nevertheless provides a description of the BEEPS indicators, illustrative examples of how the data can be used, and suggests areas where additional research is needed. In conjunction with the accompanying BEEPS-at-a-Glance report for Russia, it can facilitate independent interpretations, and complementary and more in-depth analyses, by researchers in government, civil society and academia.

One topic where additional research would be useful pertains to the validity of trends over times in the various BEEPS questions on potential obstacles to firms' operations. In Russia the number and severity of complaints in many regulatory and other areas increased between 2005 and 2008, but improved again in 2011–2012, essentially tracking the business cycle. The actual dates of each survey interview is recorded, so surveys from Russia and other countries can be used to study the impact of current economic conditions on question responses at a more finely-grained level.

On corruption more specifically, the more objective and direct experiential questions in the BEEPS generally portray a more favorable trend than the more perceptions-based and indirect ("firms like this one") questions. A more in-depth analysis of particular sub-sector (e.g. tax administration) using information from other sources might shed light on the reasons for these discrepancies. Similarly, in-depth case studies on a few of the best (e.g. Smolensk) and worst (e.g. Rostov) performing regions could add to our understanding of why there are such large variations in business climate, and on the feasibility of using the top performers as models for reforms.

Further research can also explore more intensively the question of why the regulatory burden on firms and the corruption levels they face vary so much from one region to another. The fact that performance on these aspects of the investment climate differs so much even for geographically-adjacent regions suggests that much of the variation is likely not due to "deep" historical, cultural or climatic factors. This finding can be viewed optimistically, as implying that there is more scope for improvement through policy reforms, including imitation of better-performing nearby regions in some cases.

---

[30]The President has set goals of improving Russia's global ranking on the overall Ease of Doing Business from 120th in 2011 to 50th in 2015 and 20th in 2018. See for example http://www.telegraph.co.uk/sponsored/russianow/business/9333604/vladimir-putin-russia-investment.html.

[31]For example, Timothy Frye and colleagues at the National Research University Higher School of Economics are assembling a detailed dataset of characteristics of the regional governors (Frye et al. 2011). When it is made public, that dataset can usefully add to the range of political economy explanations that are only cursorily treated here.

Perhaps most importantly, future research using the BEEPS and complementary datasets can explore the effects of regulatory burden and corruption on firm entry, revenue growth and productivity, at the firm and regional level. While cross-country studies and country-specific studies of other countries have established that there are important links, the particular forms of corruption and excessive regulation that act as binding constraints to development of private enterprise may differ somewhat in Russia from other countries, and even from region to region within Russia. Moreover, further research can investigate the extent to which distortions in various regulatory and administrative areas and transactions may be redundant, in their effects on firm entry and growth. Reforms in a limited number of areas may show disappointing results, if there are remaining distortions sufficient to deter entry or expansion. Rent-seekers may be able to substitute one regulatory barrier for another in blocking competitors.

Acknowledgments The paper was prepared by a World Bank team consisting of Gregory Kisunko (Sr. Public Sector Specialist, ECSP4) and Stephen Knack (Lead Economist, DECHD), under the overall guidance of Roumeen Islam (Advisor, ECSPE). Significant inputs were provided by Branco Ponamariov (Consultant, ECSP4) and Ricky Ubee (currently with the USICT). We are grateful for advice and directions from Yvonne Tsikata (Director for Poverty Reduction and Economic Management in the Europe and Central Asia Region), Michal Rutkowski (Country Director for Russia), Lada Strelkova (Country Program Coordinator for Russia), Kaspar Richter (Lead Economist and Country Sector Coordinator for economic policy in Russia), Sergei Ulatov (Sr. Economist, ECSP3), and Stepan Titov (Sr. Economist, ECSP3). The findings, interpretations, and conclusions expressed in this paper are entirely those of the authors. They do not necessarily represent the views of the International Bank for Reconstruction and Development/World Bank and its affiliated organizations, or those of the Executive Directors of the World Bank or the governments they represent.

Appendix 1: Selected Descriptive Indicators

See Figs. 22 and 23 and Table 2.

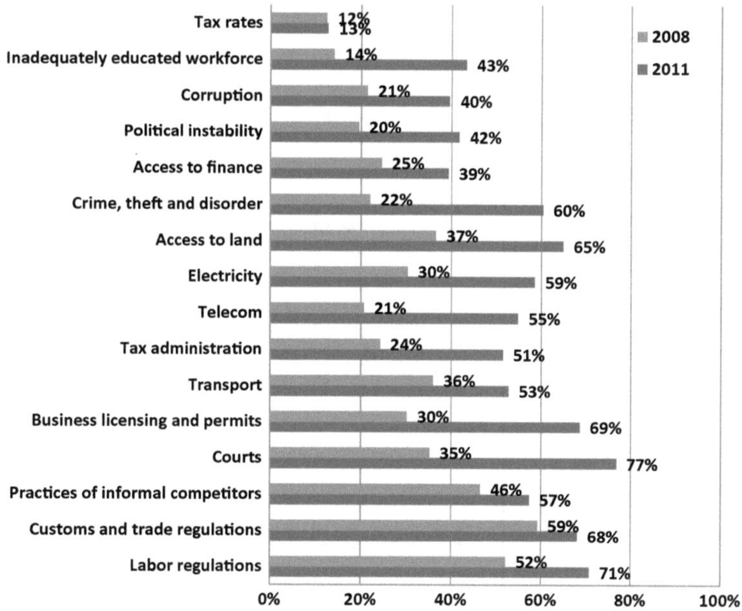

Fig. 22 Obstacles to doing business, 2008 and 2011—no obstacle (percentage of respondents indicating issue is no obstacle). *Note*: All differences are statistically significant at $P = 0.10$ or better, except "tax rates"

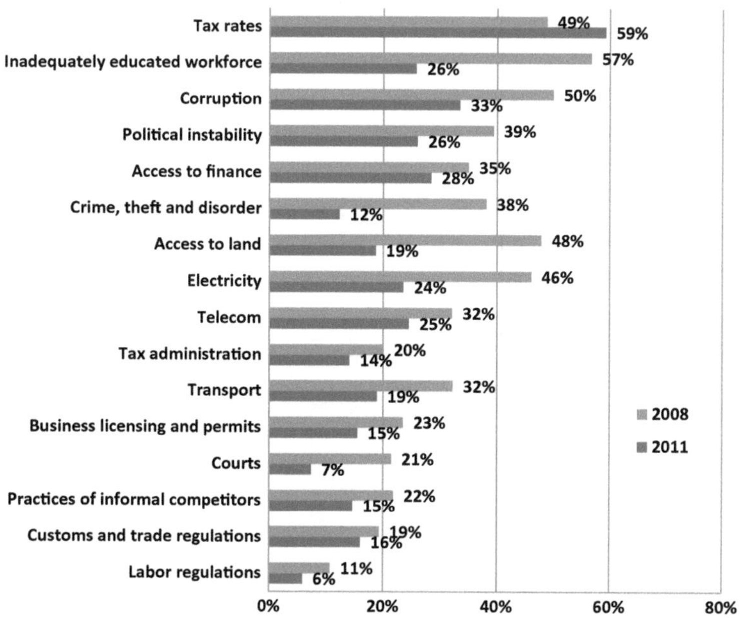

Fig. 23 Obstacles to doing business, 2008 and 2011—major or very severe obstacle (percentage of respondents). *Note*: All differences are statistically significant at $P = 0.10$ or better, except "telecommunications" (asked only of Service sector respondents in 2008), and "customs and trade regulations "

Table 2 Selected regional BEEPS indicators and 2009 GRP per capita (regions are ranked by the BEEPS ECAq44c—direct impact on business operation of private payments/gifts/other benefits to local/municipal officials)

	GRP 2009 (RRub)	Senior management's time (%)		Senior management's time spent on dealing with regulations (%)	Senior management's time—only firms with answers more than 'zero' (%)	Visited or inspected by tax officials over last year?		Number of inspections by/required meetings with tax officials over last year	Informal gift/payment expected/requested in meetings/tax inspections?		Number of days it took to obtain electrical connection	Number of days it took to obtain water connection
		No time	Some time	Mean	Mean	Yes	No	Mean	Yes	No	Mean	Mean
Khabarovsk Territory	196,252.8	20 %	80 %	15.10	18.78	56 %	44 %	3.7	2 %	98 %	124.4	28.3
Republic of Mordovia	111,903.6	25 %	75 %	12.62	16.83	59 %	41 %	3.1	4 %	96 %	60.7	14.8
Ulyanovsk Region	117,244.6	15 %	85 %	12.79	15.09	56 %	44 %	5.3	3 %	97 %	57.6	26.6
Kursk Region	140,166.1	36 %	64 %	17.96	27.92	63 %	37 %	3.2	8 %	92 %	110.2	71.8
Krasnoyarsk Territory	258,834.6	21 %	79 %	18.40	23.21	43 %	57 %	2.5	4 %	96 %	30.1	30.0
Tomsk Region	232,901.1	15 %	85 %	16.08	18.83	49 %	51 %	2.9	1 %	99 %	43.4	9.2
Samara Region	182,611.5	24 %	76 %	13.47	17.84	54 %	46 %	3.1	5 %	95 %	336.5	143.8
Kemerovo Region	181,629.5	34 %	66 %	18.10	27.33	53 %	47 %	2.7	8 %	92 %	73.4	29.5
Moscow City	679,340.7	7 %	93 %	19.36	20.79	44 %	56 %	2.5	0 %	100 %	227.4	35.3
Omsk Region	167,000.7	10 %	90 %	21.28	23.57	56 %	44 %	3.6	5 %	95 %	161.6	93.9
Voronezh Region	133,509.7	16 %	84 %	16.63	19.90	50 %	50 %	3.4	16 %	84 %	34.5	4.4
Lipetsk Region	195,126.7	14 %	86 %	16.15	18.86	59 %	41 %	3.8	12 %	88 %	97.6	56.6
Perm Territory	201,324.3	3 %	97 %	23.39	24.18	25 %	75 %	3.4	1 %	99 %	34.6	39.0

Republic of Sakha (Yakutia)	347,195.6	10 %	90 %	19.01	21.06	30 %	70 %	2.9	2 %	98 %	88.0	46.1
Stavropol Territory	102,414.9	29 %	71 %	49.23	69.05	33 %	67 %	1.8	7 %	93 %	66.3	53.1
Republic of Tatarstan	234,324.4	10 %	90 %	16.03	17.78	61 %	39 %	2.6	2 %	98 %	117.8	7.0
Kaliningrad Region	181,161.2	31 %	69 %	12.50	18.15	50 %	50 %	1.8	6 %	94 %	125.5	6.7
Yaroslavl Region	162,643.2	2 %	98 %	10.45	10.65	34 %	66 %	3.1	0 %	100 %	196.2	17.3
Smolensk Region	129,102.3	52 %	48 %	8.19	17.14	39 %	61 %	1.3	0 %	100 %	8.1	1.8
Novosibirsk Region	160,290.1	20 %	80 %	13.37	16.76	74 %	26 %	2.1	0 %	100 %	54.4	12.5
Nizhni Novgorod Region	163,840.6	22 %	78 %	10.69	13.69	25 %	75 %	3.3	12 %	88 %	31.0	
Moscow Region	227,343.2	5 %	95 %	22.14	23.25	43 %	57 %	1.8	4 %	96 %	82.6	71.3
Sverdlovsk Region	187,480.9	23 %	77 %	19.66	25.67	60 %	40 %	3.5	1 %	99 %	57.2	36.5
Leningrad Region	260,685.4	2 %	98 %	21.89	22.34	68 %	32 %	2.6	1 %	99 %	75.8	123.1
Republic of Bashko-rtostan	158,932.3	24 %	76 %	15.12	19.95	47 %	53 %	2.9	8 %	92 %	64.2	64.7

(continued)

Table 2 (continued)

	GRP 2009 (RRub)	Senior management's time (%)		Senior management's time spent on dealing with regulations (%)	Senior management's time—only firms with answers more than 'zero' (%)	Visited or inspected by tax officials over last year?		Number of inspections by/required meetings with tax officials over last year	Informal gift/payment expected/requested in meetings/tax inspections?		Number of days it took to obtain electrical connection	Number of days it took to obtain water connection
		No time	Some time	Mean	Mean	Yes	No	Mean	Yes	No	Mean	Mean
Kirov Region	103,850.7	29 %	71 %	26.11	36.95	62 %	38 %	4.9	5 %	95 %	30.6	5.5
Murmansk Region	240,346.1	27 %	73 %	24.90	33.91	39 %	61 %	2.6	3 %	97 %	10.0	65.0
Saint Petersburg	320,916.4	5 %	95 %	16.38	17.31	44 %	56 %	1.9	2 %	98 %	298.2	314.7
Chelyabinsk Region	160,939.6	34 %	66 %	15.71	23.92	34 %	66 %	2.6	1 %	99 %	29.3	9.8
Kaluga Region	156,300.9	6 %	94 %	19.51	20.75	48 %	52 %	2.2	0 %	100 %	384.3	12.6
Belgorod Region	199,229.1	50 %	50 %	2.76	5.49	57 %	43 %	2.0	2 %	98 %	9.7	9.9
Krasnodar Territory	166,469.6	21 %	79 %	10.83	13.75	57 %	43 %	1.9	4 %	96 %	31.5	30.0
Volgograd Region	145,453.6	16 %	84 %	20.24	24.24	65 %	35 %	2.7	1 %	99 %	120.9	47.1
Rostov Region	131,312.2	12 %	88 %	16.67	18.94	40 %	60 %	3.2	3 %	97 %	178.0	56.0
Tver Region	144,993.3	23 %	77 %	21.48	27.94	57 %	43 %	2.1	1 %	99 %	164.6	12.3
Irkutsk Region	181,910.9	20 %	80 %	17.49	21.83	55 %	45 %	1.9	3 %	97 %	83.3	90.0
Primorsky Territory	185,239.4	91 %	9 %	0.98	10.88	43 %	57 %	1.7	3 %	97 %	730.0	1.0

	Number of days it took to obtain a construction-related permit	Number of days it took to obtain import license	Number of days it took to obtain operating license	Corruption—obstacle to current operations	Frequency of informal payments/gifts to get things done	Frequency of unofficial payments/gifts to deal with customs/imports	Frequency of unofficial payments/gifts to deal with courts	Frequency of unofficial payments/gifts to deal with taxes and tax collection	Private payments/gifts/other benefits to local/regional officials—direct impact
	Mean	Mean	Mean	Mean	Mean	Mean	Mean	Mean	Mean
Khabarovsk Territory	330.5	7.0	45.2	1.1	2.0	1.4	1.1	1.3	1.02
Republic of Mordovia	159.7	1.0	49.2	0.9	1.8	1.1	1.2	1.3	1.08
Ulyanovsk Region	129.6		64.1	1.3	1.7	1.1	1.1	1.3	1.09
Kursk Region	163.9		39.0	1.2	2.0	1.4	1.3	1.2	1.13
Krasnoyarsk Territory	43.0		65.1	1.0	2.2	1.3	1.2	1.2	1.17
Tomsk Region	50.3		39.6	1.0	1.8	1.1	1.2	1.4	1.18
Samara Region	167.0	30.0	31.8	1.7	2.2	1.3	1.4	1.5	1.19
Kemerovo Region	71.9	180.0	34.8	1.4	1.9	1.2	1.4	1.5	1.20
Moscow City	30.4	73.0	72.1	2.0	3.0	1.5	1.2	1.9	1.21
Omsk Region	137.3		42.8	1.6	2.1	1.1	1.1	1.3	1.21
Voronezh Region	215.8	57.9	49.0	1.3	2.5	1.1	1.2	1.7	1.24
Lipetsk Region	68.6		40.0	1.0	1.8	1.1	1.2	1.4	1.24
Perm Territory	222.4	60.0	82.3	1.2	2.0	1.2	1.3	1.4	1.24

Table 2 (continued)

	Number of days it took to obtain a construction-related permit	Number of days it took to obtain import license	Number of days it took to obtain operating license	Corruption—obstacle to current operations	Frequency of informal payments/gifts to get things done	Frequency of unofficial payments/gifts to deal with customs/imports	Frequency of unofficial payments/gifts to deal with courts	Frequency of unofficial payments/gifts to deal with taxes and tax collection	Private payments/gifts/other benefits to local/regional officials—direct imp act
Republic of Sakha (Yakutia)	78.1		75.1	1.1	2.1	1.1	1.2	1.2	1.26
Stavropol Territory	58.3	30.0	22.1	1.2	1.4	1.0	1.1	1.2	1.28
Republic of Tatarstan	148.2		72.2	1.2	2.0	1.1	1.1	1.3	1.32
Kaliningrad Region	277.5	58.4	45.9	1.6	2.2	1.7	1.3	1.4	1.35
Yaroslavl Region	515.3		65.9	1.6	2.1	1.5	1.3	1.4	1.41
Smolensk Region	30.0	3.0	27.9	0.2	1.9	1.4	1.3	1.6	1.42
Novosibirsk Region	63.1	23.6	37.8	1.4	1.9	1.5	1.6	1.6	1.44
Nizhni Novgorod Region	240.0	26.2	42.8	1.1	2.6	1.2	1.3	1.4	1.50
Moscow Region	143.5	30.0	66.7	1.5	2.4	1.4	1.4	1.7	1.51
Sverdlovsk Region	83.6		48.9	1.5	2.3	1.6	1.7	1.9	1.56

Leningrad Region	176.6	80.7	60.7	2.2	2.6	1.5	1.3	1.3	1.56
Republic of Bashkortostan	71.5	60.0	64.8	1.2	2.5	1.4	1.6	1.7	1.65
Kirov Region	102.5		8.0	0.8	2.4	2.0	1.8	2.2	1.65
Murmansk Region	14.5	9.0	29.4	1.1	2.6	1.4	1.6	1.8	1.67
Saint Petersburg	84.8		51.4	2.3	2.7	1.8	1.5	1.4	1.71
Chelyabinsk Region	104.8		41.9	1.4	2.9	1.9	1.7	2.3	1.77
Kaluga Region	74.9	180.0	41.7	1.4	2.0	1.5	1.5	1.7	1.83
Belgorod Region	50.2	12.3	44.4	1.0	2.2	1.6	1.6	1.7	1.99
Krasnodar Territory	353.8	17.8	42.1	1.6	2.8	1.8	2.0	2.3	2.03
Volgograd Region	114.0		40.6	1.6	2.4	1.4	1.7	1.6	2.04
Rostov Region	82.5	7.8	60.0	2.0	3.1	2.4	2.4	2.6	2.16
Tver Region	369.5	5.0	32.4	1.6	3.0	2.6	2.5	2.6	2.17
Irkutsk Region	170.0		57.9	0.8	2.8	2.1	2.0	2.0	2.34
Primorsky Territory	350.0	14.0	50.1	1.2	3.1	2.8	2.7	2.8	3.02

Appendix 2: Composite Indexes

Methodology

Administrative Obstacles Index (AOI7) is a composite measure of selected governance obstacles faced by firms in their interactions with the state. The index utilized responses to the following seven BEEPS questions. The BEEPS questionnaire included the following question:

To what degree is XYZ an obstacle to the current operations of this establishment?

This question is being asked regarding various obstacles to firms operations and growth. Response options included: no obstacle (0), minor obstacle (1), moderate obstacle (2), major obstacle (3), and very severe obstacle (4). The index includes the following aspects:

- *customs and trade regulations (d30b);*
- *access to land (g30a);*
- *courts (h30);*
- *tax administration (j30b);*
- *business licensing and permits (j30c);*
- *corruption (j30f);*
- *labor regulations (l30a).*

The index is constructed in two steps.

1. For each of seven questions above an average regional response was calculated as a weighted mean of firms' responses (an average of 0, 1, 2, 3, and 4, i.e. numeric equivalents of the response options for specific questions).
2. An average of these regional means for all seven questions was estimated for each region.

The latter average is called the Administrative Obstacle Index (AOI7). The index can take values from 0—no burden at all (all respondents experienced no obstacle with all aspects of business-government interactions included in the index), to 4—all respondents reported very severe obstacle in every aspect of business-government interactions.

Table 3 shows that all but one correlation (tax administration and access to land) between index components are statistically significant at least at 5 % level, and all correlation coefficients are positive.

A variation of the AOI7 index is the AOI6—a narrowed-down version of the Administrative Obstacles Index that does not include the question on corruption as an obstacle to business operations, i.e. is based on six components.

Administrative Corruption Index (ACI) is a composite measure of administrative corruption. The index utilized responses to the following four BEEPS questions.

Table 3 Correlation among IAB components

		d30b	g30a	h30	j30b	j30c	j30f	l30a
d30b	Pearson correlation	1	0.512**	0.513**	0.432**	0.516**	0.639**	0.428**
g30a	Pearson correlation	0.512**	1	0.508**	0.240	0.705**	0.537**	0.557**
h30	Pearson correlation	0.513**	0.508**	1	0.717**	0.751**	0.588**	0.734**
j30b	Pearson correlation	0.432**	0.240	0.717**	1	0.459**	0.481**	0.646**
j30c	Pearson correlation	0.516**	0.705**	0.751**	0.459**	1	0.604**	0.568**
j30f	Pearson correlation	0.639**	0.537**	0.588**	0.481**	0.604**	1	0.465**
l30a	Pearson correlation	0.428**	0.557**	0.734**	0.646**	0.568**	0.465**	1

***$p < 0.01$; **$p < 0.05$; *$p < 0.1$

Thinking about officials, would you say the following statement is always, usually, frequently, sometimes, seldom, or never true? (ECAq39)

> It is common for firms in my line of business to have pay some irregular "additional payments or gifts" to get things done with regard to customs, taxes, licenses, regulations, services, etc.

Thinking now of unofficial payments/gifts that establishments like this one would make in a given year, please tell how often they would make payments/gifts for the following purposes:

- *to deal with customs/imports (ECAq41a);*
- *to deal with courts (ECAq41b);*
- *to deal with taxes and tax collection (ECAq41c).*

Response options were the same as for the previous question: always (6), usually (5), frequently (4), sometimes (3), seldom (2), or never (1).

The index is constructed in three steps.

1. For each of four questions above an average regional response was calculated as a weighted mean of firms' responses (an average of 1, 2, 3, 4, 5, and 6, i.e. numeric equivalents of the response options for specific questions).
2. An average of these regional means for the latter three questions on customs, courts and tax was estimated for each region.
3. An average of the mean estimated in the step two and the first question dealing with overall frequency of administrative corruption was calculated. In other words, the first question has a weight of 0.5 and the latter three questions are weighted at 0.17 each.

The latter average is called the Administrative Corruption Index (ACI). The index can take values from 1—additional payments/gifts have never been requested to 6—all respondents have had always make additional payments.

Table 4 shows that all components are significantly correlated at least at 5 % level, and all correlation coefficients are positive. This table also shows correlation of the components two alternative versions of the ACI—ACI3, which includes only the last three questions, and ACI4, that is calculated as a simple average of regional means of each of four questions. These versions are highly correlated as expected.

Table 4 Correlation among ACI components and different versions of the ACI

		ECAq39	ECAq41a	ECAq41b	ECAq41c	ACI	ACI4	ACI3
ECAq39	Pearson correlation	1	0.769**	0.721**	0.772**	0.947**	0.876**	0.779**
ECAq41a	Pearson correlation	0.769**	1	0.930**	0.884**	0.917**	0.957**	0.968**
ECAq41b	Pearson correlation	0.721**	0.930**	1	0.917**	0.896**	0.952**	0.978**
ECAq41c	Pearson correlation	0.772**	0.884**	0.917**	1	0.916**	0.955**	0.963**
ACI	Pearson correlation	0.947**	0.917**	0.896**	0.916**	1	0.984**	0.939**
ACI4	Pearson correlation	0.876**	0.957**	0.952**	0.955**	0.984**	1	0.985**
ACI3	Pearson correlation	0.779**	0.968**	0.978**	0.963**	0.939**	0.985**	1

***$p < 0.01$; **$p < 0.05$; *$p < 0.1$

State Capture Index (SCI) is a composite measure of state capture. The index utilized responses to the following three BEEPS questions.

It is often said that firms make unofficial payments/gifts, private payments or other benefits to public officials to gain advantages in the drafting laws, decrees, regulations, and other binding government decisions. To what extent have the following practices had direct impact on this establishment?

- *Private payments/gifts or other benefits to Parliamentarians to affect their votes.*
- *Private payments/gifts or other benefits to Government officials to the content of government decrees.*
- *Private payments/gifts or other benefits to local or regional government officials to affect their votes or content of government decrees.*

Response options were: decisive impact (5), major impact (4), moderate impact (3), minor impact (2), or no impact (1).

The index is constructed in two steps.

1. For each of three questions above an average regional response was calculated as a weighted mean of firms' responses (an average of 1, 2, 3, 4 and 5, i.e. numeric equivalents of the response options for specific questions).
2. An average of these regional means for all seven questions was estimated for each region.

The latter average is called the State Capture Index (SCI). The index can take values from 1—no impact at all to 5—decisive impact.

Components of the SCI are correlated at 1 % level. Coefficients of correlation are over 0.94.

Table 5 shows correlations between the indexes described above, the Graft Index and the overall measure of administrative corruption (ECAq39). This table shows that while ACI3 is not significantly correlated with AOI indexes, ACI and ACI4 are correlated with both of them at least at 5 % level and that, in necessary, ECAq39 can be used as a substitute for ACI index as it is highly correlated with its components, full index and is better correlated with other composite indexes than the ACI.

Table 5 Correlations among composite indexes

		ACI3	ACI	ACI4	AOI6	AOI7	GI6	SCI	ECAq39
ACI3	Pearson correlation	1	0.939**	0.985**	0.294	0.281	−0.119	0.883**	0.779**
ACI	Pearson correlation	0.939**	1	0.984**	0.398*	0.399*	−0.051	0.816**	0.947**
ACI4	Pearson correlation	0.985**	0.984**	1	0.351*	0.345*	−0.086	0.863**	0.876**
AOI6	Pearson correlation	0.294	0.398*	0.351*	1	0.989**	0.073	0.141	0.451**
AOI7	Pearson correlation	0.281	0.399*	0.345*	0.989**	1	0.047	0.121	0.464**
GI6	Pearson correlation	−0.119	−0.051	−0.086	0.073	0.047	1	−0.072	0.019
SCI	Pearson correlation	0.883**	0.816**	0.863**	0.141	0.121	−0.072	1	0.665**
ECAq39	Pearson correlation	0.779**	0.947**	0.876**	0.451**	0.464**	0.019	0.665**	1

***$p < 0.01$; **$p < 0.05$; *$p < 0.1$

For the purposes of regional ranking the following indexes will be used: AOI7, ACI, SCI, and GI6, as they measure four different and not necessarily correlated aspects of administrative burden—obstacles to doing business, administrative corruption, state capture and propensity to graft in government-private sector interactions.

Table 6 shows regional rankings on each of these four indicators. Regions are arranged in order of AOI6—with Smolensk Oblast being the best and Rostov Oblast the worst. Primorsky Kray was dead last on ACI and GCI, but fifth best on GI6, etc. In total 21 out of 37 regions appeared among top performers at least once, of which one appeared three times, and five two times. Nineteen regions were at the bottom of the list for at least one of four indicators, of which one regions was among the bottom seven four times, one three times, and four two times.

Table 7 shows a summary of Table 6 and the diversity of Russian regions—it presents only regions in the top and bottom quintiles. There is no single region among the 37 surveyed that would be in the top quintile for all four indicators. Only one—Republic of Mordovia—was a top performer on three out of four indicators, and only one region has consistently scored poorly—Krasnodar Kray. Rostov Oblast appeared among the poor performers on three indicators.

Table 6 Regional ranking on four composite indexes

Region name	Region code	AOI7	ACI	GI6	SCI
Smolensk Oblast	SML	1	13	1	20
Belgorod Oblast	BLG	2	20	20	32
Stavropol Kray	STV	3	1	17	15
Irkutsk Oblast	IRK	4	33	28	36
Republic of Mordovia	MRD	5	4	10	4
Republic of Bashkortostan	BSK	6	27	36	26
Tomsk Oblast	TOM	7	5	21	6
Nizhny Novgorod Oblast	NZN	8	22	34	21
Novosibirsk Oblast	NOV	9	15	2	22
Lipetsk Oblast	LPT	10	3	26	16
Omsk Oblast	OMS	11	9	29	5
Kirov Oblast	KRV	12	30	25	29
Murmansk Oblast	MRM	13	28	15	27
Republic of Tatarstan	TRT	14	6	8	17
Ulyanovsk Oblast	ULY	15	2	13	3
Kemerovo Oblast	KEM	16	10	23	8
Krasnoyarsk Kray	KRA	17	14	24	13
Kursk Oblast	KRS	18	11	27	2
Chelyabinsk Oblast	CHL	19	34	7	28
Khabarovsk Kray	KHA	20	8	9	1
Voronezh Oblast	VRN	21	21	36	7
Perm Kray	PER	22	12	33	11
Primorsky Kray	PRM	23	37	5	37
Tver Oblast	TVR	24	36	19	33
Kaluga Oblast	KLG	25	17	12	31
Sverdlovsk Oblast	SVD	26	26	22	24
Moscow Oblast	MSC	27	23	16	25
Yaroslavl Oblast	YRS	28	16	32	19
Moscow City	MOS	29	31	4	10
Republic of Sakha (Yakutia)	YAK	30	7	30	9
Volgograd Oblast	VGG	31	25	11	30
Kaliningrad Oblast	KNG	32	19	13	14
Saint Petersburg	LEN	33	29	3	18
Krasnodar Kray	KSN	34	32	35	34
Samara Oblast	SAM	35	18	31	12
Leningrad Oblast	SPT	36	24	6	23
Rostov Oblast	RSV	37	35	17	35

Table 7 Regions in the top and bottom quintiles

	AOI7	ACI	GI6	SCI
Top performers				
1	Smolensk Oblast	Stavropol Kray	Smolensk Oblast	Khabarovsk Kray
2	Belgorod Oblast	Ulyanovsk Oblast	Novosibirsk Oblast	Kursk Oblast
3	Stavropol Kray	Lipetsk Oblast	Saint Petersburg	Ulyanovsk Oblast
4	Irkutsk Oblast	Republic of Mordovia	Moscow City	Republic of Mordovia
5	Republic of Mordovia	Tomsk Oblast	Primorsky Kray	Omsk Oblast
6	Rep. Bashkortostan	Republic of Tatarstan	Leningrad Oblast	Tomsk Oblast
7	Tomsk Oblast	Rep. Sakha (Yakutia)	Chelyabinsk Oblast	Voronezh Oblast
Poor performers				
31	Volgograd Oblast	Moscow City	Samara Oblast	Kaluga Oblast
32	Kaliningrad Oblast	Krasnodar Kray	Yaroslavl Oblast	Belgorod Oblast
33	Saint Petersburg	Irkutsk Oblast	Perm Kray	Tver Oblast
34	Krasnodar Kray	Chelyabinsk Oblast	N. Novgorod Oblast	Krasnodar Kray
35	Samara Oblast	Rostov Oblast	Krasnodar Kray	Rostov Oblast
36	Leningrad Oblast	Tver Oblast	Rep. Bashkortostan	Irkutsk Oblast
37	Rostov Oblast	Primorsky Kray	Voronezh Oblast	Primorsky Kray

Appendix 3: Regression Results

See Tables 8, 9, 10, 11, 12, and 13.

Table 8 "Time tax" regressions (firm level)

Equation	1.1	1.2	1.3	1.4	1.5	1.6
Added regressors	(base)	Doing Business index	Tax meetings/ visits	Operating license wait	No. of " gift" chances	Graft index
Firm-level regressors						
Established 1990 or before	0.19(0.09)	−1.110(−0.58)	0.165(0.08)	4.746(1.23)	0.470(0.24)	1.974(0.99)
Retail firm	1.796(1.24)	2.339(1.33)	1.668(1.10)	3.197(1.37)	0.966(0.64)	−0.084(−0.05)
Female manager	2.241**(2.07)	2.391*(1.74)	2.184*(1.98)	6.937**(2.33)	2.305**(2.13)	4.624***(3.64)
Exporter	−1.476(−1.56)	−1.630(−1.50)	−1.159(−1.12)	−1.603(−0.64)	−1.413(−1.48)	−2.420**(−2.14)
No. of employees (log)	0.488*(1.83)	0.551*(1.69)	0.383(1.30)	−0.267(−0.37)	−0.053(−0.18)	0.096(0.26)
% Foreign owned	0.019(0.70)	−0.014(−0.47)	0.006(0.20)	−0.016(−0.27)	0.019(0.64)	0.006(0.15)
% Government owned	0.005(0.08)	0.018(0.27)	0.014(0.22)	0.042(0.83)	0.009(0.14)	−0.0003(−0.01)
No. of tax meetings			0.539**(2.33)			
Wait time for operating license (days)				0.039***(2.91)		
No. of "gift" opportunities (interactions with officials)					2.263***(0.543)	2.052***(3.55)
Graft index						3.239(1.38)
Region-level regressors						
Per capita GRP (log)	−9.428*(−1.72)	−11.792(−1.68)	−9.321*(−1.68)	1.279(0.28)	−9.433*(−1.73)	−8.768(−1.62)
Population (log)	3.985**(2.25)	4.978**(2.48)	4.050**(2.26)	1.546*(0.77)	4.209**(2.35)	4.674**(2.46)
Extractive industries as share of GRP	6.322(1.13)	8.928(1.35)	6.494(1.15)	−3.834(−0.48)	5.564(1.01)	1.152(0.21)
Distance from Moscow (ln of km)	−0.222(−0.45)	−0.607(−0.82)	−0.178(−0.36)	−0.010(−0.02)	−0.181(−0.36)	−0.051(−0.10)
Latitude	0.456(1.25)	0.392(0.94)	0.438(1.19)	0.089(0.25)	0.469(1.29)	0.600(1.57)
Doing Business index		0.512(0.24)				
No. of obs. (firms)	3,693	2,781	3,544	787	3,693	2,287
F statistic	2.79	3.20	2.28	3.98	3.90	3.36
p value of F test	0.009	0.006	0.025	0.0005	0.0006	0.0017
R^2	0.02	0.03	0.03	0.03	0.03	0.03

Dependent variable is share of senior managers' time required to deal with regulations and reporting requirements. T-statistics, reported in parentheses below point estimates, are based on standard errors adjusted for non-independence of errors within regional clusters of observations, with $^{***}p < 0.01$; $^{**}p < 0.05$; $^{*}p < 0.1$

Table 9 Regulatory burden regressions (firm level)

Equation	2.1	2.2	2.3	2.4	2.5
Dependent variable	Tax meetings		Days to obtain operating license		
Firm-level regressors					
Established 1990 or before	0.311(0.91)	0.395(0.91)	−8.238(−0.68)	−20.560(−1.27)	−21.091(0.24)
Retail firm	−0.006(−0.05)	0.029(0.18)	−6.910*(−1.80)	−6.891*(−1.94)	−6.998*(−1.83)
Female manager	−0.088(−0.63)	−0.097(−0.68)	−10.386***(−3.05)	−11.383**(−2.46)	−10.970**(−2.40)
Exporter	0.328(1.26)	0.161(0.53)	21.051(1.61)	24.977(1.52)	25.665(1.54)
No. of employees (log)	0.175***(3.85)	0.031(0.32)	6.741**(2.57)	8.702***(2.73)	8.318**(2.54)
% Foreign owned	0.019*(1.83)	0.025*(1.88)	0.282(1.61)	0.332(1.49)	0.332(1.53)
% Government owned	−0.005(−0.60)	−0.002(−0.18)	−0.200(−1.07)	−0.356**(−2.17)	−0.344**(−2.02)
Sales revenue (log)		0.195**(2.48)			
Region-level regressors					
Per capita GRP (log)	−0.622(−1.36)	−0.553(−0.98)	10.232*(1.75)	4.731(0.51)	5.768(0.82)
Population (log)	−0.003(−0.02)	−0.047(−0.25)	6.014(1.62)	4.401(0.98)	4.369(0.90)
Extractive industries as share of GRP	−0.253(−0.58)	−0.553(−0.98)	17.488(1.53)	29.702**(2.31)	26.004***(3.17)
Distance from Moscow (ln of km)	0.017(0.31)	0.020(0.30)	−0.876(−0.82)	−1.413(−1.08)	−1.329(−0.93)
Latitude	0.032(1.10)	0.050(1.28)	0.083(0.13)	−1.039(−1.19)	−0.464(−0.67)
Doing business starting a business index				−12.216**(−2.07)	
Doing business days to start a business					1.559** (2.54)
No. of obs. (firms)	3,932	2,847	864	631	631
F statistic	3.42	3.39	13.12	44.67	42.92
p value of F test	0.002	0.002	<0.0001	<0.0001	<0.0001
R^2	0.02	0.03	0.06	0.08	0.08

Dependent variable is number of tax meetings or visits reported by firm in equations 2.1 and 2.2, and number of days required to obtain an operating license reported by firms in 2.3–2.5. T-statistics, reported in parentheses below point estimates, are based on standard errors adjusted for non-independence of errors within regional clusters of observations, with ***$p < 0.01$; **$p < 0.05$; *$p < 0.1$. Intercept is included but not shown for space reasons

Table 10 Licensing and permits as an obstacle regressions (firm level)

Equation	3.1	3.2	3.3	3.4	3.5	3.6
Added regressors	(base)	Doing Business index	Days to obt. oper. license	Operating license wait	DB and BEEPS wait times	No. of "gift" chances
Firm-level regressors						
Established 1990 or before	−0.038(−0.38)	−0.020(−0.17)	−0.024(−0.20)	−0.059(−0.26)	0.056(0.23)	−0.005(−0.05)
Retail firm	0.246***(2.76)	0.252**(2.23)	0.256**(2.25)	0.211(1.29)	0.359*(1.81)	0.160*(1.82)
Female manager	−0.064(−1.30)	−0.142**(−2.59)	−0.145**(−2.64)	−0.153(−1.11)	−0.370**(−2.26)	−0.052(−1.13)
Exporter	0.120(1.34)	0.1220(1.12)	0.121(1.11)	0.162(0.73)	0.070(0.29)	0.125(1.45)
No. of employees (log)	0.098***(4.79)	0.105***(4.35)	0.104***(4.34)	−0.009(−0.20)	−0.033***(−0.66)	0.037(1.50)
% Foreign owned	−0.0003(−0.17)	−0.002(−1.49)	−0.002(−1.49)	−0.001(−0.21)	−0.004(−0.94)	−0.0002(−0.14)
% Government owned	0.0004(0.08)	0.001(0.27)	0.002(0.32)	0.010**(2.47)	0.013***(3.03)	0.001(0.26)
Wait time for operating license (days)				0.005***(3.45)	0.005***(2.94)	
No. of "gift" opportunities (interactions with officials)						0.264***(6.71)
Region-level regressors						
Per capita GRP (log)	0.386*(1.79)	0.365(1.38)	0.408(1.64)	0.568***(2.88)	0.820***(3.45)	0.380*(1.82)
Population (log)	0.033(0.32)	0.040(0.26)	0.059(0.40)	−0.097(−1.00)	−0.020(−0.17)	0.050(0.48)
Extractive industries as share of GRP	−0.496(−1.30)	−0.701*(−1.85)	−0.654(−1.60)	−0.574(−1.57)	−0.794*(−1.91)	−0.566(−1.63)
Distance from Moscow (ln of km)	0.064**(2.50)	0.079**(2.19)	0.074**(2.12)	0.041(1.27)	0.070**(1.65)	0.065**(2.58)
Latitude	0.006(0.53)	0.012(0.94)	0.014(1.15)	−0.005(−0.34)	−0.003(−0.15)	0.008(0.67)
Doing Business index		0.045(0.45)				
Doing Business days to obtain operating license			−0.007(−0.58)		−0.037**(−2.33)	
No. of obs. (firms)	3,735	2,770	2,770	859	627	3,735
F statistic	5.38	9.56	10.53	5.12	44.64	17.83
p value of F test	<0.0001	<0.0001	<0.0001	<0.0001	<0.0001	<0.0001
R^2	0.03	0.03	0.03	0.07	0.10	0.07

Dependent variable is degree to which licensing and permits are considered to be an obstacle to firm operations. T-statistics, reported in parentheses below point estimates, are based on standard errors adjusted for non-independence of errors within regional clusters of observations, with $^{***}p < 0.01$; $^{**}p < 0.05$; $^{*}p < 0.1$

Table 11 Corruption as an obstacle regressions (firm level)

Equation	4.1	4.2	4.3	4.4
Added regressors	(base)	State capture, bribe frequency	State capture, graft index	Bribe tax
Firm-level regressors				
Established 1990 or before	0.085(0.71)	0.042(0.45)	0.086(0.68)	0.225(0.89)
Retail firm	−0.216**(−2.59)	−0.140**(−1.72)	−0.160*(−1.81)	0.036(0.17)
Female manager	−0.200***(−3.06)	−0.095**(−1.57)	−0.042(−0.51)	−0.239*(−1.67)
Exporter	0.215***(2.92)	0.193***(2.81)	0.116(1.29)	0.169(1.00)
No. of employees (log)	0.024(1.31)	−0.0001(−0.01)	0.029(1.06)	0.001(0.01)
% Foreign owned	−0.002(−1.30)	−0.003*(−1.739)	−0.002(−1.08)	0.003(0.87)
% Government owned	−0.009**(−2.12)	−0.007**(−2.17)	−0.007(−1.30)	−0.013(−0.97)
State capture (regional officials)		0.096*(1.89)	0.246***(4.37)	
Bribe frequency		0.382***(15.43)		
Graft index			1.204***(8.69)	
Bribe tax (share of revenues)				0.031***(4.73)
Region-level regressors				
Per capita GRP (log)	0.280(1.34)	0.124(0.53)	0.253(0.93)	0.622**(2.01)
Population (log)	0.246***(2.77)	0.150(1.56)	0.194*(1.80)	−0.218(−1.56)
Extractive industries as share of GRP	−0.639*(−1.72)	−0.308*(−0.62)	−0.694(−1.47)	0.072(0.18)
Distance from Moscow (ln of km)	0.022(0.79)	0.007(0.21)	0.005(0.14)	−0.098*(−1.87)
Latitude	0.004(0.31)	0.008(0.54)	0.030(1.51)	−0.024(−1.14)
No. of obs. (firms)	3,891	3,025	2,024	410
F statistic	7.06	34.12	15.05	3.66
p value of F test	<0.0001	<0.0001	<0.0001	0.001
R^2	0.04	0.18	0.10	0.08

Dependent variable is degree to which corruption is considered to be an obstacle to firm operations. T-statistics, reported in parentheses below point estimates, are based on standard errors adjusted for non-independence of errors within regional clusters of observations, with $^{***}p < 0.01$; $^{**}p < 0.05$; $^{*}p < 0.1$

Table 12 State capture and bribe frequency regressions (firm level)

Equation	5.1	5.2	5.3	5.4	5.5	5.6
Dependent variable	State capture (regional officials)		Bribe frequency (common to make irregular payments to get things done)			
Firm-level regressors						
Established 1990 or before	0.081(0.98)	0.083(1.00)	0.001(0.01)	0.199(1.40)	0.013(0.10)	−0.008(−0.06)
Retail firm	−0.087(−1.18)	−0.092(−1.26)	−0.074(−0.98)	−0.134(−1.25)	−0.085(−1.10)	−0.079(−1.03)
Female manager	−0.096*(−1.83)	−0.090*(−1.66)	−0.084(−1.56)	−0.075(−1.27)	−0.078(−1.42)	−0.087(−1.55)
Exporter	−0.083(−1.49)	−0.080(−1.42)	0.139*(1.92)	0.063(0.67)	0.123*(1.74)	0.139*(1.94)
No. of employees (log)	−0.0004(−0.02)	0.001(0.08)	0.053**(2.60)	0.014(0.54)	0.050**(2.37)	0.052**(2.59)
% Foreign owned	−0.002**(−2.45)	−0.002**(−2.40)	0.002(0.91)	−0.0001(−0.05)	0.002(0.93)	−0.003(1.09)
% Government owned	0.005(1.34)	0.0045(1.08)	−0.002(−0.31)	−0.002(−0.33)	−0.012***(−2.99)	−0.002(−0.33)
No. of "gift" opportunities (interactions with officials)				0.133***(3.59)		
Graft index				1.801***(11.14)		
Region-level regressors						
Per capita GRP (log)	0.214(0.74)	0.541(1.57)	0.235(0.99)	0.157(0.88)	0.132(0.48)	0.409(1.54)
Population (log)	0.033(0.32)	0.061(0.49)	0.259**(2.47)	0.268***(3.15)	0.284***(2.68)	0.287***(2.90)
Extractive industries as share of GRP	−0.496(−1.30)	−0.732**(−2.11)	−0.720***(−2.67)	−0.628**(−2.59)	−0.606**(−2.14)	−0.774***(−2.73)
Distance from Moscow (ln of km)	0.051(0.42)	0.029(0.82)	0.053(1.46)	0.009(0.26)	0.071**(2.01)	0.026(0.76)
Latitude	−0.030(−1.31)	−0.039(−1.57)	0.010(0.56)	0.012(0.80)	0.028(1.48)	0.007(0.34)
Newspaper copies per 1,000 population		−0.001**(−2.36)				−0.001**(−2.62)
Effective freedom of information law		−0.126(−0.43)				−0.022(−0.07)
Effective freedom of information decree		−0.019(−0.06)				−0.114(−0.37)
% of citizens who were asked for unofficial payment (FOM)					0.023**(2.07)	
No. of obs. (firms)	3,277	3,277	3,771	2,380	3,680	3,771
F statistic	2.82	3.31	3.40	16.32	4.90	5.77
p value of F test	0.008	0.002	0.002	<0.0001	0.0001	<0.0001
R^2	0.04	0.05	0.03	0.13	0.04	0.03

Dependent variable in 5.1 and 5.2 is extent to which firm has been affected by unofficial payments to local or regional officials to influence votes or decrees. Dependent variable in 5.3–5.6 is frequency with which firms "in my line of business" need to make irregular payments "to get things done" with respect to regulations, etc. T-statistics, reported in parentheses below point estimates, are based on standard errors adjusted for non-independence of errors within regional clusters of observations, with $^{***}p < 0.01$; $^{**}p < 0.05$; $^{*}p < 0.1$

Table 13 Graft index, "Bribe tax" and Kickback regressions (firm level)

Equation	6.1	6.2	6.3	6.4	6.5	6.6
Dependent variable	Graft index		Bribe tax (share of revenues)		Kickback tax (share of contract value)	
Firm-level regressors						
Established 1990 or before	−0.004(−0.23)	0.017(0.84)	−0.0001(−0.01)	0.005(0.07)	−0.145(−1.22)	−0.158(−1.32)
Retail firm	−0.006(−0.42)	0.001(0.10)	−0.092***(−3.34)	−0.088***(−2.94)	−0.193(−1.25)	−0.186(−1.17)
Female manager	−0.014(−1.27)	−0.018(−1.64)	−0.064**(−2.35)	−0.068**(−2.35)	−0.214**(−2.55)	−0.200**(−2.50)
Exporter	0.049***(2.99)	0.047**(2.58)	0.030(0.61)	0.034(0.64)	0.078(0.59)	0.088(0.67)
No. of employees (log)	−0.003(−0.56)	−0.005(−0.97)	−0.030***(−2.89)	−0.028**(−2.45)	−0.040(−1.36)	−0.038(−1.26)
% Foreign owned	−0.0002(−0.65)	−0.0002(−1.26)	−0.0001(−0.19)	−0.0001(−0.09)	0.003(0.73)	0.002(0.68)
% Government owned	0.0001(0.17)	0.0001(0.04)	0.002(1.43)	0.002(1.45)	−0.003(−1.25)	−0.003(−1.36)
No. of "gift" opportunities (interactions with officials)	0.042***(6.01)	0.045***(5.65)	0.050***(3.19)	0.044**(2.53)		
Time tax				0.035**(2.30)		
Region-level regressors						
Per capita GRP (log)	−0.011(−0.73)	−0.017(−0.98)	−0.086(−1.00)	−0.085(−0.84)	−0.199(−1.45)	−0.116(−0.88)
Population (log)	0.022**(2.17)	0.005(0.65)	0.134**(2.29)	0.126*(1.92)	0.309***(3.58)	0.348***(3.81)
Extractive industries as share of GRP	0.026(1.04)	0.006(0.27)	−0.046(−0.42)	0.003(0.02)	−0.188(−0.88)	−0.308(−1.54)
Distance from Moscow (ln of km)	0.002(1.16)	0.002(0.73)	0.024*(1.74)	0.023*(1.65)	0.040(1.60)	0.052**(2.06)
Latitude	0.001(0.45)	0.0002(0.26)	0.017***(1.15)	0.014*(2.13)	0.039***(3.43)	0.038***(3.43)
Doing Business index		0.017*(1.71)				
Procurement transparency index					−0.010*(−1.81)	
Procurement transparency: completed contracts sub-index						−0.028***(−3.10)
No. of obs. (firms)	2,557	1,890	3,299	2,987	861	861
Mean, dep. var.						
F statistic	4.25	7.44	6.54	8.11	4.00	4.41
p value of F test	0.0003	<0.0001	<0.0001	<0.0001	0.0005	0.0002
R^2	0.03	0.04	0.02	0.03	0.04	0.05

Dependent variable is Graft index in 6.1 and 6.2, (log of) Bribe tax in 6.3 and 6.4, and (log of) Kickback tax in 6.5 and 6.6. T-statistics, reported in parentheses below point estimates, are based on standard errors adjusted for non-independence of errors within regional clusters of observations, with $^{***}p < 0.01$; $^{**}p < 0.05$; $^{*}p < 0.1$

References

Balsevich A, Pivovarova S, Podkolzina E (2011) Information transparency in Russian procurement: how it works in Russian regions. National Research University, Higher School of Economics, Working Paper WP BRP 01/EC/2011

Barseghyan L (2008) Entry costs and cross-country differences in productivity and output. J Econ Growth 13(2):145–167

Bruhn M (2011) License to sell: the effect of business registration reform on entrepreneurial activity in Mexico. Rev Econ Stat 93(1):382–386

Cai H, Fang H, Xu LC (2011) Eat, drink, firms, government: an investigation of corruption from entertainment and travel costs of Chinese firms. J Law Econ, University of Chicago Press, 54(1):55–78

Chirkova E, Bowser D (2005) Corruption in Russian regions. In: Hodess R et al (eds) Global corruption report 2004. Pluto Press in association with Transparency International, Berlin/London, pp 295–297

Costa S (2012) Do freedom of information laws decrease corruption? J Law Econ Organ. Published on-line 18 May 2012

Cull R, Xu LC (2005) Institutions, ownership, and finance: the determinants of investment among Chinese firms. J Financ Econ 77:117–146

Desai RM (2008) Improving the investment climate. In: Desai RM, Goldberg I (eds) Can Russia compete? Brookings Institution Press, Washington, DC, pp 91–121

Dininio P, Orttung R (2005) Explaining patterns of corruption in the Russian regions. World Polit 57:500–529

Djankov S (2009) The regulation of entry: a survey. World Bank Res Obs 24(2):183–203

Frye T, Reuter OJ, Buckley N (2011) The political economy of Russian gubernatorial election and appointment. Working Paper BRP 01/PS/2011. National Research University higher School of Economics, Moscow

Gonzalez A, Lopez-Cordova JE, Valladares EE (2007) The incidence of graft on developing-country firms. Policy Research Working Paper No. 4394. The World Bank, Washington, DC

Kaufmann D, Montoriol-Garriga J, Recanatini F (2008) How does bribery affect public service delivery? Micro-evidence from service users and public officials in Peru. World Bank Policy Research Working Paper No. 4492

Pyle W (2011) Organized business, political competition, and property rights: evidence from the Russian federation. J Law Econ Organ 27(1):2–31

Pyle W, Solanko L (2013) The composition and interests of Russia's business lobbies: testing Olson's hypothesis of the 'Encompassing Organization'. Public Choice 155(1–2):19–41

Rivas MF (2012) An experiment on corruption and gender. Bull Econ Res 65(1):10–39

Swamy A, Knack S, Lee Y, Azfar O (2001) Gender and corruption. J Dev Econ 64(1):25–55

Treisman D (2007) What have we learned about the causes of corruption from ten years of cross-national empirical research? Annu Rev Polit Sci 10:211–244

World Bank (2000) Anticorruption in transition: a contribution to the policy debate. World Bank, Washington, DC

World Bank (2011) Trends in corruption and regulatory burden in Eastern Europe and Central Asia. World Bank, Washington, DC

World Bank (2012) Doing business in Russia 2012: comparing regulation for domestic firms in 30 cities and with 183 economies. The World Bank and IFC, Washington, DC

World Economic Forum (2011) The Russia competitiveness report 2011. World Economic Forum, Geneva

Yakovlev E, Zhuravskaya E (2007) Deregulating of businesses. New Economic School, Moscow

Institutional Creativity for Happy High-Income Societies: Can Basic Income-Based Reforms Help to Build Them?

Lorenzo Bona

Abstract This paper tackles the problem of the building of a happy high-income society and develops a theoretical approach that leads to a puzzling conclusion, for developed countries engaged in debates about the opportunity of welfare state reforms. For this purpose the paper focuses on the links between cooperation, labor market and growth, taking into account two main interconnected relationships: one between happiness and economic growth and development, and another one where the focal events are employment subsidy-based reforms and basic income-based reforms in the area of welfare state. Drawing on arguments from behavioral economics and welfare state studies, the paper suggests: (a) basic income-based reforms of welfare states may in theory help the building of a happy high-income society; (b) a full development of this building process may however be impeded or delayed by the emergence of self-control dilemmas.

1 Introduction

Human creativity and happiness are the main drivers of economic growth and development. Human creativity, as suggested both by common sense and entrepreneurship literature (Schumpeter 1934; Kirzner 1973; Baumol 1990), fuels innovation in our societies; happiness encourages people to be more productive and ingenious (Oswald et al. 2009; Erez and Isen 2002). Their role is particularly critical when an economy approaches the technology frontier—i.e. when the economy exhausts the potential of the available technology—or in situations like the current conjuncture where a recovery from an economic and financial crisis is needed. As suggested by the Nobel Laureate Edmund Phelps (2007), the creation of a "good economy"—

L. Bona (✉)
Via Palestrina, 23 09189 Cagliari, Italy
e-mail: lb.1@libero.it

L. Paganetto (ed.), *Wealth, Income Inequalities, and Demography*,
DOI 10.1007/978-3-319-05909-9_4,

that is, a more performing economy focused on human satisfaction and based on higher levels of social inclusion and mobility—or, if we may say so, the transition from a high-income to a happy high-income society may, in this sense, represents a fundamental problem for many developed countries that are engaged in finding new and more sustainable paths for growth and development. Unfortunately both human creativity and happiness can't be taken for granted, since they require appropriate structures of incentives and institutions (Baumol 1990; North 1990).

Moving from these preliminary considerations, this paper tackles the problem of the building of a happy high-income society focusing on the links between cooperation, labor market and growth. For this purpose, the following paragraphs will take into account two main interconnected relationships: one between happiness and economic growth and development, and another one where the focal events are employment subsidy-based reforms and basic income-based reforms in the area of welfare state.

In particular, the second paragraph—largely related with behavioral economics arguments and heavily based on the works of Rachlin (2000, 2002) and Rachlin and Jones (2008)—deals with the emotional status of happiness and its relationship with the economic growth and development of a social system. This provides a way to look at the topic of the paper from a general perspective and in ways that may help us to focus on highly problematic conflict-situations, like those between short-term and long-term rewards, individual and social choices, selfishness and altruism. Together with this perspective it is also provided the opportunity to benefit from a review of one line of reasoning in which social cooperation and solidarity, with their value in terms of happiness, are strictly related with the emergence of self-control dilemmas and fragile institutional remedies.

The third paragraph, more specific, is about the urgency, underlined in many current debates, of newer and better alignments between efficiency and equity goals in labor markets. In this regard—greatly drawing on studies like Esping-Andersen (1990) and Sabattini (2009)—some of the most innovative proposals in the area of welfare state research are synthetically recalled and, with some simplification, especially related to the works of Van Parijis (1990, 1995, 2000) and Phelps (1997, 2000, 2007), so to consider two main ideas: the idea in favor of universal subsidies to employers limited to full-time workers at the low-wage end of the labor market; and the idea in favor of unconditional transfer payments to each citizen. Taking these ideas simply to symbolize many current calls for employment subsidy-based reforms and alternatives in favor of basic income-based reforms, it is then analyzed their relationship in a way where the emergence of a possible reconciliation between the proposed institutional innovations is a stimulus for a problematical conclusion. On the one hand—as suggested by several studies (Van Parijis 1995; Standing 2005; Jordan 2010)—basic income-based reforms of welfare states may help the building of a happy high-income society; on the other hand, a lack of self-controlled choices may however arise in this building process in ways that can delay and/or impede its full development.

The final paragraph will provide the opportunity for a brief discussion.

2 Happiness, Economic Growth and Development

2.1 Happiness and Self-Control

Among economists and other social scientists there is a growing consensus that happiness positively affects economic growth and development. For example, Hermalin and Isen (2008) propose a model of decision making that incorporates psychological findings about the existence of a relationship that runs from positive emotions to consumption. Kenny (1999), re-examining the debate about the links between income and happiness and studies like Dusenbeq (1949), Mishan (1967), and Easterlin (1974) but also more traditional works like Smith (1759) and Mill (1859), suggests that happiness can be a determinant rather than an effect of economic growth. Finally, other scholars like Fukuyama (1995) and Guven (2011) emphasize that this type of emotional status favours the diffusion of higher levels of social capital and trustful relationships, which in turn may have a positive impact on economic growth (Knack and Keefer 1997).

Accordingly this paper also embraces the view consistent with the idea that the promotion of happiness should be a central goal of public policies, given that happy people are more likely to be industrious, to expand human knowledge and to employ it ingeniously. But, what is happiness and how can we formally describe its impact on economic growth and development?

In a well-documented study closely related with these questions, Luigino Bruni (2010) provides stimulating insights when he observes that efforts about the definition of happiness and the discovery of its causes are traceable in economics and other social studies—like sociology and philosophy—in a way that reflects a tension between a ‘hedonistic’ and an ‘eudaimonistic’ approach to happiness: the first approach—heavily indebted with the philosophical insights of Epicurus and Jeremy Bentham—tends to describe well-being in terms of pleasure and to be more concerned about what people can actually do, while the same approach shows a less intense interest about how people feel; the other approach is instead deeply related with the Aristotelian school of philosophy and, consequently, with the view according to which happiness arises when an individual interacts with others within society.

Supporting this latter approach—on the basis of empirical evidences about the strong relationship between genuine sociality and self-reported happiness—the study of Bruni remarks other interesting aspects, like the fact that economists and other social scientists, although lacking a univocal definition of happiness, are more and more interested in its measurement on the basis of the answers to questionnaires; and in this sense the Subjective Well-Being Index may provide a valuable tool. On the other hand, Bruni’s work is also noteworthy because it suggests that research on economics and happiness may profit by a reconsideration of the Aristotelian tradition and by making room to the related and emerging concept of “relational good” (Gui 1987; Uhlaner 1989), i.e. goods which can be produced, exchanged and enjoyed by individuals only if they are shared with others in non-anonymous social interactions.

This kind of suggestions seems, in fact, particularly useful to shed new light on several issues underlying the problem of happiness in modern high-income societies, for example, reinforcing the message that these societies experience a decrease of individual and public happiness which can be seen as the unintentional consequence of the fact that too few relational goods are produced and consumed (Bruni 2010, p. 399).

The approach developed so far can be, however, further expanded to analyze and interpret happiness not only as a result of social and non-anonymous exchanges, but also as a product of individual behaviors which are not necessarily embedded in face-to-face interactions. In this regard we can consider the phenomenon known as sunk costs fallacy. We know that, according to standard economics, in decision processes about future investments sunk costs should be ignored: for a given present investment only costs and returns must be considered. But we also know that this approach may be problematical, as prominent works at the intersection between behavioral psychology and economics—like those of Kahneman and Tversky (1979), Phillips et al. (1991), and Rachlin (2000)—have clearly underlined. To clarify this point in the rest of the paragraph, we can usefully review some observations and insights developed in the latter one of the mentioned works.

In this light, let's imagine that it takes 5 years between the project and the completion of a mall. Let's also imagine that after 4 years of construction the costs of completion escalate and the market shrinks dramatically with an effect that can translate, for the builder, in the dilemma of whether to stop or continue the construction of the mall. For the builder's dilemma there are no easy or a priori solutions. On the one hand, the builder should certainly stop the construction of the mall if the problem is simply stated in the terms earlier introduced. On the other hand, it may be wise to consider other elements. What if the uncompleted mall will stand in the city environment as an abandoned ruin while the builder plans to stay in the business? Can, in future time, potential investors worry about a builder who doesn't complete his projects and, for this reason, choose other builders who "irrationally" complete their jobs once they are started? In other terms, what may appear as a sunk cost in a short-time perspective may appear differently when a long-time perspective is taken into account.

The sunk cost dilemma, this way, can be helpful in a fourfold way: first, to focus on conflict situations where smaller-sooner rewards (or SSR) coexist with larger-later ones (or SSR); second, to realize that the establishment of informal rules (such as "complete the job once it's started") may lead individuals towards preferred outcomes; third, to interpret happiness as a form of self-control; fourth, to consider that contrary the appearances, self-control doesn't mean the abolishment of human spontaneity, but the improvement of contexts where people can move towards higher levels of spontaneity.

Developing this line of reasoning, Rachlin's work also makes room to a set of propositions that appear particularly valuable: (a) subjective evaluation of rewards changes over time, in a way that it is functionally related—like a discount function—

with the amount of time that has to elapse for the delivery of rewards; (b) as the delay in the delivery of rewards increases, rewards become less valuable for individuals; (c) subjective evaluation of rewards grows faster when individuals are closer to their delivery than when individuals are far away; (d) unlike rational discount functions traditionally assumed in economics (where rationality is identified with consistent preferences between two or more alternatives, i.e. with discount functions that do not cross), human and non-human behavior is variable (which doesn't mean irrational) and individual choices can be better described by means of crossing discount functions hyperbolic in their forms.

The usefulness of these four propositions finds its main reflex in the fact that they can lead to the following prediction, confirmed in several experiments: when the delivery of rewards is distant for both the SSR and the LLR, the subjective view of the values of the alternatives faced by an individual tends to coincide with the objective view; the LLR is then preferred to the SSR. But when the delivery of these rewards is closer, the discount function of the smaller reward rises not only rapidly toward a point where it intersects the discount function of the larger one, but also in ways where—after this point of intersection—the value of the SSR becomes momentarily higher than that of the LLR, with a final effect that translates in a situation where it is very difficult to resist the temptation offered by the SSR.

Temptation results furthermore virtually impossible to be controlled if the conflict between the SSR and the LLR translates in a phenomenon named "complex ambivalence" (Rachlin 2000, 2002). This phenomenon occurs when two conditions are satisfied: (a) the existence of a conflict situation between a given SSR associated with particular acts of consumption and a given LLR associated with abstract patterns of acts; (b) the emergence of an *indistinct situation,* where—simultaneously—a particular act of consumption is always preferred (e.g. a drink for an alcoholic) and an abstract pattern of acts is also always preferred (e.g. sobriety for an alcoholic). When the phenomenon of "complex ambivalence" emerges, it becomes then important to find out how to encourage happiness via self-control based choices.

It is generally agreed that self-control can be encouraged restricting the set of future choices, i.e. doing something that prevents preference reversal and immediate consumption. In this sense, as summarized in Rachlin's works, three main techniques to achieve this goal are those respectively associated with the notions of "*strict commitment*", "*commitment by punishment*", and "*soft commitment*", in coherence with the idea that commitment implies a situation where freedom—interpreted in terms of potential variability of behaviors—is reduced (Rachlin 2000, pp. 125–126). The first one consists in the removal of temptations offered by the SSR; the second one, similarly, to everyday agreements, reduces the value of the SSR attaching a cost on any deviation from the LLR; the third technique consists in beginning (making an investment in) a behavioral pattern (cluster of behaviors) whose interruption is costly, so that it leads to the choice of the LLR in a way that will carry this choice over the point of preference reversal.

For a better understanding of soft commitment, we can additionally say that in *repeated prisoner's dilemmas* some people cooperate and continue to cooperate regardless of their counterparts' decisions about cooperation or defection. For these people cooperation is an intrinsically highly valuable pattern of behaviors (like for others morality, altruism, sobriety etc.), and in order to reap the related rewards case-by-case decisions must be abandoned. In these situations soft commitment is, in part, similar to punishment commitment and, in part, different. The similarity concerns the fact that there is a cost for who deviates from a commitment situation. The difference is that, on the one hand, punishment commitment is associated with costs that depend from an impulsive act and that are imposed after impulsiveness; on the other hand, soft commitment is connected with costs that are dependent from the breaking of a behavioral pattern in opposition to an impulsive act and that are imposed at the same time if not in advance of impulsiveness (Rachlin 2000, p. 109).

With regard to the mentioned techniques for self-control promotion, following Rachlin's works, it's also possible to add three other points. First "strict commitment" is rarely available in everyday life or consistent with human aspirations to a normal life: a TV addicted can surely destroy the remove-control, but not the opportunity to buy a new one. Second, "*commitment by punishment*" is efficient and common in many everyday self-control procedures—e.g. marriage and other agreements that include penalties for noncompliance—but *not very much in complex ambivalence situations*: since both a particular act of consumption and an abstract pattern of acts are always preferred, it becomes virtually impossible to find out both a right moment for the establishment of "commitment by punishment" and an effective way for its maintenance once established. Third, "*soft commitment*", although not a perfect remedy too, not only appears more compatible with a protection of people's freedom and aspirations to live a normal life than the other two commitment techniques, but it also reveals and a greater efficiency than these latter ones in complex ambivalence situations, where self-control problems appear particularly critical.

2.2 *Individual and Social Choices for Happy Lives*

We learned that self-control and soft commitment techniques are key factors in helping people to obtain more valuable rewards and achieve, in turn, higher levels of happiness. However our analysis focused on *individual choices* based on *individual delay discounting* (IDD), and it didn't say much about the relationship between *individual* and *social choices*.

This relationship is particularly crucial in our lives since the attainment of welfare enhancing outcomes frequently requires high levels of interindividual cooperation which, in turn, may call once more our attention on the great importance of self-control based behaviors.

Fiduciary and altruistic relationships—like those within a family, a group of friends or a firm—represent, for example, an important ingredient in people's lives and can stimulate a reflection on how individuals may converge toward a

Fig. 1 "Trust game"

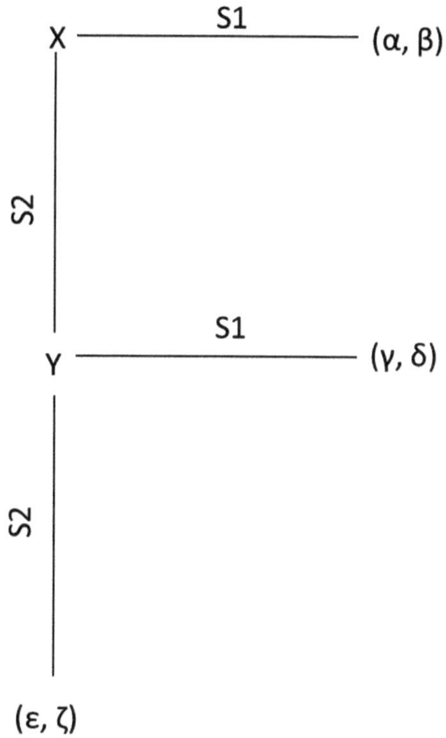

common goal to contrast temptations associated with the persistence of unfavorable or unhappy situations.

One way we can follow to introduce to this reflection is by making room to studies dealing with organizations and agency problems. In this regard one of the most valuable contribution is provided by Thaler and Shrefin (1981), who explicitly recall works like Jensen and Meckling (1976) to introduce self-control in their theory of intertemporal choice. For this purpose they characterize self-control in terms of an internal conflict that, for the individual, it is similar to the principal-agent conflict between owners and managers of a firm: both individuals and organizations may, sometimes, experience simultaneous conflicts of interests between farsighted and myopic behaviors; moreover both people and firms, to reduce these conflicts, rely on the introduction of rules and institutions—like norms that restrict the area of managerial discretion and/or the modification of incentives—like when firms control departmental inputs by means of cost accounting in ways useful to establish a link between compensation and these new input measures (Thaler and Shrefin 1981, p. 398).

To expand our reflection we can also introduce, by means of Fig. 1, what game theorists usually call a "trust game":

Figure 1—if interpreted drawing on studies like (Pelligra 2007)—illustrates how a possible interaction between two subjects, X and Y, may develop with respect to a set of outcomes that are both in relation with two alternative strategies (S1 and S2) and with a relationship fundamentally important for the nature of the game, where $\varepsilon > \alpha, \alpha > \gamma, \delta > \zeta$.

Looking at the figure we can notice that the S1 (or no-trust) strategy available to X results both rationally oriented to minimize the risk of opportunistic behaviors—since the pay-off $\delta > \zeta$ is potentially available for Y—and connected to the outcome (α, β), which in turn corresponds to a sub-game perfect Nash equilibrium. On the other hand, we can also notice that the outcome (ε, ζ) can be achieved by the subjects involved in the game only if they choose the irrational move S2 (or trust).

In other words, in situations that can be described by means of a "trust game" it is possible to discern two potential strategic moves that are not coherent with the standard principles of economic rationality. In particular, it is possible to register one strategic behavior, generally called trustful, that results: (a), vulnerable to opportunistic reaction of a counterpart; (b) based on the expectation that this latter counterpart will abstain to act opportunistically.

Furthermore, it is also possible to observe one other type of strategic behavior, generally called trustworthy, that relates, on the one hand, to subjects that make themselves vulnerable to another party and, on the other hand, to the effective satisfaction of the expectation defined in (b).

Considering several scenarios similar to the one in our figure and how outcomes such as (ε, ζ) can be reasonably achieved, even in anonymous contexts, by subjects that like X act as a first mover, various studies advanced some solutions embracing two main approaches: one based on the concepts of "reciprocity" (Rabin 1993; Dufwenberg and Kirchsteiger 2004) and a second one founded on the notion of "trust responsiveness" (Pettit 1997; Guerra and Zizzo 2004; Pelligra 2007). The "reciprocity" based approach provides experimental evidence for interpretations of social interactions according to which kind behaviors are repaid with kind behaviors and the unkind ones with unkind ones. The "trust responsiveness" approach suggests instead—via experimental procedures—that the adoption of behaviors that openly place trust in others favors an endogenous modification in the scale of preferences of these latter subjects which, in turns, concurs to the emergence of trustworthy responses.

There are however situations, as the previous section underlined, where some people cooperate and continue to cooperate regardless of their counterparts' strategies. In this respect, the relationship between *individual* and *social choices* and its further relatedness with *self-control* based behaviors may be perhaps more clearly analyzed if we think about people that are truly or radically altruistic: for example, a person who—anonymously and without any promise of reward—donates money to a charity association (Rachlin 2002).

Like the fiduciary behaviors, altruistic acts may appear completely disconnected with the economic rationality and the related cost-benefit calculus (in our example no reward exists for the donor). However, several economists advanced suggestions for the *incorporation of altruism into utility functions or discount functions* (Akerlof 1997; Becker 1981; Simon 1995), in the sense that the allocation of available goods by a given individual not only depends on current consumption and IDD (i.e.

consumption by the same individual at later times), but also on *social discounting* (SD), i.e. consumption by other individuals. Following this logic, it's been also added on the basis of experimental evidence that altruistic situations are very similar to situations associated with self-control problems. Emphasizing this point, Rachlin (2002) observes that—on a social level—self-control problems arise, in fact, when two alternative activities are simultaneously available and respectively associated with a relatively brief activity, BA (corresponding to t units of time), and a longer activity, LA (corresponding to T units of time, where $T = nt$ and $n > 1$), in accordance with the following conditions:

1. LA (in its entirety) is preferred to *n repetitions* of BA;
2. BA is preferred to a *fraction temporally defined* of LA.
   Altruistic situations arise when conditions 1 and 2 are integrated by:
3. the benefits for a group are greater when one individual member chooses a *fraction temporally defined of LA* (FLA) than when the individual's choice is in favor of BA.

Then, in situations where 1, 2 and 3 hold, altruistic acts are actions that reflect choices in favor of FLA, in ways that can also be described by means of social discount functions that are hyperbolic in their form (Rachlin and Jones 2008).

If we now return to the example about the person who—anonymously and without any promise of reward—donates money to a charity association, we can try to condense the message of these latter works on altruism and self-control in a threefold observation. First, the cost of an altruistic behavior may represent a cost (in a one-shot situation) or an opportunity cost (in a repeated situation) associated with the loss of a given preferred brief alternative. Second, reward *is obtained* only when altruistic acts are grouped in patterns which are, as a whole, intrinsically valuable (e.g. altruism for our 'charitable person'). And third, individuals like our 'charitable person' behave altruistically and in conformity with soft-commitment tactics to not incur in the costs of breaking patterns of acts with high value, i.e. to live *happy lives*.

3 The Problematic Building of a Happy High-Income Society

3.1 *The Need of Newer Alignments Between Efficiency and Equity Goals in Modern Economies: The Labor Market and the Welfare State*

The analysis outlined so far can give us a basis for trying to offer a contribution for the current debate about the policies that advanced economies should adopt to recover from the most severe socio-economic crisis since the Great Depression. More specifically, as will be suggested later in this paper, an approach *à la* Rachlin to self-control dilemmas can also help us to better understand the problem of happiness in contemporary societies, letting emerge the possibility of an application of the theoretical tools of this approach finalized to a re-examination of some of the proposals according to which a decisive step towards the building of happier and more dynamic social systems can result from a restructuring of the welfare state via institutional innovations such as subsidy-based reforms or, alternatively, basic income-based reforms.

However, before attempting to suggest more explicitly how an approach like that of Rachlin can help to analyze strategies in favor of a rapid economic recovery in advanced economies, we can usefully recall that in many debates it is generally agreed that these economies, to survive and prosper, need to move from a traditional system of mass-production towards a knowledge-based one, and—instrumentally for this longer term goal—it is often argued that governments should especially promote labour market flexibility, socio-economic inclusion and equal access to jobs and social services.

Crucially important for this transition is the problem of a better alignment between efficiency and equity goals, so to remove or reduce the negative impacts of the economic decline that translate in increasing levels of economic uncertainty and instability. A problematical alignment that may unveil several connections with many things said in the previous sections: not only about the puzzling tension between selfish and altruistic individuals' aspirations, but also about the creation of a more performing economy through both the improvement of human satisfaction and the promotion of higher levels of social inclusion and mobility.

As noted above, one of the most influential economists engaged in stressing the importance of this latter point is Phelps (1997, 2007) with proposals aiming at its incorporation as a fundamental trait of a "good economy"; an expression—this latter one—that is strictly tied with deeper ethical and moral principles concerning the essence of a "good life" and, for this reason, with considerations and controversies about how advanced economies can today regain their dynamism and promote prosperity on the basis of more or less profound institutional changes at the intersections between the private and the public sector. It is in this context, more specifically, that a broad social interest is emerging for innovations and reforms in social policies underneath the functioning of advanced societies' welfare state, where—as it is known—some of the most relevant interactions between the public, the private and the household sectors take place for the minimization problem of the economic uncertainty and instability that are generally present in social environments.

With regard to this point and in ways that can help us to approach some of the most innovative reform-based arguments in the area of welfare state research, it seems useful to summarize some of the main features of welfare state completing this section with additional observations largely based on the works of Esping-Andersen (1990) and Sabattini (2009).

In this light, we can recall that no standard procedure guided, since the late 1800s, the welfare state's gradual institutionalization in its various forms currently at work in advanced economies. Each one of these economies experienced, in fact, the establishment of a specific form of welfare state that followed, in its development, a path-dependent logic. In other terms, in these economic systems it is not possible to find fully identical forms of welfare state, since these latter ones evolved not only in different social contexts but also under the influence of earlier generations' choices about consumption and savings.

If we consider these choices, it is also useful to add that particularly important seem to be those ones concerning two main points: on the one hand, the level of welfare to supply and, on the other hand, the recipients of this welfare, or more explicitly the citizens deserving special protection in a given society. Redistributive principles, but most of all their operational translation into concrete social policy programs, play therefore a crucial role in the ways in which governments try to insure their citizens against the negative effects caused by the emergence of instable and uncertain economic situations.

It is true that, from an abstract point of view, governments could abstain from this intervention, since inter and intra-generational redistribution of social output could be obtained relying on market institutions alone, like the financial and the private insurance markets.

In the frictionless world of neoclassical economics financial markets could, in fact, work very well to achieve redistributive goals: in these markets each individual makes his or her own decisions about his or her own asset of savings, in consideration of the level of social security the same individual prefers to receive if unpredictable and involuntary situations would emerge with effects that translate in a reduction of the individual's abilities that are necessary to gain an income. On the one hand, equity and debt securities in which savings are invested may become, once appropriately converted, a form of income that individuals could use to compensate potential declines in their work abilities; on the other hand, the stock of savings cumulated by the economically active individuals may translate in available consumption for individuals who instead are not economically active.

In the same neoclassical context, private insurance markets could also work very well. Here each economically active individual obtains optimal levels of welfare relying on market mechanisms that are optimally designed for a common management of social risks through "horizontal compensations", i.e. through compensations that run from the economically active to economically 'harmed' individuals.

We know however that market failures, like those caused by moral hazard and adverse selection phenomena, are unavoidable facts in human interactions and consequently the main source of impediments in the achievement of optimal inter and intra-generational redistributions of social output for the coverage of social risks. It is essentially the recognition of this fact that in advanced economic systems provides the main justification for public sector's interventions in areas that also include the redistributions of social output and the introduction of compulsory and/or partially compulsory social security nets.

Accordingly, these systems, where the public and the private sector coexist, typically provide protection for social risks on the basis of two fundamental institutional arrangements. One of them is *social security* and finds its main peculiarity in the fact that it acts similarly to a compulsory public insurance for workers and firms against the risk of individuals' inability to gain an income after certain age limits. The other institutional arrangement is *social assistance* that, instead, it is more alike to a partially-compulsory public insurance designed to contrast the risk of individuals' inability to gain an income, if they fall in situations of unemployment, illness, injury or exclusion from the job market because of age reasons (e.g. minors).

Welfare state, in modern high-income societies, is essentially built upon these two institutional arrangements, so to provide resources—like health care, educational programs or support for permanent or temporary work inabilities—to people in ways that affect their earnings potential and in levels that, once defined, have to be financed through taxation, proportional levy on the wage bill and voluntary contributions.

Since the inability to uphold one's own livelihood represents the most crucial problem that stimulated the welfare state's expansion, it is also relevant to note that social insurance coverage is generally obtained relying on forms of solidarity that tend to oscillate between two extremes. One of these extremes corresponds to a situation of *universal solidarity*, that in turn implies that welfare is provided to all individuals within a given society; the other extreme can be associated with a situation of *occupational solidarity*, that instead denotes that welfare is provided to a greater or lesser number of individuals on the basis of their occupational activity. Moreover, both universal and occupational solidarity can develop *horizontally* and *vertically*: in the first circumstance who needs protection receives compensations from the economically active individuals; while in the second circumstance, the vulnerable obtains protection from the economically active individuals, in decreasing order with respect to the income of these latter subjects.

In the following years after World War II welfare states followed evolutionary paths which amplified their differences. However welfare research suggests the possibility for a classification of the existing welfare states with respect to the *coverage of their costs* and the *financing of their performance.* For example, considering the cost dimension, it is well known the classification articulated in Titmuss (1974), where it is possible to distinguish between three models of welfare state. According to this classification, we can have a *residual welfare model*, where temporary public intervention are envisaged when the private and the household sectors fail to provide protection to vulnerable individuals; we can also distinguish an *industrial achievement-performance model*, when public intervention integrates the market, in complementary and supplementary ways, so that the level of social protection to individuals reflects the merits and productivity of the employed population; we can finally discern an *institutional redistributive model* when public intervention is universally provided on the basis on needs principles and fully independent from what happens in the private and the household sectors.

On the other hand, if we consider many modern welfare states with respect to the financing of their performance we can recall, as a paradigmatic classification, that one introduced by Esping-Andersen (1990), who made distinctions between a *liberal*, a *social-democratic* and a *familialistic* regime. In the first regime the public intervention is minimal: although it is, in large part, in support of market mechanisms that provide protection for individuals with sufficient resources to enter market exchange relationships, this regime also provides welfare for the neediest usually on the basis of preliminary means tests. In the second regime public protection is universally provided, through taxation and in substitution of the private and the household sectors, for individuals unable to gain their original income. In the third regime public protection for vulnerable individuals is typically provided through both economic support for families and the encouragement of family solidarity.

In real world, where individualistic values prevail, the economy tends to reflect a mix between the *residual welfare model* and the *liberal* one (e.g. U.S.A., U.K., Australia); where corporative attitudes prevail, the economy tends to reveal a combination between the *industrial achievement-performance model* and the *familistic* one (e.g. Italy, Germany, the Netherlands); where community values prevail, the economy tends to mix the *institutional redistributive model* with the *social-democratic* one (e.g. Scandinavian countries).

Welfare states experienced a dramatic change between the 1950s and 1970s of the last century, when from institutional arrangements for provision of minimum levels of social protection for narrowly defined population segments, they evolved pointing towards high levels of near-universal protection. An evolution that resulted highly problematical in the second part of the 1970s, since welfare states' sustainability appeared to be possible only situations of high economic growth and full employment, like those ones existing in the initial years of their development.

In particular, the expansion of public spending for the financing of welfare state not only appeared to be excessive, but also as one of the main reasons of:

1. rigidities in the labour market functional for the persistence of unemployment levels higher than standard equilibrium;
2. rising levels of taxation functional for economic systems more and more costly, economic inputs progressively less productive and the risk of *social dumping* increasingly probable;
3. growing public deficits functional for difficulties in domestic saving, with negative effects on capital formation in the long run.

Moreover, welfare states in current days are facing new complications that concur to prolong their crisis. And in this respect we can, for example, recall a threefold fact that deserves a particular attention. First, negative or anemic economic growth combined with technological progress is increasingly translating in structural unemployment. Second, today market structures—to be competitive—are both requiring levels of flexibility higher than the present ones and promoting, as an involuntary consequence, new forms of inequalities and marginalization that are often associated with low-paid and part-time jobs. Third, the current dynamics in demography are making the management of social risks more difficult compared to situations of the past.

All this is, in essence, the reason why it is believed by many that structural reforms are a priority in the area of labor market relationships and a task that requires newer and better alignments between equity and efficiency goals.

3.2 *Restructuring the Welfare States: A Problematic Reconciliation Between Subsidy-Based and Basic Income-Based Reforms*

Criticism about the welfare state and its impact on the economy, as noted, started to emerge during the second part of the 1970s. Suggestions were then made—especially in Europe—in favor of policies for an intense restructuring of welfare states in coherence with rapid reductions of public spending.

Although it is almost impossible to refer about every single proposals advanced so far for reforms in welfare states' current arrangements, it is possible however to move further in our analysis organizing these proposals in two large groups (Sabattini 2009, pp. 125–126), in a way that, in turn, may help us to focus on a possible relationship between two subsets that can include some of the most innovative contributions to welfare state research.

One group of proposals can converge toward what we may call a '*work ethic*' *based perspective.* A fundamental trait of this perspective—supported by most mainstream economists—is the twofold view according to which self-esteem can only be achieved in work environments and that having a job is socially important, if not a right. In this light, it is stressed the idea according to which the cost of working is crucially important for the economic performance, and therefore—for competition reasons—it needs to be reduced or appropriately controlled; as a consequence and in coherence with this need, welfare states' reforms should be strategically pursued optimizing the interaction between the public, the private and the household sectors. More specifically, this renewed interaction should be promoted via institutional changes consistent with three main effects. First, *more market flexibility*—for the private sector—to increase the total demand for final goods (aggregate demand). Second, *higher levels of social protection*—for the household sector—to compensate the potential risks deriving from higher levels of market flexibility. And third, more taxpayers—for the public sector—to provide higher levels of social protection, subordinately with the preliminary emergence of both new economic activities in the reformed private sector, and higher birth rates in the reformed household sector, where decreasing levels of economic instability should contrast the phenomenon of population aging.

Proposals for universal subsidies to employers limited to full-time workers at the low-wage end of the labor market advanced by scholars like Phelps (1997, 2000, 2007) and Drèze and Malinvaud (1994) may exemplify the most innovative frontier of the 'work ethic' based perspective. The innovative character of this type of employment subsidy-based reforms (or ESbR) is largely a reflex of a tension in favor of a dynamic and flexible welfare state, whose fundamental guiding points are, on the one hand, a renewed attention for social justice claims combined with a departure from traditional schemes where inactive business-behaviors like those of the retired and the unemployed people are largely subsidized; on the other hand, a resolute fight against poverty and unemployment through the provision, on a regular basis, of permanent public subsidies for the productive activities that hire marginalized workers. In this respect, following Edmund Phelps and some his most persuasive arguments in favor of the ESbR, we may synthetically recall some of the main benefits of this type of reform by means of two groups of observations. On a pragmatic level, a properly designed subsidy, raising at higher levels the wages of low-wage workers and favoring an increase in the supply of labor of these people, could concur to reduce the impact of inequalities deriving from different social backgrounds, it could help these workers to reject a job-offer if it does not appear convincing and to move more easily towards the satisfaction of their needs (Phelps 2000). On a more abstract level, the promotion of better economic environments and better places for human fulfillment may require the preliminary or simultaneous emergence of a situation where: (a) an existence based on challenge and personal development can be conceived as the essence of a good life; (b) new efforts are constantly made in favor of a "good economy", that is a more performing economy focused on human satisfaction and based on higher levels of social inclusion and mobility (Phelps 2007, pp. 555–557).

The other large group of proposals for welfare states' reforms can instead converge toward what can be called a '*human development*' *based perspective*. This perspective reflects the twofold view according to which, on the one hand, self-esteem is largely disconnected from work environments and, on the other hand, solidarity is the most important social value. In general terms, this perspective finds support among economists who, in international development, assign importance not only to economic growth variations (in terms of GDP), but also to expansions and contractions in the set of people's choices. Fundamental, in this sense, is the idea that human labor is not like any other commodity exchanged in the market. Therefore the prevailing message of the 'human development' based perspective is that the improvements in welfare states should be pursued promoting not only efficiency, but also self-esteem and situations potentially favorable for the realization of each individual's life-plans.

One important consequence of this message concerns the *minimum wage* (MW) for workers and can be traced in another innovative frontier of welfare state research, where it is underlined that MW should be no more be associated with the marginal productivity of the labor, but with minimum levels of resources that each individual needs to realize his or her life-plans. When conceived in such a way, MW translates in a form of salary that several scholars call "*basic income*" (BI) (Van Parijis 1990, 1995, 2004; Standing 2005; Munger 2011): a sort of grant equal or below subsistence level that, within a society, it is paid to all its members on an individual basis and without means test or work requirements.

Adding that economists with diverging ideological preferences like Meade (1993), Jordan (2010), and von Hayek (1982) concurred to BI's definition and reconciliation within the economic paradigm, we can also note that its institutionalization may require the adoption of two fundamental measures: (a) a rationalization and a relabeling of existing public transfers for social protection combined with a reduction in the area of tax exemptions and rebates, to obtain the savings necessary to finance the BI; (b) determination of BI's value at a level equal or below the minimum incomes generally provided on the basis of means-tests, to favor universal social protection for individuals without discouraging job-search functional for increases in their income (Van Parijis 1990; Sabattini 2009).

In this sense, from the promotion of a basic income-based reform (BIbR), as it is often observed, may derive three important benefits, in terms of equity and efficiency, for industrial relations: in a firm-based perspective, the BIbR can support a situation where only production and its needs matter in decisions about the employment of workers; in a job-seeker/worker-based perspective, it can favor an expansion of job-seekers, employed and unemployed workers' opportunities about the acceptance or rejection of job-offers perceived as inadequate or unfair, via the independence of their decisions from bureaucracy and its discretional provision of social safety nets; finally, in a more general social perspective, the BIbR can concur to minimize the levels of social conflicts over the distribution of social product, on the basis of the higher levels of fairness that it can promote within society.

It is often recognized, both by supporters and opponents of the mentioned types of reforms, how the ESbR and the BIbR can share a great area of convergence, especially with respect to the possibility for poorly skilled people to find more easily a job in a dynamic that, in turn, can promote a better degree of social inclusion. However fundamental differences persist, with effects that seem to fuel an intense debate between opposite supporters.

Without any intention to both explore these differences in their details and to provide a conclusive solution to the mentioned debate, perhaps best symbolized by the writings of Phelps (2000) and Van Parijis (2000), we however venture to add that, on balance and in gross terms, the ESbR and the BIbR may be subject to five additional observations that can be inferred from the existing literature in ways that appear heavily related with the problem of a transition from a high-income to a happy high-income society.

First, both type of reforms, reducing the impulsiveness of people in job decisions or reinforcing self-controlled behaviors when inadequate or unfair job-offers are presented, can promote higher levels of happiness and, consequently, help the transition toward the building of a happy high-income society. Second, both type of reforms can promote freedom and, in turn, more efficient allocations of the labor force. Third, both type of reforms, enlarging the set of individual opportunities, can incentivize human creativity and, in turn, entrepreneurship, self-realization and innovation. Fourth, both types of reforms probably need to discover how overcoming social opposition in the least costly way and in coherence with the democratic institutions: since to reform means changing the 'rules of the game', it is very likely for both the ESbR and the BIbR to encounter opposition from firms, workers, citizens and other social forces who benefit from the status quo. In this logic, the BIbR can appear more costly than the ESbR, since the aim of the first type of reform translates not only in changes of material incentives but also in modifications of immaterial incentives (e.g. type of work and social status). Fifth, with respect to the abolishment of unemployment, job insecurity, poverty and other unpredictable social ills—a goal commonly shared by both type of reforms—it may be argued that ESbR and the BIbR may be subject to different performances: for example if—after the introduction of the ESbR—innovation and technological

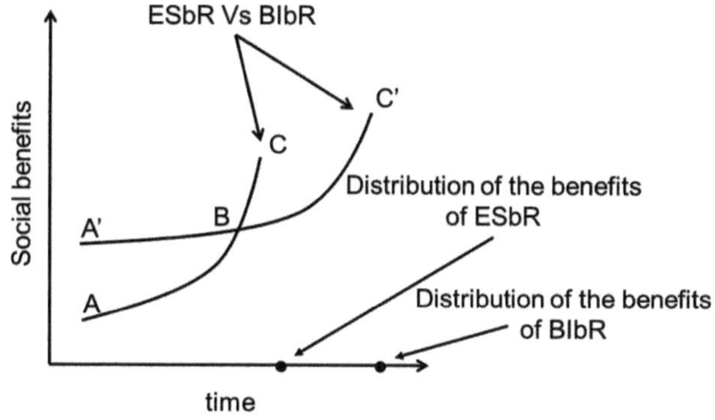

Fig. 2 Self-control problems in a transition from a high-income to a happy high-income society

progress result in unemployment levels unexpectedly high, then new institutional equilibria (new reforms) between the private, the public and the household sectors are needed again; and if this process continues, *frustration* rather than a generalized sense of *satisfaction* and *happiness* could emerge. In this temporally expanded perspective, the BIbR can appear to be more efficient than ESbR, because the introduction of a basic income for all would correspond to a structural, and not a temporary, measure for the social inclusion and happiness of the marginalized workers and the people that instead are out of the labor market.

These comparative observations, combined with the behavioral-economic arguments earlier introduced, seem appropriate to extend the idea of a possible reconciliation between the 'work ethic' and the 'human development' based perspectives within an evolutionary trajectory of the prevailing institutions that ultimately favors the institutionalization of a universal basic income (Sabattini 2009). More specifically, because of their lower cost for the overcoming of potential social resistances, the ESbR should be clearly preferred over the BIbR; but, this preference should prevail only in the short-run and in accordance with a long-run strategy in favor of the BIbR, because of the greater efficiency of this type of reform in *promoting* and *stabilizing* high degrees of social inclusion and happiness within a given social system. However this type of reconciliation, requiring a distinction between a relative short reform-path associated with the institutionalization of the ESbR and a longer one related with the institutionalization of the BIbR, may invite us also to introduce another figure (Fig. 2) that, if interpreted on the basis of works like Rachlin (2000), may help us to consider, at least, another critical aspect. The proposed reconciliation is associated with the presence of short-term and long-term goals, that trying to apply the theoretical tools earlier discussed, may somehow reintroduce the emergence of social dilemmas related with the phenomenon of complex ambivalence and the coexistence between benefits or rewards different in the amount and separated by an interval of time with respect to their delivery or distribution.

4 Discussion

All this considered, a successful reconciliation between the relative short-term path of the ESbR and the longer one of the BIbR, may be, in theory, more probable only if conceived in ways where, *à la* Rachlin, forms of continuous commitment are introduced since the beginning and each component or fraction of the longer reform-path can be put together. This would suggest, on a theoretical level, a twofold conclusion. On the one hand, if we return to Fig. 2, the highest levels of happiness within a given society would be better reached by means of an evolutionary trajectory of the prevailing institutions that can be symbolized not so much as a movement from A to B and then to C′, but rather as a transition that since its beginning is strategically oriented towards larger later rewards and that can be represented as a movement from A′ to B and then to C′; on the other hand, a full development of this transition may be delayed and/or impeded by a lack of self-controlled social choices and the unavailability, at the present time, of remedies for impulsiveness that are simultaneously not only perfectly efficient, but also consistent with the promotion of people's freedom.

Acknowledgments This paper benefited from comments received during a lecture that I had the opportunity to prepare and deliver within the Summer School in the Economics of Culture focused on the theme "Creativity, happiness and growth" and organized, in July 2012, by the School of Economics of the University of Rome "Tor Vergata". I am also in debt with Frédéric Gannon who kindly read earlier versions of this paper and helped me with useful suggestions. Furthermore, I am particularly grateful to Howard Rachlin, Gianfranco Sabattini and Pasquale Lucio Scandizzo: without their very useful comments and sometimes critical observations this paper wouldn't have been possible. All remaining errors and omissions are mine.

References

Akerlof GA (1997) Social distance and social decisions. Econometrica 65:1005–1027

Baumol WJ (1990) Entrepreneurship: productive, unproductive, and destructive. J Polit Econ 98(5):893–919

Becker GS (1981) A treatise on the family. Harvard University Press, Cambridge

Bruni L (2010) The happiness of sociality. Economics and eudaimonia: a necessary encounter. Rationality Soc 22(4):383–406

Drèze JH, Malinvaud E (1994) Growth and employment: the scope for a European initiative. Eur Econ 1:77–106

Dufwenberg M, Kirchsteiger G (2004) A theory of sequential reciprocity. Games Econ Behav 47(2):268–298

Dusenbeq J (1949) Income, saving and the theory of consumer behavior. Harvard University Press, Cambridge

Easterlin R (1974) Does economic growth improve the human lot? In: David P, Reder M (eds) Nations and households in economic growth. Academic, New York

Erez A, Isen AM (2002) The influence of positive affect on the components of expectancy motivation. J Appl Psychol 87(6):1055–1067

Esping-Andersen G (1990) The three worlds of welfare capitalism. Princeton University Press, Princeton

Fukuyama F (1995) Trust: social virtues and the creation of prosperity. Free Press, New York
Guerra G, Zizzo D (2004) Trust responsiveness and beliefs. J Econ Behav Organ 55(1):25–30
Gui B (1987) Eléments pour une definition d'économie communautaire. Notes et Documents 19–20:32–42
Guven C (2011) Are happier people better citizens? Kyklos 64(2):178–192
Hermalin B, Isen A (2008) A model of the effect of affect on economic decision making. Quant Mark Econ 6(1):17–40
Jensen MC, Meckling WH (1976) The theory of the firm: managerial behaviour, agency costs and ownership structure. J Financ Econ 3:305–360
Jordan B (2010) Basic income and social value. Basic Income Stud 5(2):1–19
Kahneman D, Tversky A (1979) Prospect theory: an analysis of decisions under risk. Econometrica 47(2):263–292
Kenny C (1999) Does growth cause happiness, or does happiness cause growth? Kyklos 52(1):3–26
Kirzner IM (1973) Competition and entrepreneurship. Chicago University Press, Chicago
Knack S, Keefer P (1997) Does social capital have an economic payoff? A cross-country investigation. Q J Econ 112(4):1251–1288
Meade JE (1993) Fifteen propositions concerning the building of an equitable, full-employment non-inflationary, free-enterprise economy. Econ Notes 22–23:402–419
Mill JS (1859) On liberty; Italian edition (1981) Saggio sulla libertà. Il Saggiatore, Milano
Mishan E (1967) The costs of economic growth. Pelican, London
Munger MC (2011) Basic income is not an obligation, but it might be a legitimate choice. Basic Income Stud 6(2):1–13
North DC (1990) Institutions, institutional change, and economic performance. Cambridge University Press, Cambridge
Oswald AJ, Proto E, Sgroi D (2009) Happiness and productivity. IZA Discussion paper No. 4645, December 2009
Pelligra V (2007) The not-so-fragile fragility of goodness: the responsive quality of fiduciary relationships. In: Bruni L, Porta PL (eds) Handbook on the economics of happiness. Edward Elgar, Northampton, pp 290–317
Pettit P (1997) Republicanism. A theory of freedom and government. Oxford University Press, New York
Phelps ES (1997) Rewarding work. Harvard University Press, Cambridge
Phelps ES (2000) Subsidize wages. Boston Review, October/November
Phelps ES (2007) Macroeconomics for a modern economy. Am Econ Rev 97(3):543–561
Phillips OR, Battalio RC, Kogut CA (1991) Sunk and opportunity costs in valuation and bidding. South Econ J 58(1):112–128
Rabin M (1993) Incorporating fairness into game theory and economics. Am Econ Rev 83(5):1281–1302
Rachlin H (2000) The science of self-control. Harvard University Press, Cambridge
Rachlin H (2002) Altruism and selfishness. Behav Brain Sci 25:239–296
Rachlin H, Jones B (2008) Discounting and delay discounting. J Behav Decis Mak 21:29–43
Sabattini G (2009) Welfare State. Nascita evoluzione e crisi. Le prospettive di riforma. Franco Angeli, Milano
Schumpeter JA (1934) The theory of economic development. An inquiry into profits, capital, credit, interest, and the business cycle. Oxford University Press, Oxford (first edition: 1911)
Simon J (1995) Interpersonal allocation continuous with intertemporal allocation. Rationality Soc 7:367–392
Smith A (1759) The theory of moral sentiments. In: Raphael DD, Macfie AL (1982), Liberty Press, Indianapolis, USA
Standing G (2005) Why basic income is needed for a right to work. Rutgers J Law Urban Policy 1(1):91–102
Thaler R, Shrefin HM (1981) An economic theory of self-control. J Polit Econ 89(2):392–406
Titmuss R (1974) Social policy. An introduction. Allen and Unwin, London

Uhlaner CJ (1989) Relational goods and participation: incorporating sociality into a theory of rational action. Publ Choice 62:253–285
Van Parijis P (1990) The second marriage of justice and efficiency. J Soc Policy 19(1):1–25
Van Parijis P (1995) Real freedom for all. Clarendon, Oxford
Van Parijis P (2000) A basic income for all. Boston Review October/November
Van Parijis P (2004) Basic income: a simple and powerful idea for the twenty-first century. Polit Soc 32(1):7–39
von Hayek FA (1982) Law, legislation and liberty. University of Chicago Press, Chicago

Crisis in the Eurozone: Some Popular Fallacies and a Few Unpleasant Remarks

Luigi Bonatti and Andrea Fracasso

Abstract Paradoxically, the fact that financial markets believed that real convergence between the Euro periphery and Euro core would have occurred as a consequence of the Euro led to real divergence and external imbalances within the Eurozone. After the outbreak of the European debt crisis, austerity policies in the peripheral countries of the Eurozone simply had no alternative, given the refusal on the part of the markets to go on financing levels of private and public expenditures structurally in excess with respect to the value of the goods and services that the peripheral countries were able to supply at competitive prices. Could the resulting recession in the periphery have been made less severe by larger inflow of funds from the rest of the Eurozone and prompter interventions of the ECB? And why the Euro periphery made only modest gains in competitiveness during the 3 years of acute recession that followed the outbreak of the crisis? This is a crucial issue since there is no possibility of sustainable long-run growth for the periphery without restoring its competitiveness vis-à-vis the Euro core and the rest of the world.

1 Introduction

After 3 years of harsh recession and rising unemployment, it appears that in the European countries struck more severely by the crisis, i.e., the so-called "periphery" of the Eurozone, hostile feelings toward the European institutions and the "core" countries of the Eurozone (Germany in particular) are spreading in alarming way, reflecting the diffuse perception that they are among the biggest culprits of the suffering inflicted on the periphery. This certainly comes from a natural tendency of individuals and groups facing hard times to search for scapegoats toward which

L. Bonatti (✉) • A. Fracasso
Department of Economics and Management & School of International Studies, University of Trento, via Inama 5, 38122 Trento, Italy
e-mail: luigi.bonatti@unitn.it; andrea.fracasso@unitn.it

L. Paganetto (ed.), *Wealth, Income Inequalities, and Demography*,
DOI 10.1007/978-3-319-05909-9_5,

to canalize their anguish and resentment. However, one should not underestimate the destructive potential of these sentiments, especially when they are fed by unscrupulous politicians. One could even argue that, in the present situation, the most concrete threat to the survival of the Euro, and possibly to the entire European project, is not any longer represented by the attitudes of the financial markets toward the periphery's debt, but by the possibility that political forces able to exploit this hostility may prevail in some key country of the Eurozone.

The intense debate that has taken place among economists on both the European sovereign debt crisis and the consequent policy responses has contributed to shape people's perceptions of these issues. Although arguments—and above all narratives of the crisis—provided by professional economists have been often misinterpreted, or instrumentally used to reach policy conclusions that go well beyond the intentions of those who originally put them forward, nevertheless they must be scrutinized in the light of their impact on the public opinion, since this has become a crucial factor in the evolution of the European crisis. The present essay is intended precisely to contribute to this task.

The remainder of the paper proceeds as follows. Section 2 outlines how the fact that financial markets believed that real convergence between the Euro periphery and Euro core would have occurred as a consequence of the Euro led to real divergence and external imbalances within the Euro zone and to the European debt crisis. Section 3 motivates why, with the outbreak of the European debt crisis, austerity policies in the peripheral countries of the Eurozone simply had no alternative, given the refusal on the part of the markets to go on financing levels of private and public expenditures structurally in excess with respect to the value of the goods and services that the peripheral countries were able to supply at competitive prices. This section discusses also whether the resulting recession in the periphery could have been made less severe by larger inflow of funds from the rest of the Eurozone and prompter interventions of the ECB. Section 4 examines why the Euro periphery made only modest gains in competitiveness during the 3 years of severe recession that followed the outbreak of the crisis, thus missing the opportunity to recreate the conditions for satisfactory and sustainable long-run growth. Section 5 concludes.

2 Causes: Financial Markets Failure and/or Poor Institutional Design?[1]

It was widely believed that the establishment of a single currency for the countries previously participating in the EMS would have eliminated the main cause of the speculative attacks that led in 1992–1993 to the crisis of the European system of semi-fixed exchange rates (see Eichengreen and Wyplosz 1993). Indeed, the conviction was that the creation of the Euro would have suppressed any intra-European

[1] This section follows closely what we wrote in Bonatti and Fracasso (2013a).

exchange-rate risk by ruling out any exchange-rate realignment within the monetary union. The lack of any legal provision for regulating the exit of a country from the monetary union reinforced this perception of irreversibility of the latter. Moreover, the tight fiscal rules of the Stability and Growth Pact, making operational the vague provisions on the Excessive Deficit procedure contained in the Maastricht Treaty, were supposed to keep in check governments' profligacy and prevent the fiscal irresponsibility that was crucial in precipitating the crisis of 1992–1993. Finally, financial markets were deemed able to discriminate properly between private and public borrowers according to their specific credit worthiness and thus to price efficiently the risk inherent in the securities issued by various debtors.

The conventional wisdom described above concerning the solidity of the European currency construction was at the origin of the widespread belief that—with the irrevocable decision made at the European Council of May 1998 to let the peripheral countries join the Euro from its establishment (1 January 1999)[2]—real convergence would have occurred between the core and the periphery, namely that peripheral countries would have displayed German-like wage moderation and low inflation in order not to lose competitiveness vis-à-vis the core. Actually, the optimistic conviction that the elimination of the nominal exchange rate as a means of adjustment within the Euro area would have forced the peripheral countries to uniform their price and wage dynamics to the more disciplined core countries was a key determinant of the investors' benign neglect attitude towards the persistent structural differences across members of the Euro zone.[3]

In retrospect, these expectations proved to be self-defeating since it was mainly because of them that the elimination of (nominal) exchange-rate risk, together with the ECB anti-inflationary credibility and the protection implicitly provided by membership in the Euro club, allowed the periphery to borrow at interest rates much lower than those observed before the establishment of the Euro. Since the late 1990s, the spreads between the yields on the long-term German bonds and peripheral securities were practically reduced to zero (Fig. 1).[4] Easy access to

[2]With the exception of Greece, that was admitted from January 1st, 2001.

[3]In the debate on the Commission's plan, two main approaches emerged: the 'monetarist view', held by France, and the 'economists' view', embraced by Germany (see Wyplosz 2006). In a nutshell, the former was against discriminating among the candidate countries on the basis of demanding entry conditions: the European institutions in charge of the monetary integration and the very same integration process would have reset past expectations and habits. The economists camp, on the contrary, considered the participation in the monetary union as the very last stage of a long-term convergence process, along which the candidate countries adopt a stability culture and more similar socio-economic systems. Notably, the adoption of the Maastricht criteria to select the members of the union was not a victory of the economists camp: the convergence criteria focused exclusively on few aspects of nominal convergence, their respect was monitored only over a short period of time before the irrevocable fixing of the exchange rates, and their interpretation was quite loose. Markets and policymakers acted as if convergence had been achieved, although—as timely argued by various scholars, such as Lane (2006) and Wyplosz (2006)—it had not.

[4]The disappearance of interest spreads between the core and the periphery of the Eurozone was also encouraged by the EU's prudential guidelines, according to which the government bonds of all

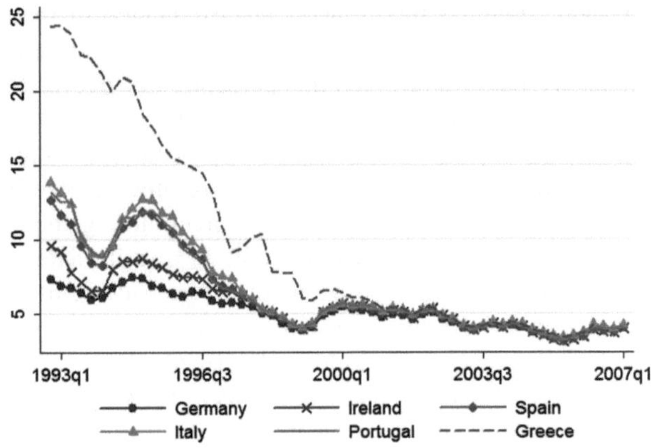

Fig. 1 Ten year government bonds yields (quarterly averages). *Source*: Eurostat

credit at low interest-rate levels, which was indeed the very EMU dividend for which the peripheral countries strived to be admitted to the Euro club, created incentives to postpone painful fiscal consolidations (Italy, Greece) and structural reforms (Greece, Italy, Portugal, Spain), or to exploit the boom of debt-financed households' consumption and housing investment (Ireland, Spain). Hence, one can conclude that—paradoxically—the very same belief that real convergence would have occurred in the Eurozone ended up feeding a process of real divergence between the core and the periphery in the years preceding the outbreak of the sovereign debt crisis: prices and unit labor costs increased much faster in peripheral countries (Fig. 2),[5] while large current account imbalances emerged within the Eurozone.

Indeed, for a certain period of time, most of the countries with large external deficits were recording high rates of growth, good fiscal results, and declining unemployment rates. In fact, this was associated with housing bubbles, large private debts (see Figs. 3 and 4), high bank-leverage and deteriorating net foreign asset positions, which did signal the existence of some structural problems. However, neither the national nor the European authorities decided to intervene as this would have risked spoiling the favorable momentum.[6] On the contrary, structural

countries belonging to the monetary union carried risk weights of 0 %, thus exempting banks and insurance companies from holding equity against periphery's bonds. Since the start, the European Central Bank accepted all the EMU government bonds at the same conditions for the conduct of its monetary policy operations, thus reinforcing the idea that they were equally secure (Ullrich 2006).

[5]From the irrevocable commitment to the Euro at the Madrid Summit of December 1995 to the Lehman Brothers' collapse of September 2008, the total rate of appreciation of the peripheral countries (Greece, Ireland, Portugal, Spain, Italy, Cyprus) taken together relative to the rest of the Eurozone was—if both price changes and exchange rate adjustments since 1995 are considered—30 %. In particular, Italian prices increased by 27 % relative to the rising prices in the rest of the Eurozone, and by 48 % relative to German prices.

[6]The European authorities could not actively intervene to ensure greater convergence, mainly because the European treaties focused on fiscal policy and neglected macroeconomic coordination

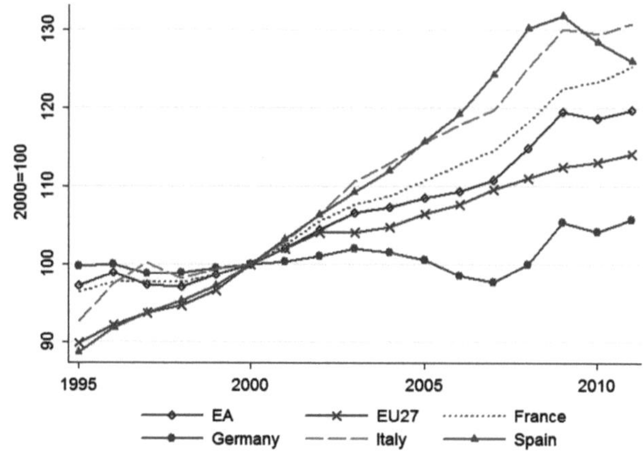

Fig. 2 Nominal unit labor costs (2000 = 100). *Source*: Eurostat

reforms and budgetary policies aimed at improving international competitiveness were implemented in the main country of the core, that is in Germany (e.g., the Hartz reforms), with a view to recovering from the negative consequences of the re-unification (see Bonatti and Fracasso 2013b).[7]

In the same years, the growing real imbalances between the Euro core and periphery were exacerbated by the emergence of new economic powers (e.g., after the accession of China to the WTO) and by the extension of the EU to Eastern Europe, which for Euro-core countries enterprises—more than for the enterprises of other countries—represented an opportunity for de-localizing some production processes in nearby low-cost countries, thereby boosting productivity and profitability. The emergence of new industrial powers in the world economy

---

and financial surveillance. Moreover, the Commission had been severely weakened in the early 2000s by its struggle against Germany and France over the adoption of excessive deficit procedures, notwithstanding the favorable judgment of the European Court of Justice in 2004. Focusing on the progressive worsening of the Greek external position, Katsimi and Moutos (2010) argue that European authorities have been unable or unwilling to intervene. If Greek budgetary data were misreported, the ongoing large current account deficits were well visible and clearly dangerous. On the disappointing performance of Portugal and the evident signs of its lack of progress over time, see Baer et al. (2013), whereas on the Spanish parabola, see Neal and García-Iglesias (2013).

[7]The reforms implemented in Germany in the first half of the 2000s in order to gain in efficiency and competitiveness are sometimes dubbed "beggar-thy-neighbor" policies by radical Keynesians. This is a theoretical mistake since undertaking structural reforms aimed at increasing productivity and efficiency is not a zero-sum game: if the peripheral countries had done the same in those years the final result would have been higher sustainable growth in the Euro area. Moreover, to dub in such a way those reforms is at odds with the foundations of modern growth theory, which recognizes in the gains in productivity and efficiency driven by competitive pressure the only source of long-run improvements in per-capita standards of living.

Fig. 3 Household mortgages over gross national disposable income. *Source*: OECD

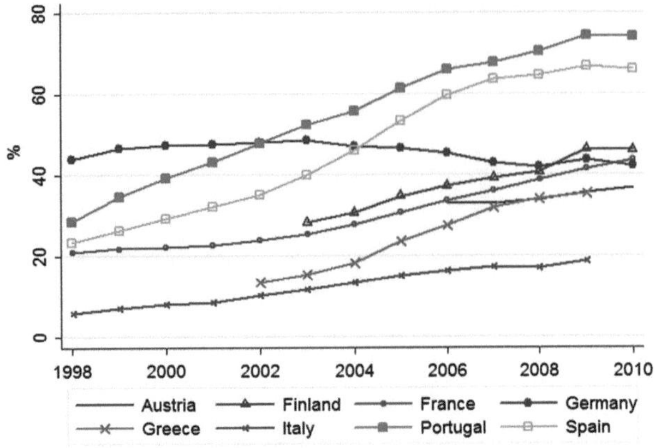

Fig. 4 Private sector debt over GDP (consolidated, non financial sectors). *Source*: Eurostat

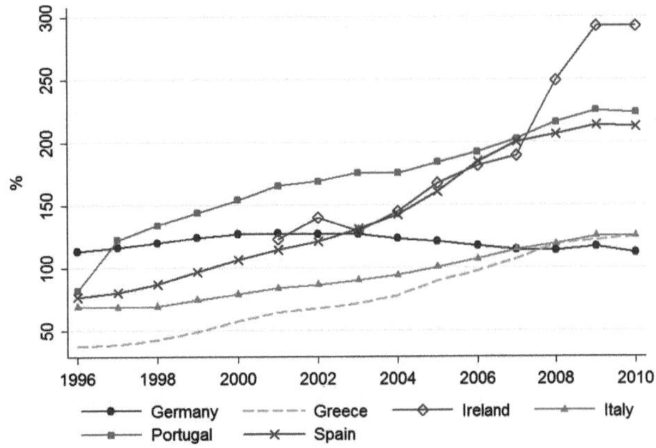

turned out to be a true asymmetric shock for the Eurozone: China was directly competing with the southern European producers specialized in labor-intensive industries (like textile), while it represented a new destination market for the German investment goods (see Chen et al. 2012; Mikkelsen and Ruiz 2012).

Summarizing, one may say that financial markets failed for years to price the risk that was inherent both in the accumulation of debt by the peripheral countries and in their declining competitiveness, thus providing these countries with cheap credits that ultimately fed the imbalances within the Eurozone and set the conditions for the subsequent crisis. National governments in the peripheral countries had no incentive to address the increasingly visible problems of excess (private and/or public) debt and poor competitiveness that affected their countries. In addition, European rules and institutions revealed their impotence in dealing with these imbalances. Focusing almost entirely on checking and restricting government deficits (as established in the Stability and Growth Pact), the European institutions dedicated little attention—and had practically no policy instrument—to tackle the cross-border private capital flows directed towards the periphery and to cure its growing problems of competitiveness.[8]

3 Austerity in the Euro Periphery: Inevitable Response to a Sudden Reversal of Capital Flows or Self-Inflicted Pain?

The absence of relevant financial market reactions in the face of growing intra-European imbalances came to an end with the worldwide crisis of the housing and banking sectors. Even if the contagion transmitted through the U.S. toxic assets hit primarily financial institutions located in Central and Northern Europe and no major Southern European bank was significantly affected by the financial turmoil, the discovery that Greek governments had regularly misreported public finance data exposed the structural weaknesses of the peripheral countries (see Lane 2012 and Shambaugh 2012). Indeed, from the moment in which the Eurozone became the epicenter of the global crisis, it has been apparent that the periphery is highly vulnerable because of its twin problems, that are closely intertwined: (1) high government debt, because of high public deficits in the past (Greece and Italy) or because of the necessity to bail out banks that lent heavily to the private sector (Ireland, Spain), and (2) depressing long-term growth prospects (Greece, Italy, Portugal and Spain), because of these countries' serious competitiveness problem exacerbated by the heavy tax burden that will long be needed to prevent their public debt from exploding.

Given the diffuse pessimism concerning the ability of the Euro periphery to deal with its twin problems, international investors started pulling their money out of these countries, thus rapidly increasing the cost of debt financing (Fig. 5) and, in some cases, undermining their ability to roll over their debt. Banks in the periphery encountered even greater troubles than their sovereigns in raising new funding and in re-financing outstanding debts, which aggravated the deleveraging process and led to a fully fledge credit crunch in their countries.[9] Hence, the fall in domestic demand that occurred in the periphery was the inevitable effect of the drying up of private capital inflows that were previously used to finance the excess of private and public expenditures in the periphery.

Clearly, it was not only the belated realization of the bad macroeconomic conditions and growth prospects in the peripheral countries that fuelled such a dramatic capital flight: this was amplified by the financial markets' tendency to overreact in periods of turbulence (see De Grauwe and Ji 2012, 2013), and by the uncertain and fragmented political response of the political leaders regarding

---

[8]For a fact-based evaluation of the performance of the main EU economic governance pillars (Stability and Growth Pact and Lisbon Strategy), see Ioannou and Stracca (2014).

[9]For an empirical assessment of the bank/sovereign spillovers see De Bruyckere et al. (2013).

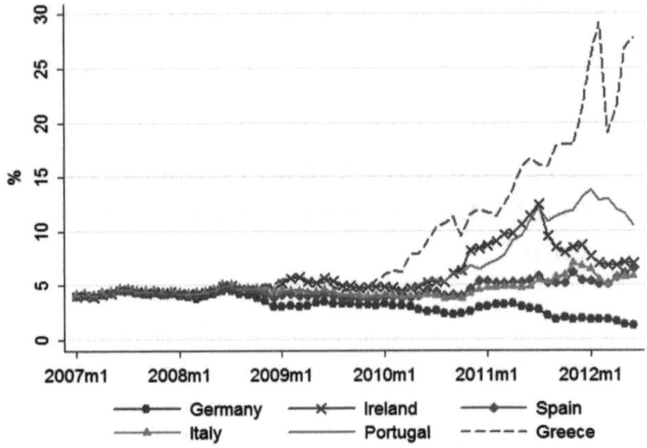

Fig. 5 Ten year government bonds yields (monthly averages). *Source*: ECB

how to deal with a possible debt restructuring/default in the EU country (so as to limit negative spillovers) and how to involve private sector (bail-in) in crisis resolution. In the case of Italy, whose current account deficit and negative net foreign asset position were relatively modest with respect to the other peripheral countries, investors' pessimism was particularly motivated by the diffuse skepticism about the government's ability to keep the high primary surplus that would have been necessary in a long-term scenario of stagnation or very low growth to avoid a rapid rise of the public debt-GDP ratio.

Consistently with the narrative above, austerity policies in the peripheral countries of the Eurozone simply had no alternative, given the refusal on the part of the markets to go on financing levels of private and public expenditures structurally in excess with respect to the value of the goods and services that the peripheral countries were able to supply at competitive prices. In this sense, these policies were one of the modalities (together with the decrease in private consumption and investment) whereby it materialized the sharp decline in absorption made inevitable by the sudden reversal of (private) capital flows previously directed towards the Euro periphery. In other words, austerity measures should be considered as part of the adjustment process that necessarily follows a structural imbalance, rather than as the result of the discretionary choice of conducting contractionary fiscal policies in the middle of a cyclical downturn.

Even if inevitable, fiscal contraction in the peripheral countries made more acute the recession that hit these countries in 2010–2013, and with negative GDP growth the government debt-GDP ratio went on increasing in spite of the fiscal cuts. Non-Keynesian effects of fiscal policy did not materialize and also the IMF recognized that fiscal multipliers were underestimated (see Blanchard and Leigh 2013). It became apparent how wrong were those claiming that austerity measures would have soon permitted to the periphery's economies to resume growth and stabilize their government debt-GDP ratio without too much pain (see Tamborini 2013).

Some observers contrasted the U.S. policy response to the financial crisis with that of the Eurozone, stressing that in the aftermath of the Lehman Brothers' bankruptcy the U.S. government let its deficit skyrocketing in order to transform bad private debt into public debt and to offset (at least partially) the fall in private demand with an increase in public demand, while the Eurozone reacted to the periphery's debt crisis by a fiscal contraction. One should not forget, however, that the U.S. government securities kept their traditional "safe heaven" status even when it looked like the U.S. financial system was at the edge of collapse,[10] thus benefiting from the "flight to quality" (so to speak), that occurred under those circumstances. In contrast, markets' attitudes towards the government securities of the Euro peripheral countries were heavily influenced after the outbreak of the debt crisis by the inherited reputation for fragility of these countries' government and institutions, as well as by the scarce confidence about their economy's long-term prospects. As a consequence, the fiscal space for reacting to the crisis was incomparably much ampler in the United States than in the Euro periphery. Differently than the latter, the Euro core had some space for a more expansionary fiscal policy in 2010–2013, which was enlarged by those capital flows entering the core from the periphery that pushed down the core's interest rates, but it did not use it.[11] In any case, it is likely that the positive spillovers to the periphery generated by a fiscal stimulus in the core would have only slightly attenuated the intensity of the consolidation efforts that the peripheral countries had to make anyway as a consequence of their imbalances (in 't Veld 2013).

Even admitting that a drastic drop in domestic spending could not be avoided in the periphery, one may argue that this drop could have been made less severe by a more substantial and timely transfers of funds to the periphery through the various European rescue facilities and the IMF, by more prompt and aggressive interventions on the part of the ECB, and by an open commitment to mutualize periphery's debt on the part of the core countries of the Euro zone.

Critics of the argument above point at the huge amounts of money that the peripheral countries got from the various official rescue packages of the Euro area as soon as they were denied access to the capital markets.[12] These critics also

[10]With regard to this, one cannot neglect the role played by officials of China and other countries holding huge reserves of U.S. government securities in reassuring the investors about their country's willingness to hold U.S. securities and go on purchasing them.

[11]For an interpretation of the German point of view towards the European debt crisis, see Bonatti and Fracasso (2013b).

[12]Since May 2010, a series of intergovernmental support mechanisms were created by the euro area Member States: the European Financial Stabilisation Mechanism (EFSM); and the European Financial Stability Facility (EFSF), followed by the European Stability Mechanism (ESM) in October 2012. Four large financial assistance programs were created to support Ireland, Greece, Portugal, and Spain. Smaller rescue packages were established to the benefit of smaller (EMU and non EMU) countries (Latvia, Hungary, Romania and Cyprus). For what Ireland is concerned, in December 2010 an Economic Adjustment Programme was agreed, which included financial assistance over 2010–2013 for €85 billion (EFSM €22.5 billion; EFSF €17.7 billion; the U.K. €3.8 billion, Sweden €0.6 billion and Denmark €0.4 billion; as well as funding from the IMF

mention the secondary market purchases of periphery's government bonds activated by the ECB through the Securities Markets Programme (SMP), which especially in the Summer of 2011—when the Italian and Spanish sovereign debt came under attack—were extremely important to calm down investors on the financial markets. Moreover, they emphasize that, after the outbreak of the Euro crisis, TARGET2[13] enabled the central banks of the peripheral countries to finance their large Balance-of-Payments deficits (especially with the Euro core) by accumulating net liabilities vis-à-vis the Eurosystem, which were mirrored by the massive accumulation of net claims on the part of the core countries' central banks.

As a matter of fact, this impressive increase in TARGET2 imbalances was fed by the two special longer-term refinancing operations (LTRO) decided by the ECB in 2011–2012 to provide liquidity to the banks in the Euro area.[14] This additional liquidity was widely used by the Italian and Spanish banks to buy their national government bonds in a period when international investors were getting rid of them, while it was deposited (and left idle) at the ECB by the banks in the Euro core (reaching in early March 2012 a historic high of circa €830 billion).[15] By lengthening the maximum maturity of its refinancing operations, as well as reducing its main refinancing rate and the minimum rating that assets must have for being accepted as collateral in these operations, the ECB made any

€22.5 billion and the Irish Treasury and National Pension Reserve Fund €17.5 billion). The resources devoted to Greece under the two adjustment programmes were about €80 billion for 2010 and 2011, and €164.5 billion for 2012–2014 (of which, €144.7 billion committed by the EU via the EFSF and €19.8 billion contributed by the IMF). Portugal could tap EU financial resources in 2011 for a 3-year programme of €78 billion (€26 billion committed by each of the following: EFSM, EFSF, IMF). In 2012–2013 Spain received financial assistance via the EFSF, and then the ESM, of up to €100 billion for backing the process of reform and stabilization of its weak banking sector.

[13]TARGET stands for "Trans-European Automated Real-Time Gross Settlement Express Transfer", which is the European transaction settlement system whereby one commercial bank of an Euro-area member country can make payments to one commercial bank of another member country. The TARGET2 balances of a country belonging to the Euro area are the claims or the liabilities of its central bank vis-à-vis the Eurosystem and are a measure of the accumulated surpluses or deficits of this country's Balance of Payments with other countries of the Euro-area (see Cecchetti et al. 2012 and Cour-Thimann 2013). In April 2012, Germany, the largest economy of the Euro core, had net claims of €644 billion, while Italy, the largest economy of the Euro periphery, had net liabilities of €279 billion. Notice that at the outbreak of the crisis both countries had TARGET2 balances close to zero (see Sinn and Wollmershäuser 2012).

[14]The ECB developed 2 special 3-year LTROs for about €1 trillion: on 21st December 2011 for €489 billion to 523 banks and on the 29th of February 2012 for €530 billion to 800 banks. In fact the net increase in liquidity was far smaller, respectively €193 and €310 billion: one is to consider the simultaneous expiration of previous operations to provide liquidity and the reduction in ordinary three month LTROs. The Bank of Italy supplied its counterparties with circa €250 billion (about €140 billion net).

[15]In 2013 this excess liquidity has diminished because the banks in the core exploited the opportunity of an early repayment (of about a quarter of) the money received with the two three-year LTROs. Unsurprisingly, this pattern was accompanied by a marked reduction also in the TARGET2 imbalances.

effort to facilitate the central banks of the euro periphery to finance their banking system's purchases of government bonds. This amounted, de facto, to a partial (and temporary) monetization of the periphery's government debt, thus weakening the popular argument according to which the European sovereign debt crisis had its main cause in the impossibility for the peripheral countries to monetize their debt.

Notice that the liquidity used by the banks in the periphery to buy government bonds represented an important portion of the net liabilities that their countries accumulated with respect to the Eurosystem. However, it is known how these large purchases of bonds issued by their own governments on the part of the periphery's commercial banks put in motion a vicious circle, in which market assessments of sovereign risk for these countries was sensitive to the possibility that periphery's commercial banks incurred large losses in case of a fall in government bonds' prices, thus obliging their governments to recapitalize them. It was to dissolve this vicious circle that the governments of the Eurozone decided to proceed towards the establishment of a banking union, and that the ECB announced the readiness to undertake "Outright Monetary Transactions" (OMT). Indeed, Mario Draghi's well-known statement of September 6th, 2012, was unanimously interpreted as an ECB's firm commitment to buy unlimited quantity of peripheral countries' government bonds (with a maturity between 1 and 3 years), conditional on the country's formal request for financial assistance from the European Stability Mechanism and its acceptance of the conditions for getting it.[16] These purchases would be done in secondary markets if necessary for "safeguarding an appropriate monetary policy transmission and the singleness of the monetary policy".

De Grauwe and Ji (2013) claim that, if the ECB's had made such an announcement at an earlier date, confidence amidst investors would have not deteriorated to the point to determine a brutal rise in the risk premia on the periphery's government debt, and consequently the austerity measures that periphery's governments were forced to implement might have been less severe. This point, however, does not fully recognize what was at stake in the difficult negotiations taking place behind the scenes which were necessary for the ECB to convince the governments of the Euro core to accept its departure from a rigid interpretation of the no-bail-out clause and to isolate the core countries' hawks. Indeed, the core governments' opposition to an ECB's open commitment to provide unlimited support to Italian and Spanish government bonds could be overcome only after that severe austerity measures were eventually undertaken by Italy and Spain: the earlier stages of the crisis had shown that the periphery's governments tended to implement harsh budgetary and reform measures only under the pressure of financial markets and that, when this pressure was temporary relieved by some interventions of the ECB or other European

[16]An additional condition is that the ESM commits to purchase these very same securities on the primary market. OMTs refer to purchases of government securities, for which the Eurosystem has no preferred creditor status.

authorities, they tended to backtrack on their previous commitments.[17] In a way, this experience conforms the problems arising from the lack of mechanisms allowing governments to credibly pre-commit to undertake some future action that will not be in their interest when the future arrives.

Euro core countries have eventually accepted to relax their pro-austerity stance and to provide temporary financial assistance to the banks and countries in trouble. However, core countries fear that a fully fledged mechanism of fiscal transfers might ultimately lead to the crystallization of the imbalances (and the related vicious incentive spirals) often observed in those depressed areas receiving substantial transfers on a permanent basis from richer areas. Together with the moral hazard problem that a mutualisation of debt in the Euro zone would create, this is the main argument for the core's opposition to it. It is hard to think that the Euro core's viewpoints on this issue will change in the future, at least until a genuinely federal European budget amounting to some non-negligible fraction of the area's GDP will be established.[18]

In spite of the core countries' refusal to accept some mutualization of the Euro zone's government debt, one cannot deny that—since the beginning of the European debt crisis—the Euro periphery has received considerable direct and indirect support from the Euro core. Adding up the various official sector's channels mentioned above from which the peripheral countries received funds, considering that under the pressure of the events the ECB ended up acting de facto as a lender of last resort, and taking into account that a banking union is under construction, some commentators are even arguing that such large amount of transfers channeled to the countries hit by the debt crisis through non-market decisions could—especially if protracted for a long period—undermine the necessary adjustment of the imbalances within the Euro zone and the re-establishment of periphery's competitiveness (see Sinn 2014). As a matter of fact, indeed, the competitiveness gains achieved by some of the peripheral countries during the years of severe recession have been quite disappointing,[19] and

[17]One can find a good example of this tendency during the months preceding the fall of the Berlusconi's government in November 2011, when the Italian government tried to backtrack on its budgetary commitments anytime that the pressure of financial markets on it was temporarily relieved thanks to some statement or action of the ECB and other European authorities in support of the Italian public debt.

[18]Let us note in passing that this would be at variance with the recent reduction in the overall EU budget due to the fierce opposition of non-Euro area countries (e.g., the U.K.) to expand the competences and the resources of the Union.

[19]Focusing on the inflation differentials since 2009, only Ireland exhibited a lower HICP inflation rate than Germany. In fact, all the other periphery countries recorded rates not below the Euro-area average. Setting the HICP indices at 100 in 2009, in 2013 the index of the Euro area (17) reaches 108.43, while Germany 107.55, Greece 108.15, Spain 109.36, Italy 109.37, Portugal 108.38 (*source*: Eurostat). The picture would improve for Greece and Portugal, were one focusing on the index excluding energy, food, alcohol and tobacco. Admittedly, these numbers are at most suggestive for three reasons: first, periphery countries decided to increase the VAT rates so as to facilitate an internal devaluation; second, external competitiveness is better captured by export prices (provided the composition and the quality of the export is unchanged); third, administered

almost only the remarkable decrease in imports due to the fall of domestic demand has allowed these countries to improve drastically their trade balance.[20] Moreover, as observed by the Commission in the Alert Mechanism Report 2014, the external sustainability of the most vulnerable economies has not yet been re-established on firm grounds. This is a very serious problem, since no sustainable growth will be possible in the Euro periphery if it does not restore its competitiveness with respect to the Euro core and the rest of the world.[21]

4 Restoring Competitiveness in the Euro Periphery: An Impossible Task Without a Nominal Exchange-Rate Depreciation?

The "classical" adjustment process that follows a balance-of-payment crisis presupposes that the fall of domestic demand necessary to eliminate the excess absorption is at least partially offset by an increase in foreign demand: labor and capital must move from the sectors protected from international competition towards the sectors exposed to it. Typically, a nominal exchange-rate depreciation facilitates this switch by making relatively more convenient to produce internationally tradable products

prices in the periphery countries increased by a very large extent also because of measures directed to raise government revenues. However, the patterns of export price deflator over the entire period not provide a different picture. Setting the indices at 100 in 2009, it reaches 108.42 for the Euro area (17), 106.36 for Germany, 107.14 for Ireland, 112.79 for Greece, 108.10 for Spain, 108.78 for Italy, 110.60 for Portugal (*source*: AMECO). Clearer improvements occurred in some peripheral countries only recently, in 2013. It must be observed, however, that these price developments hide more favorable patterns of unit labor costs, due to an increase in profit margins as well as to higher indirect taxes and administered prices. Notably, profit margins increased relatively more in the tradable sector in Portugal and Spain: though reducing price competitiveness, this does help to attract investment in these activities. Italy (and Cyprus), instead, showed no signal of sectoral price and margin adjustment.

[20]Current accounts progressively improved in several peripheral countries. Ireland moved into positive territory in 2010 and in 2013 run a surplus of 4 % over GDP (against the 2, 5.6 and 5.6 % deficits in 2009, 2008, 2007). The deficit in Greece fell from 17 % in 2008 to 2.3 % in 2013. Portugal, Italy and Spain all recorded a positive current account balance in 2013 (respectively, 1, 1 and 1.4 %) (*source*: AMECO). Although the reduction in the yields of sovereign and private securities did contribute to the improvement in the current accounts, similar patterns can be observed for the trade balance.

[21]With this we do not mean that growth and debt-sustainability in the periphery countries can be ensured only through a greater export-oriented approach, in turn requiring all EMU countries to behave even better than Germany. This conclusion would clearly suffer of a sort of fallacy of composition. Rather, as mentioned above, it suggests to recognise that higher productivity and efficiency lead not to a zero-sum game: homogenously high levels of productivity and efficiency are compatible with homogeneously high living standards, whereas heterogeneous levels of productivity and efficiency are conducive to greater divergence and hence to deep tensions within the EMU.

rather than non-internationally tradable ones and allowing domestic producers to regain some price competitiveness relatively to their foreign competitors. With no possibility of nominal exchange-rate depreciations, an area of a monetary union can regain competitiveness relatively to another area of the same union by an *internal devaluation*, i.e. by cutting its nominal wages, prices of goods and services, land and real estate prices etc. relatively to this other area.

Why has this way of restoring competitiveness revealed highly problematic and not particularly successful until now for the Euro periphery? And what are the periphery's future chances of making progress in this crucial field? On this we make some short, and certainly not-exhaustive, remarks.

It is often said that, particularly in areas with market rigidities, strong interest groups, rent-seeking activities, unions, barriers to competition in many service sectors, etc., internal devaluations require long and painful recessions (and high unemployment!) to get modest results. Therefore, it should not be surprising that this is exactly what has happened in the Euro periphery. Hence, "structural" reforms are advocated in order to make product markets more competitive and labor markets less dualistic, thus facilitating the necessary adjustment process. More in general, national governments are encouraged to implement any kind of reform that could generate gains in efficiency and productivity. However, all these reforms meet resistance and take time to achieve some success.[22]

Permanent reductions of taxation on labor and capital (by cutting public expenditures and by switching the tax burden onto consumption and property) can be of much help for regaining competitiveness and boosting long-run growth (see European Commission 2011). To be effective and sustainable in a context of high public debt, these reductions must be carefully planned over an extended time horizon and then consistently implemented, overcoming the predictable resistance to spending cuts and switches of taxation coming from special interests and populist politicians. The recent cut of taxes on residential housing that took place in Italy under the pressure of such politicians went in the opposite direction to that which is unanimously recommended for reviving economic growth, thus showing how difficult it is in the present social and political conditions of the periphery to conduct growth-promoting policies.

The comparatively high level of households' wealth in Italy and Spain is often mentioned as a factor of strength for these economies.[23] In assessing the effects of

[22]It should be noted that the effects of deep structural reforms can vary a lot over time. While the beneficial effects of structural reforms in the long term are uncontended, it is well possible that they aggravate the effects of simultaneous efforts in fiscal consolidation in the short term. See on this, among others, Barkbu et al. (2012), Bouis et al. (2012), Eggertsson et al. (2014), and Anderson et al. (2013). When this is the case, the implementation of structural reforms requires then a lot of forward-lookingness by the authorities and exceptional patience in the population.

[23]According to an oft-stated opinion, the fact that a country's households are relatively rich should reassure international investors about the long-term solvency of their governments. In principle, however, the political cost of defaulting on the debt held by foreigners is lower for a government than that of confiscating some wealth owned by domestic households in order to service the

these high levels of households' wealth on competitiveness and long run growth, it is worth considering the fact that Italian and Spanish households are richer than their German or Nordic counterparts, in spite of their lower income, because of their houses (see Tables 1 and 2, as well as Davies et al. 2011; ECB 2013).[24] Namely, Southern European households are particularly inclined to use their savings to purchase houses (both main residences and other real estate property), that is consumer durables, rather than to finance investment in productive assets.[25] Therefore, it is legitimate to suspect that in the Euro periphery the households' relatively high levels of residential housing and the endemic undercapitalization of private firms are two sides of the same coin. Preferences shaped by cultural values and habits do probably interact with distortions caused by the tax system and with imperfections of the asset markets to determine the tendency of the periphery's households to invest predominantly in houses. Similarly, one may think that the generous government transfers to the private sector in form of pensions, interest payments and subsidies, which for years have characterized a country like Italy, have allowed the households to accumulate wealth at the expenses of public goods and infrastructures that have been relatively underfinanced.

In other words, one may argue that in the periphery the provision of public goods and the investment in productive assets and public capital have been somehow sacrificed in favor of higher households' investment in residential housing. This cannot but having negative effects on periphery's competitiveness and long-run growth. In addition, a high households' wealth-GDP ratio tends to depress competitiveness and growth by raising workers' reserve wage and by discouraging labor-market participation and labor mobility (especially if households are generally the owners of the houses where they live and housing transaction costs are high). One may expect that the relatively high households' wealth-GDP ratio that characterizes the Euro periphery will slowly decline over time, as both households will gradually decumulate their wealth and house prices will fall in response to a permanently lower

---

debt held by foreigners (and also lower than the political cost of defaulting on the debt held by domestic investors). Hence, international creditors of periphery's governments have no reason to feel particularly reassured by the knowledge that periphery's households are relatively rich.

[24]According to Davies et al. (2011), for instance, the mean and the median wealth per adult (expressed in thousands of PPP $) in 2000 were equal to 115 and 39 in Germany, 150 and 80 in Italy, 117 and 72 in Spain. Table 1, which reports some empirical evidence in ECB (2013), provides a similar picture. It is worth mentioning that these figures, as well as those in Credit Suisse (2010), should be taken with caution and subject to various caveats, for the complicated accounting and surveying issues regarding data collection on wealth.

[25]According to ECB (2013), in all the Southern European countries 70 % (or more) of the households own their main residence, against a percentage between 45 and 55 in Germany, Austria, Netherlands and France (see Table 2). This is consistent with the fact that non-financial wealth in Spain and Italy tends to be larger than financial wealth, at odds with what observed in most EU countries (Credit Suisse 2010). Table 2 reports the breakdown of the fraction of households that own their residence by income and net wealth: from these figures it appears clearly that in Italy, Greece, Spain and Portugal even households with low income or low net wealth tend to purchase their residence.

Table 1 Gross and net wealth per household

		DE	GR	ES	IT	PT	FR	NL	AT	FI
All	Total assets	67.9	110.2	210.2	188.0	93.2	150.4	217.3	92.8	132.7
		5.0	2.6	5.3	4.6	3.0	3.2	9.0	9.7	2.1
	Total liabilities	12.6	14.6	36.0	15.0	31.7	18.4	89.1	13.8	29.4
		1.2	1.6	2.6	1.7	2.7	1.1	6.1	3.2	0.9
	Net wealth	51.4	101.9	182.7	173.5	75.2	115.8	103.6	76.4	85.8
		3.2	2.5	3.8	3.9	3.0	4.0	8.1	11.0	2.1
Owners	% of households	44.2	72.4	82.7	68.7	71.5	55.3	57.1	47.7	69.2
	Total assets	263.1	152.1	245.6	259.5	127.0	273.8	330.5	264.1	196.4
		9.0	4.4	4.7	3.5	4.1	3.9	9.8	9.1	2.4
	Total liabilities	61.7	20.0	43.4	31.0	40.6	44.2	132.8	30.8	56.7
		6.4	2.4	2.9	3.4	2.5	2.2	4.7	9.3	1.1
	Net wealth	215.5	136.5	214.3	250.8	106.1	238.4	214.8	241.2	153.1
		9.4	4.8	5.6	3.8	3.7	4.1	9.1	9.6	1.8
Non-owners	Total assets	13.3	7.0	9.1	12.0	5.5	9.5	25.7	13.7	5.2
		1.3	1.0	1.6	0.8	0.5	0.4	4.2	1.1	0.2
	Total liabilities	3.3	5.0	8.0	5.0	3.0	4.4	11.2	3.6	4.9
		0.4	0.9	1.1	0.2	0.9	0.3	3.4	0.5	0.4
	Net wealth	10.3	5.4	5.1	10.8	4.5	7.8	19.3	11.6	2.8
		1.2	0.7	0.9	0.8	0.6	0.4	5.3	0.9	0.3

Medians (Euro thousands) and % households. The standard errors are reported below the main figures. *Source*: Eurosystem Household Finance and Consumption Survey (ECB 2013)

Table 2 Fraction of households owning their main residence (breakdowns by income and wealth)

		DE	GR	ES	IT	PT	FR	NL	AT	FI
Total population		44.2	72.4	82.7	68.7	71.5	55.3	57.1	47.7	67.8
By income	Bottom 20 %	16.3	64.5	78.0	54.3	65.5	30.3	40.7	27.1	41.3
	20–40 %	34.7	69.0	79.2	60.5	63.3	42.9	42.8	40.8	57.2
	40–60 %	43.2	72.0	82.4	67.4	71.9	53.1	53.5	47.8	67.4
	60–80 %	55.2	73.9	84.7	78.6	75.0	70.3	71.3	53.5	82.0
	80–90 %	69.9	79.8	86.7	79.3	78.6	76.4	75.6	66.0	87.3
	90–100 %	74.4	85.6	91.9	86.2	84.9	83.1	79.0	72.9	94.7
By net wealth	Bottom 20 %	3.8	6.5	30.6	2.3	12.4	1.2	25.0	3.1	19.3
	20–40 %	6.7	73.9	92.6	54.1	66.6	13.4	22.8	3.9	34.1
	40–60 %	39.4	92.8	96.6	93.2	89.2	77.5	55.1	52.0	90.9
	60–80 %	79.0	95.0	96.9	97.2	94.5	91.1	87.3	87.9	96.5
	80–90 %	93.0	95.2	97.3	97.2	96.1	92.5	93.2	91.1	97.6
	90–100 %	91.5	93.7	96.6	96.8	93.7	93.8	97.8	92.4	98.9

Source: Eurosystem Household Finance and Consumption Survey (ECB 2013)

income trajectory. This decline will have a positive impact on competitiveness and growth, as a part of the process of internal devaluation that we discussed above. Governments should accompany this process by changing those policies that have favored over time an excessive concentration of national wealth in the hands of the households, and removing those provisions (particularly in the tax system) that have favored households' overinvestment in residential housing at the expenses of investment in productive assets. Although growth promoting, one may doubt that this policy shift will ever occur, given its unpopularity in countries with strong familistic values and the unparalleled ability of the construction sector to absorb large amount of unskilled workers.

The peripheral countries' chances of stabilizing their debt and starting again to grow are increased by a favorable external environment. In the recent past, core countries did not appear willing to accept higher inflation or more generous wage increases, but nowadays in Germany market and political forces are pushing wages up and inducing the government to run a less tight fiscal policy.[26] At the global level, many countries want to pursue an export-led growth strategy. However, in the next future, there is a realistic possibility of a (slightly) more rapid expansion in aggregate demand than we had in the recent past: the US will resume—to a limited extent—its traditional role of "consumer of last resort" and China will slowly rebalance its economy toward domestic consumption. Hence, if the peripheral economies were able to make some progress in restoring their competitiveness, they could probably fully exploit the possibilities offered by an external environment slightly more favorable than in the past to revive their growth.[27]

5 Conclusions

Southern European countries are among the losers of the globalization process of the last 20 years: the quality of their institutions and social capital, the comparative advantages that they enjoy, their role in the international division of labor have probably become inconsistent with the standards of living and aspirations of most people in these countries, and with the level of their private wealth and public entitlements. Increasing private (and in some cases public) indebtedness has permitted for some years to conceal this inconsistency. After the outbreak of the European debt crisis, a brutal and rapid downward readjustment of the living standards toward the real possibilities of these countries has occurred and is still under way. The weak legitimacy of the political class managing this collective impoverishment (especially in Greece and Italy) and the widespread perception

---

[26]Comments in the aftermath of the agreement of December 2013 that led to the formation of the Grand Coalition government headed by Ms. Merkel were along these lines (see e.g. Folkerts-Landau 2013; Barysch 2013).

[27]Notably, a more even distribution of income and wealth across agents and sectors in the peripheral countries (typically suffering of the negative impact of diffuse cronyism, corruption and rents) could not only help to tackle the distortions hindering growth on the supply side, but also improve the composition and the level of domestic demand. The rapid growth in households' indebtedness, and then aggressive deleverage, can also be partly ascribed to the compression of the purchasing power of certain groups of population. This calls for redistribution, not for larger public expenditures.

that losses and sacrifices are unfairly distributed make this painful process even more problematic. After all, it is not the first time that a long and deep recession creates social unrest and political instability. In this environment, it is easy for unscrupulous political entrepreneurs to use European institutions or the Euro-core countries as scapegoats against which to channel popular resentment towards economic hardships, and to propose populist ways out of the crisis.

Indeed, two shortcuts are quite popular and often invoked. The idea that economic growth can be reactivated in the peripheral countries by letting them to run larger public deficits in order to boost domestic demand is an old one. This notwithstanding, given the nature of the causes leading to very slow growth in these countries, it is a wrong idea. Beside the unsolved problem of how to finance such a deficit, in a context where monetary policy is already very expansionary and financial markets remain very wary of the peripheral countries, more deficit can give them only transient relief, without removing the reasons underlying their low growth potential and contributing to postpone the necessary real adjustment.

A possible return of the peripheral countries to national currencies, the other shortcut advocated by some commentators and political forces, even if agreed upon with the other countries belonging to the Euro and—to the extent that this will be possible—carefully planned, would result in major losses and risks in the near term. Above all, it would give a merely temporary relief to the exporting firms of these countries, given that production costs and prices will promptly adjust to the depreciation of the nominal exchange rate, leaving unaffected the sources of inefficiency and low productivity at the origin of their current lack of competitiveness. In addition, the return to national currencies would recreate in the peripheral countries the climate of monetary instability, lack of confidence in their ability to keep inflation under control and high interest rates that had characterized them prior to the introduction of the Euro.

All this makes even more urgent to conduct a battle of ideas in order to convince the general public of Southern Europe that people's long-term well-being depends on restoring the competitiveness of their national economies, without which there is no possibility of satisfactory economic growth over the long run: the return to a sustainable grow path requires a long, patient, painful and systematic series of interventions and reforms, which should tackle the structural causes underlying the productivity stagnation and the endemic pockets of inefficiency that burden these economies. It should also be made clear that along this arduous route there are no shortcuts.

References

Anderson D, Hunt B, Snudden S (2013) Fiscal consolidation in the Euro area: how much pain can structural reforms ease? IMF Working Paper 13/211

Baer W, Dias DA, Duarte JB (2013) The economy of Portugal and the European Union: from high growth prospects to the debt crisis. Q Rev Econ Finance 53(4):345–352

Barkbu B, Rahman J, Valdés R, a staff team (2012) Fostering growth in Europe now. IMF Staff Discussion Note 12/07

Barysch K (2013) What Germany's new coalition government means for the EU. Center for European Reform, December 16

Blanchard OJ, Leigh D (2013) Growth forecast errors and fiscal multipliers. Am Econ Rev 103(3):117–120

Bonatti L, Fracasso A (2013a) Origins and prospects of the Euro existential crisis. In: van der Harst J, Zhang L (eds) The European sovereign debt crisis and China–EU relations. Tsinghua University Press, Beijing, pp 3–19

Bonatti L, Fracasso A (2013b) The German model and the euro crisis. J Common Mark Stud 51(6):1023–1039

Bouis R, Causa O, Demmou L, Duval R, Zdzienicka A (2012) The short-term effects of structural reforms: an empirical analysis. OECD Economics Department Working Papers, No. 949

Cecchetti SG, McCauley RN, McGuire PM (2012) Interpreting Target2 balances. BIS Working Papers No. 393, Bank for International Settlements

Chen R, Milesi-Ferretti G-M, Tressel T (2012) External imbalances in the Euro area. IMF Working Paper, WP/12/236

Cour-Thimann P (2013) Target balances and the crisis in the Euro Area. CESifo Forum Special Issue, April 2013, Ifo Institute for Economic Research at the University of Munich, vol 0, pp 05–50

Credit Suisse (2010) Credit Suisse Global Wealth Databook 2010

Davies JB, Sandström S, Shorrocks A, Wolff EN (2011) The level and distribution of global household wealth. Econ J 121:223–254

De Bruyckere V, Gerhadt M, Schepens G, Vander Vennet R (2013) Bank/sovereign risk spillovers in the European debt crisis. J Bank Finance 37:4793–4809

De Grauwe P, Ji Y (2012) Mispricing of sovereign risk and macroeconomic stability in the Eurozone. J Common Mark Stud 50:866–880

De Grauwe P, Ji Y (2013) More evidence that financial markets imposed excessive austerity in the Eurozone. CEPS Commentary, February

ECB (2013) The Eurosystem Household Finance and Consumption Survey. Results from the First Wave. Statistics Paper Series No. 2

Eggertsson G, Ferrero A, Raffo A (2014) Can structural reforms help Europe? J Monetary Econ 61:2–22

Eichengreen BJ, Wyplosz C (1993) The unstable EMS. Brookings Paper Econ Activ 24(1):51–144

European Commission (2011) Internal devaluations and external imbalances. Q Rep Euro Area 10(3):22–27

Folkerts-Landau D (2013) Grand coalition – poor policies. Standpunkt Deutschland, Deutsche Bank Research, December 16

in 't Veld J (2013) Fiscal consolidations and spillovers in the Euro Area periphery and core. European Economy – Economic Papers 506, Directorate General Economic and Monetary Affairs (DG ECFIN), European Commission

Ioannou D, Stracca L (2014) Have the Euro Area and EU governance worked? Just the facts. Eur J Polit Econ 34:1–17

Katsimi M, Moutos T (2010) EMU and the Greek crisis: the political-economy perspective. Eur J Polit Econ 26(4):568–576

Lane PR (2006) The real effects of European Monetary Union. J Econ Perspect 20:47–66

Lane PR (2012) The European sovereign debt crisis. J Econ Perspect 26(3):49–68

Mikkelsen U, Ruiz EP (2012) The trade impact of China: is it even across members? IMF Working Paper, 12/221

Neal L, García-Iglesias MC (2013) The economy of Spain in the euro-zone before and after the crisis of 2008. Q Rev Econ Finance 53(4):336–344

Shambaugh JC (2012) The Euro's three crises. Brookings Paper Econ Activ 44(1):157–231, Spring

Sinn H-W (2014) Growth and inflation: remarks on the Eurozone's unsolved competitiveness problem. World Econ 37:1–13

Sinn H-W, Wollmershäuser T (2012) Target loans, current balances and capital flows: the ECB's rescue facility. Int Tax Publ Finance 19:468–508

Tamborini R (2013) Transatlantic austerity 2010-... DEM Discussion Papers 2013/10, University of Trento

Ullrich K (2006) Market discipline and the use of government bonds as collateral in the EMU, ZEW Discussion Papers, No. 06–46

Wyplosz C (2006) European Monetary Union: the dark sides of a major success. Econ Pol 21:207–261

Information Technology and Labor Market Polarization in Europe

Paolo Naticchioni and Giuseppe Ragusa

Abstract The US labor market has become increasingly polarized both in terms of jobs and wages, and the routinization explanation is well established for these trends. Recent papers have found job polarization patterns also in Europe, while few evidence is available for wages. The goal of the paper is to investigate the dynamics of unconditional and conditional—on technology—wages in Europe, using industry (EU KLEMS) data. As for unconditional wages, there are no wage polarization trends at work, as the wage structure is broadly constant over time. For the conditional polarization, we investigate the impact of ICT intensity on wages and hours worked by three skill groups by education levels. Our analysis does not provide evidence supporting the conditional polarization of wages, while we detect job polarization trends.

1 Introduction

Autor et al. (2006) have shown that the US labor market has become increasingly polarized both in terms of occupations and wage distributions. The routinization hypothesis has been advocated for explaining this empirical evidence (Autor et al. 2003): job polarization occurs because of information and communication technologies complementing the analytical tasks performed by highly educated

---

P. Naticchioni (✉)
Department of Political Science, University of Roma Tre, Rome, Italy

IZA, Bonn, Germany
e-mail: p.naticchioni@gmail.com

G. Ragusa
Department of Economics and Finance, Luiss University, Rome, Italy
e-mail: gragusa@luiss.it

L. Paganetto (ed.), *Wealth, Income Inequalities, and Demography*,
DOI 10.1007/978-3-319-05909-9_6,

workers and substituting for routine tasks generally performed by middle educated workers.

Goos et al. (2009) find job polarization patterns in Europe as well, and Goos et al. (2010) investigate the effects of technology, globalization, institutions and product demand effects on the employment dynamics for different occupations. Their results suggest that in Europe the routinization hypothesis is the most important factor behind the observed shifts in employment structure. Michaels et al. (2014) use EU KLEMS industry level data to study whether the distribution of wage bill shares in European countries has polarized and whether this is due to information and communication technology. Their findings suggest the routinization explanation applies. In a sense, Michaels et al. (2014) investigate a conditional impact of technology on wage polarization, without showing if actually unconditional wages have polarized over time in Europe.

The goal of this paper is to add to the empirical evidence on wage polarization in Europe. First, we analyze whether the unconditional wages get polarized over time in Europe. Second, we analyze the conditional impact of technology on wages, using proxies for technological change, in such a way testing the routinization explanations.

We make use of EU KLEMS industry level data, from 1980 to 2005, which contains data on value added, labor, capital, skills and ICT for various industries in OECD countries. We focus on nine countries for which the variables of interest are available (Austria, Denmark, Finland, France, Germany, Italy, Netherlands, Spain, the UK).

As far as the dynamics of unconditional wages is concerned, we show that there is no evidence of wage polarization, since the structure of wages remains rather constant over time. In particular, the wage ratio between high skilled and medium skilled, and the one between medium skilled and low skilled, remain constant over the period.

For the conditional impact of technological proxies, the evidence is more mixed. Using EU KLEMS industry data, we investigate the impact of new technology on relative wages between high and medium skilled, and between medium and low skilled. Our technological measure is Information and Communication Technology (ICT) intensity, for which we include a wide set of descriptive statistics by country, industry, and over time. Further, in the econometric analysis we point out that changes in ICT intensity has impacted the labor market through a polarizing effect in jobs. The evidence on the relation between wage polarization and ICT is much weaker. We find evidence supporting ICT as having had a weak effect on the high-skilled (HS)-medium-skilled (MS) relative wages, but no effect is found for the medium-skilled (MS)-low-skilled (LS) relative wages. We also find that the financial and postal sectors have played an important role in Europe: without this sector there is no evidence of European wages responding to changes in ICT intensity.

Apart for controlling for unobserved heterogeneity, our results are robust to an instrumental variable approach to take into account for endogeneity problems, using as instrument the value of ICT in 1980 for the US.

The paper is structured as follow. Section 2 presents the data, Sect. 3 focuses on the analysis of unconditional wages, while Sect. 4 investigates the conditional polarization of wages. Section 5 concludes.

2 Data

In this section we present aggregate evidence on the polarization of the European labor market. The analysis is based on the EU KLEMS Growth and Productivity Accounts.

The EU KLEMS database contains industry-level measures of output, inputs, and productivity for 23 European countries, Japan and the US for the period from 1970 to 2005. The database harmonizes data provided from each country's National Statistical Office. O'Mahony and Timmer (2009) provide a detailed explanation of the construction of the dataset. For a selected number of countries—Austria, Denmark, Finland, France, Germany, Italy, Japan, the Netherlands, Spain, the UK, and the US—the database collects industry-level data on wages and hours worked by skill levels: high (HS), medium (MS), and low skilled (LS). Workers are assigned to these skill levels according to their education attainment: lower than upper secondary, upper secondary and tertiary. Key to the analysis here, EU KLEMS has industry level data on Information and Communication Technology (ICT) capital compensation; we use this variable to construct a measure of industry intensity in new technologies.

There are at the time of writing four different releases of the EU KLEMS database: March 2007, March 2008, November 2009, and March 2011. We use the most recent release (March 2011) for the industry input data, and the March 2008 for the skill-level labor data. This choice is due to the fact that skill-level labor data was not updated in the last two releases. Differences in the March 2008 and March 2011 are modest and the findings of this section are not sensitive to the use of either one of the dataset. On the contrary, the March 2008 and the March 2007 releases diverge in a substantial way. As such, some of the conclusions of Michaels et al. (2014)—who uses the March 2007 release—do not survive the data upgrading.

While EU KLEMS provides unique information on industry-level economic variables and their dynamic over time, the database has some inconsistencies that should be kept in mind when interpreting the results. First, the criterion with which skill level groups are identified varies across the eleven countries. While the definition of high skilled group is basically homogeneous among countries—high skilled are those with a college degree—the medium and the low skilled groups are less uniformly defined. This results in a problem with some European countries having an unreasonably low fraction of low-skilled workers. Second, the number of industries for which skill composition variables are available varies across countries. To obviate this problem, we follow Michaels et al. (2014) and aggregate industries to the lowest possible level of aggregation for which all skill-level variables are present. Third, in EU KLEMS capital compensation measures are built using the perpetual inventory method from the underlying investment flow data for several types of capital. In this approach, the price of capital services is defined as a residual and in practice it can be negative. When this happens—and it does frequently in the agriculture industry—we set the price of capital to zero.

3 Unconditional Wage Polarization in Europe

In this section we investigate whether unconditional wages have polarized in the period 1980–2005. We focus on the wages for high skilled, medium skilled, and low skilled workers, defined as workers having a tertiary, upper secondary, and lower than upper secondary respectively.

In Fig. 1 we include the trends of wages for the three skill levels. It emerges that the dynamics of wages is pretty homogenous across skills levels. Of course, the business cycle is rather important, but it concerns all the groups in a similar way. This is confirmed in Fig. 2, where we plot the wage ratio between high skilled and medium skilled, and between medium skilled and low skilled, in such a way depurating from the impact of the business cycle. For Europe as a whole, it emerges that the wage ratio between high skilled and medium skilled is rather constant around 1.6, i.e. wages of high skilled are 60 % greater than those of medium skilled. Actually, even if slightly, this ratio decreases, and this is at odds with the polarization hypothesis, that would predict a sharp increase. As for the wage ratio between medium and low skilled, it is slightly increasing over time, from 1.4 to 1.5. Also this evidence is at odds with the polarization prediction, i.e. the wage ratio between medium and low skilled workers should decrease.

Of course, it might be the case that unconditional wages do not polarize, while conditional wages do. This would suggest that the impact of technology is consistent with the routinization assumption, but that other confounding factors—as institutions—affect unconditional wages preventing the impact of technology to emerge. Hence, we move our attention to conditional wage polarization, i.e. the impact of ICT intensity on wages.

4 Conditional Wage Polarization in Europe: The Impact of ICT Intensity

4.1 Descriptive

Figure 3 plots for Europe as a whole the by-industry 1980–2005 changes of our measure of ICT intensity: ICT capital compensation over value added (ICT/VA). The choice of value added as scaling factor is arbitrary and other variables related

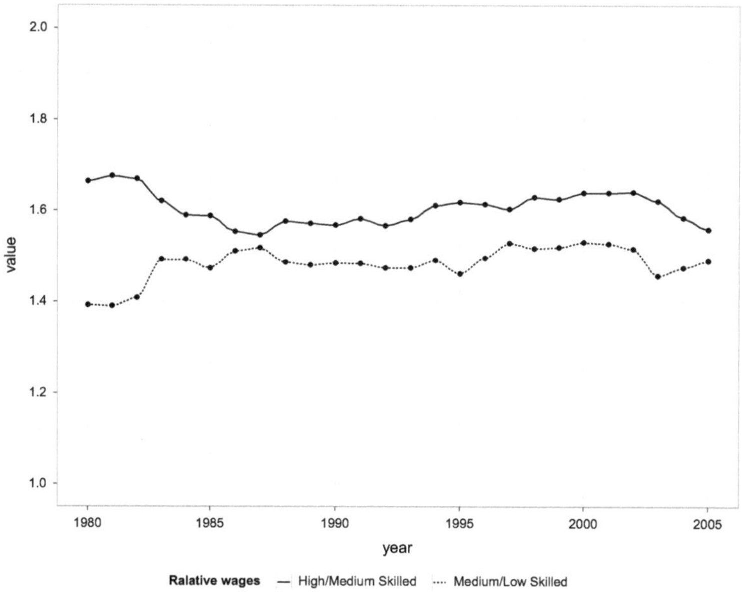

Fig. 1 European relative real wages. Wage data are obtained by aggregating over industries and over countries the total wage bill and the total hours worked. Wages are expressed in 2005 real dollars. *Source*: EU KLEMS

to the whole size of the economy could be potentially used. We use value added to be consistent with Michaels et al. (2014). The graph also distinguishes among tradable and non-tradable industries.[1] It is interesting to note that ICT increased the most in the financial and postal industries (with ratios close to 10), while in tradable industries the ratio in never greater than 3. Figure 4 includes the industry dynamics of ICT out of VA by countries. Each country has a minimum of 14 industries, with Italy and Denmark having data for 27, and Spain for 19. The number of tradable industries is limited in many countries: Austria, Finland and Netherlands have data for only three tradable industries; Germany, UK, and France for four. The highest growth in ICT/VA took place in non-tradable industries. In particular, in six of the nine countries (Denmark, Spain, Finland, France, Germany, and Netherlands) the highest growth occurred in the financial industry. And also the postal sector displays high values in most of the countries. In Finland, the ICT/VA grew for the financial industry by 25 % points. In Austria and Denmark by 15 % points. In other countries,

[1]Tradable industries are: electrical and optical equipment; pulp, paper, paper products, printing and publishing; transport equipment; machinery, nec; chemical, rubber, plastic products; wood and products of wood and cork; basic metals and fabricated metal products; non-metallic mineral products; textiles, textile products, leather and footwear; food products; agriculture, hunting, forestry, and fishing.

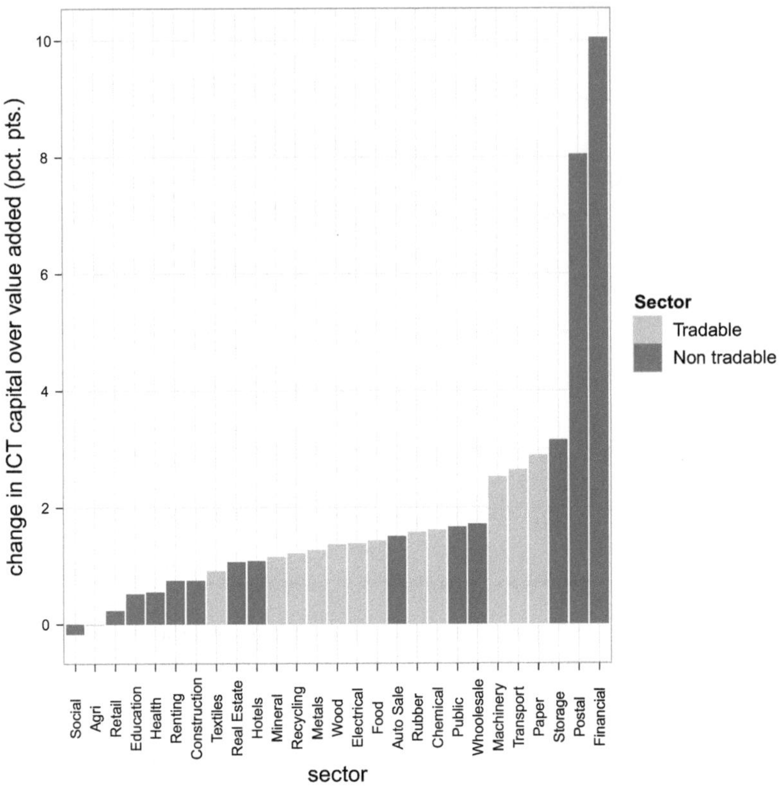

Fig. 2 By-industry 1980–2005 changes of ICT capital compensation over value added. Industries are divided in tradable and non-tradable. Country data are aggregated by weighting by 1980 share of each country's employment. *Source*: EU KLEMS

the Financial industry registered a more modest increase which is however still disproportionate with respect to the other industries.

Table 1 shows summary statistics for the 1980 level and the 1980–2005 change of the key variables. The variables are wage bill share, relative hours worked, and real wages, all broken down by skill levels; ICT and non-ICT capital over value added, and ICT capital over total capital.[2] The table makes clear that the issues with the skill identification criterion adopted by EU KLEMS may be rather severe, with remarkable differences across countries.

Finland is the country with the highest increase in the wage bill accruing to the high skilled. Countries with similar rate of growth are UK, USA, JPN, and

[2]Wages are expressed in real US dollars.

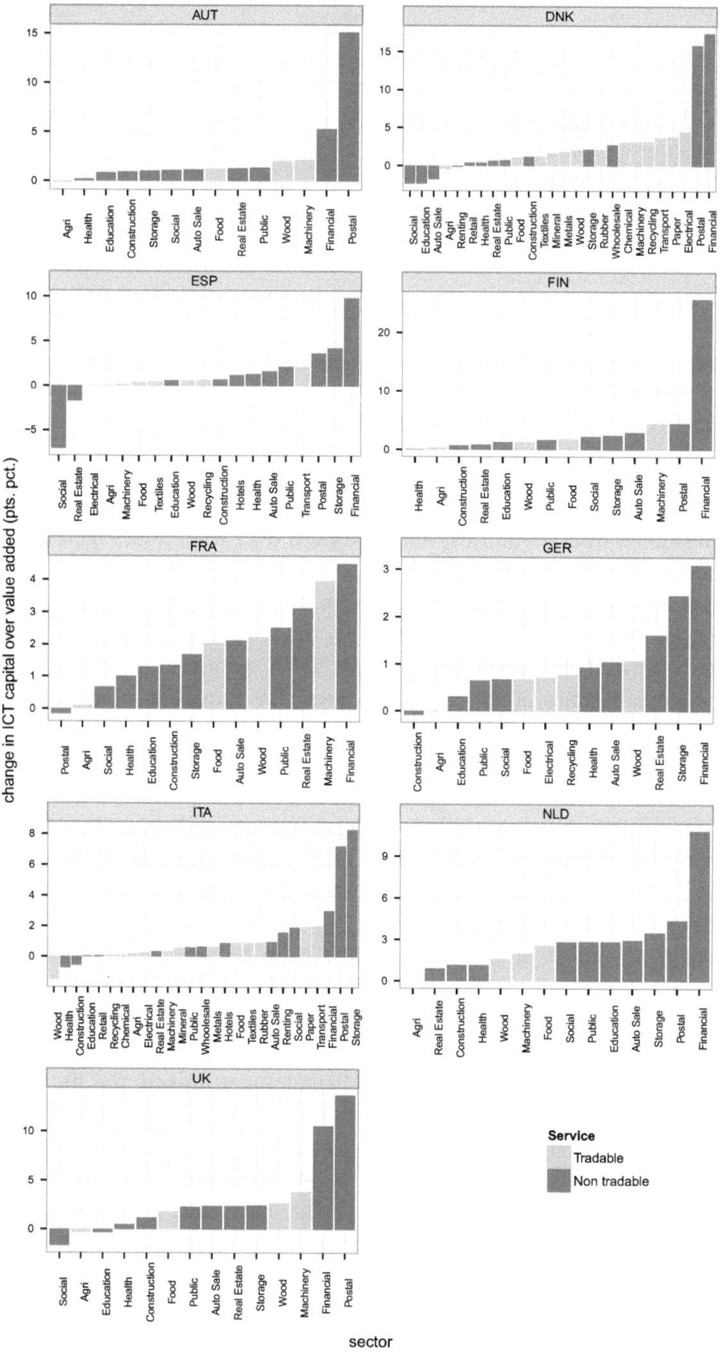

Fig. 3 By-industry 1980–2005 changes of ICT capital compensation over value added. Industries are divided in tradable and non-tradable. Tradeable industries. *Source*: EU KLEMS

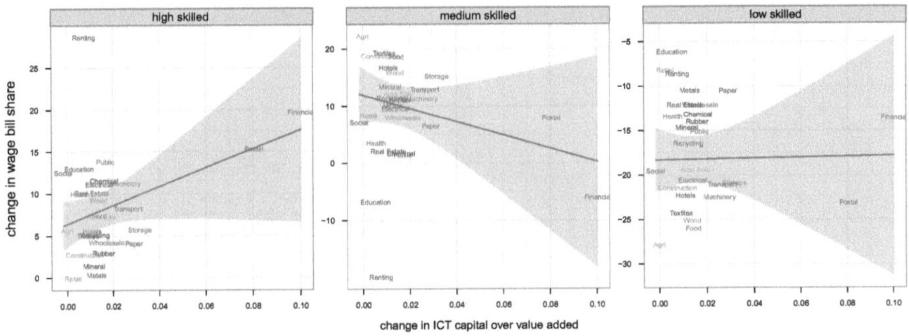

Fig. 4 Changes in 2005–1980 wage bill share versus changes in 2005–1980 ICT capital compensation over value added, by skill levels. Data by industries are obtained by summing total ICT capital compensation and total value added over countries. *Source*: EU KLEMS

Spain.[3] The wage bill accruing to the medium skilled declined only in the US and in Germany. In all countries, hours worked over total hours increased for high skilled and decreased for low skilled. ICT capital intensity increased in all countries although there are marked differences on the rate of growth. Germany, France and Italy are countries where ICT intensity grew the least over the 1980–2005 period.

Figure 5 draws 1980–2005 changes in ICT/VA against changes in the three skill groups wage bill share at the aggregate level for European countries. The wage bill share of high skilled has on average increased more in industries that have experienced higher changes in ICT/VA over the 1980–2005 period. There is instead a negative correlation between changes in wage bill share of medium skilled and changes in ICT/VA. For low skilled, changes in wage bill share do not to have any correlation with changes in ICT/VA. Remarkably, the correlation between wage bill share and ICT/VA is disproportionately influenced by the financial and postal sectors both for high skilled and medium skilled.

Figures 6, 7, and 8 plot changes in the ratio between ICT capital and value added against changes in the three skill groups wage bill share by country. Each observations (and the regression line) are weighted by each industry's 1980 share of each country's employment. The correlation is generally positive for the high skilled, negative for the medium skilled, and more mixed for the low skilled. Figures 6 and 8 for high skilled and medium skilled also point out that the ICT impact is rather homogenous across countries, at least for high skilled and medium skilled. Consistent with Fig. 5 in most countries the financial industry has experienced the largest change in ICT intensity, and, as noted in the graphs, this increase results in an outlying observation which has a strong effect on the correlations.

[3]We include USA and Japan for sake of comparison. These countries however are not considered in the econometric analysis.

Table 1 The first panel reports by-industry means of labor bill share (B_{HS}, BS_{MS}, and BS_{LS}); hours worked by skill groups over (H_{HS}, H_{MS}, and H_{LS}) over total number of hours worked in the economy (H); average hourly real wage (in 2005 USD) by skills (W_{HS}, W_{MS}, and W_{LS}); ICT (K_{ICT}) and non ICT capital (K_{NICT}) over value added (VA); the ration between ICT and total capital (K). The second panel shows level changes of the same variables over the period 1980–2005. Means are weighted by 1980 share of each country's employment

	1980											
Country	BS_{HS}	BS_{MS}	BS_{LS}	$\frac{H_{HS}}{H}$	$\frac{H_{MS}}{H}$	$\frac{H_{LS}}{H}$	W_{HS}	W_{MS}	W_{LS}	$\frac{K_{ICT}}{VA}$	$\frac{K_{NICT}}{VA}$	$\frac{K_{ICT}}{K}$
ITA	4.73	87.57	7.70	4.79	87.40	7.80	39.77	32.99	26.20	0.013	0.16	0.11
DNK	5.37	50.51	44.11	2.97	44.29	52.74	49.48	28.48	20.52	0.029	0.17	0.16
NLD	7.54	76.59	15.87	4.28	76.59	19.14	48.06	24.45	19.52	0.012	0.16	0.07
UK	8.52	52.60	38.89	5.12	53.87	41.01	30.05	18.17	17.13	0.018	0.19	0.08
AUT	8.66	55.03	36.31	5.61	50.61	43.78	29.66	16.24	11.92	0.013	0.24	0.04
GER	9.22	66.17	24.61	5.52	59.81	34.67	32.24	19.90	12.72	0.018	0.19	0.09
FRA	10.20	48.05	41.75	5.94	46.56	47.50	52.64	28.21	23.00	0.010	0.18	0.05
ESP	12.41	9.65	77.93	8.21	7.54	84.26	46.81	33.30	22.24	0.021	0.27	0.07
FIN	25.95	28.45	45.59	16.96	32.21	50.83	29.67	16.35	16.52	0.015	0.22	0.08
	1980–2005											
Country	ΔBS_{HS}	ΔBS_{MS}	ΔBS_{LS}	$\Delta\frac{H_{HS}}{H}$	$\Delta\frac{H_{MS}}{H}$	$\Delta\frac{H_{LS}}{H}$	ΔW_{HS}	ΔW_{MS}	ΔW_{LS}	$\Delta\frac{K_{ICT}}{VA}$	$\Delta\frac{K_{NICT}}{VA}$	$\Delta\frac{K_{ICT}}{K}$
ITA	4.55	2.77	−7.32	3.41	2.45	−5.85	−13.27	−10.57	−19.07	0.009	0.05	−0.01
DNK	4.55	17.31	−21.85	4.12	18.73	−22.85	−0.21	8.05	4.88	0.014	−0.03	0.08
NLD	8.90	2.91	−11.81	6.68	6.67	−13.35	4.83	6.50	2.59	0.024	0.07	0.07
UK	14.84	14.67	−29.51	10.53	16.67	−27.20	17.61	9.87	2.09	0.025	−0.02	0.14
AUT	6.26	13.35	−19.61	5.04	16.71	−21.75	10.15	7.85	5.37	0.015	0.03	0.04
GER	5.71	−0.89	−4.82	2.76	3.59	−6.35	23.87	9.98	7.41	0.009	0.02	0.03
FRA	6.74	16.97	−23.70	6.17	20.20	−26.37	−6.82	1.58	2.78	0.019	0.05	0.05
ESP	12.76	21.26	−34.02	9.41	23.15	−32.56	−19.99	−16.10	−8.10	0.011	0.06	0.02
JPN	13.74	9.73	−23.47	12.08	14.35	−26.43	17.21	11.91	11.03	0.016	0.10	0.04
FIN	15.56	13.12	−28.67	14.70	15.07	−29.77	4.26	5.61	3.47	0.021	0.01	0.11
USA	14.50	−5.34	−9.16	9.22	−0.72	−8.50	12.39	3.61	−0.61	0.029	0.03	0.09

Fig. 5 European real wages by skill levels. Wage data are obtained by aggregating over industries and over countries the total wage bill and the total hours worked. Wages are expressed in 2005 real dollars (RECHECK). *Source*: EU KLEMS

4.2 Regression Analysis

We study the impact of ICT on the log relative wage bill share and its components. The baseline regressions is given by

$$\Delta \log\left(\frac{BS_{HS}}{BS_{MS}}\right) = \beta_0^{HM} + \beta_1^{HM} \Delta K_{ICT}/VA + \beta_2^{HM} \Delta K_{NICT}/VA + \beta_Q^{HS} \Delta \ln(Q)_{ic} + \Delta \varepsilon_{ic}^{HM},$$

$$\Delta \log\left(\frac{BS_{MS}}{BS_{LS}}\right) = \beta_0^{ML} + \beta_1^{ML} \Delta K_{ICT}/VA + \beta_2^{ML} \Delta K_{NICT}/VA + \beta_Q^{ML} \Delta \ln(Q)_{ic} + \Delta \varepsilon_{ic}^{ML},$$

where Δx denotes the change of the variable x over the 1980–2005 period. Since 1980–2005 changes in the log relative high skilled/medium skilled (HS/MS) and medium skilled/low skilled (MS/LS) wage-bill shares can be decomposed as:

$$\Delta \log\left(\frac{BS_{HS}}{BS_{MS}}\right) = \Delta \log\left(\frac{W_{HS}}{W_{MS}}\right) + \Delta \log\left(\frac{L_{HS}}{L_{MS}}\right),$$

$$\Delta \log\left(\frac{BS_{MS}}{BS_{LS}}\right) = \Delta \log\left(\frac{W_{MS}}{W_{LS}}\right) + \Delta \log\left(\frac{L_{MS}}{L_{LS}}\right),$$

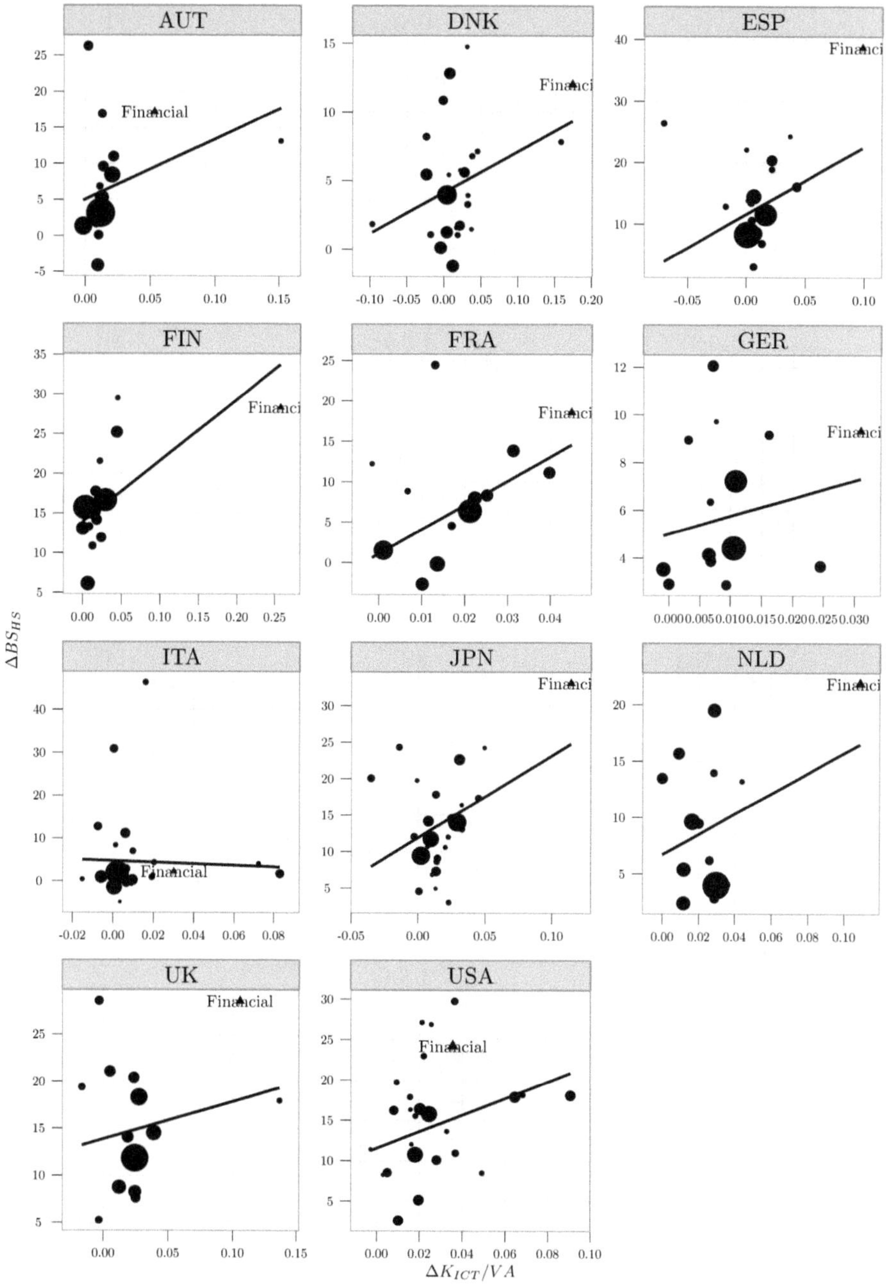

Fig. 6 High skilled wage bill share and ICT/VA

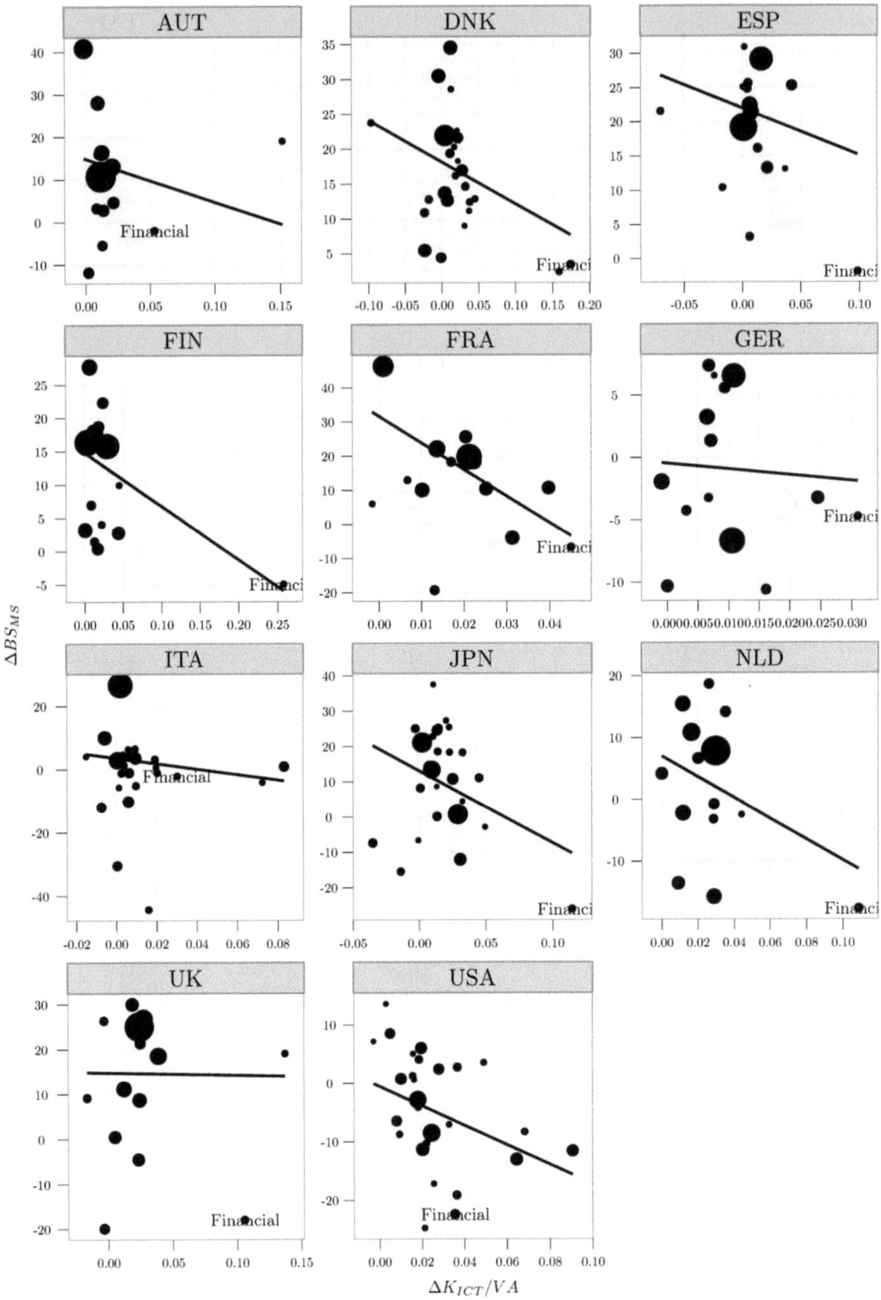

Fig. 7 Medium skilled wage bill share and ICT/VA

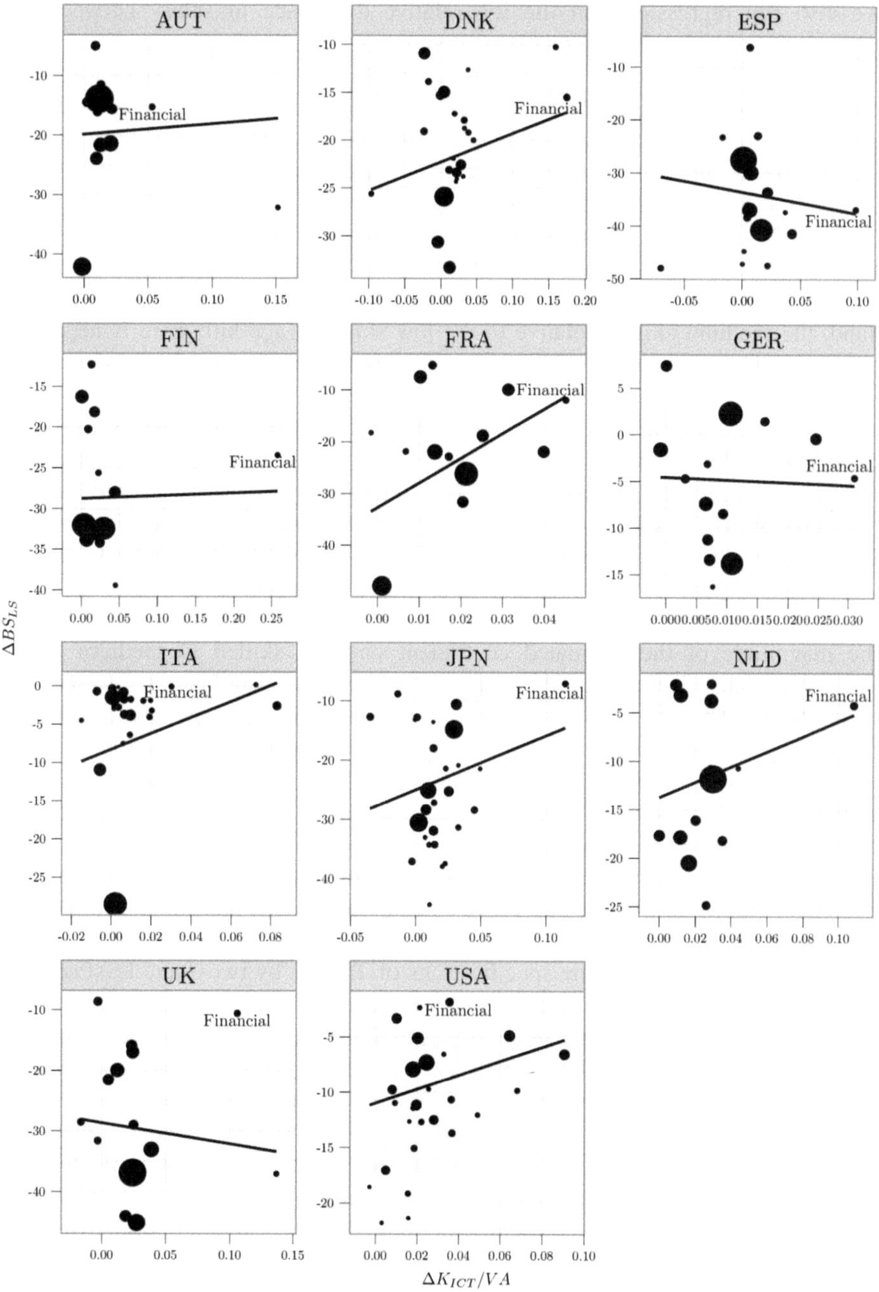

Fig. 8 Low skilled wage bill share and ICT/VA

we also run regressions on the log relative difference in salary between two education groups and the log relative difference in hours worked to appraise whether the effect of ICT intensity depends more on changes in relative hours worked or relative changes in wages. Note that our specification, which is in time difference, allows controlling for country and industry unobserved heterogeneity. Further, since we include in our specification country fixed effects, we also account for country unobserved heterogeneity in trends over time.

Table 2 Panel A presents regression results when all European countries and all industries are included. The high skilled relative to the medium skilled wage bill share is estimated to be positively correlated with ICT/VA changes. On the other hand, the medium skilled relative to the low skilled wage bill share is negatively correlated with changes in ICT/VA, but the coefficient is very small and statistically insignificant.

These first results are in line with the routinization hypothesis: the wage bill share of high skilled is positively correlated with ICT/VA, while that of medium skilled workers is negatively correlated with ICT intensity. An increase of one standard deviation in $\Delta ICT/VA$ is associated with a 12 % of a standard deviation increase in the wage bill share of high skilled. ICT capital does not have a statistically and economically significant effect on the low-skilled bill share.[4]

However, when we exclude the financial and the postal sectors, Table 2 Panel B, the magnitude of the estimated coefficient on high skilled to medium skilled wage bill share decreases rather substantially and it also becomes statistically insignificant. This suggests that much of the wage bill share polarization can be induced by industry-specific dynamics and not by a general phenomenon.

As we decompose wage bill shares into hours and wages, we find that changes in high to medium skilled wage bill share tend to be almost totally explained by changes in relative hours worked. For the medium to low skilled case, the effect of ICT on wage bill share is small and insignificant and thus interpreting the decomposition is of limited interest, if not for saying that there is no evidence of technology driven wage polarization for the countries considered here.

We also estimate the same specifications of Table 2 by two-stage least squares, instrumenting changes in ICT over value of each with the 1980 level of ICT over value added in the US. This instrument provides an indicator of the initial ICT intensity of a country, the US, which can be considered the technological leader. Notice that the observations from the US are not included in our analysis. The assumption underlying the validity of the instrument is that industry specific US technological shocks in the 1980 are predetermined, that is, are not correlated with industry specific shocks to the path of technological progress as measured by ICT intensity. The IV results are presented in Table 3. The results are similar to those obtained by OLS. The main difference with Table 2 is that the high to medium wage bill share is estimated to be positively affected by ICT even when the financial and the postal industries are excluded from the regression. However, also in the

[4]All findings are robust to the inclusion of 1980 level of value added, ICT, and non ICT capital. In the interest of space, we do no report the results of this robustness check here.

Table 2 Relative wage bill share, hours worked, and wages

	$\Delta \ln\left(\frac{BS_{HS}}{BS_{MS}}\right)$	$\Delta \ln\left(\frac{H_{HS}}{H_{MS}}\right)$	$\Delta \ln\left(\frac{W_{HS}}{W_{MS}}\right)$	$\Delta \ln\left(\frac{BS_{MS}}{BS_{LS}}\right)$	$\Delta \ln\left(\frac{H_{MS}}{H_{LS}}\right)$	$\Delta \ln\left(\frac{W_{MS}}{W_{LS}}\right)$
Panel A						
$\Delta K_{ICT}/VA$	5.870***	5.232***	0.637*	−0.329	−0.223	−0.107
	(1.772)	(1.793)	(0.378)	(1.150)	(1.077)	(0.363)
$\Delta K_{NICT}/VA$	0.833	0.434	0.400	0.557	0.254	0.303
	(0.519)	(0.465)	(0.261)	(0.372)	(0.374)	(0.272)
$\Delta \ln(VA)$	−0.0107	−0.0204	0.00970	−0.356***	−0.288***	−0.0674
	(0.117)	(0.0969)	(0.0704)	(0.0907)	(0.0855)	(0.0726)
Constant	0.269	0.396	−0.127	1.446***	1.351***	0.0954
	(0.296)	(0.291)	(0.0789)	(0.175)	(0.155)	(0.0798)
R-squared	0.353	0.385	0.384	0.771	0.682	0.740
Country FE	Yes	Yes	Yes	Yes	Yes	Yes
Financial and postal	Yes	Yes	Yes	Yes	Yes	Yes
Observations	157	157	157	157	157	157
Panel B						
$\Delta K_{ICT}/VA$	1.657	0.601	1.055	−0.372	−0.576	0.204
	(3.763)	(3.597)	(1.091)	(1.924)	(1.917)	(1.167)
$\Delta K_{NICT}/VA$	0.991*	0.590	0.400	0.744*	0.433	0.310
	(0.559)	(0.504)	(0.293)	(0.389)	(0.417)	(0.313)
$\Delta \ln(VA)$	−0.0238	−0.0346	0.0108	−0.364***	−0.296***	−0.0677
	(0.116)	(0.0975)	(0.0717)	(0.0902)	(0.0888)	(0.0745)
Constant	0.271	0.400	−0.129	1.437***	1.350***	0.0870
	(0.313)	(0.308)	(0.0856)	(0.191)	(0.172)	(0.0871)
R-squared	0.353	0.385	0.384	0.771	0.682	0.740
Country FE	Yes	Yes	Yes	Yes	Yes	Yes
Financial and postal	No	No	No	No	No	No
Observations	157	157	157	157	157	157

Robust standard errors in parentheses
*** p<0.01, ** p<0.05, * p<0.1
Dependent variable are the 1980–2005 relative log changes in relative wage bill share, relative hours worked, and relative wage. Coefficients are estimated by OLS. Robust standard errors in parenthesis. Regressions weighted by industry's 1980 share of each country's employment. Panel A: all industries, Panel B: all industries except financial and postal

IV analysis, the impact on wage bill shares is basically totally driven by changes in hours worked while the changes in wages are small in magnitude and not statistically significant.

To summarize, we interpret these results as suggesting that, as for the US, the polarizing forces of technology may have had an impact on the European labor market. The evidence from EU KLEMS indicates that technology may have affected skill employment composition. As far as wages are concerned, we find very weak evidence indicating that wages have responded as they have in the US. This weak impact totally fade out when the financial and postal industries are excluded from the analysis, suggesting that these industries play a not negligible role.

Table 3 Relative wage bill share, hours worked, and wages

	$\Delta \ln\left(\frac{BS_{HS}}{BS_{MS}}\right)$	$\Delta \ln\left(\frac{H_{HS}}{H_{MS}}\right)$	$\Delta \ln\left(\frac{W_{HS}}{W_{MS}}\right)$	$\Delta \ln\left(\frac{BS_{HS}}{BS_{MS}}\right)$	$\Delta \ln\left(\frac{H_{MS}}{H_{LS}}\right)$	$\Delta \ln\left(\frac{W_{MS}}{W_{LS}}\right)$
Panel A						
$\Delta K_{ICT}/VA$	16.99***	15.27***	1.720	−5.225	−4.698	−0.527
	(4.550)	(4.285)	(1.259)	(4.942)	(4.473)	(0.994)
$\Delta K_{NICT}/VA$	0.630	0.250	0.380	0.647*	0.336	0.310
	(0.543)	(0.483)	(0.267)	(0.369)	(0.373)	(0.277)
$\Delta \ln(VA)$	−0.0970	−0.0983	0.00129	−0.318***	−0.254***	−0.0641
	(0.128)	(0.108)	(0.0714)	(0.0975)	(0.0913)	(0.0707)
Constant	0.210	0.343	−0.133*	1.472***	1.375***	0.0976
	(0.294)	(0.290)	(0.0790)	(0.177)	(0.158)	(0.0813)
Observations	157	157	157	157	157	157
R-squared	0.217	0.267	0.372	0.749	0.650	0.739
Country FE	Yes	Yes	Yes	Yes	Yes	Yes
Financial and postal	Yes	Yes	Yes	Yes	Yes	Yes
	$\Delta \ln\left(\frac{BS_{HS}}{BS_{MS}}\right)$	$\Delta \ln\left(\frac{H_{HS}}{H_{MS}}\right)$	$\Delta \ln\left(\frac{W_{HS}}{W_{MS}}\right)$	$\Delta \ln\left(\frac{BS_{MS}}{BS_{LS}}\right)$	$\Delta \ln\left(\frac{H_{MS}}{H_{LS}}\right)$	$\Delta \ln\left(\frac{W_{MS}}{W_{LS}}\right)$
Panel B						
$\Delta K_{ICT}/VA$	34.09**	30.30**	3.787	−2.698	−5.691	2.993
	(13.52)	(12.56)	(3.152)	(7.475)	(6.894)	(4.922)
$\Delta K_{NICT}/VA$	−0.0739	−0.385	0.311	0.820*	0.601	0.219
	(0.792)	(0.674)	(0.339)	(0.454)	(0.480)	(0.384)
$\Delta \ln(VA)$	−0.0741	−0.0806	0.00658	−0.360***	−0.288***	−0.0721
	(0.146)	(0.119)	(0.0728)	(0.0886)	(0.0879)	(0.0734)
Constant	0.000340	0.152	−0.151	1.457***	1.393***	0.0637
	(0.355)	(0.343)	(0.0930)	(0.205)	(0.187)	(0.108)
Observations	140	140	140	140	140	140
R-squared		0.056	0.368	0.808	0.715	0.730
Country FE	Yes	Yes	Yes	Yes	Yes	Yes
Financial and postal	No	No	No	No	No	No

Robust standard errors in parentheses
*** $p<0.01$, ** $p<0.05$, * $p<0.1$
Dependent variable are the 1980–2005 relative log changes in relative wage bill share, relative hours worked, and relative wage. Coefficients are estimated by 2SLS. The instrument is the ICT over value added for the US in 1980. Robust standard errors in parenthesis. Regressions weighted by industry's 1980 share of each country's employment. Panel A: all industries, Panel B: all industries except financial and postal

5 Conclusions

In this paper we investigate whether there is wage polarization trends at work in Europe. In particular we investigate the trends of unconditional wages as well as the conditional impact of technology on wages, in such a way testing the routinization explanation. We produce a industry level analysis, and we make use of the EU KLEMS aggregate industry data, as in Michaels et al. (2014).

We show that unconditional wages do not polarize in the period 1980–2005. As for conditional (on technology) wage polarization, we use as technological measure the ICT intensity, for which we provide interesting descriptive evidence concerning trends by country and by sector, in the period 1980–2005. We point out that there is evidence of the impact of ICT intensity on polarization of hours worked, while the evidence on the relation between wage polarization and ICT is much weaker. Further, we show that when excluding the financial and postal sectors, the polarization of wages disappear completely. Results are robust to an instrumental variable analysis, to account for endogeneity issues.

Acknowledgments We thank Carlo Dell'Aringa, Nicole Fortin, Thomas Lemieux, Marco Leonardi, Elisabetta Magnani, Raul Ramos, for their suggestions, and the participants to seminars held at Cattolica University (MILLS Seminar, Milan), OFCE-Science Po (POLHIA meeting, Paris), CeLEG-Luiss (Rome), Padova, ECINEQ conference (Catania, 2011), AIEL conference (Milan, 2011), SIE conference (Rome), Royal Economic Society (Cambridge, 2012), Barcelona (UB), Cagliari, Napoli Partenope.

References

Autor D, Levy F, Murnane R (2003) The skill content of recent technological change: an empirical exploration. Q J Econ 118:1279–1333

Autor D, Katz L, Kearney M (2006) The polarization of the US labor market. Am Econ Rev 96:189–194

Goos M, Manning A, Salomons A (2009) Job polarization in Europe. Am Econ Rev 99:58–63

Goos M, Manning A, Salomons A (2010) Explaining Job Polarization in Europe: The Roles of Technology and Globalization. Technical report, Katholieke Universiteit Leuven Working Paper, May, revise and resubmit to the American Economic Review

Michaels G, Natraj A, Van Reenen J (2014) Has ICT polarized skill demand? Evidence from eleven countries over 25 years. Rev Econ Stat 96(1): 60–77. ISSN 0034-6535

O'Mahony M, Timmer MP (2009) Output, input and productivity measures at the industry level: the EU KLEMS database. Econ J 119:F374–F403

Sovereign Risk, Monetary Policy and Fiscal Multipliers: A Structural Model-Based Assessment

Alberto Locarno, Alessandro Notarpietro, and Massimiliano Pisani

Abstract This paper briefly reviews the literature on fiscal multipliers and then presents results for the Italian economy obtained by simulating a dynamic general equilibrium model that allows for the possibility (a) that the zero lower bound may be binding and (b) that the initial public debt-to-GDP ratio may affect the financing conditions of the public and private sectors (sovereign risk channel). The results are the following. First, the public consumption multiplier is in general less than 1. Second, it goes above 1 only under extremely strong assumptions, namely the constancy of the monetary policy rate for an exceptionally long period (at least 5 years) and full time-coincidence between the fiscal and the monetary stimuli. Third, when the sovereign risk channel is active the government consumption multiplier is much lower. Fourth, in all cases tax multipliers are lower than government consumption multipliers. Finally, we make a tentative assessment of the fiscal consolidation measures enacted in Italy in 2011–2012: the evidence is that the impact on GDP was much weaker than the IMF had expected.

1 Introduction

Until the 2007 financial crisis there was a broad consensus that discretionary fiscal policy was ineffective in stabilizing aggregate demand and fighting recessions. This position was justified by the fact that the lags in implementing fiscal policy were typically too long for it to successfully combat cyclical downturns; and it was reinforced by the econometric evidence that the fiscal multiplier was generally low, especially when the fiscal stimulus was ultimately tax-financed. The crisis shattered

A. Locarno • A. Notarpietro • M. Pisani (✉)
Modeling and forecasting Division, Bank of Italy, via Nazionale 91, 00184 Rome, Italy
e-mail: alberto.locarno@bancaditalia.it; alessandro.notarpietro@bancaditalia.it; massimiliano.pisani@bancaditalia.it

L. Paganetto (ed.), *Wealth, Income Inequalities, and Demography*,
DOI 10.1007/978-3-319-05909-9_7,

these beliefs. When monetary policy interest rates hit the dreaded zero lower bound in several countries, it became abundantly clear that the axiom of the ineffectiveness of discretionary fiscal policy was incorrect.

This paper reconsiders the effectiveness of fiscal policy as a demand-management tool, evaluating the fiscal multiplier under various macroeconomic conditions. The question is whether an increase in government consumption leads to more than a one-for-one increase in output,[1] with special attention to the reasons for supposing that the fiscal multiplier is higher in Depression-like circumstances and to the potential importance of the initial stock of public-sector debt. Our contribution is twofold. First, we survey the main theories on the size of the fiscal multiplier and discuss the empirical evidence for and against the competing views on the effectiveness of government spending. Then, using the Bank of Italy's dynamic stochastic general equilibrium (DSGE) model, we estimate the fiscal multiplier in Italy under differing assumptions concerning the monetary policy stance, the financing of the fiscal expansion and the role of sovereign risk.

We are mainly concerned with the short-term impact of fiscal expansions, but we also give an assessment of their long-term effects. Our main conclusions are the following. First, short-run fiscal multipliers are typically less than 1; in particular, tax multipliers are lower than public consumption multipliers. The latter come closer to 1 if a large share of households are liquidity-constrained. Second, public consumption multipliers are substantially greater than 1 only under highly constrictive assumptions, i.e. the constancy of the monetary policy rate for an exceptionally long period (at least 5 years in our simulations) and full time-coincidence between the fiscal and monetary stimuli. Third, under conditions similar to those now prevailing in the euro area, in countries with high public debt the stimulus produces a deterioration of the public finances and hence a rapid increase in the sovereign risk premium, which in turn substantially reduces the multiplier and the effectiveness of fiscal policy. Fourth, and symmetrically, the short-run contractionary effects of fiscal consolidation can be mitigated by a lowering of the risk premium.

The rest of the paper is organized as follows. Section 2 reviews the literature on fiscal multipliers and the related empirical evidence. Section 3 presents the model and elaborates on model calibration. Section 4 illustrates the simulation exercises and shows the results for fiscal multipliers under different macroeconomic scenarios. Section 5 concludes.

[1]Government spending is treated as pure waste in the analysis, in order to focus on the pure macroeconomic effects of fiscal policy as a determinant of aggregate demand in the short run. So it does not directly affect households' welfare or firm's productivity.

2 Theory and Evidence on the Effects of Government Spending

Government spending can boost economic activity only if it increases the employment of labour: as the capital stock cannot instantaneously adjust and technical progress is unresponsive to fiscal stimulus, in the short run output can increase only if more hours of labour are used in production. Thus, the value of the fiscal multiplier is closely linked to the effect of government spending on number of hours worked, though the channels posited differ according to whether the perspective is Keynesian or Neoclassical (i.e. real-business cycle). The value of the fiscal multiplier depends on (1) the duration of the stimulus; (2) how the budget slippage is financed; (3) whether the monetary policy responds or not (e.g. because the binding zero lower bound (ZLB) keeps the policy rate well above the desired level); (4) the country's initial conditions (i.e. the volume of resources idles due to lack of aggregate demand and the size of the public debt). Each of these factors must be taken properly into account in order to derive a reliable assessment of the macroeconomic impact of a change in the discretional component of government spending.

2.1 *Neoclassical Approaches*

In the neoclassical paradigm, a debt-financed increase in government purchases—unexpected but known immediately to be permanent—has a negative wealth effect on households, related to the expected payment of higher taxes in the future. Individuals respond by reducing consumption and leisure, as long as both are normal goods.[2] Because the increase in the labour input shifts the marginal product schedule for capital upward, investment rises and remains higher than in the no-stimulus scenario; it stops increasing only when the pre-shock capital-labour ratio is restored. In response to the jump in labour supply, the real wage declines and the rental rate of capital increases symmetrically; these factor-price movements are temporary, however, and the accumulation of capital eventually restores the original situation. According to Baxter and King (1993), the long-run fiscal multiplier is 1.16, corresponding to a 0.2 percentage-point decrease in consumption and a 0.3-point increase in investment[3]; welfare is unambiguously lower, as the representative agent consumes less and works more. When the increase in government spending is

[2]The most-cited reference on this regard is Baxter and King (1993). The numbers for the fiscal multipliers quoted in this section refer to their paper. Under fairly general conditions, there is no difference between a debt-financed and a tax-financed fiscal stimulus, provided the latter is based on lump-sum taxes. Baxter and King (1993) consider a fiscal expansion financed by lump-sum taxes.

[3]As for the change in government spending, variations in consumption and investment are measured in terms of units of output.

temporary, the results are sharply different.[4] As before, agents, who suffer a negative wealth shock, save and work more; now, however, investment falls, due to the increased government absorption of resources. On impact, output increases, though less than in the previous case. After T years, when public spending is back to the pre-stimulus level, investment goes above its long-run level and gradually declines thereafter; consumption and leisure remain below the steady-state equilibrium level and so does output. Eventually, all variables revert to their steady-state level and the original equilibrium is restored. When the fiscal stimulus is withdrawn, output falls below the pre-shock level, reducing the growth rate of the economy, and stays there indefinitely.

Government purchases financed by distortionary taxes have a radically different effect, lessening rather than expanding output. The mechanism is as follows. First, the increase in tax rates creates a gap between marginal productivity and (net) factor compensation and so reduces individuals' incentives to work and invest. Second, the fall in labour supply and capital accumulation compresses the tax base and calls for higher tax rates to balance the budget. Third, the heavier tax burden depresses output even more and forces the government to procure additional revenues. The resulting downward spiral drive output well below the pre-shock level. According to Baxter and King (1993), the fiscal multiplier may go as low as −2.5, implying that private-sector spending is completely crowded out and tax distortions discourage work and investment.

In the case of a tax-financed fiscal "stimulus" that lasts for T years, temporarily low after-tax factor rewards induce households and firms to increase leisure and to postpone investment. Output declines and remains below baseline for as long as the measure is in effect. When the "stimulus" ends (and tax rates return to their normal level), hours worked and capital accumulation immediately increase, pushing output slightly above baseline. Eventually, the initial equilibrium is restored. To summarize, the neoclassical theory provides three main insights: (1) permanent changes in government purchases have a multiplier greater than 1[5]; (2) temporary fiscal stimulus is less effective, even in terms of the impact multiplier, which tends to be less than 1[6]; (3) financing decisions are crucial, as they can not only reduce the size of the multiplier but even change its sign.

2.2 *Keynesian Approaches*

Keynesian analysis focuses on situations in which the binding constraint on production and employment is aggregate demand. The essential policy implication is that

---

[4]Once again it is assumed that the increase in government spending is unexpected but that it is immediately known to last for T years.

[5]A short-run multiplier greater than 1 is also possible if the labour supply is highly elastic.

[6]The finding that temporary stimulus is less effective than permanent is not trivial. Barro (1981) and Hall (1980) reach opposite conclusions.

any increase in aggregate spending, whatever the source, will make induce firms to expand production and draw workers into employment without requiring any change in wages or prices. Under the assumptions that (1) the economy is closed, (2) there is no capital, (3) monetary policy does not respond to the fiscal stimulus, and (4) government spending is debt-financed, then the multiplier corresponding to a permanent increase in government purchases is equal to the reciprocal of the marginal propensity to save. Allowing for foreign trade or for a monetary policy response reduces the size of the output expansion; taking capital accumulation into account has the opposite effect. Even if the fiscal stimulus is tax-financed, the multiplier remains positive and large, as the Haavelmo theorem shows.[7] If instead it is temporary, the size remains the same but it falls to zero as soon as the government stops spending. Accordingly, a temporary fiscal stimulus simply shifts aggregate demand from one period to another: first it provides a boost to growth, then it subtracts from it.

New Keynesian models generate predictions that are in between those consistent with the neoclassical and the Keynesian theories. Since New Keynesian models add sticky prices and other frictions to the real business cycle theory, neoclassical features tend to mute the Keynesian multiplier. Galí et al. (2007) show, however, that the traditional Keynesian predictions can be restored if two ingredients are added, namely: (1) a sufficiently high proportion of rule-of-thumb consumers, which helps by increasing the marginal propensity to consume[8]; and (2) an elastic labour supply, which makes workers willing to offer as many hours as firms demand.[9] Both assumptions, however, ultimately make the models heavily dependent on non-optimizing behavior and so are not entirely appealing.

2.3 ZLB, Hysteresis and (Other) Initial Conditions

Monetary policy ordinarily reacts to demand shocks that increase output and drive inflation up; thus in normal times the value of the fiscal multiplier is low, as the fiscal

[7]See Haavelmo (1945).

[8]Rule-of-thumb consumers are non-Ricardian. They consume just what they earn, regardless of the impact of government spending on the inter-temporal budget constraint. The larger the share of these non-optimizing agents, the smaller the (negative) impact of wealth effects on consumption and the higher the multiplier.

[9](u_l) must be equal to the (real) wage rate (w) times the marginal utility of consumption (u_c), i.e. $u_l = wu_c$. Households' labour-supply decision is driven by the intra-temporal equilibrium condition, which states that the marginal utility of leisure (u) must be equal to the (real) wage rate (w) times the marginal utility of consumption (u), i.e. u wu. Because of the negative wealth effect of additional government spending, consumption falls and its marginal utility increases; to restore the equilibrium, either leisure has to diminish (i.e. hours worked have to increase) and/or the real wage has to fall. In the standard Neo-classical (i.e. real business cycle model) both things happen. By preventing the real wage to change, all the adjustment is born by the labour supply, that accordingly has to increase more, boosting the output response to a fiscal stimulus.

stimulus is largely offset by the response of the central bank. In severely depressed economies, in which the policy interest rate is well above the desired level because of the zero lower bound (ZLB), this is no longer the case. A stream of the literature has recently resumed the Keynesian argument that government spending is likely to boost aggregate demand much more substantially in recession than in expansion, especially when the monetary policy rate is stuck at the ZLB (see Christiano et al. (2011), Eggertsson (2001) and Woodford (2011), among others). The sequence is as follows. When the ZLB is strictly binding, an increase in government spending leads to a rise in output, marginal costs and expected inflation; with the nominal interest rate stuck at zero, higher expected inflation decreases the real interest rate, which stimulates private spending; the increase in spending leads to a further rise in output, marginal cost, and expected inflation and a further decline in the real interest rate. The net result is a large rise in output: the increase in government consumption counteracts the deflationary spiral associated with the ZLB state. The value of the government-spending multiplier depends on how long the ZLB is expected to be binding. Christiano et al. (2011) also respond to the practical objection that using fiscal policy to counteract a contraction associated with the ZLB state is not feasible, as spending increases are subject to long lags. They argue that the case for fiscal stimulus while the constraint binds applies only where the increased government purchases will be terminated as soon as the constraint ceases to bind.[10] Christiano et al. (2011) also provide estimates of the size of the fiscal multiplier, obtained with a DSGE model: assuming government spending that lasts for 12 quarters and a constant nominal interest rate, the impact multiplier is roughly 1.6 and reaches a peak value of about 2.3. However, the high estimates of the spending multiplier implicitly depend on the assumption that non-standard monetary policy measures cannot stimulate aggregate demand and prevent a deflationary spiral.

Another possible factor is hysteresis, especially in the labour market. The concept of hysteresis, borrowed by economists from its original application to physical systems, is that transitory causes may have permanent effects. First used by Blanchard and Summers (1986), it has been revived by DeLong and Summers (2012), who argue that in a depressed economy hysteresis is important and once it is taken into account, the impact of additional government purchases on output can become so strong as to be self-financing. They define a depressed economy as one in which many workers are jobless for an extended period of time, undermining both their skills and their morale. A depressed economy is marked by low investment, slow if any accumulation of capital, and little entrepreneurial exploration. These factors can affect potential output, which means that a temporary shortage of aggregate demand may permanently reduce aggregate supply. Any policy that averts this outcome is therefore worth being pursued; in particular, a temporary increase in government spending can not only raise output significantly and help end the

[10]Woodford (2011) adds an additional condition, namely that the tax increase required to finance the budget deficit also lasts only as long as the constraint binds.

recession but can also ensure permanent output gains at no financial cost.[11] As Blanchard and Leigh (2013) note, hysteresis characterizes the transmission of fiscal impulses in general and is particularly marked during severe downturns.

Besides the business cycle, other initial conditions also matter, in particular the public finances and debt. Blanchard (1990) proposes a model in which the size of the fiscal multiplier may be inversely related to the ratio of debt to GDP. A budget consolidation affects expectations, hence consumption, in two ways. First, the inter-temporal redistribution of taxes from the future to the present is likely to increase the tax burden of current taxpayers and reduce their consumption. This is the conventional effect, and its strength depends on how far the economy departs from the benchmark of Ricardian equivalence. Second, by taking measures today, the government avoids larger, more disruptive adjustments in the future, which averts the danger of low output and thus increases consumption. Third, consolidation may be associated with a substantial reduction of uncertainty, which should decrease precautionary saving and lower the option value of waiting by consumers to buy durables and by firms to invest. The last two mechanisms are unconventional and may explain non-Keynesian effects of tighter fiscal policies. Symmetrically, if an increase in government purchases is perceived as threatening the sustainability of the public finances, it may have very little or even a negative effect on output. Sutherland (1997) presents a model that shows how the power of fiscal policy to affect consumption can vary with the level of the public debt. At moderate levels of debt, fiscal policy has the standard Keynesian effects: current consumers discount future taxes because they may not live until the next debt stabilization. But when debt reaches extreme values, current consumers know that they are very likely to be present for the next stabilization programme, and in these situations a fiscal deficit can have a contractionary effect on consumer spending. Nickel and Tudyka (2013) provide empirical evidence on the negative correlation between the fiscal multiplier and the level of public debt. As indebtedness rises the private sector has increasingly Ricardian features: for low debt ratios, consumers and firms ignore the government's inter-temporal budget constraint, but for higher debt ratios they appear to internalize the tax burden that is inevitably associated with an expansion of government spending.

2.4 *Empirical Evidence on the Size of the Fiscal Multiplier*

2.4.1 Pre-Crisis Estimates of the Multiplier

Until recently, it was widely agreed that the government-spending multiplier was not much greater than 1. Hall (2009) holds that in the US the multiplier is between

[11] DeLong and Summers (2012) provide an example: an incremental $1.00 of government spending raises future output permanently by $0.015 if (1) the fiscal multiplier is 1.5; (2) the average income tax rate is 33 %; (3) the real interest rate on long-term government debt is fixed at 1 %.

0.7 and 1.0, while Ramey (2011a) estimates it at closer to 1.2.[12] In both studies the estimates are obtained by using structural VAR models, which suffer from serious identification problems.[13] Moreover, studies using aggregate data measure what happens on average when government spending changes: to assess the effect of a deficit-financed stimulus, one needs either to focus on periods in which taxes did not change significantly or to control for tax effects, which is no simple matter, given that the estimates of tax multipliers range from −0.5 to −5.0.[14]

Similar evidence is obtained with DSGE models: in standard new-Keynesian models the government-spending multiplier can be somewhat above or below 1 depending on the exact specification of agents' preferences, while in frictionless real-business-cycle models this multiplier is typically less than 1.[15] Accordingly, due to its limited fire-power, lags in implementation and financing costs, until just a few years ago fiscal policy was viewed as a poor tool for aggregate demand management. Things have changed since the 2007–2008 financial crisis, owing among other things to the perceived impotence of monetary policy, stuck at the ZLB.

2.4.2 Recessions, Depressions and the ZLB

The evidence on the size of the multiplier when monetary policy is at the ZLB derives both from calibrated DSGE models and from more standard (and data-based) econometric techniques. Christiano et al. (2011) use a DSGE model whose parameters match the response of ten US macro variables to (1) a neutral technology shock, (2) a monetary impulse, and (3) a capital-embodied technology shock. They

---

[12]Leigh et al. (2010) present estimates for 15 developed countries, including the US. However, they consider not the standard government-purchases multiplier but average multipliers, referring to fiscal packages consisting of a mixture of transfers, taxes and purchases. They find that on average a fiscal consolidation equal to 1 percentage point of GDP reduces output after 2 years by half a point and increases the unemployment rate by 0.3 points.

[13]The critical issue is to distinguish variations in government spending that represent real changes in the fiscal policy stance from those due to economic events. One solution is to focus on military buildups, on the assumption that this type of spending is the least likely to respond to economic events. Nevertheless, as Ramey (2011b) points out, there is always the possibility that the events that lead to these buildups—e.g. the onset of World War II or the Cold War—could have other effects on the economy, apart from those on government spending, that could bias the estimates of the multiplier. For example, during World War II a surge of patriotism could have expanded the labour supply by more than would have been predicted by economic incentives alone, increasing the multiplier. By contrast, rationing and capacity constraints could have held it down.

An additional factor complicating identification is that government spending shocks are most often anticipated, implying that the econometrician does not have all the information that economic agents may have. That is, individual agents' expectations may not be based just on past information from the variables in the empirical model. So errors of expectation or forecasting cannot be the residuals of the econometrician's model and the shocks to be studied may not be forecast errors and may be non-fundamental. See Ramey (2011b) and Perotti (2011).

[14]Ramey (2011b) lists a number of studies dealing with this issue.

[15]See e.g. the evidence in Cogan et al. (2010) and Coenen et al. (2012).

find, first, that when the central bank follows a Taylor rule the government spending multiplier is less than 1, in line with most of the literature; second, when the nominal interest rate does not respond to the rise in spending the multiplier is much larger[16]; third, the value of the multiplier depends critically on how much of the government spending comes during the period when the nominal interest rate is constant. The evidence cited by Christiano et al. (2011) has been criticized for improperly linearizing around the steady-state for a case study—the effects of fiscal policy when interest rates are at the ZLB—that is necessarily some distance from the steady-state. According to Braun et al. (2012), this mistake accounts for about half of the estimated size of the fiscal multiplier. Auerbach and Gorodnichenko (2012) use regime-switching models and find large differences in the values of spending multipliers between recessions and expansions: the response in expansions never rises above 1 and soon falls below 0, whereas in recessions it rises steadily to peak at more than 2.5 after 20 quarters.[17] Some aspects of their analysis are unconvincing, however, and cast a shadow over their results: first, the peak of the GDP response is reached 20 periods after the shock, at the end of the forecasting window, when output is apparently gaining further momentum; second, the government shock is still 1 percentage point of GDP higher than in the baseline after 20 periods, suggesting that the shock is permanent rather than transitory; third, the output and tax responses in expansions are quite implausible: at period 4, with taxes 1.5 percentage point of GDP below and government spending 2 points above baseline, output is by and large unchanged.

The evidence in Ramey (2012) does not support the thesis that the multiplier is higher when there is slack in the economy or when interest rates are at the ZLB. For the period 1933–1951, characterized by very low interest rates and very high unemployment rates, she estimates the following regression on monthly data:

$$\frac{\Delta Y_t}{Y_{t-1}} = \beta_0 + \beta_1 \frac{\Delta G_t}{Y_{t-1}} + \beta_2 \frac{\Delta Y_{t-1}}{Y_{t-2}} + I_t \left[\beta_3 + \beta_4 \frac{\Delta G_t}{Y_{t-1}} + \beta_5 \frac{\Delta Y_{t-1}}{Y_{t-2}} \right] + \varepsilon_t$$

where Y_t is output, G_t government spending and I_t a dummy variable equal to 1 in periods with high unemployment rates (i.e. larger than 7 %) and zero otherwise. Unlike Auerbach and Gorodnichenko (2012), she finds that $\beta_4 \simeq 0$. Evidence reported in Ramey (2012) is supported by Owyang et al. (2013), who estimate essentially the same model but use (1) a longer sample period and (2) a "news" variable (viz. the change in the expected present value of government spending in response to military events) rather than G_t: the multiplier is always below unity and, if anything, is slightly lower during the high unemployment state. Owyang et al.

[16]For example, for a 12-quarter increase in government spending the impact multiplier is roughly 1.6, with a peak value of about 2.3.

[17]Note that none of the recessions in their sample (except possibly the last) qualifies as a depression, in which the policy interest rate is at (or close to) the zero lower-bound.

(2013) estimate the same model also on Canadian data, finding this time results that are closer to those of obtained by Auerbach and Gorodnichenko (2012).

More recently, an article by Blanchard and Leigh in the IMF's October 2012 World Economic Outlook, presents evidence that the fiscal multiplier in the advanced economies may be considerably greater than had been assumed when fiscal austerity was instituted in most economies in 2010.[18] Using a sample including 28 advanced economies, Blanchard and Leigh regress the forecasting error for real GDP growth during 2010–2011 on forecasts of fiscal consolidation for 2010–2011 that were made in early 2010. Under rational expectations, and assuming that the forecasting model is the right one, the coefficient for planned fiscal consolidation should be 0. Blanchard and Leigh instead find it to be large, negative, and significant: the baseline estimate suggests that a planned consolidation of 1 % of GDP is associated with a growth forecasting error of about 1 percentage point (the estimates range from 0.4 to 1.2 points). As the multipliers underlying the growth forecasts made in early 2010 were about 0.5, these results indicate that the multipliers have actually been between 0.9 and 1.7. Blanchard and Leigh's study drew a good deal of attention and criticism. First, the estimates seem to depend significantly on the results for Greece and Germany. Second, the results were presented as general, but are limited to the specific time period chosen: the 2010 forecasts of deficits are not good predictors of errors in growth forecasts for 2010 or 2011 when the years are analyzed individually; and the 2011 forecasts are not good predictors of anything.[19] Third, the fiscal consolidation efforts assumed by the IMF in early 2010 were smaller than the measures actually implemented. Fourth, the correlation between growth forecast errors and changes in the fiscal stance breaks down when increases in sovereign bond yields are included in the regression.[20] Fifth, the analysis does not distinguish between budget expansions (in place in 2010) and fiscal tightenings (mostly enacted in 2011): usually the former are temporary, while the latter are permanent. The European Commission (2012a) estimates the same regression as the IMF for consolidating countries only and finds no correlation between growth forecast errors and changes in the fiscal stance. Sixth, multipliers differ greatly across countries and take different values depending on the credibility of the consolidation effort and on the response of sovereign risk premia.[21]

Blanchard and Leigh (2013) respond to these criticisms partially but not fully. They argue that their results are extremely robust and in particular do not depend on the inclusion of Germany and Greece; moreover, they assert that it is no surprise that estimating their model in different periods yields inconsistent results, as economic theory itself predicts that the fiscal multiplier depends on business cycle conditions

[18]In this case the fiscal multiplier does not refer to government purchases but measures the output response to all the fiscal consolidation measures on both the revenue and the expenditure sides adopted in the sample countries.

[19]On these two points, see Financial Times (2012).

[20]On the third and fourth point, see European Commission (2012a).

[21]See European Central Bank (2012).

and on the monetary policy stance; finally, they posit that sovereign risk premia respond to growth prospects, not to the fiscal stance, and accordingly consolidation measures, by weakening aggregate demand and economic activity, raise the cost of borrowing for governments and increase the multiplier.

2.4.3 Hysteresis

The evidence on hysteresis is scanty at best. With respect to DeLong and Summers (2012) it is worth stressing that while the magnitude of the hysteresis effects they assume—just $0.015 for each dollar of additional temporary government purchases—may seem small, actually it is not. In their example, the gains from fiscal stimulus are permanent and their present value, with a discount rate equal to the real interest rate they use for US long-term bonds, is 1.5, which is larger than the shock itself.

2.4.4 Fiscal Multipliers in High-Debt Countries and the Sovereign Risk Channel

The evidence on the relevance of a country's debt/deficit position to the size of the fiscal multiplier is mostly casual. The sovereign debt crisis has clearly shown that the leeway for governments in setting the fiscal policy stance is limited: any action that is perceived as jeopardizing debt sustainability immediately triggers a punitive response by the financial markets. In particular, for countries with dangerously weak finances it is to be expected that any attempt to increase public expenditure may spark a jump in the risk premium on their debt, reducing the output response to the fiscal stimulus, while the contrary is likely to happen for fiscal consolidation attempts.

The studies of Perotti (1999) and Corsetti et al. (2012b) are worth mentioning, however. Perotti (1999) lays out a simple model where government expenditure shocks have a positive, Keynesian correlation with private consumption in normal times and a negative, non-Keynesian correlation in bad times. Symmetrically, tax shocks have a negative, Keynesian correlation in normal times and a positive, non-Keynesian correlation in bad times. What is needed to rationalize state-dependent fiscal multipliers of the type described above is a model in which the correlation between private consumption and shocks to government expenditure and revenues changes, depending on the initial conditions. The empirical model uses a 30-year panel of 19 OECD member countries and distinguishes good periods and bad periods by the size of the cyclically-adjusted public debt and the probability of re-election of the incumbent government. The empirical evidence supports the thesis that expenditure shocks have Keynesian effects at low levels of debt and non-Keynesian effects at high levels. The evidence of a similar switch in the effects of tax shocks is less strong. Corsetti et al. (2012b), on a sample of 17 OECD countries for the period 1975–2008, investigate the determinants of government spending multipliers, inquiring into the way in which the fiscal transmission mechanism depends on the economic environment. The conditioning factors considered are on the exchange rate regime, the level of the public debt and deficit, and the occurrence of a financial crisis. They obtain four principal findings: (1) multipliers are virtually 0 under normal conditions; (2) the exchange rate regime matters; (3) the fiscal multiplier increases markedly during financial crises, rising from 2.3 on impact to 2.9 at peak; (4) fiscal strains may take the multiplier into negative territory (the cumulative effects over the first 2 years are strongly negative but weaken over longer horizons). The study is subject to the usual caveat about cross-country studies with small samples. Moreover, the finding on the impact of financial crises may be due to reverse causality; that is, it may simply reflect the fact that in times of financial crisis both output and government spending fall. Finally, the response to a crisis should differ substantially internationally, as larger countries have more fiscal leeway for counter-cyclical policies.

While it is clear that in some circumstances an increase in spending (or a reduction in taxation) may not only boost aggregate demand but also raise borrowing costs, thus lowering the fiscal multiplier, the evidence on this link is limited. Most empirical studies focus on countries with negligible default risk and postulate linear relationships, as if the initial stock of public debt were irrelevant. For the United States Laubach (2009) finds that a 1-percentage-point increase in the projected ratio of deficit (debt) to GDP raises long-term yields on Treasury bonds by 20–30 (3–4) basis points. Gruber and Kamin (2012) obtain similar results for OECD countries but find no support for the hypothesis that changes in fiscal balances affect yields through their effect on perceived default risk. Attinasi et al. (2010), for the pre-2010 period, estimate even lower responses of euro-area sovereign spreads to anticipated changes in government deficit and debt. Belhocine and Dell'Erba (2013) find a greater elasticity of sovereign risk premia to public finance conditions; for 26 emerging countries they estimate the response of the yield to maturity of sovereign bonds to changes in the primary budget balance (ratio to GDP), allowing the response to depend on the level of the debt. They find that for countries whose debt is greater than 45 % of GDP, a 1-point worsening of the primary balance from its debt-stabilising level increases the cost of borrowing by 53.69 basis points.

3 The Model

We have seen the findings of the previous literature on fiscal multipliers. In particular, their size depends on the monetary policy stance and the response of credit spreads to changes in the public debt and deficit. To further assess the role of these channels, we will show the fiscal multipliers obtained by simulating a DSGE model of the Italian economy. Its main features are illustrated here.

We model a world economy composed of three regions: Italy, the rest of the euro area (REA) and the rest of the world (RW). In each region there is a continuum of symmetric households and symmetric firms. Italian households are indexed by $j \in [0; s]$, REA households by $j^* \in (s; S]$, RW households by $j^{**} \in (S; 1]$.[22]

Italy and the REA have the same currency and monetary authority, which sets the nominal interest rate according to euro-area-wide variables. The presence of the RW allows us to assess the role of the nominal exchange rate and extra-EA trade in transmitting shocks. In each region there are households and firms. Households consume a final good, which is a composite of intermediate non-tradable and tradable goods. The latter are either domestically produced or imported. Households trade a one-period nominal bond, denominated in euro. They also own domestic firms and use another final good (different from the final consumption good) to invest in physical capital. The latter is rented to domestic firms in a perfectly competitive market. All households supply differentiated labour services to domestic firms and act as wage setters in monopolistically competitive labour markets by charging a markup over their marginal rate of substitution between consumption and leisure.

On the production side, there are perfectly competitive firms that produce the two final goods (consumption goods and investment goods) and monopolistic firms that produce the intermediate goods. The two final goods are sold domestically and are produced combining all available intermediate goods by a constant-elasticity-of-substitution (CES) production function. The two resulting bundles can differ in composition. Intermediate tradable and non-tradable goods are produced by combining domestic capital and labour, which are assumed to be mobile across sectors. Intermediate tradable goods can be sold both domestically and abroad. Because intermediate goods are differentiated, firms have market power and restrict output in order to create excess profits. We also assume that the markets for tradable goods are segmented, so that firms can set three different prices, one for each market. Like other DSGE models of the euro area (e.g. Christoffel et al. (2008) and Gomes et al. (2012)), our model includes adjustment costs on real and nominal variables, ensuring that consumption, production and prices respond gradually to shocks. On the real side, habit preferences and quadratic costs prolong the adjustment of households' consumption and investment, respectively. On the nominal side, quadratic costs make wages and prices sticky.[23]

In the following section we describe in detail the fiscal policy setup (the public sector budget constraint and the sovereign spread), the monetary policy setup, and households' problem in the case of Italy. Similar equations, not reported to save on space, hold for other regions. The only exception is the equation for the spread, which holds for Italy alone.[24]

---

[22]The parameter s is the size of the Italian population, which is also equal to the number of firms in each Italian sector (final non-tradable, intermediate tradable and intermediate non-tradable). Similar assumptions hold for the REA and the RW.

[23]See Rotemberg (1982).

[24]The rest of the model is set out in the appendix.

3.1 The Fiscal Authority

Initially we report the budget constraint and the fiscal rule of the public sector, and subsequently the sovereign spread.

3.1.1 Budget Constraint and Fiscal Rule

Fiscal policy is set at the regional level. The government budget constraint is:

$$\left[\frac{B_{t+1}^{g}}{R_t^H} - B_t^g\right] = (1+\tau_t^c)P_{N,t}C_t^g + Tr_t - T_t \tag{1}$$

where $B_t^g \geq 0$ is nominal public debt. It takes the form of a one-period nominal bond issued in the EA market and paying the gross nominal interest rate R_t^H. The variable C_t^g represents government purchases of goods and services, $Tr_t > 0$ ($<$ 0) are lump-sum transfers to (lump-sum taxes on) households. Consistent with the empirical evidence, C_t^g is fully biased towards the intermediate non-tradable good. Hence it is multiplied by the corresponding price index $P_{N,t}$.[25]

We assume that the same tax rates apply to every household. Total government revenues T_t from distortionary taxation are given by the following identity:

$$T_t \equiv \int_0^s \left(\tau_t^\ell W_t(j) L_t(j) + \tau_t^k \left(R_t^k K_{t-1}(j) + \frac{\Pi_t^P}{s}\right) + \tau_t^c P_t C_t(j)\right) dj - \tau_t^c P_{N,t} C_t^g \tag{2}$$

where τ_t^ℓ is the tax rate on individual labor income $W_t(j) L_t(j)$, τ_t^k on capital income $R_t^k K_{t-1}(j) + \Pi_t^P/s$ and τ_t^c on consumption $C_t(j)$. The variable $W_t(j)$ represents the individual nominal wage, $L_t(j)$ is individual hours worked, R_t^k is the rental rate of existing physical capital stock $K_{t-1}(j)$, Π_t^P stands for dividends from ownership of domestic monopolistic firms (they are equally shared across households) and P_t is the price of the consumption bundle.

The government follows a fiscal rule defined on a single fiscal instrument that serves to bring the ratio of public debt to GDP, $b^g > 0$, into line with its target $\bar{b}^g$ and to limit the increase in the ratio of public deficit to GDP (b_t^g/b_{t-1}^g)[26]:

[25] See Corsetti and Mueller (2006, 2008).

[26] The definition of nominal GDP is:

$$GDP_t = P_t C_t + P_t^I I_t + P_{N,t} C_t^g + P_t^{EXP} EXP_t - P_t^{IMP} IMP_t \tag{3}$$

where P_t, P_t^I, P_t^{EXP}, P_t^{IMP} are prices of consumption, investment, exports and imports, respectively.

$$\frac{i_t}{i_{t-1}} = \left(\frac{b_t^g}{\bar{b}^g}\right)^{\phi_1} \left(\frac{b_t^g}{b_{t-1}^g}\right)^{\phi_2} \tag{4}$$

where i_t is one of the five fiscal instruments (three tax rates $(\tau_t^\ell, \tau_t^k, \tau_t^c)$ and the two expenditure items (C_t^g, Tr_t)). Parameters ϕ_1, ϕ_2 are less than 0 when the rule is defined on an expenditure item calling for a reduction in expenditures whenever the debt level is above target and/or there is a positive change in the debt. They are greater than 0 when the rule is on tax rates.

3.1.2 Sovereign Spread

The interest rate paid by the Italian government and Italian households is determined as a spread over the EA risk-free nominal interest rate (set by the ECB). In the spirit of Corsetti et al. (2012a) the spread reflects the default risk, and any policy measure that changes public-sector deficit and debt affects the sovereign risk premium (whose response depends, among other things, on the size of the outstanding debt). We make two additional assumptions: (1) after the initial adjustment, the spread returns to its pre-shock value: the reversion is gradual and is completed when the fiscal stimulus (or consolidation effort) terminates; (2) in case of permanent fiscal measures, households and firms do not fully anticipate the duration of the spread change.[27] These assumptions permit taking account, in our otherwise perfect-foresight framework, of the uncertainty surrounding the sustainability of public finances and the duration of the discretionary measures.

The assumption that even temporary changes in the fiscal stance affect the sovereign risk premium can be justified on the grounds that any deterioration or improvement in net borrowing pushes the economy closer to or further from the fiscal limit, i.e. the point at which taxes and spending can no longer adjust to stabilize debt and the government has no choice but to default on the debt: the closer the fiscal limit, the more likely it is that a recessionary shock will trigger a run on the sovereign debt.[28] The higher probability of default calls for an increase in the sovereign risk premium, which does not disappear until the stimulus is withdrawn and the economy is back to the original position.

Specifically, we formalize the spread as follows:

$$spread_t^H \equiv \begin{cases} f\left(b_t^g / b_{t-1}^g\right) \; for\; t = 1 \\ \rho * spread_{t-1}^H \; for\; t > 1 \end{cases} \tag{5}$$

where $b_t^g > 0$ is the Italian public debt-to-GDP ratio at the end of period t.

---

[27] This assumption is deliberately conservative, because it allows us to rule out large and counterfactual macroeconomic responses associated with perfect anticipation of permanent changes in the cost of borrowing. In this respect, the estimated contribution of the sovereign risk channel to our results should be taken as a lower bound.

[28] See for instance Leeper (2013).

As such, the (gross) interest rate R^H paid by the Italian government is:

$$R_t^H \equiv R_t * spread_t^H \tag{6}$$

where R_t is the (gross) risk-free nominal interest rate. The spread also affects the intertemporal choices of Italian households through the standard Euler equation, as reported later.

3.2 Monetary Authority

The monetary authority controls the short-term policy rate R_t according to a Taylor rule of the form:

$$\left(\frac{R_t}{\bar{R}}\right) = \left(\frac{R_{t-1}}{\bar{R}}\right)^{\rho_R} (\Pi_{EA,t})^{(1-\rho_R)\rho_\pi} \left(\frac{GDP_{EA,t}}{GDP_{EA,t-1}}\right)^{(1-\rho_R)\rho_{GDP}} \tag{7}$$

The parameter ρ_R $(0 < \rho_R < 1)$ captures inertia in interest rate setting, while the term $\bar{R}$ represents the steady state gross nominal policy rate. The parameters ρ_π and ρ_{GDP} are respectively the weights of the euro-area CPI inflation rate $(\Pi_{EA,t})$ and GDP $(GDP_{EA,t})$. The CPI inflation rate is a geometric average of CPI inflation rates in Italy and the REA (respectively Π_t and Π_t^*) with weights equal to the correspondent country size (as a share of the EA):

$$\Pi_{EA,t} \equiv (\Pi_t)^{\frac{s}{s+S}} \left(\Pi_t^*\right)^{\frac{S}{s+S}} \tag{8}$$

The EA GDP, $GDP_{EA,t}$, is the sum of the Italian and REA GDPs (respectively GDP_t and GDP_t^*):

$$GDP_{EA,t} \equiv GDP_t + rer_t * GDP_t^* \tag{9}$$

where rer_t is the bilateral real exchange rate between Italy and REA, defined as the ratio of REA to Italian consumer prices. In some simulations, the interest rate will be held constant at its steady-state value for several periods, instead of following the Taylor rule (7), which eventually kicks in. In this way we can assess the role of the monetary policy stance for the size of fiscal multipliers.

3.3 Households

Households' preferences are additively separable in consumption and labor effort. The generic Italian household j receives utility from consumption C and disutility from labor L. The expected value of the lifetime utility is:

$$E_0\left\{\sum_{t=0}^{\infty}\beta^t\left[\frac{(C_t(j)-hC_{t-1})^{1-\sigma}}{(1-\sigma)}-\frac{L_t(j)^{1+\tau}}{1+\tau}\right]\right\} \tag{10}$$

where E_0 denotes the expectation conditional on information set at date 0, β is the discount factor ($0 < \beta < 1$), $1/\sigma$ is the elasticity of intertemporal substitution ($\sigma > 0$) and $1/\tau$ is the labor Frisch elasticity ($\tau > 0$). The parameter h ($0 < h < 1$) represents external habit formation in consumption.

The budget constraint of household j is:

$$\begin{aligned}\frac{B_t(j)}{(1+R_t^H)} - B_{t-1}(j) \leq (1-\tau_t^k)\left(\Pi_t^P(j) + R_t^K K_{t-1}(j)\right) + \\ +(1-\tau_t^\ell)W_t(j)L_t(j) - (1+\tau_t^c)P_tC_t(j) - P_t^I I_t(j) \\ +Tr_t(j) - AC_t^W(j)\end{aligned}$$

As is commonly assumed in the literature, Italian households hold a one-period nominal bond, B_t, denominated in euro ($B_t > 0$ is a lending position). The short-term nominal rate R_t^H is paid at the beginning of period t and is known at time t.[29] We assume that government and private bonds are traded in the same international market. Households own all domestic firms and there is no international trade in claims on firms' profits. The variable Π_t^P includes profits accruing to the Italian households. The variable I_t is the investment bundle in physical capital and P_t^I the related price index, which differs from the consumer price index because the two bundles are different in composition.[30] Italian households accumulate physical capital K_t and rent it to domestic firms at the nominal rate R_t^k. The law of motion of capital accumulation is:

$$K_t(j) = (1-\delta)K_{t-1}(j) + \left(1 - AC_t^I(j)\right)I_t(j) \tag{11}$$

where δ is the depreciation rate. Adjustment cost on investment AC_t^I is:

$$AC_t^I(j) \equiv \frac{\phi_I}{2}\left(\frac{I_t(j)}{I_{t-1}(j)} - 1\right)^2, \phi_I > 0 \tag{12}$$

Finally, Italian households act as wage setters in a monopolistic competitive labor market. Each household j sets its nominal wage taking into account labor demand and adjustment costs AC_t^W on the nominal wage $W_t(j)$:

[29] A financial friction μ_t is introduced to guarantee that net asset positions follow a stationary process and the economy converge to a steady state. Revenues from financial intermediation are rebated in a lump-sum way to households in the REA. See Benigno (2009).

[30] For details see the appendix.

$$AC_t^W(j) \equiv \frac{\kappa_W}{2}\left(\frac{W_t(j)}{W_{t-1}(j)} - 1\right)^2 W_t L_t, \kappa_W > 0 \tag{13}$$

The costs are proportional to the per-capita wage bill of the overall economy, $W_t L_t$.

The sovereign risk channel (see Eq. (6)) affects households' choices via the interest rate R_H in the Euler equation (obtained by maximizing utility subject to the budget constraint with respect to bond holdings B_t):

$$(C_t(j) - hC_{t-1})^{-\sigma} = \beta E_t\left(R_t^H (C_{t+1}(j) - hC_t)^{-\sigma}\right) \tag{14}$$

The larger the spread, the higher the interest rate R_t^H and the greater the incentive for households to postpone consumption.

Similar relations hold in the rest of the euro area and the world, with two exceptions, in correspondence with two simplifying assumptions. First, the spreads paid by Italian households and government are rebated as a lump sum way to households in the REA. Second, neither the public sector nor the private sector in the REA and RW pay the spread on their borrowing. So what appears in the corresponding Euler equations is the riskless interest rate.

Finally, it is assumed that the bond traded by households and governments is in worldwide zero net supply. The implied market clearing condition is:

$$-B_t^g + \int_0^s B_t(j)\,dj - B_t^{g*} + \int_s^S B_t(j^*)\,dj^* - B_t^{g**} + \int_S^1 B_t(j^{**})\,dj^{**} = 0 \tag{15}$$

where $B_t^{g*}, B_t^{g**} > 0$ are respectively the borrowing of the REA and RW public sectors, and $B_t(j^*)$ and $B_t^{**}(j^{**})$ are respectively the per capita bond positions of their households.

3.4 Calibration

The model is calibrated at quarterly frequency. We set some parameter values so that steady-state ratios are consistent with the 2010 national accounts data, the latest and most complete available. For the remaining parameters we use previous studies and estimates.[31]

Table 1 gives the parameters that regulate preferences and technology. Parameters with "*" and "**" are related to the REA and the RW, respectively. Throughout we assume perfect symmetry between the REA and the RW, unless otherwise indicated. We assume that discount rates and elasticities of substitution have the

[31] Among others, see Forni et al. (2009, 2010a,b).

Table 1 Parametrization of Italy, the rest of the euro area and the rest of the world

Parameter	IT	REA	RW
Discount rate β	0.993	0.993	0.993
Intertemporal elasticity of substitution $1/\sigma$	1.0	1.0	1.0
Inverse of Frisch elasticity of labor supply τ	2.0	2.0	2.0
Habit h	0.6	0.6	0.6
Depreciation rate of (private and public) capital δ	0.025	0.025	0.025
Tradable intermediate goods			
Substitution between factors of production $\xi_T, \xi_T^*, \xi_T^{**}$	0.93	0.93	0.93
Bias towards capital $\alpha_T, \alpha_T^*, \alpha_T^{**}$	0.56	0.46	0.46
Non-tradable intermediate goods			
Substitution between factors of production $\xi_N, \xi_N^*, \xi_N^{**}$	0.93	0.93	0.93
Bias towards capital $\alpha_N, \alpha_N^*, \alpha_N^{**}$	0.53	0.43	0.43
Final consumption goods			
Substitution between domestic and imported goods $\phi_A, \phi_A^*, \phi_A^{**}$	1.50	1.50	1.50
Bias towards domestic tradable goods a_H, a_F^*, a_G^*	0.68	0.59	0.90
Substitution between domestic tradables and non-tradables $\rho_A, \rho_A^*, \rho_A^{**}$	0.50	0.50	0.50
Bias towards tradable goods a_T, a_T^*, a_T^{**}	0.68	0.50	0.50
Final investment goods			
Substitution between domestic and imported goods $\phi_E, \phi_E^*, \phi_E^{**}$	1.50	1.50	1.50
Bias towards domestic tradable goods υ_H, υ_F^*	0.50	0.49	0.90
Substitution between domestic tradables and non-tradables ρ_E, ρ_E^*	0.50	0.50	0.50
Bias towards tradable goods υ_T, υ_T^*	0.78	0.70	0.70

Note: *IT* = Italy; *REA* = rest of the euro area; *RW* = rest of the world

same value in all three regions. The discount factor β is set to 0.9927, so that the steady-state real interest rate is equal to 3.0 % on an annual basis. The value for the intertemporal elasticity of substitution, $1/\sigma$, is 1. The Frisch labor elasticity is set to 0.5. The depreciation rate of capital δ is set to 0.025. Habit is set to 0.6.

In the production functions of tradables and non-tradables, the elasticity of substitution between labor and capital is set to 0.93. The bias towards capital in the production function of tradables is set 0.56 in Italy and 0.46 in the REA and in the RW. The corresponding values in the production function of non-tradables are 0.53 and 0.43. In the final consumption and investment goods functions the elasticity of substitution between domestic and imported tradable is 1.5, that between tradables and non-tradables 0.5. In the consumption bundle the bias to the domestic tradeable is 0.68 in Italy, 0.59 in REA and 0.90 in RW. The bias towards the composite tradeable is 0.68 in Italy and 0.5 in REA and RW. For the investment basket, the bias towards the domestic tradable is 0.50 in Italy, 0.49 in REA and 0.90 in RW. The bias towards the composite tradable is 0.78 in Italy, 0.70 in REA and RW. The biases towards the domestically produced good and composite tradable good are chosen to match the import-to-GDP ratios of Italy and REA.

Table 2 reports gross markup values. In the Italian tradable and non-tradable sectors and in the Italian labour market the markup is set to 1.08, 1.30 and 1.60, respectively (the corresponding elasticities of substitution across varieties are set to

Table 2 Gross markups

	Markups and elasticities of substitution		
	Tradables	Non-tradables	Wages
IT	1.08 ($\theta_T = 13.32$)	1.30 ($\theta_N = 4.44$)	1.60 ($\psi = 2.65$)
REA	1.11 ($\theta_T^* = 10.15$)	1.24 ($\theta_N^* = 5.19$)	1.33 ($\psi^* = 4$)
RW	1.11 ($\theta_T^{**} = 10.15$)	1.24 ($\theta_N^{**} = 5.19$)	1.33 ($\psi^{**} = 4$)

Note: *IT* = Italy; *REA* = rest of the euro area; *RW* = rest of the world; source: OECD (2012)

Table 3 Real and nominal adjustment costs

Parameter	IT	REA	RW
Real adjustment costs			
Investment $\phi_I, \phi_I^*, \phi_I^{**}$	6.00	6.00	6.00
Households' financial net position $\phi_{b1,}\phi_{b2}$	0.00055, 0.00055	–	0.00055, 0.00055
Nominal adjustment costs			
Wages $\kappa_W, \kappa_W^*, \kappa_W^{**}$	200	200	200
Italian produced tradables $\kappa_H, k_H^*\ k_H^{**}$	300	300	50
REA produced tradables $\kappa_H, k_H^*\ k_H^{**}$	300	300	50
RW produced tradables $\kappa_H, k_H^*\ k_H^{**}$	50	50	300
Non-tradables $\kappa_N, \kappa_N^*, \kappa_N^{**}$	500	500	500

Note: *IT* = Italy; *REA* = rest of the euro area; *RW* = rest of the world

13.32, 4.44 and 2.65). In the REA these gross markups are respectively set to 1.11, 1.24 and 1.33 (the corresponding elasticities are set to 10.15, 5.19 and 4.00). Similar values are chosen for the corresponding parameters in the RW.

Table 3 gives the parameters that regulate the dynamics. Adjustment costs on investment change are set to 6. Nominal wage quadratic adjustment costs are set to 200. In the tradable sector, we set the nominal adjustment cost parameter to 300 for Italian tradables sold domestically and in REA; and to 50 for Italian goods sold in RW. The same parameterization is adopted for REA, while for the rest of the world we set the adjustment cost on goods exported to Italy and REA to 50. Nominal price adjustment costs are set to 500 in the non-tradable sector. The parameters are calibrated to generate dynamic adjustments for the euro area similar to those obtained with the New Area Wide Model (NAWM, see Christoffel et al. 2008) and Euro Area and Global Economy model (EAGLE, see Gomes et al. 2012). The two parameters regulating the adjustment cost to private agents on their net financial position are set to 0.00055 so that they do not greatly affect the model dynamics.

Table 4 reports the parametrization of the systemic feedback rules followed by the fiscal and monetary authorities. In the fiscal policy rule (4) we set $\phi_1 = \pm 0.05$, $\phi_2 = \pm 1.01$ for Italy and $\phi_1 = \phi_2 = \pm 1.01$ for the REA and the RW. Their sign is positive when the fiscal instrument in the rule is a tax rate, negative when it is expenditure. The central bank targets contemporaneous EA wide consumer price inflation (this parameter is set to 1.7) and the output growth (parameter 0.1). The interest rate is set in an inertial way, so its previous-period value enters the rule with

Table 4 Fiscal and monetary policy rules

Parameter	IT	REA	EA	RW
Fiscal policy rule				
$\phi_1, \phi_1^*, \phi_1^{**}$	± 0.05	± 1.01	–	± 1.01
$\phi_2, \phi_2^*, \phi_2^{**}$	± 1.01	± 1.01	–	± 1.01
Common monetary policy rule	–	–		
Lagged interest rate at t-1 ρ_R, ρ_R^{**}	–	–	0.87	0.87
Inflation ρ_Π, ρ_Π^{**}	–	–	1.70	1.70
GDP growth $\rho_{GDP}, \rho_{GDP}^{**}$	–	–	0.10	0.10

Note: *IT* = Italy; *REA* = rest of the euro area; *EA* = euro area; *RW* = rest of the world

Table 5 Main macroeconomic variables (ratio to GDP) and tax rates

	IT	REA	RW
Macroeconomic variables			
Private consumption	61.0	57.1	64.0
Private investment	18.0	16.0	20.0
Imports	29.0	24.3	4.3
Net foreign asset position	0.0	0.0	0.0
GDP (share of world GDP)	0.03	0.17	0.80
Public expenditures			
Public purchases	20.0	20.0	20.0
Interests	4.0	2.0	2.0
Public investment	2.0	3.0	3.0
Debt (ratio to annual GDP)	119	79	79
Tax rates			
on wage	42.6	34.6	34.6
on rental rate of capital	34.9	25.9	25.9
on price of consumption	16.8	20.3	20.3

Note: *IT* = Italy; *REA* = rest of the euro area; *RW* = rest of the world. Sources: European Commission (2012b); tax rates (in percent) are from Eurostat (2012)

a weight equal to 0.87. The same values hold for the corresponding parameters of the Taylor rule in RW.

Table 5 reports the actual GDP ratios and tax rates, which are matched in the steady state under our baseline calibration. We assume zero steady-state net foreign asset positions, which means that in each region the net financial position of the private sector is equal to the public debt. The Italian and REA GDPs are set to 3 and 17 %, respectively, of world GDP.

As for fiscal policy variables, the public consumption-to-GDP ratio is set to 0.20. The tax rate on wage income τ^ℓ is set to 42.6 % in Italy and to 34.6 in the REA. The tax rate on physical capital income τ^k is set to 34.9 in Italy and 25.9 in the REA, while the tax rate on consumption τ^c is equal to 16.8 in Italy and to 20.3 in the REA. The public debt-to-yearly GDP ratio is calibrated to 119 % for Italy and to 0.79 for the REA. Variables of the RW are set to values equal to those of corresponding REA variables.

Finally, for Italy we calibrate the relationship between the fiscal policy stance and the spread on the sovereign debt (5). Absent operational estimates of the link between fiscal conditions and risk premia, we turn to the literature on this issue, in particular Belhocine and Dell'Erba (2013), and posit that an increase in government spending of 1 percentage point of GDP maps into a 75-basis-point rise in the sovereign risk premium. The greater sensitivity of borrowing costs with respect to their estimates is justified by the fact that the Italian debt ratio is much higher than the threshold Belhocine and Dell'Erba find for emerging economies. Moreover, in a way this value is consistent with market developments since June 2011. At that time the spread between Italian and German 10-year bond yields was about 180 basis points, close to the level reached in the aftermath of the Lehman crisis. During the summer it soared brusquely: the exacerbation of the euro-area sovereign debt crisis fuelled fears for the sustainability of the public finances in the peripheral countries. The political mishandling of the crisis further heightened market tensions, and by mid-November the spread had reached 553 basis points, 370 more than 5 months earlier.[32] It took three fiscal consolidation packages for a total of 4.8 percentage points of GDP to stop the escalation of borrowing costs. Hypothesizing that a budget adjustment of that size is what the financial markets expected to keep the re-pricing of Italian sovereign risk at just 370 basis points, we can gauge the cost (benefit) of increasing (reducing) the public-sector deficit by 1 percentage point of GDP at about 75 basis points.[33] This estimate is admittedly rough and highly tentative; and it fails to distinguish sovereign risk from redenomination risk. Even so it appears reasonable, more plausible than the alternatives. Furthermore, we carry out a robustness check, calibrating the initial spread increase according to the estimates of Borgy et al. (2011). A number of assumptions are required in order to map the observed variations in long-term government bond yields onto our model-based quarterly interest rate. We follow the common practice and take the return on 10-year government bonds as the most representative long-term market rate. We design a procedure to map a given change in that yield onto variations in R_t^H. We follow the common practice and take the return on 10-year government bonds as the most representative long-term market rate. We design a procedure to map a given change in that yield onto variations in R_t^H. For simplicity we assume that changes in the return on any given maturity are transmitted in equal measure to all maturities, so that the shape of the term structure is unchanged. Hence, a change in the yield on 10-year bonds corresponds simply to an upward or downward shift in

[32]Spikes came immediately after the downgrade of Portugal in July, the release of the bail-in plan for Private Sector Involvement at the EU summit of 21–22 July, and the announcement of the Greek referendum on 1st November. Domestic events, i.e. the tensions generated by the uncertainty over the fiscal consolidation m also played some role. For a detailed account of the impact of news on the BTP-Bund spread between June 2011 and March 2012, see Pericoli (2012).

[33]The decrease in the spread in the initial months of 2012 and since August is not considered in the computation, as it most likely depends on monetary policy.

the entire yield curve, with no effect on its slope. This reflects the implicit definition of the model-based long-term interest rate as a weighted average of expected future short-term rates, via the expectation hypothesis and the Euler equation. In our model an expected change in the short-term rate would affect the returns paid at different maturities equally, so that the shape of the term structure of interest rates would remain unchanged.

4 The Results

In what follows we simulate the model to assess the fiscal multipliers for Italy under standard monetary policy, constant monetary policy rate and alternative responses of the credit spread. All simulations assume perfect foresight: shocks are fully anticipated by households and firms, with the exception of the initial shock in the first period.

4.1 *Benchmark Fiscal Multipliers*

Table 6 shows the short-term (first and second year) results of increasing Italian public consumption by 1 % of the pre-stimulus baseline GDP. For the permanent fiscal shock, the table also reports the long-run multipliers.[34] Monetary policy is conducted according to the Taylor rule (7), while public debt is stabilized by raising lump-sum taxes according to the fiscal rule (4).[35] After the end of the stimulus, public consumption returns immediately to its initial steady-state value.

The first two columns of Table 6 report multipliers of Italian public consumption when it is increased for 1 year. In the first year GDP increases by 0.86 % of its baseline value. Household consumption and investment decrease slightly. The nominal policy rate does not increase, because it is set at the euro-area level and reacts to EA-wide inflation and output, which are not significantly affected by the increase in Italian GDP and even less by the rise in the CPI. With the small increase in Italian prices, the real exchange rates of Italy against the REA and the RW appreciate slightly, so Italy's terms of trade vis-à-vis those areas improve slightly. Accordingly, tradables produced in the REA and in the RW become cheaper than those produced in Italy. Italy's net exports diminish (gross exports decrease and gross imports increase).[36] Spillovers towards the REA and RW are small, given

[34] For temporary shocks the long-run multiplier is 0.

[35] The implications of distortionary taxation for the spending multiplier are considered below.

[36] This is true for bilateral exports and imports to and from REA and RW (not reported for space reasons). Exports decrease more towards the RW, as their prices increase by more than those of the exports towards the REA (the former are more flexible than the latter).

Table 6 Public consumption multipliers

	1 year-stimulus		2 year-stimulus		5 year-stimulus		Permanent stimulus		
	1st year	2nd year	1st year	2nd year	1st year	2nd year	1st year	2nd year	LR
Italian variables									
GDP	0.86	−0.10	0.80	0.67	0.78	0.56	0.69	0.52	0.59
Consumption	−0.04	−0.06	−0.08	−0.17	−0.15	−0.32	−0.51	−0.80	−0.79
Investment	−0.05	−0.13	−0.03	−0.25	0.34	0.31	0.57	1.03	0.54
Exports	−0.42	−0.18	−0.56	−0.73	−0.62	−0.98	−0.48	−0.69	−0.30
Imports	0.05	0.00	0.09	0.06	0.22	0.30	0.01	0.11	−0.16
Terms of tr. REA (+ = deterior.)	−0.13	−0.11	−0.21	−0.35	−0.27	−0.54	−0.20	−0.38	−0.20
Terms of tr. RW (+ = deterior.)	−0.35	−0.12	−0.44	−0.55	−0.47	−0.69	−0.36	−0.49	−0.20
Real exc. rate REA (+ = depr.)	−0.05	−0.05	−0.09	−0.16	−0.13	−0.27	−0.09	−0.20	−0.15
Real exc. rate RW (+ = depr.)	−0.06	−0.05	−0.10	−0.16	−0.15	−0.29	−0.12	−0.21	−0.15
Inflation (annualized)	0.08	−0.03	0.15	0.02	0.20	0.11	0.14	0.07	0.00
Real int. rate (annualized)	−0.03	0.04	−0.12	0.04	−0.18	−0.07	−0.12	−0.05	0.00
Nominal int. rate (annualized)	0.01	0.00	0.01	0.02	0.01	0.01	0.01	0.00	0.00
Labor	1.34	−0.18	1.22	0.99	1.17	0.74	1.02	0.66	0.46
Pub. def. (%gdp)	0.72	−0.10	0.75	0.84	0.76	0.90	0.84	0.98	0.00
Prim. pub. def. (%gdp)	0.73	−0.13	0.76	0.82	0.78	0.89	0.85	0.97	0.00
REA GDP	0.00	0.00	0.00	0.00	−0.01	−0.02	−0.02	−0.01	0.00
RW GDP	0.00	0.00	0.00	0.00	0.00	0.00	0.00	0.00	0.00

Note: *LR* = long run, *REA* = rest of the euro area; *RW* = rest of the world. All variables as % dev. from initial steady state, inflation, interest rate, public deficit/GDP and primary public deficit/GDP as % point dev. from initial steady state

Italy's small share of the world economy and the relatively strong home bias in the REA and RW consumption and investment baskets.[37]

The remaining columns of Table 6 report the multipliers for the first 2 years for 2-year, 5-year and permanent fiscal stimuli (for the last, the long-run multiplier is also reported). In the first year GDP increases by 0.80, 0.78 and 0.69 %, respectively; in the second, by 0.67, 0.56 and 0.52. In the case of a permanent fiscal stimulus, the long-run multiplier is 0.59. The responses of the output components change with the scenario. The longer the duration of the stimulus, the larger the decrease in private

[37]REA and RW consumption and investment (not reported) fall slightly to finance the increase in Italian borrowing associated with the fiscal stimulus and the consumption smoothing of Italian households.

Table 7 Public consumption multipliers: Labor tax-based financing

	1 year-stimulus		2 year-stimulus		5 year-stimulus		Permanent stimulus		
	1st year	2nd year	1st year	2nd year	1st year	2nd year	1st year	2nd year	LR
Italian variables									
GDP	0.83	−0.14	0.74	0.54	0.66	0.27	0.49	0.14	−0.33
Consumption	−0.05	−0.09	−0.11	−0.24	−0.22	−0.50	−0.85	−1.33	−1.76
Investment	−0.07	−0.18	−0.09	−0.41	0.23	−0.07	0.45	0.67	−0.13
Exports	−0.47	−0.26	−0.68	−0.97	−0.83	−1.46	−0.58	−0.97	−1.31
Imports	0.05	0.00	0.09	0.06	0.22	0.28	−0.19	−0.19	−0.42
Terms of tr. REA (+ = deterior.)	−0.16	−0.15	−0.27	−0.48	−0.37	−0.82	−0.26	−0.56	−0.89
Terms of tr. RW (+ = deterior.)	−0.39	−0.18	−0.54	−0.73	−0.62	−1.03	−0.43	−0.68	−0.88
Real exc. rate REA (+ = depr.)	−0.07	−0.07	−0.12	−0.22	−0.18	−0.43	−0.13	−0.32	−0.65
Real exc. rate RW (+ = depr.)	−0.07	−0.07	−0.13	−0.23	−0.22	−0.46	−0.16	−0.33	−0.65
Inflation (annualized)	0.10	−0.03	0.20	0.04	0.29	0.20	0.20	0.13	0.00
Real int. rate (annualized)	−0.05	0.04	−0.17	0.03	−0.29	−0.15	−0.20	−0.12	0.00
Nominal int. rate (annualized)	0.01	0.00	0.01	0.02	0.01	0.01	0.00	0.00	0.00
Labor	1.29	−0.26	1.11	0.76	0.97	0.23	0.68	0.01	−0.68
Pub. def. (%gdp)	−0.31	−0.11	−0.29	−0.22	−0.27	−0.13	−0.12	0.03	0.00
Prim. pub. def. (%gdp)	−0.29	−0.11	−0.26	−0.20	−0.24	−0.10	−0.10	0.05	0.00
GDP REA	0.00	0.00	−0.01	−0.01	−0.02	−0.03	−0.02	−0.02	−0.01
GDP RW	0.00	0.00	0.00	0.00	0.00	−0.01	0.00	0.00	0.00

Note: *LR* = long run, *REA* = rest of the euro area; *RW* = rest of the world. All variables as % dev. from initial steady state, inflation, interest rate, public deficit/GDP and primary public deficit/GDP as % point dev. from initial steady state

consumption and the smaller the decrease in private investment; the latter increases when the stimulus lasts for 5 years or longer. Differences in household demand responses are associated with the strength of the negative wealth effect of current and expected public spending. The more resources appropriated to public consumption, the larger the negative wealth effect, the more households cut consumption and increase labour supply. The increase in labour supply makes capital more productive and induces investment and capital accumulation. Accordingly the aggregate supply can match the persistently higher public consumption demand.

For comparison, Table 7 reports the values of the public consumption multipliers when both public spending and labour income taxes are increased. The increase in the labour tax rate is such that the corresponding revenues are equal to 1 % of pre-stimulus GDP, so that the fiscal stimulus is ex ante revenue-neutral. The multiplier

Table 8 Tax multipliers: Italian GDP and inflation

	Labor tax			Capital tax			Consumption tax		
	1st year	2nd year	LR	1st year	2nd year	LR	1st year	2nd year	LR
1 year-stimulus	0.02	0.04	0.00	0.02	0.02	0.00	0.34	0.07	0.00
2 year-stimulus	0.06	0.13	0.00	0.08	0.11	0.00	0.30	0.37	0.00
5 year-stimulus	0.11	0.29	0.00	0.23	0.47	0.00	0.28	0.30	0.00
Permanent stimulus	0.19	0.37	0.89	0.17	0.53	2.51	0.08	0.15	0.37
Inflation									
1 year-stimulus	−0.02	0.00	0.00	0.00	0.00	0.00	0.06	−0.01	0.00
2 year-stimulus	−0.04	−0.02	0.00	0.00	−0.01	0.00	0.09	0.03	0.00
5 year-stimulus	−0.09	−0.08	0.00	0.04	−0.03	0.00	0.11	0.07	0.00
Permanent stimulus	−0.06	−0.07	0.00	0.00	−0.05	0.00	−0.02	−0.03	0.00

Note: LR = long run. GDP as % dev. from initial steady state, inflation as annualized % point dev. from initial steady state

is now lower than in the case of higher lump-sum taxes. There is less incentive to increase labour effort than in the previous case, as the increase in distortionary labour taxes reduces the net real wages. The differences are large for the second year, in particular for long-lasting stimuli.

The foregoing simulations have shown the multipliers associated with public consumption spending. Table 8 reports the multipliers associated with stimuli consisting in lowering tax rates on labour income, capital income and consumption. The reduction in tax revenues is 1 % of pre-stimulus GDP and lasts for either 1, 2, 5 years or permanently. After the stimulus, the public debt is stabilized by increasing lump-sum taxes according to the fiscal rule (4); public consumption is held constant at its pre-stimulus level. In the short run tax multipliers are less than 1 and lower than public consumption multipliers; they are larger in the second year than in the first (the only exception is consumption tax), because household consumption and investment react smoothly, given the assumptions of habit persistence and adjustment costs on investment. Finally, in the case of labour and capital income taxes, the longer the duration of the stimulus, the larger the multipliers, because households have more incentive to increase labour effort, the more long-lasting the decrease in taxes on their labour or capital income. In particular, in the long run the GDP multiplier associated with a permanent reduction in the capital tax rate is greater than 1.

Figure 1 shows the dynamic response of the main macroeconomic variables in the benchmark case of a public consumption increase financed by lump-sum taxes. Figure 2 reports the responses to the labour tax cut. In both cases the stimulus lasts for 1 year. Interestingly, the increase in public consumption raises GDP immediately, whereas the labour tax cut does so only gradually, as consumption and investment increase smoothly because of external habit formation in consumption and adjustment costs for investment.

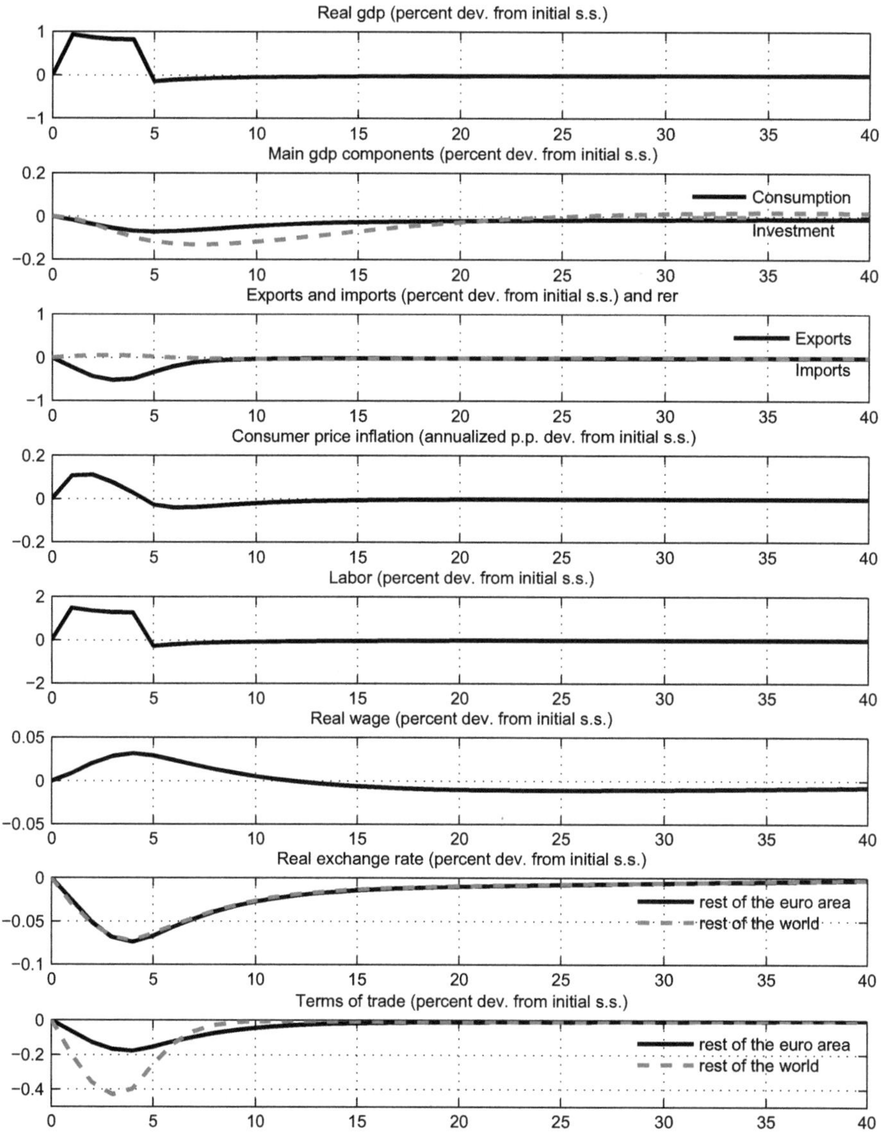

Fig. 1 Italian public consumption shock. Note: 1-year increase in public consumption of 1 % of (pre-shock) Italian GDP. *Horizontal axis*: quarters

Overall, the results suggest that fiscal multipliers are less than 1 and that for short-lived shocks the multipliers associated with taxation are lower than those associated with public spending, as public consumption affects aggregate demand directly while the negative wealth effects on consumption are rather muted. By contrast,

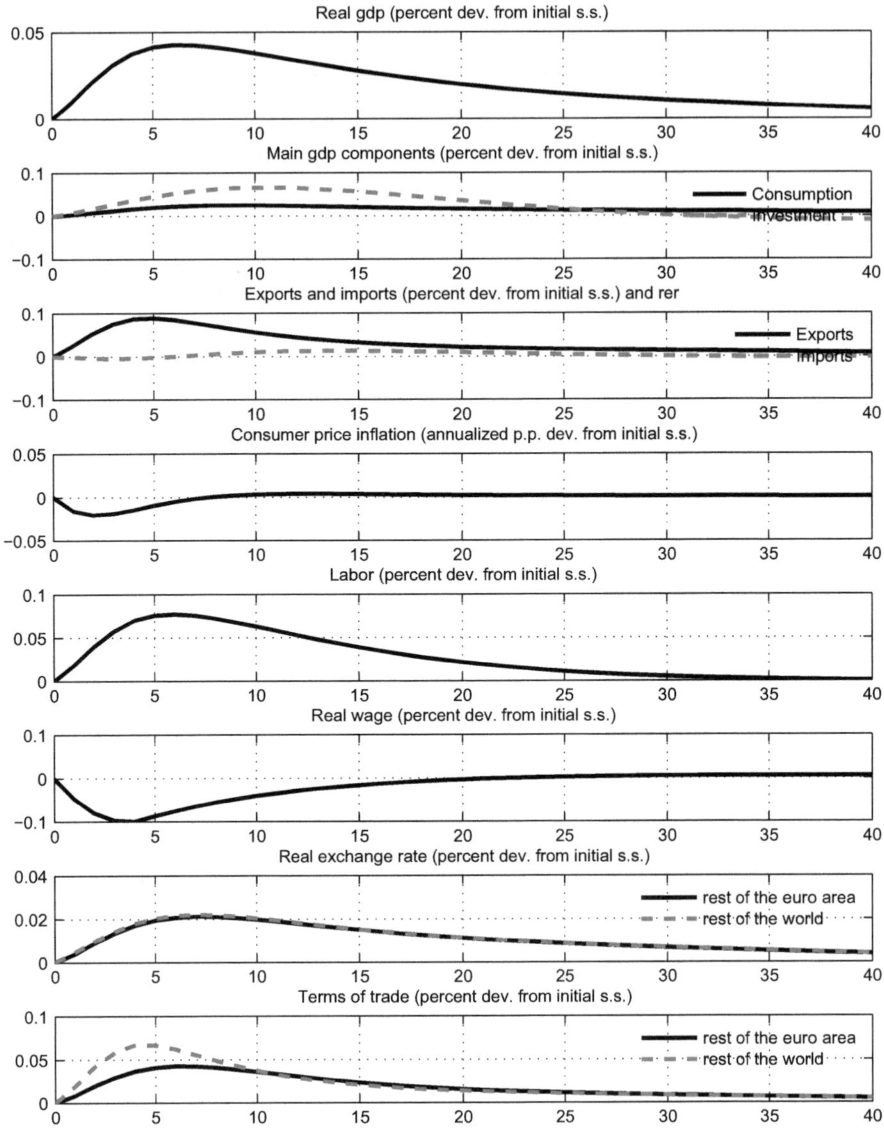

Fig. 2 Italian labor tax shock. Note: 1-year reduction in labor taxation of 1 % of (pre-shock) Italian GDP. *Horizontal axis*: quarters

in the case of permanent measures the wealth effects become large, implying that in the long run, when private spending fully adjusts to a given shock, the taxation multiplier is larger than the public consumption multiplier.

Table 9 Public consumption multipliers: Constant monetary policy rate

	1 year-stimulus		2 year-stimulus		5 year-stimulus		Permanent stimulus		
	1st year	2nd year	1st year	2nd year	1st year	2nd year	1st year	2nd year	LR
Italian variables									
GDP	0.88	−0.09	0.86	0.73	1.37	1.13	0.79	0.62	0.59
Consumption	−0.02	−0.05	−0.01	−0.11	0.50	0.22	−0.40	−0.71	−0.79
Investment	−0.02	−0.09	0.09	−0.09	1.43	1.80	0.77	1.29	0.54
Exports	−0.40	−0.17	−0.50	−0.70	−0.17	−0.71	−0.40	−0.64	−0.30
Imports	0.06	0.01	0.15	0.13	0.77	0.92	0.11	0.22	−0.16
Terms of tr. REA (+ = deterior.)	−0.13	−0.11	−0.22	−0.35	−0.29	−0.55	−0.20	−0.38	−0.20
Terms of tr. RW (+ = deterior.)	−0.36	−0.12	−0.47	−0.55	−0.75	−0.69	−0.41	−0.49	−0.20
Real exc. rate REA (+ = depr.)	−0.05	−0.05	−0.09	−0.16	−0.13	−0.27	−0.09	−0.20	−0.15
Real exc. rate RW (+ = depr.)	−0.03	−0.04	0.00	−0.11	0.75	0.16	0.04	−0.13	−0.15
Inflation (annualized)	0.10	−0.03	0.21	0.05	0.81	0.44	0.25	0.12	0.00
Real int. rate (annualized)	−0.06	0.03	−0.19	0.00	−0.78	−0.35	−0.23	−0.09	0.00
Nominal int. rate	0.00	0.00	0.00	0.00	0.00	0.00	0.00	0.00	0.00
(annualized) Labor	1.37	−0.16	1.34	1.09	2.21	1.62	1.21	0.82	0.46
Pub. def. (%gdp)	0.69	−0.12	0.70	0.78	0.42	0.54	0.77	0.92	0.00
Prim. pub. def. (%gdp)	0.72	−0.13	0.73	0.79	0.48	0.60	0.80	0.92	0.00
REA GDP	0.02	0.01	0.07	0.06	0.58	0.53	0.09	0.08	0.00
RW GDP	0.00	0.00	0.00	0.00	0.00	0.00	0.00	0.00	0.00

Note: *LR* = long run, *REA* = rest of the euro area; *RW* = rest of the world. All variables as % dev. from initial steady state, inflation, interest rate, public deficit/GDP and primary public deficit/GDP as % point dev. from initial steady state

4.2 Constant Monetary Policy Rate

So far we have assumed that monetary policy follows the Taylor rule (7). Now we assume instead an accommodative monetary policy stance. Table 9 reports the results for increases in public consumption by 1 % of GDP for 1, 2, and 5 years and on a permanent basis when the nominal policy rate is constant during the fiscal stimulus; for the permanent stimulus, the accommodative stance lasts for 5 years.[38] After the stimulus, monetary policy is standard (the Taylor rule kicks in). As in

[38] In what follows, we assume that the central bank does not or cannot steer the short-term nominal interest rate of the monetary union for a certain amount of time. Unlike much of the literature (see for example Corsetti et al. 2012a), we do not posit an exogenous recessionary shock that takes the

previous simulations the public debt is stabilized by increasing lump-sum taxes according to rule (4).

In the case of 1- and 2-year stimuli the GDP multiplier is comparable to that under the standard monetary policy stance (Table 6). The multiplier increases to well above 1 when the stimulus lasts for 5 years. It is 1.37 in the first year and 1.13 in the second. The monetary policy rate is similar in all scenarios, as we see by comparing Tables 6 and 9. For the standard stance, it increases by a few basis points. In the case of the 5-year fiscal stimulus and accommodative monetary policy, in conjunction with the Italian fiscal stimulus inflation increases substantially in Italy and in the rest of the euro area (not reported). The implied reduction in the real interest rate favors the crowding-in of private demand and thus enhances the effectiveness of the stimulus.

When the fiscal stimulus is permanent and monetary policy is accommodative for 5 years (Table 9), the lack of full overlap between monetary and fiscal policy implies that the multiplier is only slightly greater than under standard monetary policy (0.79 and 0.62 in the first 2 years vs. 0.69 and 0.52). The results are qualitatively in line with those reported in Woodford (2011), who finds that both fiscal stimulus and accommodative monetary policy have to be retained for an exceptionally long period in order to generate large multipliers, as inflation expectations need to be high enough to reduce the ex ante real interest rate. Note also that the 5-year mix of expansionary Italian fiscal policy and constant EA policy rate affects the REA activity and inflation positively, through trade spillovers. When the interest rate is constant for a sufficiently long time and there is full overlap with the fiscal stimulus, the inflation expectations of REA households become high enough to reduce the ex ante real interest rate significantly, stimulating household consumption and investment demand. This favours Italian exports, partially offsetting the loss of competitiveness due to the appreciation in the real exchange rate.

Table 10 reports the results under the assumption that the policy rate remains constant for half as long as the fiscal stimulus (2.5 years in the case of the 5-year and permanent fiscal stimuli). Multipliers are lower than in Table 9, as the monetary policy now accommodates the public consumption shock to a lesser extent. If the shock lasts 5 years, the multipliers are 0.88 in the first year and 0.65 in the second (instead of 1.37 and 1.13).

Table 11 reports the results for tax-rate multipliers. For 1- and 2-year stimuli, assuming constant interest rate, the multipliers are similar to those under standard monetary policy (Table 8). For 5-year and permanent stimuli the capital income and consumption tax multipliers are higher under no monetary-policy response than under standard monetary policy. In particular, the capital income tax multiplier rises above 1. On the other hand, the labour income tax multiplier decreases in the case of 2- and 5-year stimuli, because of the large initial positive response on the supply side, which lowers inflation expectations and, given the absence of monetary policy

---

monetary policy rate down to the ZLB. The reason is that the ZLB holds at EA level and so can be taken as exogenous with respect to changes in Italian economic conditions.

Table 10 Public consumption multipliers: Partial monetary policy accommodation

	1 year-stimulus		2 year-stimulus		5 year-stimulus		Permanent stimulus		
	1st year	2nd year	1st year	2nd year	1st year	2nd year	1st year	2nd year	LR
Italian variables									
GDP	0.87	−0.09	0.81	0.68	0.88	0.65	0.71	0.55	0.59
Consumption	−0.03	−0.06	−0.06	−0.16	−0.04	−0.23	−0.48	−0.78	−0.79
Investment	−0.04	−0.11	0.00	−0.22	0.52	0.55	0.62	1.09	0.54
Exports	−0.41	−0.17	−0.54	−0.73	−0.55	−0.93	−0.46	−0.68	−0.30
Imports	0.06	0.00	0.11	0.07	0.31	0.40	0.04	0.14	−0.16
Terms of tr. REA (+ = deterior.)	−0.13	−0.11	−0.21	−0.35	−0.27	−0.54	−0.20	−0.38	−0.20
Terms of tr. RW (+ = deterior.)	−0.35	−0.12	−0.45	−0.55	−0.52	−0.69	−0.38	−0.49	−0.20
Real exc. rate REA (+ = depr.)	−0.05	−0.05	−0.09	−0.16	−0.13	−0.27	−0.09	−0.20	−0.15
Real exc. rate RW (+ = depr.)	−0.04	−0.05	−0.07	−0.15	0.00	−0.22	−0.08	−0.19	−0.15
Inflation (annualized)	0.09	−0.03	0.16	0.03	0.30	0.16	0.16	0.08	0.00
Real int. rate (annualized)	−0.05	0.03	−0.15	0.03	−0.29	−0.13	−0.15	−0.06	0.00
Nominal int. rate (annualized)	0.00	0.00	0.00	0.01	0.00	0.00	0.00	0.00	0.00
Labor	1.36	−0.17	1.25	1.01	1.35	0.89	1.07	0.70	0.46
Pub. def. (%gdp)	0.70	−0.11	0.72	0.82	0.69	0.83	0.82	0.96	0.00
Prim. pub. def. (%gdp)	0.72	−0.13	0.75	0.81	0.73	0.84	0.84	0.96	0.00
REA GDP	0.01	0.01	0.01	0.01	0.09	0.07	0.01	0.01	0.00
RW GDP	0.00	0.00	0.00	0.00	0.00	0.00	0.00	0.00	0.00

Note: *LR* = long run, *REA* = rest of the euro area; *RW* = rest of the world. All variables as % dev. from initial steady state, inflation, interest rate, public deficit/GDP and primary public deficit/GDP as % point dev. from initial steady state

response, raises the real interest rate. Consumption and investment fall accordingly, as monetary policy is no longer accommodative.

Overall, the public consumption multiplier is well above 1 only when monetary policy remains accommodative for a very long time; otherwise the multipliers do not differ greatly from the case of standard monetary policy response and remain generally below 1.

4.3 Sovereign Risk Premium

The macroeconomic effects of a fiscal stimulus depend not only on monetary policy but also on the response of financial markets. As our review of the literature shows

Table 11 Tax multipliers: Constant monetary policy rate—Italian GDP and inflation

	Labor tax			Capital tax			Consumption tax		
	1st year	2nd year	LR	1st year	2nd year	LR	1st year	2nd year	LR
1 year-stimulus	0.02	0.04	0.00	0.02	0.02	0.00	0.35	0.08	0.00
2 year-stimulus	0.05	0.12	0.00	0.09	0.12	0.00	0.36	0.42	0.00
5 year-stimulus	0.00	0.17	0.00	0.45	0.68	0.00	0.80	0.80	0.00
Permanent stimulus	0.39	0.56	0.89	1.44	1.75	2.51	0.16	0.23	0.37
Inflation									
1 year-stimulus	−0.02	0.00	0.00	0.00	0.00	0.00	0.07	−0.01	0.00
2 year-stimulus	−0.05	−0.03	0.00	0.02	−0.01	0.00	0.14	0.05	0.00
5 year-stimulus	−0.22	−0.15	0.00	0.25	0.08	0.00	0.64	0.36	0.00
Permanent stimulus	0.14	0.04	0.00	1.32	0.65	0.00	0.06	0.02	0.00

Note: *LR* = long run. GDP as % dev. from initial steady state, inflation as annualized % point dev. from initial steady state

(Sect. 2), if investors are worried about the solvency of the government, they will demand a higher premium in response to a fiscal expansion. Moreover, the sovereign risk premium will be quickly transmitted to the borrowing cost of domestic households and firms, crowding out their spending decisions (this is the sovereign-risk channel of fiscal policy; see Corsetti et al. 2012a). Accordingly, this sovereign-risk channel may reduce the fiscal multiplier in times of financial turbulence. This conjecture is supported by some recent empirical evidence. Laubach (2012) studies the dependence of the sovereign spread on the current level of fiscal indicators (such as the surplus-to-GDP or the debt-to-GDP ratios) for a panel of EA countries and finds that the elasticity is small or nil in non-crisis periods but increases rapidly and dramatically at times of financial stress.

This section reports the model results for an increase in public consumption of 1 % of pre-stimulus GDP for 1, 2 and 5 years and permanently. Consistent with Eq. (5), we assume that the fiscal expansion entails an immediate 75-basis-point rise in the sovereign premium, hence in the interest rate on Italian government bonds. The effects of the stimulus depend crucially on the dynamics of the sovereign risk premium. We assume that after the initial rise the spread declines linearly, returning to baseline level by the time the stimulus is withdrawn.[39] In line with the empirical evidence for Italy (see Albertazzi et al. 2012, Neri 2013 and Zoli 2013), the increase in sovereign risk is fully passed through in one quarter to the borrowing rate for the Italian private sector. Monetary policy follows the standard Taylor rule and public debt is stabilized by lump-sum taxes after the end of the fiscal stimulus. The output multipliers are reported in Table 12: 0.78, 0.61, 0.27 and 0.18 in the first year when, respectively, the stimulus is for 1, 2, and 5 years and permanent; in the second year, they fall to −0.12, 0.57, 0.07 and 0.03 respectively. The values are lower than in the scenarios where the sovereign channel is lacking (Table 6), because

[39] In the case of a permanent stimulus, we assume this takes 5 years.

Table 12 Public consumption multipliers: Spread increase

	1 year-stimulus		2 year-stimulus		5 year-stimulus		Permanent stimulus		
	1st year	2nd year	1st year	2nd year	1st year	2nd year	1st year	2nd year	LR
Italian variables									
GDP	0.78	−0.12	0.61	0.57	0.27	0.07	0.18	0.03	0.59
Consumption	−0.22	−0.10	−0.48	−0.36	−1.19	−1.28	−1.55	−1.75	−0.73
Investment	−0.20	−0.21	−0.51	−0.67	−1.51	−2.35	−1.28	−1.64	0.56
Exports	−0.37	−0.15	−0.42	−0.62	−0.15	−0.33	−0.01	−0.04	−0.37
Imports	−0.12	−0.06	−0.35	−0.23	−1.17	−1.37	−1.37	−1.56	−0.08
Terms of tr. REA (+ = deterior.)	−0.12	−0.10	−0.17	−0.30	−0.09	−0.25	−0.02	−0.09	−0.25
Terms of tr. RW (+ = deterior.)	−0.31	−0.10	−0.33	−0.47	−0.10	−0.21	0.01	−0.01	−0.25
Real exc. rate REA (+ = depr.)	−0.05	−0.05	−0.07	−0.14	−0.05	−0.15	−0.02	−0.07	−0.18
Real exc. rate RW (+ = depr.)	−0.05	−0.05	−0.08	−0.14	−0.06	−0.15	−0.03	−0.07	−0.18
Inflation (annualized)	0.07	−0.03	0.12	0.03	0.07	0.09	0.00	0.05	0.00
Real int. rate (annualized)	−0.03	0.03	−0.10	0.02	−0.07	−0.12	−0.01	−0.09	0.00
Nominal int. rate (annualized)	0.01	0.00	0.01	0.01	0.00	−0.01	−0.01	−0.02	0.00
Labor	1.21	−0.19	0.91	0.88	0.36	0.13	0.21	0.05	0.44
Pub. def. (%gdp)	1.27	−0.03	1.46	1.30	1.73	1.91	1.81	1.99	0.00
Prim. pub. def. (%gdp)	0.78	−0.14	0.87	0.86	1.08	1.15	1.16	1.23	0.00
GDP REA	0.00	0.00	−0.01	−0.01	−0.03	−0.03	−0.03	−0.03	0.00
GDP RW	0.00	0.00	0.00	0.00	−0.01	−0.01	−0.01	0.00	0.00

Note: *LR* = long run, *REA* = rest of the euro area; *RW* = rest of the world. All variables as % dev. from initial steady state, inflation, interest rate, public deficit/GDP and primary public deficit/GDP as % point dev. from initial steady state

of the larger crowding-out effect on private-sector spending due to higher interest rates. Moreover, the longer the stimulus, the slower the decrease in the spread, the greater the reduction in the multiplier. In the case of the 5-year stimulus, private consumption decreases by 1.19 % in the first year and 1.28 % in the second, private investment by 1.51 and 2.35 %. Absent the sovereign risk channel (Table 6), private consumption would fall by 0.15 % in the first year and 0.32 % in the second, while private investment would increase.

Figure 3 sums up the results given here and in the previous section. The government-consumption multiplier depends heavily on the monetary policy response and on the change of the sovereign risk premium; in particular, it can be greater than 1 only if the monetary policy rate is held constant for an extended period. Moreover, monetary policy should remain accommodative for the duration

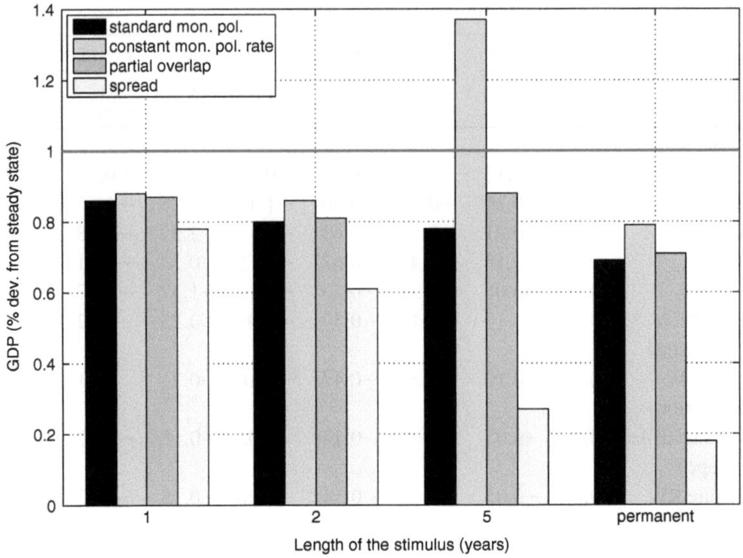

Fig. 3 First year-GDP multiplier associated with public consumption

of the fiscal stimulus (compare the bars for accommodative monetary policy and partial overlap). Otherwise, multipliers are less—possibly much less—than 1, if the sovereign risk premium increases.

4.4 Fiscal Consolidation and Sovereign Risk

The foregoing results suggest that in times of financial stress fiscal consolidation may reduce borrowing costs for households and firms. If the consolidation is credible, financial markets, anticipating that the public finances will become fully sustainable, might demand a lower sovereign risk premium. With quick and complete pass-through of the premium to the private sector borrowing rate, the decrease in the borrowing cost for households and firms should at least partially offset the contractionary effects of the consolidation.

This section analyzes the output effects of fiscal consolidation when the sovereign risk channel is operative. The policy tightening may be induced by an abrupt increase in the sovereign spread as a result of financial market turbulence, as it was in Italy in late 2011. Our results on fiscal consolidation should be compared, ideally, to a benchmark scenario in which there is no fiscal plan.

Table 13 reports the results of permanently reducing the debt-GDP ratio by 1 percentage point. As in Italy's fiscal package in the second half of 2011, public spending is reduced permanently by 0.25 percentage points while taxation (on labour income, capital income and consumption) is increased by 0.75 percentage

Table 13 Fiscal consolidation and spread reduction: Italian GDP

	Standard monetary policy		5 year constant mon. pol. rate	
	1st year	2nd year	1st year	2nd year
No spread	−0.29	−0.40	−0.69	−0.79
Spread: −75 bp on impact, 0 bp after 1 year	−0.21	−0.38	−0.62	−0.78
Spread: −75 bp on impact, 0 bp after 2 years	−0.10	−0.30	−0.51	−0.70
Spread: −75 bp on impact, 0 bp after 3 years	0.02	−0.17	−0.38	−0.56
Spread: −75 bp on impact, 0 bp after 5 years	0.22	0.10	−0.04	−0.16

Note: GDP as % dev. from initial steady state

points.[40] The sovereign spread responds as follows: on impact it narrows by 75 basis points (the reduction observed in Italy following the announcement of the consolidation in the autumn of 2011) and then gradually returns to its baseline value after 1, 2, 3 or 5 years. We simulate both a standard monetary policy response and a constant rate for 5 years. The sharpest reduction in output is 0.69 % in the first year and 0.79 in the second. This occurs when the monetary policy rate is held constant and there is no sovereign risk channel. The smallest reduction in output is 0.04 % in the first year and 0.16 in the second, which occurs when the decrease in the risk premium is durable (5 years). In this case, households benefit from a lower real interest rate, partially offsetting the increase in distortionary taxation.[41] As a limiting case, the effect on output can even be positive in the first year if the spread comes back to the baseline value in 3 or 5 years. For a permanent spread reduction, the effects would be larger still. Our assumptions are deliberately conservative, because they preclude large—and probably counterfactual—macroeconomic effects associated with perfect anticipation of permanent changes in spreads. In this respect, the estimate of the sovereign risk effect should be taken as a lower bound.

Simulation results suggest that under conditions of financial stress, when the sovereign risk channel is active the negative impact of fiscal consolidation can be quite modest, certainly less than under normal conditions.

4.5 *Sensitivity Analysis*

This section reports the sensitivity analysis for the public consumption multipliers (see Table 6). We now assume that the share of liquidity-constrained households

---

[40] See Ministero dell'Economia e delle Finanze (2012).

[41] Note that public spending decreases, helping to crowd in household consumption and investment spending.

Table 14 Sensitivity on public consumption multipliers: Italian GDP and inflation

	Benchmark			ROT households			Fiscal coord.			Fiscal coord. + constant m.p.		
	1st year	2nd year	LR	1st year	2nd year	LR	1st year	2nd year	LR	1st year	2nd year	LR
GDP												
1 year-stimulus	0.86	−0.10	0.00	0.98	−0.13	0.00	0.85	−0.10	0.00	0.99	0.00	0.00
2 year-stimulus	0.80	0.67	0.00	0.90	0.75	0.00	0.75	0.63	0.00	1.31	1.13	0.00
5 year-stimulus	0.78	0.56	0.00	0.88	0.61	0.00	0.60	0.35	0.00	6.96	6.14	0.00
Permanent stimulus	0.69	0.52	0.59	0.76	0.56	0.68	0.53	0.37	0.56	1.56	1.34	0.56
Inflation												
1 year-stimulus	0.08	−0.03	0.00	0.09	−0.04	0.00	0.12	−0.02	0.00	0.22	0.01	0.00
2 year-stimulus	0.15	0.02	0.00	0.17	0.02	0.00	0.20	0.07	0.00	0.71	0.30	0.00
5 year-stimulus	0.20	0.11	0.00	0.22	0.12	0.00	0.17	0.17	0.00	6.76	3.57	0.00
Permanent stimulus	0.14	0.07	0.00	0.14	0.06	0.00	0.04	0.03	0.00	1.09	0.58	0.00

Note: *LR* = long run; GDP as % dev. from initial steady state, inflation as annualized % point dev. from initial steady state

is 30 % of the Italian population and, alternatively, that the increase in public consumption is implemented simultaneously in Italy and the REA, under standard or accommodative monetary policy. Finally, we report the multipliers when the spread increases by 37 basis points, in line with the estimates provided by Borgy et al. (2011).

4.5.1 Liquidity Constrained Households

Table 14 shows the results when liquidity constraints affect 30 % of Italian households instead of none.

Following Campbell and Mankiw (1989) and Galí et al. (2004, 2007), we assume that in each period liquidity-constrained households consume their entire after-tax disposable income. That is, the budget constraint of the generic liquidity-constrained household j is:

$$(1 + \tau_t^c) P_t C_t(j) = (1 - \tau_t^\ell) W_t(j) L_t(j)$$

We assume liquidity-constrained households' wages and hours of labour are the same as those of unconstrained households, as are the tax rates on labour income and consumption.

The multipliers are now larger, owing to the income effect associated with the liquidity-constrained households, who increase consumption immediately as they do not save but spend their entire available wage income. The latter increases because firms expand employment, to serve increased aggregate demand. The differences with respect to the benchmark scenarios are not particularly great. In any event, the multipliers remain below 1.

4.5.2 Simultaneous Fiscal Stimulus in the EA

We assess the extent to which Italian fiscal multipliers change when the stimulus is implemented simultaneously in Italy and the REA. We assume an increase in public consumption by 1 % of pre-shock GDP for 2 years. The monetary policy is conducted according to the Taylor rule or is accommodative (policy rate held at its baseline level during the fiscal stimulus).

The results are reported in Table 14. Under standard monetary policy, the multipliers are slightly smaller for EA-wide stimulus than for unilateral Italian stimulus. As in the case of unilateral Italian stimulus, the multiplier is less than 1. Italian net exports (not reported) now diminish less, because the Italian exchange rate vis-à-vis the REA appreciates less. The monetary policy rate now rises more, given the increase in EA-wide aggregate demand. Accordingly, the real interest rate falls more modestly when the fiscal stimulus is coordinated, crowding out relatively more Italian household and business demand.

The Italian multipliers are greater than 1 when the monetary policy is accommodative and the fiscal stimulus lasts for 2 years at least. The constant interest rate stimulates REA aggregate demand by lowering the real interest rate. Italian gross exports decrease less, thanks to greater aggregate REA demand. The Italian GDP multiplier is 1.31 % in the first year. For unilateral Italian stimulus and accommodative monetary policy lasting 2 years, it is 0.86 % (Table 9). This suggests that the accommodative monetary policy is more effective in driving the multiplier above 1 when the fiscal stimulus comes simultaneously at EA level.

4.5.3 Spread Increase

Table 15 reports the public consumption multipliers when the spread increases immediately by 37 basis points, in line with estimates provided by Borgy et al. (2011). The multipliers are in general slightly lower than benchmark (see Table 6), but they are now larger than in the case of a 75-basis-point increase in the spread (Table 12). The smaller increase in the spread implies less crowding-out of household and business spending, which therefore does not contract as much. Overall, the multipliers do not differ greatly in the different scenarios, in particular for stimuli of plausible duration. Only for protracted stimulus (5 years or permanent) do the multipliers increase substantially.

Finally, we exploit the calibration implicitly suggested by Borgy et al. (2011) to simulate the 2011 Italian fiscal consolidation again. The spread decreases on impact by 37 basis points, then returns to its baseline value after 1, 2, 3 or 5 years. Table 16 shows the results. The effects are larger than in the benchmark case (Table 13). The spread decreases less, giving households and firms less incentive to increase

Table 15 Sensitivity: Public consumption multipliers—Spread increase

	1 year-stimulus		2 year-stimulus		5 year-stimulus		Permanent stimulus		
	1st year	2nd year	1st year	2nd year	1st year	2nd year	1st year	2nd year	LR
Italian variables									
GDP	0.82	−0.11	0.70	0.62	0.52	0.31	0.43	0.27	0.59
Consumption	−0.13	−0.08	−0.28	−0.27	−0.68	−0.81	−1.04	−1.29	−0.76
Investment	−0.13	−0.17	−0.27	−0.46	−0.59	−1.04	−0.36	−0.33	0.55
Exports	−0.39	−0.16	−0.49	−0.67	−0.38	−0.65	−0.24	−0.36	−0.33
Imports	−0.04	−0.03	−0.13	−0.09	−0.49	−0.55	−0.69	−0.73	−0.12
Terms of tr. REA (+ = deterior.)	−0.13	−0.11	−0.19	−0.33	−0.18	−0.39	−0.11	−0.23	−0.22
Terms of tr. RW (+ = deterior.)	−0.33	−0.11	−0.39	−0.51	−0.28	−0.45	−0.17	−0.25	−0.22
Real exc. rate REA (+ = depr.)	−0.05	−0.05	−0.08	−0.15	−0.09	−0.21	−0.06	−0.13	−0.16
Real exc. rate RW (+ = depr.)	−0.05	−0.05	−0.09	−0.15	−0.11	−0.22	−0.07	−0.14	−0.16
Inflation (annualized)	0.08	−0.03	0.13	0.03	0.13	0.10	0.07	0.06	0.00
Real int. rate (annualized)	−0.03	0.03	−0.11	0.03	−0.13	−0.10	−0.07	−0.07	0.00
Nominal int. rate (annualized)	0.01	0.00	0.01	0.02	0.00	0.00	0.00	−0.01	0.00
Labor	1.27	−0.19	1.07	0.94	0.76	0.43	0.61	0.35	0.45
Pub. def. (%gdp)	1.00	−0.07	1.10	1.07	1.25	1.41	1.33	1.49	0.00
Prim. pub. def. (%gdp)	0.75	−0.13	0.82	0.84	0.93	1.02	1.01	1.10	0.00
GDP REA	0.00	0.00	−0.01	0.00	−0.02	−0.02	−0.02	−0.02	0.00
GDP RW	0.00	0.00	0.00	0.00	0.00	0.00	0.00	0.00	0.00

Note: *LR* = long run, *REA* = rest of the euro area; *RW* = rest of the world. All variables as % dev. from initial steady state, inflation, interest rate, public deficit/GDP and primary public deficit/GDP as % point dev. from initial steady state

Table 16 Sensitivity: Fiscal consolidation and spread reduction—Italian GDP

	Standard monetary policy		5 year constant mon. pol. rate	
	1st year	2nd year	1st year	2nd year
No spread	−0.29	−0.40	−0.69	−0.79
Spread: −37 bp on impact, 0 bp after 1 year	−0.25	−0.39	−0.65	−0.78
Spread: −37 bp on impact, 0 bp after 2 years	−0.19	−0.35	−0.60	−0.74
Spread: −37 bp on impact, 0 bp after 3 years	−0.14	−0.29	−0.54	−0.67
Spread: −37 bp on impact, 0 bp after 5 years	−0.03	−0.15	−0.36	−0.47

Note: GDP as % dev. from initial steady state

consumption and investment. Even if the monetary policy rate is held constant for 5 years, the implied multiplier continues to be less than 1.[42]

5 Conclusions

This paper estimates the size of fiscal multipliers in Italy under various assumptions concerning the reaction of the central bank and the sovereign risk premium. There are four main conclusions. First, short-run fiscal multipliers are typically less than 1, and tax multipliers are lower than public consumption multipliers. Second, public consumption multipliers are substantially greater than 1 when the monetary policy rate is kept constant for an exceptionally extended period (5 years in our simulations). Third, under conditions similar to those currently prevailing in the euro area, in countries with a high public debt ratio the stimulus causes a worsening of the public finances and consequently a rapid increase in the sovereign risk premium, which in turn substantially reduces the multiplier and diminishes the effectiveness of fiscal policy. Fourth, the short-run contractionary effects of fiscal consolidation can be mitigated by a lowering of the sovereign risk premium. Overall, our results suggest that the magnitude of fiscal multipliers differs between normal times and periods of financial distress, insofar as initial public finance conditions and the stance of monetary policy can be decisive to the financing conditions of to the private sector.

Acknowledgements We thank Fabio Canova, Francesco Nucci and participants at Villa Mondragone International Economic Seminar 2013 for useful comments. The views expressed in this paper are those of the authors and do not necessarily represent those of the Bank of Italy.

Appendix

In this appendix we report a detailed description of the model, excluding the fiscal and monetary policy part and the description of the households optimization problem that are reported in the main text.[43]

There are three countries, Italy, the rest of the euro area (REA) and the rest of the world (RW). They have different sizes. Italy and the REA share the currency and the monetary authority. In each region there are households and firms. Each household consumes a final composite good made of non-tradable, domestic tradable and

[42]We have also experimented by calibrating the spread on the basis of Corsetti et al. (2012a). According to our elaborations, the spread would increase by 20 basis points in response to a 1-percentage-point expected increase in the public debt-GDP ratio. The results, available upon request, are intermediate between zero-spread case and the case considered in the sensitivity analysis.

[43]For a detailed description of the main features of the model see also Bayoumi (2004) and Pesenti (2008).

imported intermediate goods. Households have access to financial markets and smooth consumption by trading a risk-free one-period nominal bond, denominated in euro. They also own domestic firms and capital stock, which is rent to domestic firms in a perfectly competitive market. Households supply differentiated labor services to domestic firms and act as wage setters in monopolistically competitive markets by charging a markup over their marginal rate of substitution.

On the production side, there are perfectly competitive firms that produce the final goods and monopolistic firms that produce the intermediate goods. Two final goods (private consumption and private investment) are produced combining all available intermediate goods according to constant-elasticity-of-substitution bundle. The public consumption good is a bundle of intermediate non-tradable goods.

Tradable and non-tradable intermediate goods are produced combining capital and labor in the same way. Tradable intermediate goods can be sold domestically or abroad. Because intermediate goods are differentiated, firms have market power and restrict output to create excess profits. We assume that goods markets are internationally segmented and the law of one price for tradables does not hold. Hence, each firm producing a tradable good sets three prices, one for the domestic market and the other two for the export market (one for each region). Since the firm faces the same marginal costs regardless of the scale of production in each market, the different price-setting problems are independent of each other.

To capture the empirical persistence of the aggregate data and generate realistic dynamics, we include adjustment costs on real and nominal variables, ensuring that, in response to a shock, consumption and production react in a gradual way. On the real side, quadratic costs and habit prolong the adjustment of the investment and consumption. On the nominal side, quadratic costs make wage and prices sticky.

In what follows we illustrate the Italian economy. The structure of each of the other two regions (REA and the RW) is similar and to save on space we do not report it.

Final Consumption and Investment Goods

There is a continuum of symmetric Italian firms producing final non-tradable consumption under perfect competition. Each firm producing the consumption good is indexed by $x \in (0, s]$, where the parameter $0 < s < 1$ measures the size of Italy. Firms in the REA and in the RW are indexed by $x^* \in (s, S]$ and $x^{**} \in (S, 1]$, respectively (the size of the world economy is normalized to 1). The CES production technology used by the generic firm x is:

$$
\begin{aligned}
&A_t(x) \\
&\equiv \left(a_T^{\frac{1}{\phi_A}} \left(a_H^{\frac{1}{\rho_A}} Q_{HA,t}(x)^{\frac{\rho_A - 1}{\rho_A}} + a_G^{\frac{1}{\rho_A}} Q_{GA,t}(x)^{\frac{\rho_A - 1}{\rho_A}} (1 - a_H - a_G)^{\frac{1}{\rho_A}} Q_{FA,t}(x)^{\frac{\rho_A - 1}{\rho_A}} \right)^{\frac{\rho_A}{\rho_A - 1} \frac{\phi_A - 1}{\phi_A}} \right. \\
&\qquad \left. + (1 - a_T)^{\frac{1}{\phi_A}} Q_{NA,t}(x)^{\frac{\phi_A - 1}{\phi_A}} \right)^{\frac{\phi_A}{\phi_A - 1}}
\end{aligned}
$$

where Q_{HA}, Q_{GA}, Q_{FA} and Q_{NA} are bundles of respectively intermediate tradables produced in Italy, intermediate tradables produced in the REA, intermediate tradables produced in the RW and intermediate non-tradables produced in Italy. The parameter $\rho_A > 0$ is the elasticity of substitution between tradables and $\phi_A > 0$ is the elasticity of substitution between tradable and non-tradable goods. The parameter a_H $(0 < a_H < 1)$ is the weight of the Italian tradable, the parameter a_G $(0 < a_G < 1)$ the weight of tradables imported from the REA, a_T $(0 < a_T < 1)$ the weight of tradable goods.

The production of investment good is similar. There are symmetric Italian firms under perfect competition indexed by $y \in (0, s]$. Firms in the REA and in the RW are indexed by $y^* \in (s, S]$ and $y^{**} \in (S, 1]$. Output of the generic Italian firm y is:

$$E_t(y) \equiv \left(v_T^{\frac{1}{\phi_E}} \left(v_H^{\frac{1}{\rho_E}} Q_{HE,t}(y)^{\frac{\rho_E-1}{\rho_E}} + v_G^{\frac{1}{\rho_E}} Q_{GE,t}(y)^{\frac{\rho_E-1}{\rho_E}} + (1-v_H-v_G)^{\frac{1}{\rho_E}} Q_{FE,t}(y)^{\frac{\rho_E-1}{\rho_E}} \right)^{\frac{\rho_E}{\rho_E-1}\frac{\phi_E-1}{\phi_E}} + (1-v_T)^{\frac{1}{\phi_E}} Q_{NE,t}(y)^{\frac{\phi_E-1}{\phi_E}} \right)^{\frac{\phi_E}{\phi_E-1}}$$

Finally, we assume that public consumption C^g is composed by intermediate non-tradable goods only.

Intermediate Goods

Demand

Bundles used to produce the final consumption goods are CES indexes of differentiated intermediate goods, each produced by a single firm under conditions of monopolistic competition:

$$Q_{HA}(x) \equiv \left[\left(\frac{1}{s} \right)^{\theta_T} \int_0^s Q(h,x)^{\frac{\theta_T-1}{\theta_T}} dh \right]^{\frac{\theta_T}{\theta_T-1}} \tag{16}$$

$$Q_{GA}(x) \equiv \left[\left(\frac{1}{S-s} \right)^{\theta_T} \int_s^S Q(g,x)^{\frac{\theta_T-1}{\theta_T}} dg \right]^{\frac{\theta_T}{\theta_T-1}} \tag{17}$$

$$Q_{FA}(x) \equiv \left[\left(\frac{1}{1-S} \right)^{\theta_T} \int_S^1 Q(f,x)^{\frac{\theta_T-1}{\theta_T}} df \right]^{\frac{\theta_T}{\theta_T-1}} \tag{18}$$

$$Q_{NA}(x) \equiv \left[\left(\frac{1}{s} \right)^{\theta_N} \int_0^s Q(n,x)^{\frac{\theta_N-1}{\theta_N}} dn \right]^{\frac{\theta_N}{\theta_T-1}} \tag{19}$$

where firms in the Italian intermediate tradable and non-tradable sectors are respectively indexed by $h \in (0, s)$ and $n \in (0, s)$, firms in the REA by $g \in (s, S]$ and firms in the RW by $f \in (S, 1]$. Parameters $\theta_T, \theta_N > 1$ are respectively the elasticity of substitution across brands in the tradable and non-tradable sector. The prices of the intermediate non-tradable goods are denoted $p(n)$. Each firm x takes these prices as given when minimizing production costs of the final good. The resulting demand for intermediate non-tradable input n is:

$$Q_{A,t}(n,x) = \left(\frac{1}{s}\right)\left(\frac{P_t(n)}{P_{N,t}}\right)^{-\theta_N} Q_{NA,t}(x) \tag{20}$$

where $P_{N,t}$ is the cost-minimizing price of one basket of local intermediates:

$$P_{N,t} = \left[\int_0^s P_t(n)^{1-\theta_N} dn\right]^{\frac{1}{1-\theta_N}} \tag{21}$$

We can derive $Q_A(h,x)$, $Q_A(f,x)$, $C_A^g(h,x)$, $C_A^g(f,x)$, P_H and P_F in a similar way. Firms y producing the final investment goods have similar demand curves. Aggregating over x and y, it can be shown that total demand for intermediate non-tradable good n is:

$$\int_0^s Q_{A,t}(n,x)\,dx + \int_0^s Q_{E,t}(n,y)\,dy + \int_0^s C_t^g(n,x)\,dx$$
$$= \left(\frac{P_t(n)}{P_{N,t}}\right)^{-\theta_N} \left(Q_{NA,t} + Q_{NE,t} + C_{N,t}^g\right)$$

where C_N^g is public sector consumption. Italy demands for (intermediate) domestic and imported tradable goods can be derived in a similar way.

Supply

The supply of each Italian intermediate non-tradable good n is denoted by $N^S(n)$:

$$N_t^S(n) = \left((1-\alpha_N)^{\frac{1}{\xi_N}} L_{N,t}(n)^{\frac{\xi_N-1}{\xi_N}} + \alpha^{\frac{1}{\xi_N}} K_{N,t}(n)^{\frac{\xi_N-1}{\xi_N}}\right)^{\frac{\xi_N}{\xi_N-1}} \tag{22}$$

Firm n uses labor $L_{N,t}^p(n)$ and capital $K_{N,t}(n)$ with constant elasticity of input substitution $\xi_N > 0$ and capital weight $0 < \alpha_N < 1$. Firms producing intermediate goods take the prices of labor inputs and capital as given. Denoting W_t the nominal wage index and R_t^K the nominal rental price of capital, cost minimization implies:

$$L_{N,t}(n) = (1-\alpha_N)\left(\frac{W_t}{MC_{N,t}(n)}\right)^{-\xi_N} N_t^S(n) \tag{23}$$

$$K_{N,t}(n) = \alpha\left(\frac{R_t^K}{MC_{N,t}(n)}\right)^{-\xi_N} N_t^S(n)$$

where $MC_{N,t}(n)$ is the nominal marginal cost:

$$MC_{N,t}(n) = \left((1-\alpha)W_t^{1-\xi_N} + \alpha\left(R_t^K\right)^{1-\xi_N}\right)^{\frac{1}{1-\xi_N}} \tag{24}$$

The productions of each Italian tradable good, $T^S(h)$, is similarly characterized.

Price Setting in the Intermediate Sector

Consider now profit maximization in the Italian intermediate non-tradable sector. Each firm n sets the price $p_t(n)$ by maximizing the present discounted value of profits subject to the demand constraint and the quadratic adjustment costs:

$$AC_{N,t}^p(n) \equiv \frac{\kappa_N^p}{2}\left(\frac{P_t(n)}{P_{t-1}(n)} - 1\right)^2 Q_{N,t}\ \kappa_N^p \geq 0$$

paid in unit of sectorial product $Q_{N,t}$ and where κ_N^p measures the degree of price stickiness. The resulting first-order condition, expressed in terms of domestic consumption, is:

$$p_t(n) = \frac{\theta_N}{\theta_N - 1} mc_t(n) - \frac{A_t(n)}{\theta_N - 1} \tag{25}$$

where $mc_t(n)$ is the real marginal cost and $A(n)$ contains terms related to the presence of price adjustment costs:

$$A_t(n) \approx \kappa_N^p \frac{P_t(n)}{P_{t-1}(n)}\left(\frac{P_t(n)}{P_{t-1}(n)} - 1\right)$$
$$-\beta\kappa_N^p \frac{P_{t+1}(n)}{P_t(n)}\left(\frac{P_{t+1}(n)}{P_t(n)} - 1\right)\frac{Q_{N,t+1}}{Q_{N,t}}$$

The above equations clarify the link between imperfect competition and nominal rigidities. As emphasized by Bayoumi et al. (2004), when the elasticity of substitution θ_N is very large and hence the competition in the sector is high, prices closely follow marginal costs, even though adjustment costs are large. To the contrary, it may be optimal to maintain stable prices and accommodate changes in demand through supply adjustments when the average markup over marginal costs is relatively high. If prices were flexible, optimal pricing would collapse to the standard pricing rule of constant markup over marginal costs (expressed in units of domestic consumption):

$$p_t(n) = \frac{\theta_N}{\theta_N - 1} mc_{N,t}(n) \tag{26}$$

Firms operating in the intermediate tradable sector solve a similar problem. We assume that there is market segmentation. Hence the firm producing the brand h chooses $p_t(h)$ in the Italian market,a price $p_t^*(h)$ in the REA and a price $p_t^{**}(h)$ in the RW to maximize the expected flow of profits (in terms of domestic consumption units):

$$E_t \sum_{\tau=t}^{\infty} \Lambda_{t,\tau} \begin{bmatrix} p_\tau(h)\, y_\tau(h) + p_\tau^*(h)\, y_\tau^*(h) + p_\tau^{**}(h)\, y_\tau^{**}(h) \\ -mc_{H,\tau}(h)\left(y_\tau(h) + y_\tau^*(h) + y_\tau^{**}(h)\right) \end{bmatrix}$$

subject to quadratic price adjustment costs similar to those considered for non-tradables and standard demand constraints. The term E_t denotes the expectation operator conditional on the information set at time t, $\Lambda_{t,\tau}$ is the appropriate discount rate and $mc_{H,t}(h)$ is the real marginal cost. The first order conditions with respect to $p_t(h)$, $p_t^*(h)$ and $p_t^{**}(h)$ are:

$$p_t(h) = \frac{\theta_T}{\theta_T - 1} mc_t(h) - \frac{A_t(h)}{\theta_T - 1} \tag{27}$$

$$p_t^*(h) = \frac{\theta_T}{\theta_T - 1} mc_t(h) - \frac{A_t^*(h)}{\theta_T - 1} \tag{28}$$

$$p_t^{**}(h) = \frac{\theta_T}{\theta_T - 1} mc_t(h) - \frac{A_t^{**}(h)}{\theta_T - 1} \tag{29}$$

where θ_T is the elasticity of substitution of intermediate tradable goods, while $A(h)$ and $A^*(h)$ involve terms related to the presence of price adjustment costs:

$$\begin{aligned} A_t(h) \approx {} & \kappa_H^p \frac{P_t(h)}{P_{t-1}(h)} \left(\frac{P_t(h)}{P_{t-1}(h)} - 1 \right) \\ & -\beta \kappa_H^p \frac{P_{t+1}(h)}{P_t(h)} \left(\frac{P_{t+1}(h)}{P_t(h)} - 1 \right) \frac{Q_{H,t+1}}{Q_{H,t}} \\ A_t^*(h) \approx {} & \theta_T - 1 + \kappa_H^p \frac{P_t^*(h)}{P_{t-1}^*(h)} \left(\frac{P_t^*(h)}{P_{t-1}^*(h)} - 1 \right) \\ & -\beta \kappa_H^p \frac{P_{t+1}^*(h)}{P_t^*(h)} \left(\frac{P_{t+1}^*(h)}{P_t^*(h)} - 1 \right) \frac{Q_{H,t+1}^*}{Q_{H,t}^*} \end{aligned}$$

$$A_t^{**}(h) \approx \theta_T - 1 + \kappa_H^p \frac{P_t^{**}(h)}{P_{t-1}^{**}(h)} \left(\frac{P_t^{**}(h)}{P_{t-1}^{**}(h)} - 1 \right)$$
$$- \beta \kappa_H^p \frac{P_{t+1}^{**}(h)}{P_t^{**}(h)} \left(\frac{P_{t+1}^{**}(h)}{P_t^{**}(h)} - 1 \right) \frac{Q_{H,t+1}^{**}}{Q_{H,t}^{**}}$$

where $\kappa_H^p, \kappa_H^{p\,*}, \kappa_H^{p\,**} > 0$ respectively measure the degree of nominal rigidity in Italy, in the REA and in the RW. If nominal rigidities in the (domestic) export market are highly relevant (that is, if is relatively large), the degree of inertia of Italian goods prices in the foreign markets will be high. If prices were flexible ($\kappa_H^p = \kappa_H^{p*} = \kappa_H^{p**} = 0$) then optimal price setting would be consistent with the cross-border law of one price (prices of the same tradable goods would be equal when denominated in the same currency).

Labor Market

In the case of firms in the intermediate non-tradable sector, the labor input $L_N(n)$ is a CES combination of differentiated labor inputs supplied by domestic agents and defined over a continuum of mass equal to the country size ($j \in [0, s]$):

$$L_{N,t}(n) \equiv \left(\frac{1}{s} \right)^{\frac{1}{\psi}} \left[\int_0^s L_t(n, j)^{\frac{\psi-1}{\psi}} dj \right]^{\frac{\psi}{\psi-1}} \tag{30}$$

where $L(n, j)$ is the demand of the labor input of type j by the producer of good n and $\psi > 1$ is the elasticity of substitution among labor inputs. Cost minimization implies:

$$L_t(n, j) = \left(\frac{1}{s} \right) \left(\frac{W_t(j)}{W_t} \right)^{-\psi} L_{N,t}(j) \tag{31}$$

where $W(j)$ is the nominal wage of labor input j and the wage index W is:

$$W_t = \left[\left(\frac{1}{s} \right) \int_0^s W_t(h)^{1-\psi} dj \right]^{\frac{1}{1-\psi}} \tag{32}$$

Similar equations hold for firms producing intermediate tradable goods. Each household is the monopolistic supplier of a labor input j and sets the nominal wage facing a downward-sloping demand, obtained by aggregating demand across Italian firms. The wage adjustment is sluggish because of quadratic costs paid in terms of the total wage bill:

$$AC_t^W = \frac{\kappa_W}{2}\left(\frac{W_t}{W_{t-1}} - 1\right)^2 W_t L_t \tag{33}$$

where the parameter $\kappa_W > 0$ measures the degree of nominal wage rigidity and L is the total amount of labor in the Italian economy.

The Equilibrium

We find a symmetric equilibrium of the model. In each country there is a representative agent and four representative sectorial firms (in the intermediate tradable sector, intermediate non-tradable sector, consumption production sector and investment production sector). The equilibrium is a sequence of allocations and prices such that, given initial conditions and the sequence of exogenous shocks, each private agent and firm satisfy the correspondent first order conditions, the private and public sector budget constraints and market clearing conditions for goods, labor, capital and bond holdings.

References

Albertazzi U, Ropele T, Sene G, Signoretti FM (2012) The impact of the sovereign debt crisis on the activity of Italian banks. Questioni di Economia e Finanza (occasional papers), no. 133, Bank of Italy

Attinasi MG, Checherita-Westphal C, Nickel C (2010) What explains the surge in euro area sovereign spreads during the financial crisis of 2007–09? Public Finance Manag 10:595-645

Auerbach A, Gorodnichenko Y (2012) Measuring the output responses to fiscal policy. Am Econ J Econ Policy 4(2):1–27

Barro R (1981) Output effects of government purchases. J Polit Econ 83(6):1113–1144

Baxter M, King R (1993) Fiscal policy in general equilibrium. Am Econ Rev 83(3):315–334

Bayoumi T (2004) GEM: a new international macroeconomic model. IMF occasional paper no. 239

Bayoumi T, Laxton D, Pesenti P (2004) Benefits and spillovers of greater competition in europe: a macroeconomic assessment. NBER working paper no. 10416

Belhocine N, Dell'Erba S (2013) The impact of debt sustainability and the level of debt on emerging markets spreads. IMF working paper no.13/93, May

Benigno P (2009) Price stability with imperfect financial integration. J Money Credit Bank 41(1):121–149

Blanchard OJ (1990) Comment on Giavazzi-Pagano. In: NBER macroeconomics annual. National Bureau of Economic Research, Cambridge

Blanchard OJ, Leigh D (2013) Growth forecast errors and fiscal multipliers. IMF working paper no. 13/1, January

Blanchard OJ, Summers LH (1986) Hysteresis and the European unemployment problem. In: NBER macroeconomic annual. National Bureau of Economic Research, Cambridge

Borgy V, Laubach T, Mésonnier JS, Renne JP (2011) Fiscal sustainability, default risk and the euro area sovereign bond spreads. Banque de France Document de Travail no. 350

Braun AR, Körber LM, Waki Y (2012) Some unpleasant properties of log-linearized solutions when the nominal rate is zero. Federal Reserve Bank of Atlanta working paper no. 2012–5a

Campbell JY, Mankiw NG (1989) International evidence on the persistence of economic fluctuations. J Monet Econ 23(2):319–333
Christiano L, Eichenbaum M, Rebelo S (2011) When is the government spending multiplier large? J Polit Econ 119(1):78–121
Christoffel K, Coenen G, Warne A (2008) The new area-wide model of the euro area: a micro-founded open-economy model for forecasting and policy analysis. ECB working paper series no. 944
Coenen G, Erceg C, Freedman C, Furceri D, Kumhof M, Lalonde R, Laxton D, Lind J, Mourougane A, Muir D, Mursula S, de Resende C, Roberts J, Roeger W, Snudden S, Trabandt M, in't Veld J (2012) Effects of fiscal stimulus in structural models. Am Econ J Macroecon 4(1):22–68
Cogan JF, Cwik T, Taylor JB, Wieland V (2010) New Keynesian and old Keynesian government spending multipliers. J Econ Dyn Control 34(3):281–295
Corsetti G, Mueller GJ (2006) Twin deficits: squaring theory, evidence and common sense. Econ Policy 21(48):597–638
Corsetti G, Mueller GJ (2008) Twin deficits, openness and the business cycle. J Eur Econ Assoc 6(2–3):404–413
Corsetti G, Kuester K, Meier A, Mueller GJ (2012a) Sovereign risk, fiscal policy, and macroeconomic stability. IMF working papern no. 12/33
Corsetti G, Meier A, Müller GJ (2012b) What determines government spending multipliers? Econ Policy 27(72):521–565
DeLong JB, Summers LH (2012) Fiscal policy in a depressed economy. Presented to BPEA, March 2012
Eggertsson G (2001) Real government spending in a liquidity trap. Mimeo
European Central Bank (2012) Monthly Bullettin, December, Box 6
European Commission (2012a) European Economic Forecast, Box 1.5, Autumn
European Commission (2012b) AMECO Database
Eurostat (2012) Taxation Trends in the European Union
Financial Times (2012) Robustness of IMF Data Scrutinised, October
Forni L, Monteforte L, Sessa L (2009) The general equilibrium effects of fiscal policy: estimates for the euro area. J Public Econ 93(3–4):559–585
Forni L, Gerali A, Pisani M (2010a) The macroeconomics of fiscal consolidations in euro area countries. J Econ Dyn Control 34(9):1791–1812
Forni L, Gerali A, Pisani M (2010b) Macroeconomic effects of greater competition in the service sector: the case of Italy. Macroecon Dyn 14(5):677–708
Galí J, López-Salído JD, Vallés J (2004) Rule-of-thumb consumers and the design of interest rate rules. J Money Credit Bank 36(4):739–764
Galí J, López-Salído JD, Vallés J (2007) Understanding the effects of government spending on consumption. J Eur Econ Assoc 5(1):227–270
Gomes S, Jacquinot P, Pisani M (2012) The EAGLE: a model for policy analysis of macroeconomic interdependence in the euro area. Econ Model 29(5):1686–1714
Gruber JW, Kamin SB (2012) Fiscal positions and government bond yields in OECD countries. J Money Credit Bank 44(8):1563–1587
Haavelmo T (1945) Multiplier effects of a balanced budget. Econometrica 13(4):311–318
Hall R (1980) Labor supply and aggregate fluctuations. In: Carnegie-Rochester Conference Series on Public Policy, vol 12
Hall R (2009) By how much does GDP rise if the government buys more output? Brookings Papers Econ Act 40(2):183–249
Laubach T (2009) New evidence on the interest rate effects of budget deficits and debt. J Eur Econ Assoc 7(4):858–885
Laubach T (2012) Fiscal policy and interest rates: the role of sovereign default risk. Mimeo
Leeper EM (2013) Fiscal limits and monetary policy. Mimeo

Leigh D, Devries P, Freedman C, Guajardo J, Laxton D, Pescatori A (2010) Will it hurt? Macroeconomic effects of fiscal consolidation. World Economic Outlook, October, International Monetary Fund
Ministero dell'Economia e delle Finanze (2012) Documento di economia e finanza 2012
Neri S (2013) The impact of the sovereign debt crisis on bank lending rates in the euro area. Questioni di Economia e Finanza (occasional papers), no. 170, Bank of Italy
Nickel C, Tudyka A (2013) Fiscal stimulus in times of high debt: reconsidering multipliers and twin deficits. ECB working paper, no. 1513, February
OECD (2012) Structural Analysis Database. Available at http://www.oecd.org/industry/ind/stanstructuralanalysisdatabase.htm
Owyang MT, Ramey VA, Zubairy S (2013) Are government spending multipliers greater during periods of slack? In: Evidence from 20th Century Historical Data, AEA Papers and Proceedings, (forthcoming)
Pericoli M (2012) News, political uncertainty and the Italian sovereign risk premium from June 2011 to March 2012. Mimeo
Perotti R (1999) Fiscal policy in good times and bad. Q J Econ 114(4):1399–1436
Perotti R (2011) Expectations and fiscal policy: an empirical investigation. GRASP working paper no. 19
Pesenti P (2008) The global economy model (GEM): theoretical framework. IMF Staff Papers 55(2):243–284
Ramey VA (2011a) Identifying government spending shocks: it's all in the timing. Q J Econ 22:1–50
Ramey VA (2011b) Can government purchases stimulate the economy? J Econ Literature 49(3):673–685
Ramey VA (2012) Discussant Comments on Fiscal Policy in a Depressed Economy, by J.B. DeLong and L.H. Summers
Rotemberg JJ (1982) Monopolistic price adjustment and aggregate output. Rev Econ Stud 49(4):517–531
Sutherland A (1997) Fiscal crises and aggregate demand: can high public debt reverse the effects of fiscal policy? J Public Econ 65(2):147–162
Woodford M (2011) Simple analytics of the government expenditure multiplier. Am Econ J Macroecon 3(1):1–35
Zoli E (2013) Italian sovereign spreads: their determinants and pass-through to bank funding costs and lending conditions. IMF working paper no. 13/84, April

Perspectives for Growth and Income Equality in the European Monetary Union: 2012–2025

Fred Campano, Alberto Costantiello, and Dominick Salvatore

Abstract Using national accounts data obtained from the United Nations Statistical data base, GDP by expenditure was projected to the year 2025 for each of the countries belonging to the Eurozone (excluding Estonia and Slovakia) and added to get a total for the group. The projections were based on the trends that were prevailing from 1995 to 2011 in each of the countries assuming there would be a recovery from the recessionary period of 2008 to 2009 and a return to the trend. Per capita GDP projections were obtained by dividing the projected GDP by the population projections produced by the United Nations Population Division. A projection of the labor force for each country was obtained by extrapolating the labor participation rates given by the ILO and applying them to the projected population. Unemployment was then projected to the year 2025 and consequently the unemployment rate for each year in the projected period was estimated. Income distribution and inequality was captured through the use of income share by quintile of population data available for each of the countries. The per capita GDP of the poorest and richest quintiles was projected to 2025.

F. Campano
Department of Economics, Fordham University, New York, NY, USA
e-mail: campano@fordham.edu

A. Costantiello
Department of Economics, LUM, Bari, Italy
e-mail: a.costantiello@gmail.com

D. Salvatore (✉)
Department of Economics, Fordham University, New York, NY, USA

Department of Economics, LUM, Bari, Italy
e-mail: salvatore@fordham.edu

L. Paganetto (ed.), *Wealth, Income Inequalities, and Demography*,
DOI 10.1007/978-3-319-05909-9_8,

1 Introduction

The method used in projecting the long-term growth for the group of Eurozone countries as a whole, is based upon projections to the year 2025 of each of the member countries that share the same currency. While it is impossible to predict anything that far into the future, our main interest in this exercise is the prognosis for income distribution in the group, both between countries and within countries if the savings behavior and import propensities that were prevailing in the 1995–2011 period were to continue for the next 15 years. We would argue that savings behavior is cultural and that households in Europe will strive to maintain their historical savings patterns. Globalism has led to more and more dependence on trade and it is our opinion that this tendency is not going to reverse itself before 2025. Hence, the region will continue to see an increasing share of imports in GDP, but we also believe that this share cannot increase without complementary increases in exports, and in fact this exercise indicates an export surplus for the region as a whole over the entire period. Another assumption pertains to investment shares in GDP. We will take the trend in that share as exogenous even though the recent recession led to a deviation from the trend. We believe that investment share will rise again to trend levels once confidence is restored in the regional economy. The resulting projections of GDP will be used with projections of population from the United Nations and observed income distribution data for the member countries. This gives us the ability to compare the incomes of the poorest populations with the richest population within the countries and the region as a whole.

2 The Economic Model

In projecting the supply side of the economy, we will make the assumption that labor is not a constraint in the region. That is, there is a surplus of labor in almost any country and the only real constraint to production is capital. In this case, the Harrod–Domar production is a good stand-in for the more commonly used constant elasticity of substitution (CES) type of function, such as the Cobb-Douglas, which uses labor as an input. The identities and equations of the model are based on the expenditure table of the national accounts and have the following form:

Identities:	$Y = FC + I + X - M$, where Y is GDP, FC is final consumption, I is gross capital formation, X is exports and M is Imports.
	$S = Y - FC$, where S is national savings.
	$X - M =$ net exports which equals $S - I$
	$B = M - X = I - S =$ national borrowings
Behavioral:	$S = a + b\,Y$ and $M = a + bX + cY$
Harrod–Domar:	$Y_{t+1} = a + b \sum I_t$
Investment trend:	$I_t/Y_t = a + b$ Year

Fig. 1 GDP trend for the Eurozone (millions of 2005 Euros)

The estimated parameters are found in the Appendix 1; further details regarding the estimates will be provided by the authors upon request. The projection of GDP for region as a whole is shown in Fig. 1. The projected trend reflects recovery path from the 2008 recession when each country moves back on its 1995–2011 trend. The level of GDP rises from about 7.5 trillion in 2000 to about 11 trillion Euros (constant in base year 2005) in 2025.

Table 1 shows how the assumptions about savings and imports project into the future. National savings hovered around 24% of GDP for most of the historical period. However, during the recession, the rate dropped to about 20.7%. The equation for the savings function raises the savings rate to 23.1% in first projected year and the rate steadily increase to 24.1% over the projected period. Likewise the import function continues the increasing trend in imports as a share of GDP reaching 48.9% in 2025. However, the net export share remains positive and reaches 3.7% in 2025. At this the level it is slightly below the 4% average level that prevailed before the 2008 recession. Investment shares in GDP are almost constant, only rising one tenth of a percent from about 20.3% to about 20.4%. Final consumption shares in GDP are the residual, and these remain around 76% for the whole projected period. However, there is a slight decrease of 1% from the beginning of the period to the end of the period. Since final consumption is the sum of both private and public consumption, that decline of 1% may come from one or both of these sectors. In some sense the GDP trend seems a bit optimistic, but it really is not. The historical growth rate of GDP for the Eurozone, using regression growth rates, was 1.84% for the 2000–2008 period. The projected growth rate of the trend from 2012 to 2025 is less, only 1.59%. Of course the reality may be higher or lower, but in this scenario we prefer to error on the low side rather than on the high side. That is for the purpose of this exercise we prefer to be more pessimistic about the growth of GDP than more optimistic. The projected growth rate falls in between 1.84 and 1.23% which is the growth rate in the historical period if the recession years of 2009–2011 are included.

Table 1 Historical and projected shares in gross domestic product

	Eurozone (2005 Euros)						
Year	Y	FC	I	X	M	S	Net X
Historical							
2000	100.0	77.9	23.1	35.5	34.2	24.4	3.6
2001	100.0	77.9	22.5	36.1	34.2	24.4	4.2
2002	100.0	78.4	22.3	36.3	34.7	23.9	3.9
2003	100.0	78.4	22.4	37.1	35.6	23.9	3.9
2004	100.0	78.1	22.5	38.8	37.1	24.2	4.1
2005	100.0	77.7	22.9	40.3	38.6	24.6	4.0
2006	100.0	76.7	23.6	41.8	39.9	25.6	4.2
2007	100.0	76.6	24.0	42.8	41.1	25.7	4.0
2008	100.0	78.2	23.1	41.7	40.7	24.1	3.3
2009	100.0	79.2	19.3	39.3	37.8	20.8	1.5
2010	100.0	78.7	19.4	42.2	40.3	21.3	1.9
2011	100.0	79.3	19.6	40.6	39.4	20.7	1.2
Projected							
2012	100.0	76.9	20.3	43.3	40.5	23.1	2.8
2013	100.0	76.8	20.3	44.1	41.2	23.2	2.9
2014	100.0	76.7	20.3	44.8	41.9	23.3	3.0
2015	100.0	76.6	20.3	45.6	42.5	23.4	3.0
2016	100.0	76.5	20.3	46.3	43.2	23.5	3.1
2017	100.0	76.5	20.3	47.1	43.9	23.5	3.2
2018	100.0	76.4	20.4	47.8	44.5	23.6	3.3
2019	100.0	76.3	20.4	48.5	45.2	23.7	3.3
2020	100.0	76.2	20.4	49.2	45.8	23.8	3.4
2021	100.0	76.2	20.4	49.9	46.5	23.8	3.5
2022	100.0	76.1	20.4	50.6	47.1	23.9	3.5
2023	100.0	76.0	20.4	51.3	47.7	24.0	3.6
2024	100.0	76.0	20.4	51.9	48.3	24.0	3.6
2025	100.0	75.9	20.4	52.6	48.9	24.1	3.7

Now if we exogenously include the United Nations Population projections for the Eurozone, we obtain the per capita GDP figures of 26,540 Euros in 2012 and 31,890 Euros in 2025. These will of course vary from country to country, but there is a real increase in every country (see Table 2).

3 Projecting the Unemployment Rate

Data on labor force and employment were obtained from the International Labour Organization's LABORSTA data file. Their coverage is from 1999 to 2008, just enough to allow us to estimate a simple model for unemployment. The models that we used are based on the contributions to unemployment from the size of

Table 2 Projected per capita GDP (constant 2005 Euros)

Country	2012	2025	Country	2012	2025
Austria	33,118	41,698	Italy	23,976	26,504
Belgium	31,469	38,737	Luxembourg	68,018	93,375
Cyprus	14,313	19,608	Malta	13,434	16,195
Finland	32,463	42,959	Netherlands	34,345	42,351
France	29,284	34,076	Portugal	14,884	17,449
Germany	30,726	36,865	Slovenia	16,179	23,562
Greece	16,542	21,571	Spain	21,211	27,432
Ireland	38,559	50,013	*Eurozone*	26,540	31,890

the population and the size of the gross domestic product. In principle, the larger the population, the larger the labor force, the larger the potential for unemployed members in the labor force. On the other hand, the larger the gross domestic product, the more participants of the labor force are needed for production and the lower the unemployment rate. Therefore, we tested models of the following form:

$$\text{Unemployment} = \text{f}\,(\text{population}, \text{GDP}) \text{ and}$$
$$\text{Unemployment} = \text{f}\,(\text{labor force}, \text{GDP}),$$

where GDP has a 1-year lag. That is the size of the unemployment is related to the size of GDP of the previous year. We used two specifications, one in double logarithms and the other in linear form. The results of the regression are shown below:

$$\text{LN}\,(\text{Unemp}) = -71.9213 + 9.395831\,\text{LN}\,(\text{pop}) - 2.41133\,\text{LN}\,(\text{Y}_{t-1}),\ \text{R}^2 = 0.493$$
$$(t = -1.65)\quad (t = 2.03)\qquad\qquad (t = -2.39)$$
$$\text{Unemp} = -87{,}347 + 0.41833\,\text{pop} - 0.00539\,\text{Y}_{t-1},\ \text{R}^2 = 0.555$$
$$(t = -1.96)\quad (t = 2.36)\qquad (t = -2.73)$$

$$\text{aLN}\,(\text{Unemp}) = 10.87596 + 1.229098\,\text{LN}\,(\text{LF}) - 1.02681\,\text{LN}\,(\text{Y}_{t-1}),\ \text{R}^2 = 0.233$$
$$(t = -1.02)\quad (t = 0.586)\qquad\qquad (t = -0.972)$$
$$\text{Unemp} = 8{,}800.543 + 0.121068\,\text{LF} - 0.00224\,\text{Y}_{t-1},\ \text{R}^2 = 0.247$$
$$(t = 0.611)\qquad (t = 0.651)\qquad (t = -1.02).$$

The equations involving the labor force as an explanatory variable did not fit as well as the ones using total population. However, the signs are correct and when we projected with these coefficients our results are not much different than what is shown in Table 3. Nevertheless, we used the total population equations rather than the labor force equations. The latter are more appealing from a theoretical point of view, but it is not surprising that they do not fit as well as the former. Estimating who is included in the labor force is the most difficult challenge for labor statisticians. The population estimates, both historical and projected are made by the Population Division of the United Nations. These are more predictable. However, we made

Table 3 Historical and projected labor force and unemployment in the Eurozone

			Historical		
Year	Population (× 1,000)	Labor force	Labor participation rate (%)	Number unemployed	Unemployment rate (%)
1999	312,769	139,171	44.5	13,553	9.7
2000	313,552	140,659	44.9	12,228	8.7
2001	315,259	141,368	44.8	11,109	7.9
2002	317,018	143,308	45.2	11,819	8.2
2003	318,777	144,479	45.3	12,720	8.8
2004	320,536	145,418	45.4	13,225	9.1
2005	322,347	148,299	46.0	13,131	8.9
2006	323,912	150,180	46.4	12,408	8.3
2007	325,476	152,924	47.0	11,207	7.3
2008	327,039	154,840	47.3	11,432	7.4
			Projected (log equat.)		
Year	Population (× 1,000)	Labor force	Labor participation rate (%)	Number unemployed	Unemployment rate (%)
2009	328,603	155,646	47.4	12,203	7.8
2010	330,166	157,399	47.7	14,217	9.0
2011	330,981	158,802	48.0	13,858	8.7
2012	331,796	160,210	48.3	13,698	8.6
2013	332,610	161,622	48.6	13,035	8.1
2014	333,424	163,040	48.9	12,845	7.9
2015	334,238	164,463	49.2	12,656	7.7
2020	337,219	171,098	50.7	11,379	6.7
2025	339,128	177,265	52.3	9,905	5.6
			Projected (linear eq.)		
Year	Population (× 1,000)	Labor force	Labor participation rate (%)	Number unemployed	Unemployment rate (%)
2009	328,603	155,646	47.4	12,162	7.8
2010	330,166	157,399	47.7	14,481	9.2
2011	330,981	158,802	48.0	14,081	8.9
2012	331,796	160,210	48.3	13,885	8.7
2013	332,610	161,622	48.6	13,076	8.1
2014	333,424	163,040	48.9	12,807	7.9
2015	334,238	164,463	49.2	12,528	7.6
2020	337,219	171,098	50.7	10,503	6.1
2025	339,128	177,265	52.3	7,725	4.4

the projection of the total labor force by estimating a trend equation for the labor participation rate. The resulting equation is:

$$\begin{aligned} \mathrm{LF} &= -568.499 + 0.306553\ \mathrm{YEAR},\ \mathrm{R}^2 = 0.936 \\ &\quad (\mathrm{t} = -10.04) \qquad (\mathrm{t} = 10.85)\,. \end{aligned}$$

Table 3 shows the projections comparing estimates of the projected period with the historical data. The labor force participation rate in the Eurozone increased from 44.5% of the population in 1999 to 47.3% in 2008. Our trend equation continues this incremental increase to 2025 when it reaches 52.3%. This increasing trend in the labor force participation rate may reflect cultural changes in the Eurozone relating to higher education of women and immigration. Highly educated women are more likely to pursue a career at the completion of their studies rather than the traditional role of stay-at-home mother and housewife. Immigrants are likely to have a higher labor participation rate because often the motive to migrate is to find work. The projections of the unemployment rate under the two models are shown in Table 3. Even though the labor participation rate is increasing, the unemployment rate decreases after an increase in 2009. The model indicates that there will be a return to pre-recession unemployment rates as the Eurozone returns to long-turn trend in GDP. Another factor in the decreasing unemployment rate is the slowing down of population growth. Unless there is a huge surge in migration, the demographics are working favorably for the Eurozone in terms of future unemployment rates. That is, for the period from 2012 to 2025, the slow moving population growth rate is keeping the unemployment rate in check, however, at some point further in the century, this trend may be cause the dependency ratio to rise to the point where those working will not be able to support those on pension.

4 Projecting the Distribution of Income

While the national level of per capita income is of great interest, the difference in the per capita income between the richest and poorest populations is even of more interest. In order to capture the income distribution we use the population quintile shares of income distribution that are available for each of the countries. Since the units of money are in 2005 constant Euros, the starting year for the quintiles is observation for the year 2005 when available. If no data for 2005 are available, we use the year for that country which is closest to 2005. These data are obtained from a number of sources, including the data bases of the United Nations, i.e., The United Nations University (Wider), International Labour Office, and The World Bank, as well as European sources such as The Luxembourg Income Study, and the Eurostat Database. Our source of preference is the country's national statistical office. Appendix 2 shows the complete data base of the quintile shares and the share of the richest decile. We used this data to disaggregate the projected the per capita income into per capita income by quintile and then use the ratio of the lowest quintiles average income to the highest quintiles average income as a measure of inequality. We looked at two scenarios, the first assuming no change in the quintiles over the 15 year period, and the second assuming the shares will gradually change according to the level of development, also known as the Kuznets' hypothesis. Scenario 1 is given in Table 4. For the Eurozone as a whole, the per capita GDP of the poorest quintile will increase from 8,652 to 10,936 Euros per

Table 4 Projected per capita GDP of poorest and richest quintiles

	Q1	Q5	Q1/Q5		Q1	Q5	Q1/Q5
Austria				Italy			
2012	12,088	61,433	0.1968	2012	8,152	51,909	0.1570
2025	15,220	77,350	0.1968	2025	9,012	57,382	0.1570
Belgium				Luxembourg			
2012	11,015	65,928	0.1671	2012	26,016	137,838	0.1887
2025	13,558	81,154	0.1671	2025	35,716	189,224	0.1887
Cyprus				Malta			
2012	4,552	31,861	0.1429	2012	4,010	28,133	0.1425
2025	6,235	43,646	0.1429	2025	4,834	33,913	0.1425
Finland				Netherlands			
2012	9,771	86,658	0.1128	2012	11,849	69,377	0.1708
2025	12,930	114,679	0.1128	2025	14,611	85,550	0.1708
France				Portugal			
2012	12,153	55,786	0.2179	2012	4,912	33,487	0.1467
2025	14,142	64,915	0.2179	2025	5,758	39,258	0.1467
Germany				Slovenia			
2012	12,136	56,689	0.2141	2012	8,259	27,230	0.3033
2025	14,562	68,016	0.2141	2025	12,028	39,655	0.3033
Greece				Spain			
2012	4,632	36,394	0.1273	2012	5,939	45,391	0.1308
2025	6,040	47,458	0.1273	2025	7,681	58,704	0.1308
Ireland				Eurozone			
2012	7,133	91,771	0.0777	2012	8,652	56,862	0.1522
2025	9,252	119,030	0.0777	2025	10,396	68,323	0.1522

Constant quintile shares scenario (constant 2005 Euros)

year, while the richest quintile will increase from 56,862 to 68,323 Euros per year. Furthermore, the lowest quintile is projected to have about 15.2% of the income of the highest quintile. These ratios refer to GDP per person in the quintile, and in this sense it is similar to but not the same as before tax household income. It is similar because it is a gross figure before taxes are deducted, but not the same because it is GDP and not household income. The EU Survey on Income and Living Conditions (EU-SILC) also does a similar computation but on household ***Equivalised Income***. This is an estimation based on dividing disposable household income by the equivalised household size, which is calculated using an Equivalence scale. This provides an estimate of how much of the income can be attributed to each member of the household. For example, if the disposable household income is 48,000 Euros and the equivalised household size is 2.4, then the equivalised income for the for this household is 20,000 and applied to each member of a household. The important difference here is that after tax household income is used and this will indicate more equality between the quintiles than GDP per person.

Under the constant quintile shares scenario, the long-term outlook for living standards is not bad for the poorest quintile, even though the trend in GDP is somewhat pessimistic. In every country, real GDP per capita is increasing, and hence so are living standards. However, quintile shares do change over time. In the next section we will look at the possible outcomes for equality and real per capita incomes of the quintiles if that happens.

While all countries show increasing per capita incomes, this scenario still projects a considerable degree of inequality between countries, for example, the lowest per capita income in Q1 (Malta) is estimated to be about 46.3% of the Eurozone Q1.

5 Changing Quintile Shares Scenario

The difficult question is in what direction will they change and how fast? Unless there is a dramatic shock to the country's political system, change will probably be gradual and relatively small from 1 year to the next. One way to simulate the possible change in quintile shares of total income is estimate cross-country equations on each of the quintile shares and per capita GDP. This is the method used by the World Bank in a celebrated paper by Ahluwalia et al. (1979). The specification of the equation is in conformity with the Kuznets' hypothesis Kuznets (1955, 1963) which suggests that these shares will change with the level of development. If we use per capita income as a proxy for level of development, then the Kuznets' hypothesis predicts that income distribution will be relatively equal at very low levels of Y/P, and then start to become more unequal as the development process introduces modern and better paid industrial sectors to the economy. That is, the portion of the labor force still working in the traditional sectors will have lower incomes than those who are working in the modern sectors, but for the country as a whole, Y/P will be increasing. However, when enough of the labor force is absorbed into the modern sectors, household incomes will begin to become more equal again. Hence the change in the shares of income in the quintiles is best modeled as a quadratic equation. Using the data in Appendix 2 we estimated the equations in Table 5 and used them to change the quintile shares over the projected period. The specification of the regression equation is of the following form:

$$Q = a + b\,LN\,(Y/P) + c[LN\;Y/P]^2,$$

where Q is the quintile share and LN(Y/P) is the natural logarithm of the observed countries per capita GDP. Other specifications have been tried in the literature but most of them do not yield acceptable t-tests, especially when the Gini coefficient is used as the endogenous variable. One might argue that per capita GDP does not sufficiently describe level of development and that perhaps some other indicator may be more appropriate, i.e., per capita income modified by purchasing power parity, or the United Nations Human Development Index. However, for a cross-country regression with the number of observations number that are contained in Appendix 2, these t-tests are quite robust. Likewise the signs of the coefficients are in agreement with the Kuznets hypothesis.

Table 5 Quintile (D10 is the share of the top 10%) share equations

D10=	−30.1349	+	18.49346	LN Y/P	+	−1.27853	$[\text{LN Y/P}]^2$
	(t = −1.779)		(t = 4.436)			(t = −5.113)	Adj. $R^2 = 0.33$
Q1=	26.32189	+	−5.37639	LN Y/P	+	0.335518	$[\text{LN Y/P}]^2$
	(t = 5.411)		(t = −4.491)			(t = 4.672)	Adj. $R^2 = 0.11$
Q2=	30.949	+	−5.87249	LN Y/P	+	0.394023	$[\text{LN Y/P}]^2$
	(t = 5.871)		(t = −4.526)			(t = 5.0626)	Adj. $R^2 = 0.26$
Q3=	33.42415	+	−5.57745	LN Y/P	+	0.389803	$[\text{LN Y/P}]^2$
	(t = 6.615)		(t = −4.484)			(t = 5.225)	Adj. $R^2 = 0.36$
Q4=	30.99089	+	−3.27903	LN Y/P	+	0.249124	$[\text{LN Y/P}]^2$
	(t = 6.893)		(t = −2.963)			(t = 3.753)	Adj. $R^2 = 0.37$
Q5=	−20.9826	+	19.92785	LN Y/P	+	−1.35732	$[\text{LN Y/P}]^2$
	(t = −1.2)		(t = 4.629)			(t = −5.256)	Adj. $R^2 = 0.31$

Table 6 Projected per capita GDP of poorest and richest quintiles

	Q1	Q5	Q1/Q5		Q1	Q5	Q1/Q5
Austria				Italy			
2012	12,255	60,586	0.2023	2012	8,087	52,246	0.1548
2025	16,300	71,915	0.2267	2025	9,146	52,495	0.1613
Belgium				Luxembourg			
2012	11,324	64,345	0.1760	2012	27,534	130,460	0.2111
2025	14,652	75,614	0.1938	2025	41,233	162,620	0.2536
Cyprus				Malta			
2012	4,538	31,935	0.1421	2012	4,080	27,736	0.1471
2025	6,612	41,601	0.1589	2025	5,099	32,435	0.1572
Finland				Netherlands			
2012	9,973	85,634	0.1165	2012	11,954	68,847	0.1736
2025	14,290	107,844	0.1325	2025	15,553	80,830	0.1924
France				Portugal			
2012	12,127	55,921	0.2169	2012	4,917	33,456	0.1470
2025	14,551	62,837	0.2316	2025	5,939	38,272	0.1552
Germany				Slovenia			
2012	12,474	54,958	0.2270	2012	8,301	27,004	0.3074
2025	15,553	62,975	0.2470	2025	18,712	36,063	0.3522
Greece				Spain			
2012	4,592	36,613	0.1254	2012	5,967	45,243	0.1319
2025	6,377	45,661	0.1397	2025	8,254	55,714	0.1482
Ireland				Eurozone			
2012	7,164	91,616	0.0782	2012	8,764	56,271	0.1558
2025	10,549	112,558	0.0937	2025	10,994	65,201	0.1686

Changing quintile shares scenario (constant 2005 Euros)

We used these equations to obtain the quintile shares found in Table 6. Since these countries are developed countries, the change in quintile share is in the direction of more equality. So in contrast to the constant share scenario of Table 5, Table 6 shows a gradual increase of poorest quintile in the total income and a slight decline in the richest quintile of their share. The changes are incremental, and not very large from 1 year to the next, but they reflect a tendency for greater equality over the projected period. For the Eurozone region as a whole, the ratio of the share of the bottom quintile to the top quintile (Q1/Q5) increases from 15.58 to 16.86%, or about 1%. Now this is an optimistic scenario. It is quite possible that the shares of developed countries become more *unequal* rather than more equal as has happened in the United States for a decade. However, the changes in the United States may be attributed to rapid restructuring of the economy with new technology, thereby creating a new potential path for GDP and new "modern sectors" and hence differentiated wages in the modern and traditional sectors. Also, the real mean household income has been declining in the United States since the year 2000 (see *Income, Poverty, and Health Insurance Coverage in the United States: 2011,* **Current Population Reports,** U.S. Department of Commerce, P60-243, Sept. 2012.) Real per capita income in the United States increased from 2000 to 2007, but declined from 2008 to 2009 and then slightly increased in 2010 and 2011, but it did not reach the level of 2007.

6 Conclusions

In the recovery period from the "Great recession", that is, the years from 2012 to 2025, the gross domestic product of the group of countries which form the Eurozone will probably return to its historical growth rate. The growth rates used in this study are about one-half of a per cent less than the growth rates that prevailed in these countries before the recession, which in our opinion is probably a bit too pessimistic. But, even with this conservative growth rate, if households in the Eurozone continue to save and import with the same propensities as they have since 1995, then living standards will continue to rise and unemployment rates will go back to historical levels. The increase in living standards is not only true on the average, but it is true for all population quintiles. The increases will be gradual, and there is no tendency for closing the gap between the richest and the poorest quintiles, but some improvement in the differences may occur if Kuznets hypothesis is correct. However, these projections are based on GDP per person, which ignores the transfers that occur through government redistribution. Our estimates of final consumption indicate that its share in GDP is completely consistent with the historical period. Hence, unless there is a surge in government spending, the social expenditure that has been put in place for health care, welfare, etc., should be plausible over the projected period. Especially since the group as a whole has a surplus on the external (and internal) balances. In all probability the group will grow faster than our projections, and that of course should provide even more resources for redistribution. Nevertheless, even the poorest quintiles of population in the group are far better off than the poor in every other part of the world. This is true because of higher incomes for the lower quintiles of population, and generous redistribution in the form of social expenditure that is not found anywhere else.

Appendix 1: Estimated Parameters

	Savings		Imports		
Country	a	b	a	b	c
Austria	−43, 710.49	0.4114	44, 701.25	0.860	−0.117
Belgium	−38, 031.89	0.3521	24, 585.66	0.803	0.184
Cyprus	2, 431.56	0.0081	−2, 653.41	0.657	0.362
Finland	−13, 384.91	0.3265	−36, 147.50	0.357	0.408
France	67, 638.95	0.1559	−666, 516.56	0.190	0.190
Germany	−760, 699.50	0.5030	−288, 898.25	0.648	0.200
Greece	1, 958.77	0.0992	−7, 936.42	1.200	0.101
Ireland	−5, 884.35	0.3976	−28, 200.68	0.158	0.705
Italy	140, 238.39	0.1295	−546, 676.94	0.615	0.409
Luxembourg	−4, 974.03	0.6002	−1, 274.28	0.815	0.021
Malta	1, 845.45	−0.1437	−0.14	0.841	0.065
Netherlands	−37, 616.76	0.3314	−90, 241.41	0.700	0.272
Portugal	30, 749.09	−0.0139	−47, 118.03	0.469	0.485
Slovenia	−4, 203.31	0.3762	−4, 774.48	0.651	0.360
Spain	68, 225.08	0.1785	−258, 516.64	0.175	0.483

	Harrod–Domar Model			Investment	Shares
Country	a	b	ICOR	a	b
Austria	246, 986.20	0.0883	11.325	5.22265	−0.00249
Belgium	312, 758.75	0.0844	11.848	−0.69207	0.00045
Cyprus	12, 275.41	0.1643	6.086	−1.26402	0.00073
Finland	150, 308.98	0.1193	8.382	−1.37967	0.00079
France		0.0820	12.195	−3.13389	0.00166
Germany		0.0683	14.641	3.39664	−0.00160
Greece	179, 423.67	0.1099	9.099	1.96835	−0.00088
Ireland	127, 452.89	0.1618	6.180	10.90044	−0.00533
Italy		0.0403	24.814	−0.55932	0.00038
Luxembourg	25, 904.74	0.1680	5.952	−3.66980	0.00194
Malta	4, 695.25	0.1218	8.210	20.45110	−0.01012
Netherlands	526, 142.38	0.0967	10.341	2.61712	−0.00121
Portugal	166, 482.22	0.0521	19.194	7.46593	−0.00361
Slovenia	26, 109.70	0.1172	8.532	−2.38425	0.00132
Spain	852, 913.25	0.0937	10.672	−2.25956	0.00126

Appendix 2

	Quintiles					Top 10%	Survey	GDP per capita Constant
	Q1	Q2	Q3	Q4	Q5	D10	year	2005 US$
Algeria	2.3	6.6	12.1	21	57.9	40.5	1968	3, 793
Argentina	5.1	9.3	13.1	18.6	53.9	40.7	1961	4, 418
Argentina	4.4	9.7	14.1	21.5	50.3	35.2	1970	5, 376
Australia	3.8	12.2	18.3	26	39.7	30.9	1976	5, 376
Australia	6.4	12.7	18.1	24.2	38.7	29.4	1979	23, 633
Australia	4.4	11.1	17.5	24.8	42.2	25.8	1985	18, 659
Australia	5.9	12	17.2	23.6	41.3	25.4	1994	25, 337
Austria	5.1	10.3	15.4	22.5	46.7	30.5	1974	15, 009
Austria	4.7	9.5	16.5	24.1	45.1	28.7	1976	15, 809
Austria WB	8.1	13.2	17.3	22.9	38.5	23.5	1997	30, 808
Austria	7.3	13.4	18.2	24.0	37.1	21.8	2010	40, 717
Bangladesh	6.6	11	15.1	21.1	46.3	31.2	1974	378
Bangladesh	6.2	10.9	15	21	46.9	32	1977	357
Bangladesh	6.2	10.5	14.6	20.8	48.1	33	1982	327
Bangladesh	9.5	13.4	17	21.6	38.6	24.6	1988	370
Barbados	4	10.7	15.8	22.6	46.9	31.1	1970	3, 692
Belgium	4.5	10.5	15.8	22.4	46.8	31.1	1975	19, 749
Belgium	7.9	13.7	18.6	23.8	36	21.5	1978	25, 178
Belgium WB	8.3	14.1	17.7	22.7	37.3	22.6	1996	32, 846
Belgium	7	12.2	16.6	22.4	41.9	26.8	2001	25, 095
Bolivia	5.6	9.7	14.5	22	48.2	31.7	1990	1, 011
Bolivia WB	4	9.2	14.8	22.9	49.1	32	1999	1, 172
Botswana	4	7.5	11	17.1	60.4	46.5	1975	992
Botswana	4.3	7.7	12	18.4	57.6	42	1982	1, 438
Botswana	3.6	6.9	11.4	19.2	58.9	42.9	1985	1, 148
Brazil	2	5	9.4	17	66.6	50.6	1972	1, 885
Brazil	2.3	5.9	10.3	17.9	63.7	48.3	1982	3, 380
Brazil	2.1	4.9	8.9	16.8	67.5	51.3	1989	3, 669
Brazil WB	2	5.7	10	18	64.4	46.7	1998	5, 820
Bulgaria	10.4	13.9	17.3	22.2	36.2	21.9	1992	1, 327
Canada	3.8	10.7	17.9	25.6	42	23.4	1977	23, 236
Canada	4.6	11	17.7	25.2	41.6	25	1981	23, 245
Canada	5.7	11.8	17.7	24.6	40.2	24.1	1987	24, 496
Canada	5.1	11.7	17.4	24.1	41.7	25.7	1995	24, 699
Chile	3.7	6.8	10.3	16.2	62.9	48.9	1989	3, 475
Chile WB	3.3	6.6	10.5	17.4	62.2	47	2000	5, 657
China	6.4	11	16.4	24.4	41.8	24.6	1990	498
Colombia	2.8	7	12.1	18.6	59.4	44.6	1970	1, 965
Colombia	3.6	7.6	12.6	20.4	55.8	39.5	1991	2, 301

(continued)

	Quintiles					Top 10%	Survey	GDP per capita Constant
	Q1	Q2	Q3	Q4	Q5	D10	year	2005 US$
Colombia WB	2.7	6.6	10.8	18	61.8	46.5	1999	3,030
Costa Rica	4.8	9.5	13.6	21.7	50.4	33.8	1971	2,874
Costa Rica	4	9.1	14.3	21.9	50.8	34.1	1989	3,188
Costa Rica	4.2	8.9	13.7	21.7	51.5	34.8	2000	4,586
Cote d'Ivoire	3.9	6.7	11.2	19.7	58.5	41.5	1970	1,139
Cote d'Ivoire	7.3	11.9	16.3	22.3	42.2	26.9	1988	1,308
Cyprus	4.5	11.5	17.5	24.4	42.1	25.9	1984	7,364
Cyprus	6.4	11.3	15.8	22.1	44.5	29.0	2009	21,370
Czech Rep. WB	10.3	14.5	17.7	21.7	35.9	22.4	1996	7,570
Denmark	5.4	12	18.4	25.6	38.6	22.3	1981	22,561
Denmark WB	8.3	14.7	18.2	22.9	35.8	21.3	1997	38,162
Dom. Rep.	4.5	8.2	12.1	18.6	56.5	41.7	1977	2,775
Dom. Rep.	4.2	7.9	12.5	19.7	55.6	39.6	1989	1,681
Dom. Rep WB	5.1	8.6	13	20	53.3	37.9	1998	2,862
Egypt	7.2	12.2	16.5	22.2	41.9	26.9	1990	875
El Salvador	5.5	10	14.8	22.4	47.4	29.5	1977	566
El Salvad.	2.9	7.4	12.4	20.2	57.1	40.6	2000	1,246
Ethiopia	6.4	10.9	14.9	19.9	48	36.3	1970	342
Ethiopia	8.6	12.7	16.4	21.1	41.3	27.5	1981	304
Fiji	5.1	9.7	14.7	22.8	47.7	30.6	1972	2,210
Finland	2.7	10	17.3	26.4	43.6	21.2	1977	18,508
Finland	6.3	12.1	18.4	25.5	37.6	21.7	1981	20,659
Finland WB	9.6	14.1	17.5	22.1	36.7	22.6	2000	26,537
France	4.3	9.8	16.3	22.7	46.9	30.4	1970	11,596
France	4.2	10	15.7	23	47.1	30.7	1975	19,661
France	5.6	11.8	17.2	23.5	41.9	26.1	1989	24,997
France WB	7.2	12.6	17.2	22.8	40.2	25.1	1995	32,417
France INSE	8.3	13.4	17.5	22.7	38.1	23.5	2008	40,754
Germany	5.9	10.5	15.3	22.7	45.6	29.1	1970	10,986
Germany	7	11.8	17.1	23.9	40.3	24.4	1988	25,843
Germany	6	12	17.9	24.5	39.6	24	1978	22,595
Germany	7.9	13.8	18.1	23.3	36.9	22.1	2004	34,133
Ghana	7	11.3	15.8	21.8	44.1	29	1988	887
Greece	6.6	12.5	16.2	20.9	43.8	29.5	1974	8,787
Greece WB	7.1	11.4	15.8	22	43.6	28.5	1998	14,522
Greece	5.6	11.3	16.3	22.8	44.0	28.2	2005	21,468
Guatemala	3.6	7.7	11.6	19.1	58	35.8	1970	1,281
Guatemala	5.3	8.4	11.9	18	56.4	42.1	1981	2,038
Guatemala	2.1	5.8	10.5	18.6	63	46.6	1989	1,235
Guatemala	2.6	5.9	9.8	17.6	64.1	48.3	2000	1,725
Guinea-Bissa	2.1	6.5	12	20.6	58.9	42.4	1991	835

(continued)

	Quintiles					Top 10%	Survey	GDP per capita Constant
	Q1	Q2	Q3	Q4	Q5	D10	year	2005 US$
Honduras	2.7	6	10.2	17.6	63.5	47.9	1989	1,864
Honduras WB	2.7	6.7	11.8	19.9	58.9	42.2	1999	1,224
Hungary	9.1	15	19	23.5	33.4	19.1	1975	3,508
Hungary	10.9	14.8	18	22	34.4	20.8	1989	4,420
Hungary WB	8.9	12.3	16	21.2	41.6	27.4	1999	5,428
India	7	9.2	13.9	20.5	49.4	35.2	1975	481
India	8.8	12.5	16.2	21.3	41.3	27.1	1989	505
Indonesia	6.8	10.5	13.4	17.3	52	40.7	1971	330
Indonesia	6.6	7.8	12.6	23.6	49.4	34	1976	836
Indonesia	8.7	12.1	15.9	21.1	42.3	27.9	1990	940
Iran	2.7	5.5	9.6	16.8	65.4	51.2	1975	4,441
Ireland	4.6	10.8	16.9	24.4	43.3	26.5	1980	13,160
Ireland WB	7.1	11.8	15.8	22	43.3	27.6	1996	24,529
Ireland	3.7	9.3	15.4	24.0	47.6	30.0	2005	48,761
Israel	5.6	12.4	18	24.5	39.5	23.5	1976	12,533
Israel	6	12.1	17.8	24.5	39.6	23.5	1979	13,002
Israel WB	6.9	11.4	16.3	22.9	44.3	28.2	1997	22,765
Italy	6.5	11.7	16.6	23	42.2	26.6	1976	11,074
Italy	6.8	12	16.7	23.5	41	25.3	1986	17,334
Italy WB	6.5	12	16.8	22.8	42	26.8	2000	21,838
Italy	6.8	11.8	16.1	22.0	43.3	28.2	2006	30,711
Jamaica	6	9.9	14.5	21.3	48.4	32.6	1990	2,821
Japan	8.2	12.7	17	22.8	39.3	24.2	1972	11,014
Japan	8.7	13.2	17.5	23.1	37.5	22.4	1979	20,619
Japan WB	10.6	14.2	17.6	22	35.7	21.7	1993	45,603
Jordan	9	14.4	18.3	23	35.3	21	1986	3,374
Jordan	6.5	10.3	14.6	20.9	47.7	32.6	1991	1,557
Kenya	4.7	10.2	14	20.1	51	36.1	1977	1,057
Kenya	3.4	6.7	10.7	17.3	61.8	47.9	1992	536
Korea	8.1	13.1	17.1	22.4	39.3	24.2	1981	3,643
Korea	7.7	12.8	16.7	22.4	40.3	25.1	1985	3,949
Korea	7.4	12.3	16.3	21.8	42.2	27.6	1988	6,808
Korea WB	7.9	13.6	18	23.1	37.5	22.5	1998	9,182
Lesotho	2.9	6.4	11.3	19.5	60	43.6	1986	304
Lesotho	1	4.6	10.1	19.5	64.8	47.8	1988	406
Malawi	2.3	5	8	13.9	70.9	58.1	1980	572
Malaysia	3.5	7.7	12.5	20.3	56	39.9	1970	1,408
Malaysia	4.6	8.3	13	20.4	53.7	37.9	1989	3,407
Malaysia WB	4.4	8.1	12.9	20.3	54.3	38.4	1997	5,871
Mauritania	3.5	10.7	16.2	23.3	46.3	30.2	1987	1,210
Mauritius	4	7.5	11	17	60.5	46.7	1981	2,297

(continued)

	Quintiles					Top 10%	Survey	GDP per capita Constant
	Q1	Q2	Q3	Q4	Q5	D10	year	2005 US$
Mexico	3.5	7.9	13.2	21.6	53.8	39.1	1977	4,162
Mexico	4.1	7.8	12.3	19.9	55.9	39.5	1984	4,600
Mexico WB	3.1	7.2	11.7	19	59.1	43.1	2000	7,180
Morocco	3.4	7.8	12.7	20	55.9	40.2	1971	1,180
Morocco	6.6	10.5	15	21.7	46.3	30.5	1990	1,611
Nepal	6.5	10.8	14.9	20.9	47	31.9	1977	281
Nepal	9.1	12.9	16.7	21.8	39.5	25	1984	260
Netherland	8.1	13.3	17.7	22.8	38.1	23.3	1977	22,790
Netherland	7.1	13.8	17.7	23.1	38.9	23.9	1981	20,553
Netherland	8.2	13.1	18.1	23.7	36.9	21.9	1988	24,613
Netherland	7.3	12.7	17.2	22.8	40.1	25.1	1994	28,680
Netherland	6.9	12.4	17.2	23.1	40.4	25.2	2010	42,289
New Zealand	5.7	12.1	17.2	23.7	41.3	25.4	1972	12,067
New Zealand	5.1	10.8	16.2	23.2	44.7	28.7	1981	15,279
New Zealand	5.3	11.5	17	23.6	42.6	26.7	1988	20,523
New Zealand	6.4	11.4	15.8	22.6	43.8	27.8	1997	21,618
Niger	4.7	9.6	14.6	21.8	49.4	33.3	1973	455
Nigeria	5.4	9.2	13.3	19.2	52.9	38.7	1970	829
Norway	4.3	11.3	18.1	25.2	41	24.3	1976	24,902
Norway	6.2	12.8	18.9	25.3	36.7	21.2	1979	29,492
Norway	5	12	17.9	25.1	40	23.7	1982	27,153
Norway WB	9.6	14	17.2	22	37.2	23.4	2000	42,241
Pakistan	8	12.5	16.1	22.1	41.4	27	1971	832
Pakistan	7.4	11.5	15.2	20.9	45	30.3	1979	703
Pakistan	8.4	12.9	16.9	22.2	39.7	25.2	1991	604
Panama	4.6	10.6	15.5	21.9	47.4	32.2	1972	3,347
Panama	2	6.3	11.6	20.3	59.8	42.1	1989	3,394
Panama WB	2.4	6.5	11.2	19.6	60.3	43.3	2000	4,431
Peru	1.9	5.1	11	21	61	42.9	1972	1,952
Peru	4.9	9.2	13.7	21	51.4	35.4	1985	1,219
Philippines	5.5	9.2	12.9	19.1	53.3	38.8	1975	1,202
Philippines	6.5	10.1	14.4	21.2	47.8	32.1	1988	1,069
Poland WB	7.3	11.8	16.2	22.2	42.5	27.4	1999	5,041
Portugal	5.9	11.2	14.6	20.1	48.2	34.4	1974	6,211
Portugal WB	5.8	11	15.5	21.9	45.9	29.8	1997	13,386
Portugal	6.6	11.3	15.5	21.6	45	29.8	2005	18,196
Rwanda	9.7	13.1	16.7	21.6	38.9	24.6	1983	506
Senegal	3.5	7	11.6	19.3	58.6	42.8	1991	1,072
Singapore	6.5	10.3	14	20	49.2	34.4	1978	8,500
Singapore	5.1	9.9	14.6	21.4	48.9	33.5	1982	11,324

(continued)

	Quintiles					Top 10%	Survey	GDP per capita Constant
	Q1	Q2	Q3	Q4	Q5	D10	year	2005 US$
Spain	5.9	11.8	16.8	23.1	42.4	26.8	1974	8,715
Spain	6.9	12.5	17.3	23.4	40	24.6	1981	12,623
Spain WB	7.5	12.6	17	22.6	40.3	25.2	1990	18,535
Spain	5.6	11.6	16.7	23.2	42.8	27.1	2005	26,058
Sri Lanka	7.3	12	16.1	21.8	42.8	30.6	1973	818
Sri Lanka	6.1	10.8	15	21.2	46.9	31.7	1981	568
Sri Lanka	8.9	13.1	16.9	21.7	39.3	25.2	1990	655
Sweden	5.2	11	16.2	23.5	44.1	27.5	1970	18,098
Sweden	8	13.2	17.4	24.5	36.9	20.8	1981	27,745
Sweden WB	9.1	14	17.6	22.7	36.6	22.2	2000	31,457
Switzerland	5.2	11.7	16.4	22.1	44.6	29.8	1982	30,069
Switzerland w	6.9	12.7	17.3	22.9	40.3	25.2	1992	49,229
Thailand	5.1	8.2	11.7	17.9	57.1	42.8	1976	1,147
Thailand	3.4	6.7	10.5	17.1	62.2	47.8	1986	1,328
Thailand	6.1	9.4	13.5	20.3	50.7	35.3	1988	1,718
Trinidad & amp; Tobago	4.2	9.1	13.9	22.8	50	33	1975	7,216
Trinidad & amp; Tobago WB	5.5	10.3	15.5	22.7	45.9	29.9	1992	5,755
Tunisia	4.2	8.1	12.3	19	56.3	41.2	1975	2,510
Tunisia	5.9	10.4	15.3	22.1	46.3	30.7	1990	2,288
Uganda	5	8.9	12.8	19	54.3	35.8	1970	573
Uganda	8.5	12.1	16	21.5	41.9	27.2	1989	462
U.K.	5.8	11	17.6	24.7	41	24.8	1982	15,727
U.K. WB	6.1	11.4	16	22.5	44	28.5	1999	29,518
U.R. Tanzani	5.3	9	13.1	19.2	53.4	39.4	1975	714
U.R. Tanzani	2.4	5.7	10.4	18.7	62.7	46.5	1991	316
U.S.A.	4.2	10.8	17.1	24.5	43.3	27.1	1975	8,755
U.S.A.	4.2	10.3	16.2	24.9	44.4	27.7	1980	13,061
U.S.A.	3.9	9.6	15.6	24	46.9	30.1	1990	31,431
U.S.A.	3.6	9	14.8	22.8	49.9	33.3	2000	39,498
U.S.A.	3.4	8.7	14.7	23.2	50.4	33	2005	42,330
U.S.A.	3.3	8.5	14.6	23.4	50.3	33.4	2010	41,858
Uruguay	6	10.9	15.5	22.3	45.3	29.3	1983	3,292
Venezuela	3.6	9.4	14.2	20.8	52	36.4	1971	5,385
Venezuela	4.8	9.5	14.4	21.9	49.5	33.2	1989	3,101
Venezuela	3	8.4	13.7	21.6	53.4	36.3	1998	4,556
Zambia	5.6	9.6	14.2	21	49.7	34.2	1991	559
Zimbabwe	4.5	7.4	10.6	15.5	61.7	49.3	1975	2,266
Zimbabwe	4	6.3	10	17.4	62.3	46.9	1990	1,551

References

Ahluwalia MS, Carter NG, Chenery HB (1979) Growth and poverty in developing countries. J Dev Econ 6:307–342

Kuznets S (1955) Economic growth and income inequality. Am Econ Rev 45:1–28

Kuznets S (1963) Quantitative aspects of the economic growth of nations: VIII. Distribution of income by size. Econ Dev Cult Change 11(2):1–80

Effort and Hours over the Business Cycle

Domenico J. Marchetti and Francesco Nucci

Abstract Despite the importance of work effort very little is known about its cyclical behavior. While models with labor hoarding predict a pro-cyclical effort, other models reach an opposite conclusion and recent contributions emphasize the increase of workers' effort in the US economy during the Great recession. By using high-quality, firm-level data, we obtain an estimate of change in labor effort from a dynamic cost minimization set-up and provide some evidence that the relationship between effort and hours can be non monotonic. We find that, below a certain number of hours per employee, the marginal hour is worked with an increasing hourly effort. During expansions, however, if a critical level of hours per employee is reached, then every additional hour is worked with decreasing effort, arguably due to physical and mental fatigue from long hours.

1 Introduction

A notable feature of the Great recession in the US economy over the period 2007–2009 is the increase of labor productivity. As reported by Lazear et al. (2013), between the start of the recession in 2007:Q4 and the first quarter after the recession (2009:Q3), aggregate output declined by 7.2 % in nonfarm business but hours worked fell by relatively more, with a corresponding rise of labor productivity of about 3.2 %. This evidence is consistent with the vanishing pro-cyclicality of labor

D.J. Marchetti
Financial Intelligence Unit, Bank of Italy, Rome, Italy
e-mail: domenico.marchetti@bancaditalia.it

F. Nucci (✉)
Department of Economics and Law, Sapienza University, Rome, Italy
e-mail: francesco.nucci@uniroma1.it

L. Paganetto (ed.), *Wealth, Income Inequalities, and Demography*,
DOI 10.1007/978-3-319-05909-9_9,

productivity in the US economy since mid-1980s, a finding which has been recently documented in the literature.[1]

According to Lazear et al. (2013), the rise of productivity during recessions arises from the increased effort of the employees. In particular, when the probability of unemployment rises during downturns and the workers' alternatives decline, employees are induced to put forth a higher level of effort as the firm "makes do with less", i.e. seeks to obtain the same output from fewer workers. This is in line with the prediction of some efficiency wage models where effort is an adjustable variable and varies over the business cycle. In this case, unemployment acts as a threat, a "discipline device", and the correlation between effort and employment is therefore negative (see, Uhlig and Xu 1996, Chatterji and Sparks 1991, Riggi 2012 and the seminal contribution by Shapiro and Stiglitz 1984).

Another explanation for the rise of effort during downturns is provided by Bils et al. (2014), who develop a Mortensen-Pissarides matching model of employment that features wage flexibility for new hires but wage stickiness within matches. They show that if wages are rigid in the short run and the firm and workers bargain each period on the level of effort, then, during a recession, the firm requires more tasks from their employees who therefore provide extra effort and produce more, causing productivity to increase.[2]

By contrast, models of labor hoarding predict that effort co-moves positively with employment as it tends to increase in booms and decrease in recessions. In this class of models adjustment costs typically affect firms' decisions on hiring and firing and labor is therefore utilized more intensively in expansions than in recessions. Cyclical variation in labor utilization (i.e. work effort) may act as an important shocks' propagation mechanism in the economy (see, e.g., Burnside et al. 1993 and Burnside and Eichembaum 1996). Besides business cycle models, a relevant strand of literature where varying workers' effort has a potentially significant impact is that on production function regressions, that seek to investigate market structure, the extent of returns to scale and the existence of external effects (see, e.g., Burnside 1996).

[1]According to Galí and Gambetti (2009) the unconditional correlation between labor productivity and hours changes from 0.18 in the pre-1984 period to −0.46 in the post-1984 period. Similarly, the correlation between labor productivity and hours conditional on non-technology shocks undergoes a dramatic shifts: while in the pre-1984 period labor productivity responds positively to non-technological shocks, exhibiting a procyclical profile, in the post-1984 period it responds negatively, thus becoming countercyclical conditional to non-technology shocks (see also Barnichon 2010, Galí and Van Rens 2014).

[2]There are other theoretical explanations for the evidence that labor productivity is no longer procyclical. Galí and Van Rens (2014) show that the reduced labor market turnover in the US economy, by lowering hiring frictions, has allowed firms to adjust employment more easily in response to shocks. Nucci and Riggi (2013) show that the vanishing procyclicality of productivity originates from an increased flexibility of wages driven by a higher incidence of performance-related pay schemes.

In spite of its importance and notwithstanding the attempts made in the literature to control for it, very little is known about the cyclical behaviour of work effort. In the empirical literature the unobservability of effort is dealt with in a number of ways. Fay and Medoff (1985) directly ask firms a number of questions on labor hoarding and how work effort varies during expansions. Abbott et al. (1988) approximate labor utilization by the number of hours worked per employee, whereas Caballero and Lyons (1992) use data on overtime hours and the ratio of production to non-production workers. Shea (1990) obtains information on the intensity of labor use from data on accident rates, while Basu (1996) use materials input growth as an indicator of cyclical factor utilization. Lazear et al. (2013) document that an increase in the local unemployment rate of 5 percentage points is conducive to a 3.9 % rise of worker effort (see also Schor 1987).[3]

Against this background, we seek to analyse some dimensions of the cyclical behavior of effort. Unlike most contributions in the literature, we make use of data at the firm level. In particular, we rely on high-quality panel information on a representative sample of Italian manufacturing firms and investigate how the effort exerted by employees at work is affected by the evolution of hours worked, which typically reflects the firm-specific business cycle.

Our approach to the identification of work effort builds upon the work by Basu, Fernald and Kimball (2006). In order to identify technology shocks, they adopt a fairly general production function approach that accommodates variations in effort and capital utilization as well as departures from perfect competition and constant returns. They use optimal conditions stemming from a dynamic cost-minimization problem to derive proxies of changes in effort and capital utilization based on observed variables (see Marchetti and Nucci 2005, for an application to firm-level data). The important insight of their approach is that, in choosing the optimal amount of labor input, a firm operates simultaneously on both the observed margin (hours per worker) and the unobserved margin (effort expended per hour).

We derive a model-based measure of labor effort at the firm level along these lines and analyse on empirical grounds the relation between effort and hours per worker. The result from the baseline empirical set-up is that a rise at the margin of hours per employee is conducive to a lower effort expended per hour. While this finding is consistent with the view that effort is countercyclical, we argue however that the relation between effort per hour and the number of hours is more complex. In a very insightful contribution, Becker (1977) points to an important role of workers' fatigue from long hours and argues that the relation between effort and hours can be positive under some conditions and negative under others. He asserts convincingly that "there is no single "the" relation, not only in magnitude but also in sign" (1977,

[3]Other contributions take a different approach to this measurement problem, extracting information on work effort by imposing optimality conditions on the behavior of economic agents. In Bils and Cho's (1994) model, workers simultaneously adjust leisure at work and leisure at home, thus implying a close relationship between effort and the length of the workweek. Sbordone (1996) derives effort within a cost minimization set-up based on a compensation scheme with wages increasing more than proportionally with effort.

p. 19). Along these lines, the hypothesis that we investigate in this paper is that the physical and mental fatigue is likely to set in beyond a given level of hours, growing at rising rates as hours worked continue to rise. Eventually effort per hour may decline as hours increase.

We provide some evidence consistent with the view that below a certain number of hours per employee, the marginal hour is worked with an increasing hourly effort. In other words, when firms face increasing demand, they typically respond by increasing both man-hours and the intensity of the effort per hour exerted by each employee. However, our findings are also consistent with the hypothesis that if the number of hours per worker increases sharply and reaches a critical threshold value, for example because new hiring is difficult owing to labor market rigidities or technological factors (e.g., the need for workers with very specific skills), then physical and mental fatigue sets in, and the marginal hour is worked with decreasing work effort. Therefore, if hours per employee are below a critical value, the empirical relation between hours and hourly effort is estimated to be positive; otherwise it is negative.[4]

The empirical investigation is conducted by using the generalized method of moments (GMM) estimator for panel data developed by Arellano and Bond (1991). We first compute our firm-level, time-varying measure of change in work effort by estimating the elasticity of effort per hour with respect to hours. Subsequently, we provide evidence that the empirical relation between hourly effort and hours per worker is non-monotonic. This evidence on a hump-shaped relation is obtained by separately estimating the sign of the hours elasticity of effort under different stages of the firm-specific business cycle. The latter are identified based on the observed level and dynamics of hours at the firm level. In addition, we also provide evidence that the effort function is strictly concave around the mean value of hours per employee. We do so by estimating the structural parameters of a second-order Taylor approximation of the effort function around that value. We also find that the firm's provision of wage premia linked to performance is not conducive to a sign switch, from negative to positive, in the hours elasticity of work effort.

The remainder of the paper is organized as follows. The next section outlines the theoretical framework for identifying effort and investigating the relation between effort and hours. Section 3 illustrates the data and the methodology used for estimation. Section 4 reports the empirical findings. Section 5 contains some concluding remarks.

---

[4]Basu and Kimball (1997) estimate a positive response of unobserved effort to hours per worker. By contrast, Bils and Chang (2003) show that, if wages are rigid, a technology improvement would result in an increase in hours and a decline of effort.

2 Theoretical Framework

2.1 A Model for Deriving Work Effort

Following Marchetti and Nucci (2005), let us consider the following production function, $Y_{it} = F(L_{it}, \tilde{K}_{it}, M_{it}, Z_{it})$, where Y_{it} is gross output. L_{it} denotes effective labor services and can be expressed as the product of the number of employees, N_{it}, the number of hours per employee, H_{it}, and the amount of effort expended per hour, E_{it}. Analogously, $\tilde{K}_{it}$ is effective capital services and is the product of the installed capital stock, K_{it}, and its rate of utilization, U_{it}. M_{it} is the volume of intermediate inputs and Z_{it} indexes technology.

If we differentiate, after taking logs, the production function with respect to time, we obtain

$$dy = \frac{\partial F}{\partial L}\frac{L}{Y}(dn + dh + de) + \frac{\partial F}{\partial \tilde{K}}\frac{\tilde{K}}{Y}(dk + du) + \frac{\partial F}{\partial M}\frac{M}{Y}dm + dz, \qquad (1)$$

where lower-case letters represent logs and the elasticities of output with respect to each input are the weights on the rate of growth of that input; the output elasticity with respect to technology is normalized to one.

Output elasticities, for example the one with respect to labor, L, can be expressed as $\frac{\partial F}{\partial L}\frac{L}{Y} = \mu\frac{P_L L}{PY} = \mu s_L$, where P_L is the labor input price, μ is the mark-up ratio of price over marginal costs and s_L is the revenue-based share of labor. Output elasticities can also be expressed as

$$\frac{\partial F}{\partial L}\frac{L}{Y} = \gamma c_L; \qquad \frac{\partial F}{\partial \tilde{K}}\frac{\tilde{K}}{Y} = \gamma c_K; \qquad \frac{\partial F}{\partial M}\frac{M}{Y} = \gamma c_M; \qquad (2)$$

where γ is the returns-to-scale parameter, and c_L, c_K and c_M are the cost-based factor shares.

By replacing the output elasticities in (1) with γ times the factor shares, one obtains an equation that still has two unobservable variables: the growth rate of effort, *de*, and that of capital utilization, *du*.

In order to control for these aspects, we follow Basu et al. (2006) and consider the following dynamic cost minimization problem set-up featuring adjustment costs of increasing (decreasing) the labor force and the capital stock (see also Marchetti and Nucci 2005):

$$\underset{H,E,A,I,U,M}{Min} \int_0^{\infty} \left[NWG(H,E) + NW\Psi\left(\frac{A}{N}\right) + P_I KJ\left(\frac{I}{K}\right) + P_M M \right] e^{-rt} dt \qquad (3)$$

subject to

$$Y = F(NHE, UK, M, Z)$$

$$\overset{\circ}{N} = A \quad and \quad K = I - \delta(U)K.$$

According to (3), the firm's costs in each period are total payments for labor and intermediate inputs as well as expenditure for investment goods and for undertaking net hiring. W denotes the base wage; $WG(H, E)$ is the total compensation of each employee and varies with the number of hours and the amount effort exerted. As in Basu and Kimball (1997), these payments to each employee are assumed to be shaped by implicit contracts, so that their actual evolution may not be observed. A is hiring net of separations, while $NW\Psi\left(\frac{A}{N}\right)$ represents the cost of varying the number of employees. The total cost of investment is given by $P_I K$ times the adjustment costs evolving through the function $J\left(\frac{I}{K}\right)$; P_I denotes the price of investment goods, δ is the rate of capital depreciation and, as in Basu and Kimball (1997), it increases with capital utilization, U. P_M denotes the price of intermediate inputs.

The intratemporal first-order conditions for cost minimization are reported in appendix. By combining the optimal conditions with respect to hours, H, and effort per hour, E, the following equation is derived

$$\frac{EG_E(H,E)}{G(H,E)} = \frac{HG_H(H,E)}{G(H,E)}. \tag{4}$$

The above relation implicitly defines effort, E, as a function of hours, H. Following Basu et al. (2006), we define ζ as the elasticity of effort with respect to hours, evaluated at the steady state ($\zeta \equiv H^*E'(H^*)/E(H^*)$) and log-linearizing, we obtain $de = \zeta dh$. Hence, the following equation holds for changes in effective labor input:

$$dl = dn + dh + de = dn + (1+\zeta)\,dh. \tag{5}$$

Combining Eqs. (1), (2), (5) and (A.13), we obtain the following regression specification:

$$\begin{aligned} dy_{it} = {} & \beta_1 dx_{it} + \beta_2(c_{Lit}dh_{it}) + \beta_3\left[c_{Kit}\left(dp_{M,it} + dm_{it} - dp_{Iit} - dk_{it}\right)\right] \\ & + \beta_4\left[c_{Kit}(di_{it} - dk_{it})\right] + \beta_5' W_{it} + dz_{it}, \end{aligned} \tag{6}$$

where dx_{it} denotes changes in the observed component of inputs, each weighted by the corresponding cost-based input shares: $dx_{it} = c_{Lit}(dn_{it} + dh_{it}) + c_{Kit}dk_{it} + c_{Mit}dm_{it}$. The specification above also includes a vector of dummy variables, W_{it}, referring to the sector of manufacturing industry, the year, the firm's size and the occurrence of an extraordinary corporate operation (i.e. a merger, acquisition or break-up). The term dz_{it} denotes technology variation.

Basu et al. (2006) and Marchetti and Nucci (2005, 2007) measure technology growth, dz_{it}, as the residual from estimating an equation similar to (6) and then investigate the effect on input use of a technology improvement. On the contrary, our focus in this paper is on labor effort and, in order to measure it, we need to recover the elasticity of hourly effort with respect to hours, ζ. The unknown coefficients to estimate in Eq. (6) are β_1, β_2, β_3, β_4 and β_5'. By considering Eqs. (1), (2) and (5), the first parameter, β_1, represents the degree of internal returns to scale, while the second parameter, β_2, allows us to derive the hours elasticity of effort, ζ, since $\beta_2 = \beta_1 \cdot \zeta$. Once this information is available, our model-based measure of changes in hourly effort is obtained for each firm as $de_{it} = \zeta \cdot dh_{it}$. In the next section, we investigate in more detail the relation between effort and hours.

2.2 The Effort-Hours Equilibrium Relation

In the previous section, we introduced the effort function, $e(h)$, as implicitly defined by the firm's optimal condition (5). Building on that equation, one obtains

$$e'(h) = \frac{H}{E}\frac{G_H + HG_{HH} - EG_{EH}}{G_E + EG_{EE} - HG_{EH}}. \tag{7}$$

It is clear from this equation that the slope of $e(h)$ is determined by the shape of the compensation function, $G(H, E)$, which, in turn, depends on workers preferences. In particular, from the perspective of employers, effort and hours enter symmetrically into production and, in negotiating with each worker, employers care about effective labor service, i.e. the product of E and H. Along similar lines Becker (1977) argues convincingly that firms buy a package of effort and hours from each worker and the compensation is tied to the package rather than separately to units of hour or effort.

Arguably, the way workers achieve any particular level $E \cdot H$ hinges on how hourly effort and hours enter the utility function, which has implications for the compensation arrangement. We consider workers with preferences defined over consumption, hours of work and effort per hour at work. In particular, we assume that a representative worker has time-separable preferences and maximizes expected lifetime utility over an infinite horizon

$$\max\ E_t \sum_{\tau=0}^{\infty} (\frac{1}{1+\rho})^{\tau} U(C_{t+\tau}, H_{t+\tau}, E_{t+\tau}) \tag{8}$$

$s.t.$

$$a_{t+\tau+1} = (1+r)a_{t+\tau} + W_{t+\tau}G(H_{t+\tau}, E_{t+\tau}) - C_{t+\tau} \qquad \tau = 0, 1, 2...$$

where $C_{t+\tau}$ and $a_{t+\tau}$ are consumption and financial wealth, r is the interest rate and ρ is the pure rate of time preference. The latter two entities are assumed to be constant. The instantaneous utility at time $t + \tau$ of this individual is given by:

$$U(C_{t+\tau}, H_{t+\tau}, E_{t+\tau}) = \ln(C_{t+\tau}) - V(H_{t+\tau}, E_{t+\tau}) \tag{9}$$

where consumption enters favorably in utility while hours and effort generate disutility. The utility function is separable in consumption and labor and the term describing the disutility of working is the following

$$V(H, E) = \frac{\alpha}{1+\sigma}(\ln H)^{1+\sigma} + \beta \ln H \ln E \tag{10}$$

where α, β and σ are positive parameters, with $\sigma > 1$, and the time index is omitted for expositional clarity. Thus, preferences are chosen so that, for a given level of effort per hour, the marginal disutility of hours worked rises with hours and the marginal disutility of effort rises with the number of hours. This latter feature is due to a "fatigue factor" that we believe is crucial in identifying the equilibrium relationship between hourly effort and hours. In particular, we now show that these preferences give raise to a hump-shaped effort function, $e(h)$, because the physical and mental fatigue associated with work imply that, in equilibrium, the effort-hours relationship is not monotonic, being upward-sloping for relatively low values of H and downward-sloping for relatively high values.

For the derivations that matter for our purposes, intratemporal optimal conditions are sufficient. In particular, the optimization conditions that we need to analyse are the following:

$$C: \qquad \lambda = \frac{1}{C}, \tag{11}$$

$$H: \qquad \lambda W G_H(\cdot) = \alpha \frac{1}{H}(\ln H)^{\sigma} + \beta \frac{1}{H} \ln E, \tag{12}$$

$$E: \qquad \lambda W G_E(\cdot) = \beta \frac{1}{E} \ln H, \tag{13}$$

where λ is the multiplier on the constraint in (8). If we multiply Eqs. (12) and (13), respectively, by H and E and then use the equilibrium condition (4) from cost minimization dictating that $\frac{E}{H} = \frac{G_H(H,E)}{G_E(H,E)}$, we can combine the two equations and obtain

$$\ln E = \ln H - \alpha(\ln H)^{\sigma}. \tag{14}$$

From the above optimization condition, we can easily derive the elasticity of hourly effort with respect to hours

$$\frac{d \ln E}{d \ln H} = \frac{de}{dh} = 1 - \alpha\sigma h^{\sigma-1}. \tag{15}$$

According to the above expression, if the parameter α of the utility function (10) is greater than zero and σ is greater than one, then the equilibrium effort function, $e(h)$, can indeed be strictly concave and hump-shaped, consistently with our argument on the fatigue factor inherent to work. Below a certain level of hours, the workers exert an increasing hourly effort in the marginal hour. However, if the number of hours per worker reaches a critical threshold level, then the marginal hour is worked with decreasing effort. If hours per worker are below that critical value, the relationship between hours and effort is positive; otherwise it is negative. On the other hand, by contrast, if the parameter α from individual preferences is equal to zero, then the elasticity of effort with respect to hours would be invariant and equal to one.

The implications of this effort-hours relationship for effective labor services $(h + e)$ are the following. If for values of hours per worker, h, greater than the critical value the elasticity of effort with respect to hours is negative but less than one in absolute value, then effective labor services are positively related to the number of hours for any value of h. In particular, the change in total effective work would be more than proportional to the change in hours per employee for low values of h and less than proportional for high values of h.

The hump-shaped effort function is therefore rationalized within our theoretical framework. It is a testable implication of our model that lends itself to empirical investigation, to which we now turn.

3 Data and Estimation

We use firm-level data on a panel of Italian manufacturing firms which are drawn from two main sources: the Bank of Italy's Survey of Investment in Manufacturing (henceforth, SIM) and the Company Accounts Data Service reports (henceforth, CADS). With regard to SIM data, at the beginning of every year since 1984 about 1,000 firm are surveyed. The data are of extremely high quality, owing to the representativeness of the sample, stratified by industry, firm size and location, and to the professional expertise of the interviewers, who are officials of the Bank of Italy with long-run relationships with firms' managers (see Marchetti and Nucci 2005, 2007). Because of difficulties in ensuring the quality standard in data collection, small firms, defined as those with less than 50 employees, are excluded from the SIM sample.

CADS is a dataset compiled by a consortium of the Bank of Italy and a pool of Italian banks. CADS is the primary source of data on the balance sheets and income statements of Italian firms, collecting detailed information from the annual accounts of more than 30,000 firms. Data are reclassified to ensure comparability across firms. We merged the information from the two sources to produce an unbalanced panel of slightly fewer than 1,000 firms. The balanced panel consists of less than 300 firms. Data include about 8,000 observations and range from 1984 to 1997.

Output, Y, is firm-level gross output deflated by the corresponding industry output deflator computed by the National Statistical Institute (Istat). Employment, N, is the firm-level average number of employees over the year; man-hours, H, are also firm-level and do include overtime hours. The amount of intermediate inputs, M, is firm-level net purchases of energy, materials and business services, deflated by the sectoral Istat deflator. Investment, I, is firm-level total fixed investment in buildings, machinery, equipment and vehicles, deflated by the industry investment deflator released by Istat. Capital stock, K, is the beginning-of-period stock of capital in equipment and non-residential buildings at 1997 prices. It was computed by applying the perpetual inventory method, taking as the benchmark the value of firm-level capital stock in 1997 (valued at replacement cost), which was made available by a special section of the Bank of Italy Survey conducted for that year. The capital deflator at sectoral level, P_K, was used (source: Istat). In order to compute the cost-based capital share, c_K, and the other cost-shares, the series for payments to capital, $rP_K K$, was constructed. Importantly, we could rely on firm-level estimates of the user cost of capital, r, as obtained by De Mitri, Marchetti and Staderini (1998) up to the year 1997 within a Bank of Italy's research project. They used SIM and CADS data as well as data from the Credit Register (CR), a statistical source maintained by a special unit of the Bank of Italy (*Centrale dei Rischi*) that provides detailed information on bank-firm contracts. The user cost of capital is computed according to the Hall-Jorgenson approach, as developed by Auerbach (1983) for firms that rely on both equity and debt as sources of finance.

In deriving the model-based measure of effort variation, Eq. (6) represents the baseline empirical specification (see Marchetti and Nucci 2005). The error term of the equation, dz_{it}, is assumed to have finite moments with $E(dz_{it}) = E(dz_{it}dz_{is}) = 0$, for all $t \neq s$; we allow in the specification for unobserved fixed effects, that capture the time-invariant latent heterogeneity. When it is estimated, the firm-level technology, dz_{it}, is likely to be correlated with changes in effective labor and capital services and in intermediate inputs. To control for this endogeneity of regressors, we rely on the generalized method of moments (GMM) approach developed for panel data by Arellano and Bond (1991). This methodology is shown to be efficient within the class of instrumental variable estimators. In the estimation, the instruments we use are the lagged values of the endogenous explanatory variables dated $t-2$ and $t-3$. Moreover, we also rely on external instruments that are commonly used in production function regressions (see, for example, Hall 1988, Burnside 1996, Basu et al. 2006).[5]

[5]These instruments are the contemporaneous growth rate of material input prices and of real exchange rate, the expected variations in sectoral order-book levels (drawn from the business

Table 1 Baseline model for estimating effort changes GMM estimates on firm-level panel data

Dependent variable: dy_{it}	
dx_{it}	1.054** (0.056)
$c_{Lit}dh_{it}$	−0.404* (0.210)
$c_{Kit}(dp_{Mit} + dm_{it} - dp_{Iit} - dk_{it})$	0.582** (0.190)
$c_{Kit}(di_{it} - dk_{it})$	−0.069** (0.033)
Sargan test of over-identifying restrictions	62.4** (0.67)
Implied estimate of the structural parameter, ζ	
$\zeta = \frac{\beta_2}{\beta_1}$	−0.384* (0.20)
Number of observations	5,861

Legend: the sample period is 1984–1997. Variables, parameters and the instrument set are defined in the text. Heteroscedasticity-consistent standard errors for parameter estimates are shown in brackets. The specification also comprises the control dummy variables discussed in the text; values of Wald tests for the joint significance of these control variables are not reported. The value of the Sargan test of over-identifying restrictions is reported with p-value in parentheses. Asterisks (*) and (**) indicate significance at the 10 and 5 % levels, respectively (based on Marchetti and Nucci 2005, p. 1146)

4 Results

4.1 Evidence from the Baseline Model

The results from estimating Eq. (6) are reported in Table 1 (see Marchetti and Nucci 2005). The first four rows of Table 1 refer to the reduced form parameters (β_1, β_2, β_3 and β_4) and we also report the implied values of the structural parameters, ζ ($\zeta = \frac{\beta_2}{\beta_1}$). The estimate of the returns-to-scale parameter, β_1, is not statistically different from one, i.e. the hypothesis of constant returns to scale is not rejected by our micro-data (β_1 is estimated at 1.054, with a standard error of 0.056). This finding is in line with most microeconomic evidence reported in the literature (see, for example, Baily et al. 1992, for US firms).

Our chief focus of interest is the parameter ζ, representing the elasticity of effort that an employee exerts in one hour of work in response to a change in the number of hours worked. In other words, it is the variation of hourly effort (de) when a unit percentage change in hours per employee, h, takes place. Thus, using the information on ζ, it is possible to trace the information on the change in hourly effort for each firm: $de_{it} = \zeta \cdot dh_{it}$. On the other hand, variation in total effective work per employee is measured by $(dh + de)$.

The estimated value of ζ is −0.384, with a standard error of 0.20. That is, if the number of hours worked by an employee increases by 10 %, then her hourly effort

surveys of ISAE, a public institution providing support on economic analysis to the Italian Treasury), and a measure of unanticipated monetary shock based on a vector autoregression (VAR) model (see Marchetti and Nucci 2005).

declines by about 4 %, while total effective work per employee, $e \cdot h$, increases by roughly 6 % $(1 + \zeta)$. Increasing hours at the margin would lead to a reduction in the effort exerted during the marginal hour.

4.2 Work Effort and Hours

Although the evidence presented in Table 1 indicates that the relation between hourly effort and the number of hours per worker is on average negative as the estimated coefficient associated to $c_L dh_{it}$ is negative, this result may not hold in general. Indeed, it seems reasonable to argue that, for moderate level of hours, an increase in the number of hours is accompanied by an increase, rather than a decrease, in work effort. This is consistent with the broadly recognized fact that, to avoid adjustment costs in hiring and firing, firms hoard labor during cyclical slowdowns and recessions. When the expansion begins, firms face increasing demand by augmenting both the number of hours worked and the hourly effort required. In this case, a positive relation may emerge between hours worked and effort per hour. However, as argued in Sect. 2, simple considerations regarding the physical and mental fatigue associated with the work effort suggest that there might be a critical value of hours per worker beyond which every additional hour is worked with decreasing effort. If this threshold value is reached—for example because new hiring is difficult due to labor market rigidities or technological factors (the need for specific skills) or because of a very fast acceleration in demand—then a negative relation may emerge at the margin between hours worked and hourly effort. Which of the two cases obtains will depend on both cyclical conditions and the features of the labor market. For example, the positive elasticity estimated by Basu and Kimball (1997) with data for US sectors may ultimately be due to the fact that the US labor market is less rigid than the Italian one. In this interpretation, US firms resort to new hiring more easily and more often than Italian ones, and are therefore less likely to over-step the critical threshold value of hours per employee.

We seek to investigate whether the relation between hourly effort and hours can be captured by a non-monotonic function such as the one in Fig. 1. To this end, we first argue that the effort-hours relation depends on the business cycle conditions in which the firm is operating. These conditions can be characterized through differences in the level and dynamics of hours per employee across various firm-specific cyclical phases. Arguably, situations where effort is increasing in hours per worker (i.e., where firms operate to the left of point A in Fig.1) should presumably satisfy two conditions. First, they are likely to occur during recovery from a demand slowdown or a recession, when firms utilize the hoarded labor more intensively, increasing both the hours and the effort required. Second, in order to maintain a positive relation between effort and hours per worker, the latter variable must not increase excessively (otherwise, hours per worker, h, would reach and eventually exceed its critical value). These two conditions can be characterized in terms of the behavior of hours per employee. In particular, in order to capture the first condition,

Fig. 1 The relation between effort per hour and hours

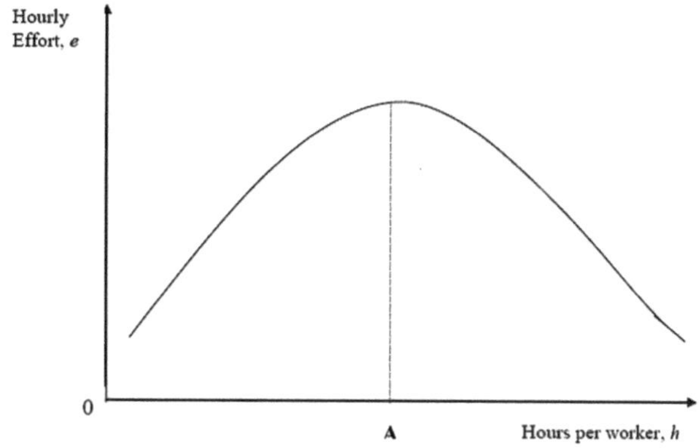

we considered observations where the *level* of hours per employee in the previous period is below a "normal" amount, as measured by the firm-specific average of h over time. In order to capture the second condition, we selected the subset of data where the *variation* in hours per employee is positive but not unusually large, e.g. not exceeding the firm-specific 75-th percentile. Accordingly, we constructed two dummy variables: the first, *D_left*, is equal to one if (i) the number of hours per employee in the previous period does not exceed the firm mean ($h_{it-1} \leqslant h_i^{mean}$), and (ii) the contemporaneous variation in hours per employee is positive but does not exceed the firm's 75-th percentile ($0 < dh_{it} \leqslant pctile75(dh_i)$). Otherwise, *D_left* is equal to zero. The second dummy, *D_right*, is equal to 1 − *D_left*, i.e. it takes the value of one when at least one of the above conditions does not hold.

In Table 2 we report the estimates obtained by including among the regressors the interaction between each of the two dummies and the variable $c_L dh_{it}$. While the first column refers to the case where condition (i) is captured by $h_{it-1} \leqslant h_i^{mean}$, in the second column we report results based on condition (i) defined as $h_{it-1} \leqslant h_i^{median}$. The evidence provides support for the hypothesis that work effort increases or decreases as hours per worker increase depending on the firm-specific cyclical phase. Indeed, the elasticity ζ is estimated to be positive in situations where the firm is presumably operating to the left of point A in Fig. 1 and negative elsewhere. Focusing on the results reported in the first column, the parameter estimates associated to $D\_left \cdot c_L dh_{it}$ and $D\_right \cdot c_L dh_{it}$ are of opposite sign and they are equal to, respectively, 1.660 (with a standard error of 0.932) and –0.688 (with a standard error of 0.141).

Of course, the cut-off values for defining the two dummy variables and characterizing the two different cyclical phases may seem to be *ad hoc*. For this reason, we also experimented with a number of alternative cut-off values for the construction of the dummies. In Table 3, we report results from defining the two dummy variables using different cut-off values and the results remain qualitatively unchanged. For example, we expressed the first condition as ($h_{it-1} \leqslant pctile25(h_i)$), that is using the 25th percentile, instead of the mean or the median, and left the second condition unchanged (i.e., $0 < dh_{it} \leqslant pctile75(dh_i)$). The results in column 1 indicate that

Table 2 The relation between effort and hours under different firm-specific cyclical conditions GMM estimates on firm-level panel data

Dependent variable: dy_{it}	(1)	(2)
dx_{it}	1.003** (0.045)	0.986** (0.044)
$D\_left \cdot c_{Lit}dh_{it}$	1.660* (0.932)	1.499** (0.669)
$D\_right \cdot c_{Lit}dh_{it}$	−0.688** (0.141)	−0.762** (0.154)
$c_{Kit}(dp_{Mit} + dm_{it} - dp_{Iit} - dk_{it})$	0.901** (0.123)	0.854** (0.118)
$c_{Kit}(di_{it} - dk_{it})$	0.009 (0.022)	0.011 (0.022)
Sargan test of over-identifying restrictions	83.7** (0.61)	83.53** (0.62)
Number of observations	5,886	5,886

Legend: See Table 1. In column (1), $D\_left = 1$ if $h_{it-1} \leqslant h_i^{mean}$ and $0 < dh_{it} \leqslant pctile75(dh_i)$; D_left is equal to zero otherwise. $D\_right = 1 - D\_left$.
In column (2), $D\_left = 1$ if $h_{it-1} \leqslant h_i^{median}$ and $0 < dh_{it} \leqslant pctile75(dh_i)$. The specification also comprises the control dummy variables of the baseline specification; values of Wald tests for the joint significance of these control variables are not reported. Asterisks (*) and (**) indicate significance at the 10 and 5 % levels, respectively

Table 3 The relation between effort and hours: alternative cut-off values for defining different firm-specific cyclical conditions GMM estimates on firm-level panel data

Dependent variable: dy_{it}	(1)	(2)	(3)
dx_{it}	0.932** (0.054)	0.960** (0.054)	0.937** (0.055)
$D\_left \cdot c_{Lit}dh_{it}$	2.551** (1.045)	7.355* (3.954)	6.312* (3.757)
$D\_right \cdot c_{Lit}dh_{it}$	−0.480** (0.193)	−0.584** (0.163)	−0.539** (0.170)
$c_{Kit}(dp_{Mit} + dm_{it} - dp_{Iit} - dk_{it})$	0.964** (0.174)	0.950** (0.159)	1.018** (0.154)
$c_{Kit}(di_{it} - dk_{it})$	−0.059* (0.031)	−0.075** (0.030)	−.095** (0.031)
Sargan test of over-identifying restrictions	81.5** (0.21)	78.5** (0.28)	76.7** (0.33)
Number of observations	5,861	5,861	5,861

Legend: See Table 1. In column (1), $D\_left = 1$ if $h_{it-1} \leqslant pctile25(h_i)$ leaving the second condition unchanged (that is, $0 < dh_{it} \leqslant pctile75(dh_i)$). D_left is equal to zero otherwise and $D\_right = 1 - D\_left$. In column (2), $D\_left = 1$ if $h_{it-1} \leqslant h_i^{mean}$ and $0 < dh_{it} \leqslant dh_i^{median}$. D_left is equal to zero otherwise and $D\_right = 1 - D\_left$. In column (3), $D\_left = 1$ if $h_{it-1} \leqslant h_i^{median}$ and $0 < dh_{it} \leqslant dh_i^{median}$. D_left is equal to zero otherwise and $D\_right = 1 - D\_left$. The specification also comprises the control dummy variables of the baseline specification; values of Wald tests for the joint significance of these control variables are not reported. Asterisks (*) and (**) indicate significance at the 10 and 5 % levels, respectively

the coefficient associated to $D\_left \cdot c_L dh_{it}$ is positive and statistically significant (2.551 with a standard error of 1.045) while the one associated to $D\_right \cdot c_L dh_{it}$ is negative and significant (−0.480 with a standard deviation of 0.193).

In column 2 we report results defining D_left as equal to 1 if the following two conditions hold: (i) $h_{it-1} \leqslant h_i^{mean}$ and (ii) and $(0 < dh_{it} \leqslant dh_i^{median})$. Again the estimated coefficient for $D\_left \cdot c_L dh_{it}$ is positive and significant (7.355 with a standard error of 3.954) while the one estimated for $D\_right \cdot c_L dh_{it}$ is negative and significant (−0.584 with a standard error of 0.163). A similar result (see column 3) is obtained when the cut-off values for distinguishing among firms' observations are such that *D_left* is equal to 1 if (i) $h_{it-1} \leqslant h_i^{median}$ and (ii) and $(0 < dh_{it} \leqslant dh_i^{median})$.

We also investigate if the effort function, $e(h)$, is strictly concave in the neighborhood of the mean value of h_{it} over the entire sample. To this end, we pursue the following approach. We consider a Taylor approximation of the effort function and, in particular, of its time variation, $de_{it} = e_{it} - e_{it-1}$.[6] Let h^* be the average value of h_{it} across firms and periods in our sample and consider the following second-order approximation around this value:

$$e(h_{it}) \approx e(h^*) + e'(h^*)(h_{it} - h^*) + e''(h^*)\frac{(h_{it} - h^*)^2}{2!}. \tag{16}$$

If we compute the same approximation for $e(h_{it-1})$ and subtract its expression from the above equation, we obtain

$$de \approx e'(h^*)dh + e''(h^*)\frac{1}{2!}[h_{it}^2 - h_{it-1}^2 - 2h^*(h_{it} - h_{it-1})], \tag{17}$$

where $e'(h^*) = \frac{de}{dh}|_{h=h^*}$ is equal to ζ. Therefore, in our regression framework, instead of inserting ζdh alone to represent de as we do in Eq. (6), we use the above approximation for defining de (recall that $\beta_2 dh = \gamma\zeta dh = \gamma de$). As a result, the basic specification is augmented with another variable, namely the term $\frac{1}{2}[h_{it}^2 - h_{it-1}^2 - 2h^*(h_{it} - h_{it-1})]$, pre-multiplied by the labor share c_L. The empirical specification of the new equation is therefore the following:

$$\begin{aligned} dy_{it} = {} & \beta_1 dx_{it} + \beta_2(c_{Lit}dh_{it}) + \beta_{2,A}c_{Lit}\frac{1}{2}[h_{it}^2 - h_{it-1}^2 - 2h^*(h_{it} - h_{it-1})] + \\ & \beta_3\left[c_{Kit}\left(dp_{Mit} + dm_{it} - dp_{Iit} - dk_{it}\right)\right] + \beta_4\left[c_{Kit}(di_{it} - dk_{it})\right] \\ & + \beta_5' W_{it} + dz_{it}. \end{aligned} \tag{18}$$

The coefficient, $\beta_{2,A}$, associated with the new regressor corresponds to the value of $\gamma e''(h^*) = \gamma\frac{d^2e}{dh^2}|_{h=h^*}$; the sign of this parameter provides insights on the curvature of the effort function in the neighborhood of h^*. If this coefficient, $\beta_{2,A}$, is estimated to be negative, and β_2 continues to be negative, then the data would support the conclusion that—around the average value of h—the effort function, $e(h)$, is downward-sloping and strictly concave. That is, for values of hours per worker close to h^*, as hours increase effort would decline at an increasing rate.

The results of this regression are reported in Table 4. The explanatory variables are those of Table 1 plus the additional term that allows the curvature of the effort function to be estimated at the value of h^*. The results support a nonlinear, strictly concave shape of the effort function in the neighborhood of h^*, since the

---

[6]We thank Miles Kimball for suggesting this approach.

Table 4 The shape of the effort function around the mean value of hours, h GMM estimates on firm-level panel data

Dependent variable: dy_{it}	
dx_{it}	0.959** (0.024)
$c_{Lit}dh_{it}$	−0.517** (0.084)
$c_{Lit}\frac{1}{2}[h_{it}^2 - h_{it-1}^2 - 2h^*(h_{it} - h_{it-1})]$	−0.237** (0.111)
$c_{Kit}(dp_{M,it} + dm_{it} - dp_{Iit} - dk_{it})$	0.958** (0.084)
$c_{Kit}(di_{it} - dk_{it})$	−0.020 (0.015)
Sargan test of over-identifying restrictions	170.2** (0.40)
Number of observations	5,886

Legend: See text and Table 1. Asterisks (*) and (**) indicate significance at the 10 and 5 % levels, respectively

coefficient of the new variable is negative (−0.237, with a standard error of 0.111) and the parameter estimate associated with $c_L dh$ remains negative and statistically significant (−0.517, with a standard error of 0.084). The parameter estimates for the other variables are also qualitatively invariant.

In principle, our theoretical set-up incorporates implicit agreements between workers and the firm with regard to hours worked and effort expended. In practice, work effort may respond not only to physical conditions but also to other factors, including economic incentives such as overtime premia and performance bonuses. These elements should be already taken into account by the $G(H, E)$ function included in our theoretical set-up. However, the availability of data from the SIM survey on wage premia allows us to explicitly investigate whether economic incentives have an additional impact beyond that captured in our analytical framework. In particular, the 1999 survey provides information on whether firms pay wage premia and on the extent to which these are linked to the firm's performance. Thus, we focused on the panel of firms included in the 1999 survey and split the sample into two groups: firms that pay labor premia entirely based on performance and all the others (respectively, 40 and 60 % of the sample). To this end we constructed a dummy variable, *D_premia*, that is equal to one for firms in the former group and zero otherwise. We found that the provision of performance-based wage incentives affects the relationship under investigation to a statistically significant extent. Interestingly, however, the payment of these incentives does not suffice to establish a positive relation between effort and hours per employee. For this group of firms the estimated elasticity of effort with respect to hours per employee remains negative, although close to zero. In particular, as we document in Table 5, while the parameter associated to $c_L dh$ is estimated to be −0.782 with a standard error of 0.20 in situations where wage premia are not paid or are not entirely linked to performance ($D\_premia = 0$), conversely, it is estimated to be −0.009 with a standard error of 0.140 in situations where wage premia are entirely linked to performance ($D\_premia = 1$).

Arguably, another possible critique of our interpretation of the results in this section is that an increase in hours per worker may be obtained from a combination

Table 5 The elasticity of effort with respect to hours: the role of wage premia linked to firm's performance GMM estimates on firm-level panel data

Dependent variable: dy_{it}	
dx_{it}	0.966** (0.029)
$c_{Lit}dh_{it}$	−0.782** (0.200)
$D\_premia \cdot c_{Lit}dh_{it}$	0.773** (0.229)
$c_{Kit}(dp_{Mit} + dm_{it} - dp_{Iit} - dk_{it})$	0.757** (0.093)
$c_{Kit}(di_{it} - dk_{it})$	−0.014 (0.018)
Sargan test of over-identifying restrictions	84.1** (0.60)
Number of observations	2,545

Legend: See Table 1. *D_premia* is equal to one for firms that pay labor premia entirely based on performance and zero otherwise. Asterisks (*) and (**) indicate significance at the 10 and 5 % levels, respectively

of more hours worked by employees already working overtime plus an increase in the proportion of employees who work overtime. While in the first case the negative effect of physical and mental fatigue on marginal effort is quite clear, in the second case it is much less so. In particular, if the increase in hours worked is obtained by raising the number of employees working overtime, workers would be less likely to reach the threshold beyond which marginal effort declines. However, it is well established that workers within a given firm do not all work the same number of hours (Trejo 1993), i.e. overtime work is persistently concentrated on a subset of employees. Furthermore, workers who are not routinely asked to work overtime are possibly the less productive ones. Thus, the additional effort of these marginal overtime workers would be typically smaller than that of workers who regularly work overtime. Therefore, even if the increase in hours per worker partly reflects a compositional change due to an enlargement of the pool of employees working overtime, the effort exerted in the marginal hour might still be decreasing.

5 Conclusions

Cyclical variations in work effort are commonly recognized as a key feature of business fluctuations. In spite of this, and notwithstanding the explicit inclusion of labor utilization in business cycle models or the addition of proxies in production function regressions, very little is known on empirical grounds on the behavior of work effort over the cycle. This is largely due to its intrinsic unobservability. In the paper we investigate the matter using firm-level data. We use a measure of change in labor effort based on a theoretical set-up that takes into account potential deviations from constant returns and perfect competition as well as cyclical variation in effort and capital utilization. Our empirical framework is estimated on panel data at the firm level, thus avoiding aggregation bias.

Due to physical and mental fatigue from long hours, we argue that the relation between hours and work effort is rather complex. In particular, we provide some evidence that the linear relationship between hours and effort can be seen as a particular case of a non-monotonic, hump-shaped relationship between the two variables. During an economic expansion, if the number of hours per worker reaches a critical level, for example because of the combination of a sharp increase in demand with hiring rigidities, every additional hour is worked with decreasing effort, arguably owing to physical and mental fatigue. We support this claim on empirical grounds by estimating the relation between effort and hours under different firm-specific business cycle conditions. We also provide evidence that—around the average value of hours per employee in our sample—the effort function is downward-sloping and strictly concave.

The implications of our results are twofold. First, while labor effort remains an important amplification mechanism of shocks, in some cases the magnification effect may be lower than it is typically assumed in models with variable factor utilization. This can occur, for example, during sudden demand accelerations and in economies characterized by labor rigidities. Second, with regard to the literature on production function regressions, our results suggest that the evidence on market structure and (internal or external) returns to scale derived from standard empirical specifications where effort is proxied linearly, or even not considered, may suffer from omitted variable bias.

Acknowledgements We thank Andrea Brandolini, Miles Kimball, Ned Phelps, Valerie Ramey and seminar participants at the University of Siena and the International Economic Association Conference in Lisbon for insightful suggestions and helpful discussions. The views expressed in this paper are those of the authors and do not necessarily reflect those of the institutions with which they are affiliated.

Appendix: Optimality Conditions

The derivation of the first-order conditions of the constrained optimization problem (3) in the text follows closely Basu and Kimball (1997) and Basu, Kimball and Fernald (2006). They are the following:

$$H: \quad \lambda \frac{\partial F}{\partial L} NE = NW \frac{\partial G}{\partial H} \tag{A.1}$$

$$E: \quad \lambda \frac{\partial F}{\partial L} NH = NW \frac{\partial G}{\partial E} \tag{A.2}$$

$$U: \quad \lambda \frac{\partial F}{\partial \tilde{K}} K = qK \frac{\partial \delta}{\partial U} \tag{A.3}$$

$$M: \quad \lambda \frac{\partial F}{\partial M} = P_M \tag{A.4}$$

$$A: \quad \phi = W\Psi' \tag{A.5}$$

$$I: \quad q = P_I J' \tag{A.6}$$

where λ, ϕ, and q are the Lagrange multipliers associated, respectively, with the first, second and third constraints. The Euler equations for the quasi-fixed factors are:

$$N: \quad \overset{\circ}{\phi} = r\phi - \lambda \frac{\partial F}{\partial L} HE + WG + W(\Psi - \frac{A}{L}\Psi') \tag{A.7}$$

$$K: \quad \overset{\circ}{q} = (r + \delta)q - \lambda \frac{\partial F}{\partial \tilde{K}} U + P_I (J - \frac{I}{K} J'). \tag{A.8}$$

Combining condition (A.3) with the expression for marginal product of capital stemming from Eq. (2) in the text ($\frac{\partial F}{\partial \tilde{K}} = \mu s_K \frac{Y}{UK}$) yields

$$U \frac{\partial \delta}{\partial U} = \frac{\lambda}{q} \mu s_K \frac{Y}{K}; \tag{A.9}$$

similarly, the joint consideration of condition (A.4) and of the expression for marginal product of intermediate inputs gives

$$\lambda \mu = \frac{P_M M}{s_M Y}; \tag{A.10}$$

if we combine the expression for marginal productivity of capital with (A.10), the following relation holds:

$$\lambda \frac{\partial F}{\partial \tilde{K}} = \frac{s_K}{s_M} \frac{P_M M}{UK}; \tag{A.11}$$

putting together Eqs. (A.9), (A.10) and condition (A.6) yields

$$U \frac{\partial \delta}{\partial U} = \frac{s_K}{s_M} \frac{P_M M}{P_I J' K}. \tag{A.12}$$

If we differentiate the above equation with respect to time and divide both sides by $U\frac{\partial\delta}{\partial U}$, we obtain

$$du = \frac{1}{1+\Delta}(dp_M + dm - dp_I - dk) - \frac{\xi}{1+\Delta}(di - dk), \qquad \text{(A.13)}$$

where the parameter Δ denotes the elasticity of marginal depreciation with respect to capital utilization ($\Delta = \frac{U\delta''}{\delta'}$) and the parameter ξ is the elasticity of marginal costs of adjustment with respect to the accumulation rate ($\xi = \frac{\delta J''}{J'}$). Following Basu, Fernald and Kimball (2006) and Basu and Kimball (1997), we define these elasticities in terms of steady-state variables and consider them as constant (also using the fact that, in steady-state, $(\frac{I}{K})^*$ equals δ^*). If we insert Eqs. (5) and (A.13) into Eq. (1) and use the expressions (2) for output elasticities, we obtain Eq. (6) in the text.

References

Abbott TA, Griliches Z, Hausman J (1988) Short-run movements in productivity: market power versus capacity utilization. Paper presented at NBER summer institute, Cambridge, MA

Arellano M, Bond SR (1991) Some tests of specification for panel data: Monte Carlo evidence and an application to employment equations. Rev Econ Stud 58:277–297

Auerbach AJ (1983) Corporate taxation in the United States, vol 2. Brookings papers on economic activity, Washington DC, pp 451–513

Baily MN, Hulten C, Campbell D (1992) Productivity dynamics in manufacturing plants. Brookings papers on economic activity (Microeconomics), Washington, DC, pp 187–267

Barnichon R (2010) Productivity and unemployment over the business cycle. J Monet Econ 57(8):1013–1025

Basu S (1996) Procyclical productivity: increasing returns or cyclical utilization. Q J Econ 111:720–751

Basu S, Kimball MS (1997) Cyclical productivity with unobserved input variation. NBER working paper, no. 5915

Basu S, Fernald JG, Kimball M (2006) Are technology improvements contractionary? Am Econ Rev 96(5):1418–1448

Becker G (1977) A theory of the production and allocation of effort. NBER working paper, no. 184

Bils M, Chang Y (2003) Welfare costs of sticky wages when effort can respond. J Monet Econ 50:311–330

Bils M, Chang Y, Kim S (2014) How sticky wages in existing jobs can affect hiring. NBER working paper, no. 19821

Bils M, Cho J (1994) Cyclical factor utilization. J Monet Econ 33:319–354

Burnside C (1996) Production function regressions, returns to scale, and externalities. J Monet Econ 37:177–201

Burnside C, Eichembaum M (1996) Factor-hoarding and the propagation of business-cycle shocks. Am Econ Rev 86:1154–1174

Burnside C, Eichenbaum M, Rebelo S (1993) Labor hoarding and the business cycle. J Polit Econ 101:245–273

Caballero R, Lyons RK (1992) External effects in U.S. procyclical productivity. J Monet Econ 29:209–226

Chatterji M, Sparks R (1991) Real wages, productivity, and the cycle: an efficiency wage model. J Macroecon 13(3):495–510

De Mitri S, Marchetti D, Staderini A (1998) Il costo d'uso del capitale nelle imprese manufatturiere Italiane: un'analisi con dati panel. Mimeo, Rome

Fay JA, Medoff JL (1985) Labor and output over the business cycle: some direct evidence. Am Econ Rev 75:638–655

Galí J, Gambetti L (2009) On the Sources of the great moderation. Am Econ J Macroecon 1:26–57

Galí J, van Rens T (2014) The vanishing procyclicality of labor productivity. Barcelona graduate school of economics, working papers, no. 489

Hall R (1988) The relation between price and marginal cost in U.S. industry. J Polit Econ 96: 921–947

Lazear E, Shaw K, Stanton C (2013) Making do with less: working harder during recessions. NBER working paper, no. 19328

Marchetti DJ, Nucci F (2005) Price stickiness and the contractionary effect of technology shocks. Eur Econ Rev 49:1137–1163

Marchetti DJ, Nucci F (2007) Pricing behavior and the response of hours to productivity shocks. J Money Credit Bank 39(7):1587–1611

Nucci F, Riggi M (2013) Performance pay and changes in U.S. labor market dynamics. J Econ Dyn Control 37(12):796–2813

Riggi M (2012) Capital destruction, jobless recoveries and the discipline device role of unemployment. Temi di Discussione, Bank of Italy working paper, no. 871

Sbordone AM (1996) Cyclical productivity in a model of labor hoarding. J Monet Econ 38: 331–361

Schor J (1987) Does work intensity respond to macroeconomic variables? evidence from British manufacturing, 1970–86. Harvard institute of economic research discussion paper no. 1379

Shapiro C, Stiglitz J (1984) Equilibrium unemployment as a worker discipline device. Am Econ Rev 74(3):433–444

Shea J (1990) Accident rates, labor effort and the business cycle. Wisconsin madison - social systems, working papers, no. 90–28

Trejo SJ (1993) Overtime pay, overtime hours, and labor unions. J Labor Econ 11(2):253–278

Uhlig H, Xu Y (1996) Effort and the cycle: cyclical implications of efficiency wages. Tilburg university, center for economic research discussion paper, no. 1996–49

Policy Prescriptions for a Good Economy

Luigi Paganetto and Pasquale Lucio Scandizzo

Abstract The prevailing interpretations of the recent economic crisis tend to regard it as a manifestation of recessionary cycle, albeit unusual for its long duration. This would not only triggered a recession, but essentially linked to the financial crisis of 2008. The available evidence suggests, however, that we are faced with something other than a cyclical phase of a prolonged recession. The unwillingness to look at the structural changes taking place, drawing the consequences in terms of economic policy, is likely to further aggravate the structural crisis, pushing the process of economic recovery far beyond what is socially sustainable. The economic policy measures to be taken to support development cannot fail to take account of this context as well as the new economic realities that accompany it. Two important elements appear undeniable, even though they are ignored by any short-term vision of the economic policy problem: (a) the progressive deterioration of income distribution, with ever more acute concentration of wealth on the one hand and of impoverishment and social exclusion on the other; (b) the unsustainable nature of the traditional welfare state.

1 The Crisis: Cyclical Phase or Structural Change?

The prevailing interpretations of the recent economic crisis tend to regard it as a manifestation of recessionary cycle, albeit unusual for its long duration. This would not only triggered a recession, but essentially linked to the financial crisis of

L. Paganetto (✉)
Tor Vergata Foundation for Economic Research, Rome, Italy
e-mail: luigi.paganetto@uniroma2.it

P.L. Scandizzo
Rome Tor Vergata University, Rome, Italy
e-mail: scandizzo@economia.uniroma2.it

L. Paganetto (ed.), *Wealth, Income Inequalities, and Demography*,
DOI 10.1007/978-3-319-05909-9_10,

2008. The available evidence suggests, however, that we are faced with something other than a cyclical phase of a prolonged recession. Despite efforts by the U.S. authorities for the reduction of unemployment, the goal of a return to an unemployment rate both "natural" and socially acceptable has not been achieved. European unemployment, which seemed contained, in a first phase, has worsened in the past 2 years in all but Germany. Italy, in particular, continues to show not only one of the highest rates of youth unemployment but, more importantly fails to increase the employment rate, which is structurally very low, particularly in the case of women's work. Social inequalities have also increased dramatically over the past 50 years, especially if we consider the so called primary distribution of income, given by income before the impact of taxes and subsidies.

Negative changes in the overall performance are accompanied by structural changes that have profoundly altered the relationship between advanced and emerging countries, with massive shifts in the international distribution of wealth and allocation of production activities. These outcomes are related not only to the massive wage differentials between the two areas and the effects of technological change, but also to the dynamism in emerging countries of a labor force dominated by younger age classes. This does not mean that the financial crisis of 2008 is not the origin of the recession that followed. There is no doubt, however, that the unwillingness to look at the structural changes taking place, drawing the consequences in terms of economic policy, is likely to further aggravate the structural crisis, pushing the process of economic recovery far beyond what is socially sustainable. The economic policy measures to be taken to support development cannot fail to take account of this context as well as the new economic realities that accompany it.

The consensus on the economic policies to be adopted, which in the past has supported the collaboration between economists and policy makers is difficult to recover, especially on the role of fiscal discipline and expansionary policies. Two important elements appear undeniable, even though they are ignored by any short-term vision of the economic policy problem: (a) the progressive deterioration of income distribution, with ever more acute concentration of wealth on the one hand and of impoverishment and social exclusion on the other; (b) the unsustainable nature of the traditional welfare state, more and more caught in the contradiction between increasing demand and decreasing availability of public resources. The policies of market liberalization and reduction of public debt and taxation, although necessary, are part of this contradiction. The liberalization of markets, while increasing the dynamism of the economy, in fact, tend to accentuate the features of inequality and concentration of wealth. The reduction of the public debt, on its part, contains an intrinsic drive to the contraction of social spending, which tends to further reduce the ability of the welfare state to address the growing social inequalities.

Long-term economic policies are thus necessary, to address the structural problems of the crisis, through the engines of economic and social dynamism, and starting with the determinants of productivity growth that directly affect growth of GDP and employment. To identify these policies, first consider the changes brought about by globalization, which document the failure of short-term visions and point to the fact that the best results were obtained by countries who have focused on knowledge and long-term industrial policies. We also need to reconsider the theoretical foundations at the base of the past 50 year economic policies, taking into account the new system variables: environment and climate change, growth sustainability, and the increasing importance of intangible assets, such as trust, social justice and harmony with nature, in determining the well-being of populations.

It is in this context that data on economic performance should be interpreted. Europe has experienced a period up to the mid-1980s in which productivity grew more than the U.S. Then the trend reversed and with it went a slower pace of GDP growth in Europe. Italy had a record negative performance with a total productivity growth close to zero in the past 15 years. This slowdown has also been accompanied by a deterioration in the performance of other determinants of well-being, such as social and economic dynamism, participation and social justice.

More generally, the whole world has been characterized by uneven growth and, as a worrisome accompanying phenomenon, by growing inequality from shifting wealth. A recent report by the OECD (2012) documents the enormous importance and magnitude of redistribution of international wealth (Shifting Wealth), which has been mainly determined in recent years by the rapid growth of emerging countries. The thesis of the report is that from cross country uneven growth a four-tier world is emerging, one tier still plagued by poverty, one affluent, one of middle-income countries that have less than twice the average OECD rate of growth and one of those converging toward OECD average GDP, with a growth rate of more than double.

Shifting wealth has led to substantial changes in the international allocation of assets, changing economic trends and the system of convergence for entire areas, starting with Europe and probably affecting also the capacity to react and adjust to crisis, as witnessed by the fact that most of the economies with high per-capita income are still experiencing high rates of unemployment, weak and uncertain growth rates, accompanied by the adoption of policies of fiscal consolidation and economic austerity. In contrast, in 2010 the exports of Asian countries had returned to the levels prior to the crisis and returns of foreign direct investment into emerging economies had recovered much faster than investment in high-income countries (Figs. 1, 2, and 3).

Globalization and shifting wealth are certainly part of the causes of the increase inequality in income distribution detected by the OECD (Divided we stand). The activities that arise from production reallocation tend to be intensive in skilled labor from the point of view of emerging countries and not skill intensive from the point of view of the advanced countries. The result is a greater demand for skills and a drive towards greater inequality of profitability in both groups of countries. At the same time the activities associated with low productivity and wages tend to be supplanted in advanced countries by import of products low in skills from low-wage countries. Increasing income inequalities also result from lower employment or reduction of wages of low skilled workers in advanced countries. Further impulse toward income

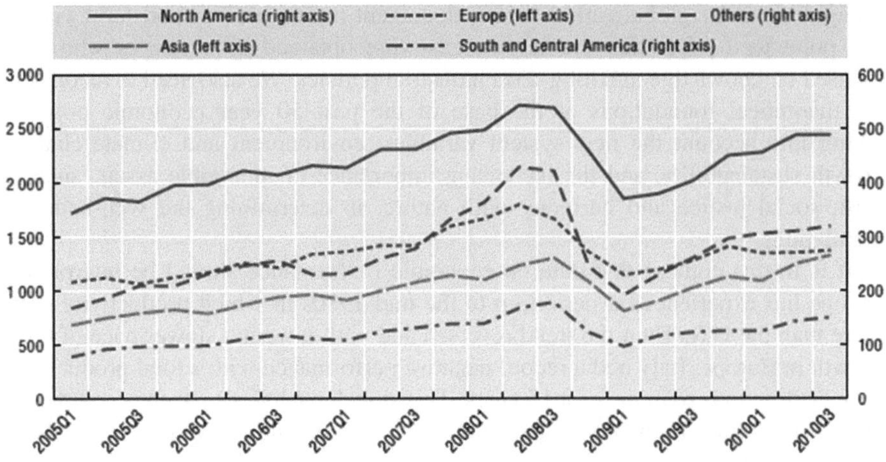

Fig. 1 Export flows in billion USD. *Note*: Others includes African and Middle Eastern countries

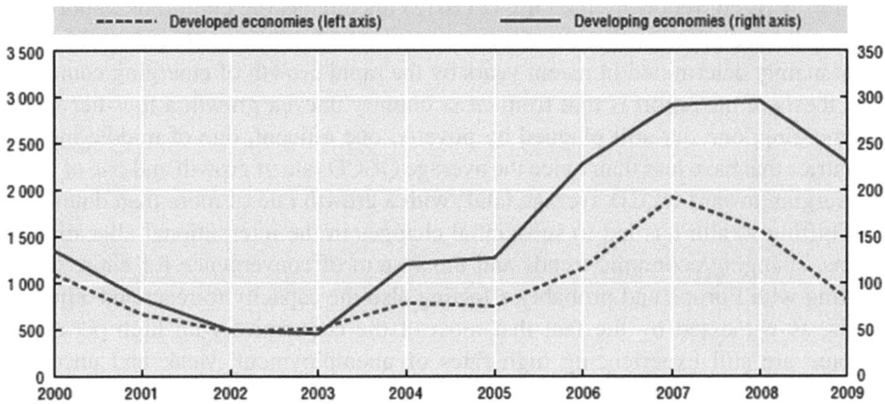

Fig. 2 Foreign direct investment flows to developed and emerging economies

inequality has also occurred because of the high level of technological change that has characterized the economic cycle in recent years, increasing further the premium on highly qualified labor (Figs. 4 and 5).

The gap between the rich and the poor has grown significantly over the years (Figs. 6, 7 and 8) and the dynamics of higher incomes have greatly influenced inequalities. However, the redistributive effect of the welfare system on average has reduced by a quarter inequalities and the quality of and access to public services. It should be noted, however, that if in Italy, France, Belgium and Finland, the inequality that stems from the labor market is less than the average of the majority of

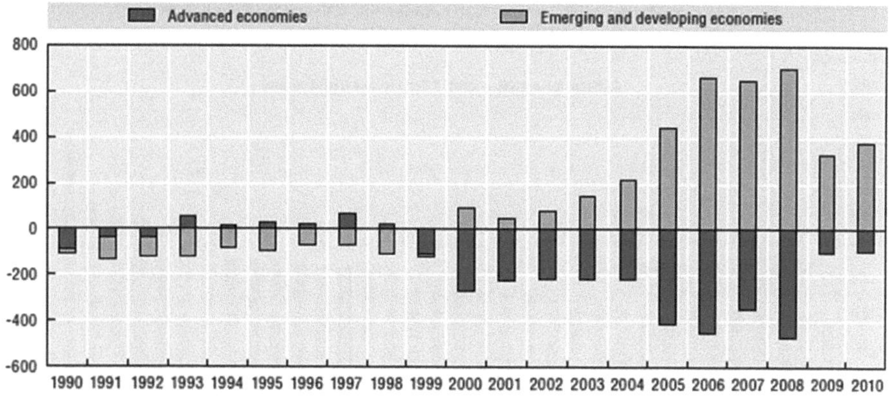

Fig. 3 Balance of payment current accounts

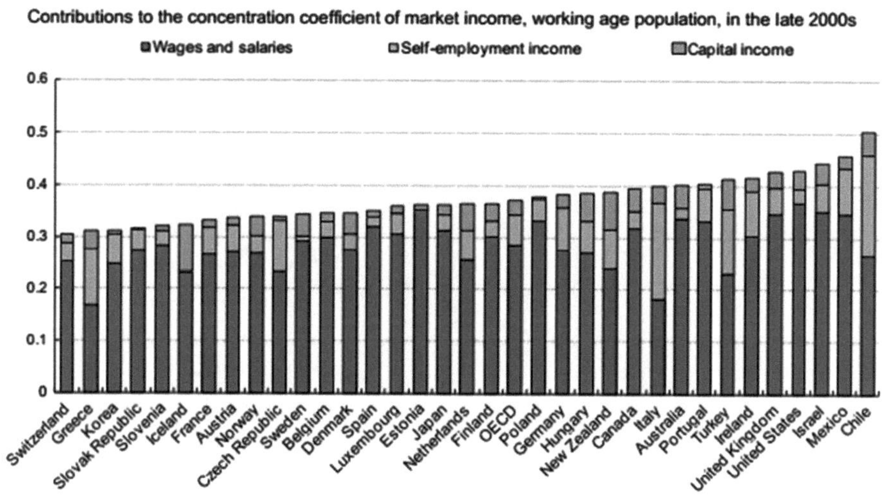

Fig. 4 Labour income inequality as the main contributor to the dispersion in household market incomes. *Source*: OECD Income Distribution and Poverty, OECD Social Expenditure Statistics (database). *Note*: Contributions to overall household market income inequality are derived by multiplying the concentration coefficients of each income source by their weight in total market income. The data for Greece, Hungary, Mexico and Turkey are net of taxes. Data for France and Ireland refer to the mid-2000s. The concentration coefficient of market income is computed as the Gini index with individuals ranked by household disposable income

the other countries considered, while the part that comes from the lower employment rate is higher (Figs. 9 and 10).

The relationship between economic growth and income distribution remains controversial, both for the ambiguity of the empirical evidence, and because the causal relation between the two phenomena is necessarily bi-directional. Economic growth in developed countries, however, seems to be associated more recently

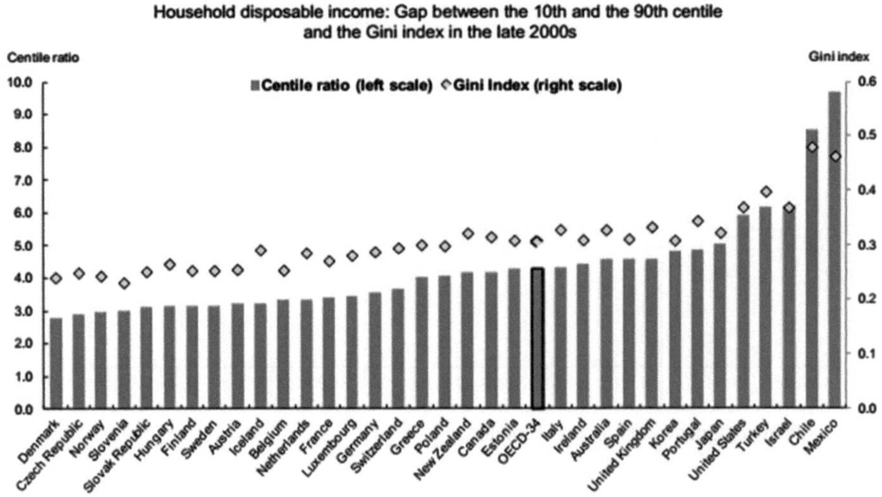

Fig. 5 Gap between rich and poor. *Source*: OECD Income Distribution and Poverty Database, OECD Social Expenditure Statistics (database). *Note*: The Gini index ranges from zero (perfect equality) to one (one individual or household receives all the income and the others receive none). Data for France and Ireland refer to the mid-2000s instead of the late 2000s

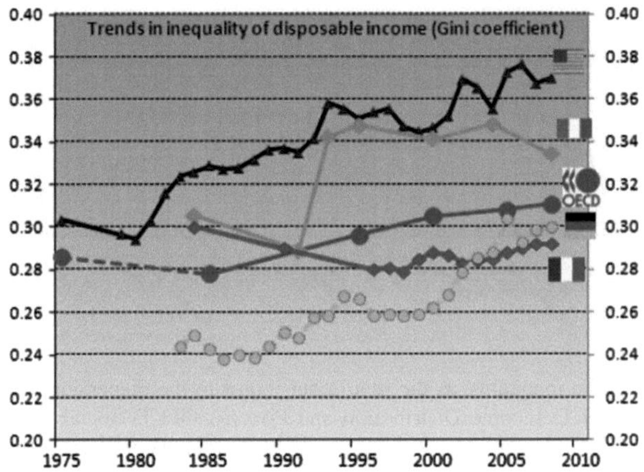

Fig. 6 Income inequality has increased in most OECD countries. *Source*: OECD (2012), Divided we Stand. *Note*: Incomes are net incomes of the working-age population

with increasing inequality, although, according to the conclusions of the OECD, policies that achieve a better distribution of income are often associated with greater development. The OECD recognizes, however, that the data do not reveal a simple bond between the measures of inequality and development (Fig. 11).

In conclusion, the present economic model presents three structural problems that do not seem to be approachable with the traditional economic policies: growing social injustice, individual loss of dignity and dynamism, progressive alienation

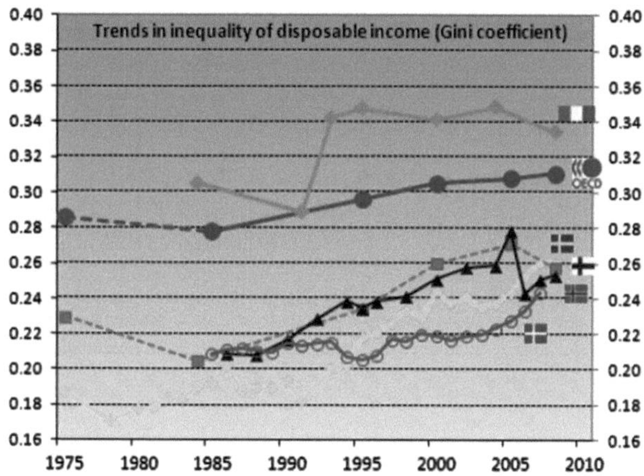

Fig. 7 Income inequality has increased in most OECD countries in the past, even those characterized by low levels of inequality. *Source*: OECD (2012), Divided we Stand. *Note*: Incomes are net incomes of the working-age population

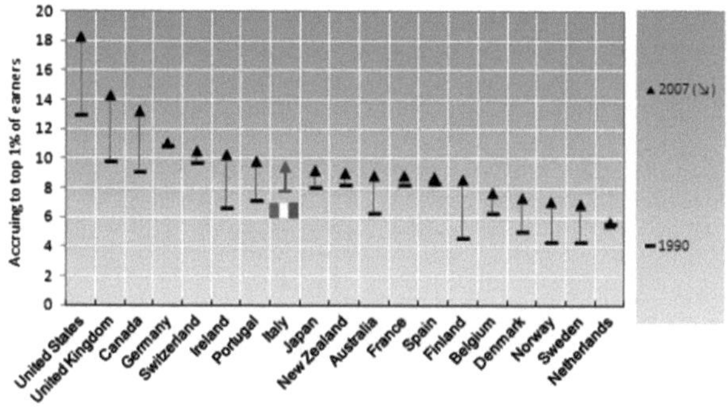

Fig. 8 The dynamics of higher incomes have greatly influenced the inequalities. *Source*: Scarpetta 2011

from nature and nurture. These three problems have become more visible during the recent, and persistent, economic and financial crisis, but they run much more deeply and date much longer than the seemingly endless recession, which may be just a manifestation of their evolving importance.

2 Sharing Prosperity and the Good Economy

Hacker and Loewentheil published their paper "Prosperity Economics: Building an economy for all" and liberal think tank Economic Policy Institute (EPI) launched their "Agenda for Shared Prosperity", both in 2012 sharing practically the

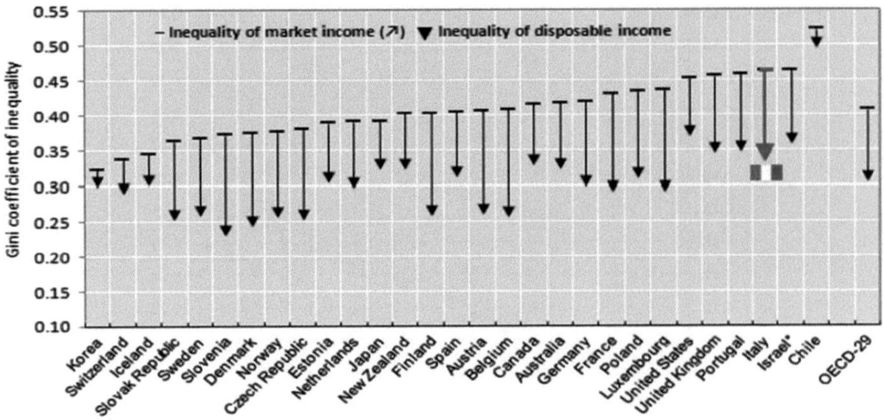

Fig. 9 The redistributive effect of the welfare systems varies widely among OECD countries. *Source*: OECD (2012), Divided we Stand. *Note*: Incomes are net incomes of the working-age population

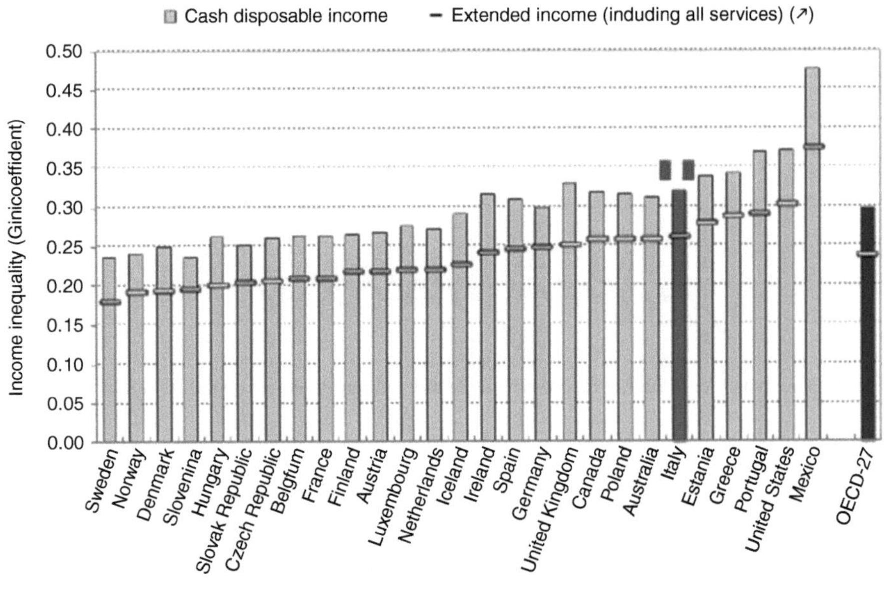

Fig. 10 The redistributive capacity also depends on access to public services and their quality. *Source*: OECD (2012), Divided we Stand. *Note*: Services include public services for education, health, social housing, child care and elderly care

same arguments. Prosperity based on three pillars: *innovation-led growth;* greater *security* for workers, the *environment* and government finances; and *greater democratic voice*, inclusivity, and accountability. While the concept of "shared prosperity" is heterogeneous, two recurrent themes are *growth, and equity*. More recently,

Fig. 11 The trends in the shared prosperity index: SCPI = (1 − Gini) × GDP

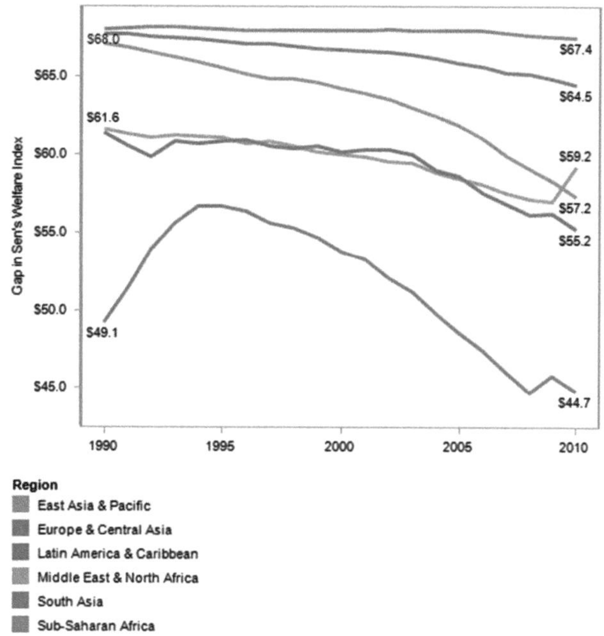

sustainability and inter-generational fairness have also become central themes. Also important are good jobs, citizen security, technological change & innovation, infrastructure.

Has shared prosperity (SP) increased and how has shifting wealth impacted on it? Figure 11 shows the evolution of a simple index (SPI) defined as (1 – Gini coefficient) × GDP, by the country regions according to the World Bank classification. Using as a benchmark the top ten countries in terms of Sen's Welfare Index in 2000, the diagram documents the different performances of joint growth and equality for areas of the world that are somewhat similar in history, development and culture. The Sub-Saharan African region (AFR) shows the largest gap and has experienced the slowest convergence rate to the benchmark. The South Asia Region (SAR), in spite of its better economic performance, as compared with AFR, also had a slow rate of convergence. The Eastern Asia and Pacific (EAP) area, on the other hand, showed the greatest dynamism both in terms of growth and decreasing inequality, with a high rate of convergence to the benchmark. The Middle East and North Africa Region (MENA) had a slow convergence rate, and in recent years diverged from the benchmark. The Latin American and Caribbean Region (LAC) experienced a moderate convergence rate that accelerated since 2005, due to good growth and falling inequality. The Eastern Europe and Central Asia Region (ECA) diverged in the early 1990s, but since mid-1990s has started to converge and now is closest to the benchmark.

The "Good Economy" is a broader concept of that encompasses the idea of sharing prosperity, but goes beyond the mere combination of growth and equality.

The term "Good Economy" has recently entered into the language of economists through the work of E. Phelps, who adopts it to define what, in his view, is an innovative and dynamic system with inclusion, creativity, self-fulfillment, satisfaction and personal development. The "good economy" is thus a more just and sustainable economic system and has much in common with the concept of pre-distribution as it aims to implement economic policies to "build" sustainable forms of social justice, rather than to repair the injustices determined by the current mechanisms of competition and democracy. It follows John Rawls' ideas on social justice in denouncing the traditional welfare-state capitalism, which " ... rejects the fair value of the political liberties, and while it has some concern for equality of opportunity, the policies necessary to achieve that are not followed. It permits very large inequalities in the ownership of real property (productive assets and natural resources) so that the control of the economy and much of political life rests in few hands. And although, as the name 'welfare-state capitalism' suggests, welfare provisions may be quite generous and guarantee a decent social minimum covering the basic needs, a principle of reciprocity to regulate economic and social inequalities is not recognized" (Rawls 2001, pp. 137–138).

The "Good Economy" approach emphasizes certain aspects of individual and institutional behaviors that can lead to greater economic and social dynamism, on the basis of the following main goals:

1. The increase in the incidence of inclusion in the labor market and in the relations between citizens and the state in a more just society and sustainable economic point of view as a pre-condition for development;
2. The propensity to invest in human capital, and in particular on new capabilities, as the most important investment decision;
3. The reduction of inequalities in income distribution as a key to greater economic dynamism;
4. A more inclusive social security system for the poor, the elderly and immigrants;
5. Investment decisions in the private and public budget, that should discourage the short-term view and encourage long-term concern with the role of human capital and knowledge;
6. Discourage excessive compensation differentials between the highest paid and the others, considering it a phenomenon that makes it obvious exclusion and reduces inclusion;
7. Encourage responsible capitalism and workers' participation in decision-making mechanisms, and of citizens in public affairs, to improve both market and social integration;
8. Combat corruption and corporatism that create enclaves of privilege unacceptable and contrary to the very idea of inclusion and development.

More generally, the idea behind the "good economy" is that the goal of economic development is a form of realization of the potential of people, as individuals and as communities, which goes beyond the mere ability to produce material goods. On the one hand, it is associated to the conservation and enhancement of environmental and human resources, according to the classical concept of "eudaimonia", interpreted as a person's ability to develop her potential an deploy her skills and her better qualities in an excellent way. On the other hand, the "good economy" is a form of takeover ("empowerment") by the members of civil society, especially those who tend to be excluded from traditional power structures, such as, for example, women, immigrants, the poor, and generally the weakest and most vulnerable of the population.

From a political perspective, one can trace the idea of a good economy to a radical critique to the welfare—capitalism model of economic growth which has dominated the history of most of the world in the past half a century. In spite of its impressive accomplishments, this model ultimately does not appear to be able to create development, inclusion and employment, because it fails to provide an adequate system of social security, and sustained investment in human capital and knowledge. This critique points also to an economic policy geared to the long term and in favor of creativity 'and industrial innovation, in a framework that accounts for broader goals for human kind such as peace and justice, as well as the need for international institutions' (Rawls 2001).

A Good Economy, however, has nothing to do with an "idealistic" conception of the world, but reaffirms the ethics inspiring A. Smith in his work on the Theory of Moral Sentiments, where he introduced the principle of sympathy, which involves identifying oneself with the passions and feelings of others, but differs from benevolence and altruism while not replacing selfishness. From this point of view, individualism (Maffettone 2011) as the methodological foundation of the economy, becomes close to selfishness if does not leave any space to the ethics of sacrifice of self-interest with respect to some social value. In the words of Rawls, individuals are both "rational", as hypothesized by economic theory, and 'reasonable', that is, 'willing to adjust their "rational" behavior to take into account both the effects on themselves and on others' (Rawls 1971).

Even supporters of "pure" liberism have to deal with this apparent contradiction of economics: while market economy rewards those who have talent, take risks, innovate and succeed, this same process generates inequality with negative results on well being. In order to work, 'the market economy', and this is the thesis of the Good Economy, must find remedies that allow to balance inequalities with social inclusion and cohesion (Lawson 2013). For example, J. Stiglitz points out (Stiglitz 2012), with reference to the U.S., that today the price of inequality is 'too high given that the 1 % of Americans own 40 % of the total wealth and receives 25 % of total annual income and at the same time the incomes of the top managers have grown by 18 % while those of the middle class have fallen. Phelps claims that efficiency and optimal allocation of resources are not sufficient to define the functions of the market and the economy. They can be fully realized when an economy is innovative and dynamic so that it generates inclusion, creativity, self-fulfillment, satisfaction and personal development. Only this combination of accomplishments will determine the conditions for increasing well-being of the community'.

The idea of inclusive development can be articulated in very different ways, as development that accompanies the increase of opportunities or reduction of inequalities or, alternatively, the increase of employment or non-monetary benefits.

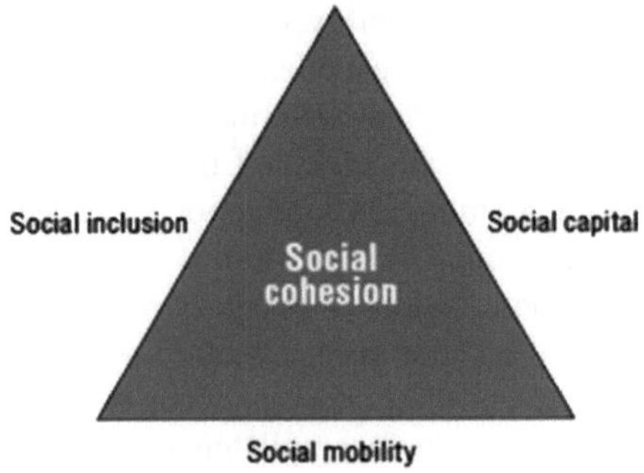

Fig. 12 The components of social cohesion

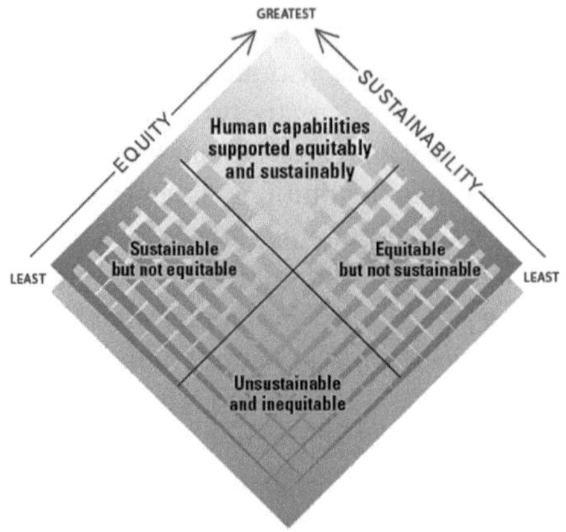

Fig. 13 Equity and sustainability

The basic concept is, however, that greater inclusion associated with an increased share of capital (Fig. 12) as claimed by the OECD (OECD 2012), and greater equity accompanied by sustainability (Fig. 13), as suggested by the 'UN, are pre-conditions for social cohesion'. These, in turn, are decisive for employment and the economic and social dynamism.

3 Pre-distribution: A New Policy Paradigm?

Pre-distribution is a neologism coined by Hacker, J., of Yale University in *The institutional foundations of middle-class democracy*, Policy Network, 6.5.2011. The theory of pre-distribution, however, can be attributed to the thought of two scholars, Meade and Rawls, who in their proposal of a *property ownership democracy*, hypothesized an alternative foundation of democracy in the redistribution of power of citizens, implemented through a wider ownership of human and non human capital, on the basis of public policy, legislation or the assignment of productive resources. Pre-distribution is thus the transfer of power to citizens, through various actions including legislation, regulation, taxation, redistribution and protection proactive rights. It includes a wide sharing of ownership for all types of capital and other means of production and the creation of options that extend the range of choices, especially to the most vulnerable ones, with less access to economic resources.

The idea of the pre-distribution is an interesting proposal, though still vague and not very operational to stimulate the economy and build a more just form of distribution of wealth, giving ex ante increases productivity. Pre-distribution thus addresses a set of economic policies that aim to improve the mechanisms of formation of the primary income, i.e. wages and profits in a more incisive and before that the mechanisms of the welfare state from attempting to apply their corrections. The main government levers for these policies are: (1) control over the structure of the tax system, which can be used to incentivize particular forms of corporate behavior while penalizing others; (2) changes in direct regulation, which can forbid certain activities, mandate others, or raise or lower the costs of particular business strategies; (3) the purchasing power of government procurement, which can be deployed with a broader eye on economic, environmental and social sustainability.

But pre-distribution also can be interpreted as a general re-orientation of social policies towards a system of individual entitlements, directed to all citizens, but especially to the most vulnerable social groups, and aimed to construct a just society by encouraging inclusive growth. From the point of view of law making, pre-distribution involves a re-legislating of rights, with more power to citizens, workers, women, the poor and other weaker subjects, trying to avoid a priori imbalances that lead, in retrospect, to the uneven distribution of income and wealth we see in modern societies. The politics of education and the right to study, for example, are crucial in determining investment in human capital which, a priori should aim in a decisive manner to a widening of access to schools and universities for the most vulnerable, but also a greater incentive of educational processes within companies and administrations.

Pre-distribution also implies the aggressive promotion of the inclusion of disadvantaged people in decision-making that affects them, from the labor market to the use of essential public services, such as education, health care, social security and transport. On market regulation, pre-distribution reconsiders strategic correction of tendencies to concentrate power and remuneration through the imposition of wage caps, and the participation of the workers compensation committees of companies. This also implies the monitoring and surveillance of the abuse of dominant positions, which extended to the labor market and the professions. In terms of taxation, pre-distribution involves more significantly the assets, in two different ways. First, taxation should aim to distribute more equally the means of production, especially human and non human capital. Second, it should aim to pre-distribute entitlements, increasing the rights of the weakest and reducing the power of the stronger subjects, including through taxes on properties related to market dominance and resource control.

References

Hacker JS, Loewentheil N (2012) Prosperity economics building an economy for all

Lawson N (2013) Europe as a good society – The joint transformation of the social democratic and European projects. Social Europe Occasional paper, July 2013

Maffettone S (2011) Toward a moral dimension of economics. In: 9th annual conference: philosophical foundations of economics and the good economy: individual values, human pursuits, self-realization and becoming, The Centre on capitalism and society

OECD (2012) Income inequality and growth: the role of taxes and transfers. OECD. Economics Department Policy Notes, No. 9. January 2012

Rawls J (1971) A theory of justice. Harvard University Press, Cambridge

Rawls J (2001) Justice as fairness: a restatement. Harvard University Press, Cambridge

Scarpetta S (2011) Trade integration and income inequality: links and policy responses. OECD global forum on trade conference, ICITE: trade, jobs and inclusive growth, 8–9 November 2011

Shifting Wealth. Perspectives on global development 2010. OECD Development Centre

Stiglitz J (2012) The price of inequality: how today's divided society endangers our future. W. W. Norton & Company, New York

The Measurement of Underground Economy in Italy

Amedeo Argentiero and Carlo Andrea Bollino

Abstract This paper presents a theoretical contribution to model and dynamically analyze the underground economy.

We build a quarterly DSGE model for the Italian economy with an homogenous good which can be produced by both a sunlight firm and an underground firm. The sunlight firm is subject to distortionary taxation, whereas the underground firm evades taxation.

The economy is subject to stochastic uncorrelated technology shocks on total factor productivity on private sectors.

The demand side of the economy is populated by an infinite number of households with preferences defined over legal good consumption, public expenditure and labor services on a period-by-period basis.

We simulate the model for the Italian economy over the sample 1974:01–2011:02 analyzing the effects of productivity shocks.

We find that in Italy GDP share of underground economy is on average about 23 %.

The dynamic behavior of the model shows that: (a) sunlight production has a greater relative volatility with respect to underground production, showing a sort of stable "parallel unobserved economic structure" in Italy; (b) all variables of the underground sector appear to be negatively correlated with the corresponding ones of regular economy. This implies that underground activities are a sort of buffer for the economy, whenever the business cycle is in downturn phases.

A. Argentiero • C.A. Bollino (✉)
Department of Economics, University of Perugia, Perugia, Italy
e-mail: amedeo.argentiero@unipg.it; carloandrea.bollino@unipg.it

L. Paganetto (ed.), *Wealth, Income Inequalities, and Demography*,
DOI 10.1007/978-3-319-05909-9_11,

1 Introduction

Underground economy is the set of goods and services which, although not violating any criminal law, are deliberately concealed from the tax authorities for one or more of the following reasons: to avoid the payment of taxes and social security contributions; not having to be subject to certain legal requirements such as the minimum wage, quality standards, safety in the workplace and maximum hours of work. There are also activities that can be partially included in the underground sector as they are in part declared to the tax authorities, whereas the remainder part is hidden. An example of this fact could be a firm that under-reports its revenues in order to obtain a tax saving or declaring a number of employed workers less than effective to pay less social security contributions.

According to Shneider et al. (2010) in 2007, the underground economy accounted on average for more than 1/3 of GDP for 162 Eastern Europe, Central Asia and high income per capita OECD countries.

The estimation techniques adopted by the empirical literature for underground economy are divided into direct methods, indirect methods and MIMIC (multiple indicators-multiple causes) models.

Direct methods are based on inductive microeconomic approaches that include sample surveys with voluntary response on production, labor, expenditure, income tax audits. Results validity depends crucially on sample quality and on respondents willingness to cooperate, which is not always granted. In any case, direct investigation may provide detailed information about the underground economic structure, which is not recoverable with other methods.

The reluctance of respondents to cooperate is fully overcome by the method of fiscal controls. The discrepancy between income declared for tax purposes and income detected by selective controls provides an estimate of the underground economy. Notice that these direct methods can only provide point estimates. Thus, there is a lack of knowledge of underground economy growth in time.

Indirect methods are based on macro-economic approaches which use, as a benchmark for the underground economy, the performance of some macroeconomic fundamental variables. For instance, an estimate of the underground economy can be obtained measuring the discrepancy between national expenditure and income statistics. Given the fundamental national accounting equality between aggregate income and expenditure, the gap between this latter and the measured income can be used as an indicator of the extension of the underground economy. The reliability of this estimate, however, is strongly affected by all errors and omissions typical of national accounts.

Another approach is based on transaction analysis (Feige and Pearce 1979; Feige 1990, 1994). Assuming a constant relationship over time between transactions and official GDP, as summarized by the well-known Fisher's quantity equation:

$$M * V = p * T \tag{1}$$

(M = money supply/demand, V = velocity of money circulation, p = absolute level of price T = total transactions), the difference between total transactions and GDP can provide an estimate of the underground economy.

The currency demand approach assumes that underground transactions are carried out only with cash payments (Cagan 1958 and later Tanzi 1980, 1983). This implies that an increase in underground economy volume would necessarily yield an increase in currency demand. Econometric estimation of this excess in money demand provides the basis to estimate underground economy. This approach had great success in the past, applied in many OECD countries, although it has been subjected to harsh criticism, because of the risk of overestimate the phenomenon: in fact also criminal economy transactions make use of money.

The physical input method (Kaufmann and Kaliberda 1996) is based on electricity consumption, which is considered a reliable estimate of overall economic activity within a country, given the well known universal correspondence between economic activity and electric power consumption. Thus, subtracting from this latter quantity the official GDP estimates an estimate of the underground economy can be obtained.

Indeed, an increase in cash demand or an increase in electricity use is not necessarily due to an increase in underground economy.

It is by now clear that direct and indirect approaches are somewhat partial and thus unsatisfactory, because of the failure to jointly consider all the effects of the underground economy, which occur simultaneously on production, labor market and money markets. The MIMIC model approach (Giles 1999) attempts to overcome this difficulty, taking into account the stochastic nature of unobserved variables. In particular, the MIMIC model assumes that underground economy is a latent variable, explainable by determinants (indicators and causes) such as burden of taxation and regulation, citizen propensity to join the irregular sector, monetary transactions, labor market participation and production level in the regular sector. Structural equations typically define the relationships between observed and non observed variables providing a more realistic representation of the underground economy. However, there remain concerns about reliability of these variables and computation difficulties.

Schneider (2005) attributes the formation of the underground economy mainly to structural reasons: high burden of taxation and labor market regulation would push entrepreneurs to operate in the shadows. Social solidarity measures (such as unemployment benefits) may have a perverse effect when they are excessive. Too severe worker protection legislation could push employers to hire illegal workers or an overly generous welfare system might induce beneficiaries to work in the black economy. A study by Bajada and Schneider (2009) on the interaction between underground economy and official labor market confirms precisely this point: there is a definite positive correlation between the high level of social security system and the extent of the underground economy.Other causes of underground economy are (Zizza 2002) the industrial structure, as small firms are more easily hidden to the authorities, the increasing volatility of the economy as new technologies may help to conceal production activities, the increase of personal services, tourism and recreational activities, as self-employed activities are more easily concealable.

A theoretical contribution analyzing underground economy effects is the model proposed by Busato and Chiarini (2004), which considers explicitly real business cycle implications of the underground economy.

Given the contribution of non-registered production to national income, it is difficult to understand the cyclical fluctuations without knowing the underground economy effects. Real Business Cycle (RBC) standard models do not take account this important aspect. The model includes explicit definition of the underground economy as an alternative productive sector. Agents are able to shift production resources between the official and underground sectors.

In this way it is possible to appreciate the cyclical properties of the underground economy. The irregular sector, in fact, helps economic agents to cope with downturn phases experienced by the official economy, allowing agents to perform consumption smoothing through optimal allocation of labor between the two sectors.

Another key contribution analyzing the underground economy effect on the economic system is offered by Orsi et al. (2014). They construct and estimate, using a Bayesian approach, a DSGE model that explicitly takes into account hidden transactions. They provide estimation of the irregular economy size, study the trend of the phenomenon and test the effects of alternative fiscal policies in an economic environment characterized by tax evasion. They use a structural econometric approach, which has solid theoretical foundation and allows to derive estimates of the variables that are not observed from the equilibrium conditions of a theoretical model.

They estimate the model using quarterly data for Italy in the time interval 1982–2006.

The results of the Bayesian estimates show that the underground size in Italy amounts on average to 23 % of GDP.

The dynamic properties of the model show a negative correlation between the cyclical component of the shadow economy and official output. Policy implication is that Italy could improve its fiscal position by reducing taxes or alternatively strengthening fiscal enforcement. The optimal solution, however, would be a mix of the two policies resulting in both welfare improvement and permanent increase tax revenues.

This paper aims to apply the *theory for measurement technique* to quarterly quantify the size of underground economy in Italy over the sample 1974:01-2011:02. Following the seminal works of Ingram et al. (1997) on house-production, Busato and Chiarini (2004) and Orsi et al. (2014) on underground economy, Argentiero et al. (2008) and Bagella et al. (2009) on money laundering, we construct a dynamic stochastic general equilibrium model (DSGE) in which there are two productive sectors:

1. a sunlight firm, which produces a legal good and pays taxes and social security contributions;

2. an underground firm which, although producing the same legal good as the sunlight firm, if it is undetected it won't pay any form of tax and therefore has a higher profit than the sunlight firm; if, instead, it is discovered evading, it will pay taxes and social security contributions as the sunlight firm together with a fine.

The economy is subject to stochastic uncorrelated technology shocks on total factor productivity on both these sectors.

The demand side of the economy is populated by an infinite number of households with preferences defined over legal good consumption, public expenditure and labor services on a period-by-period basis.

The Government collects taxation and fines from the economy and uses them for public expenditure, so that in each period public budget is balanced.

Then, under an appropriate parameterization, we simulate the model with productivity shocks; we perform this analysis for Italy over the sample 1974:01–2011:02.

The choice of Italy is related to the dimension of the underground economy in this country, much higher than other developed countries.

We find that in Italy underground economy has an average weight on total GDP of 23 %, a value about 6 % higher than Italian National Statistical Office (ISTAT) last estimations (2010). Notice, however, that ISTAT estimations are mainly based on labor input and do not directly take into account capital stock as we do in our model.

The model dynamics shows that sunlight production has a greater relative volatility with respect to regular production: this result is driven by sunlight capital stock, that is much more volatile than underground capital stock; sunlight labor input, instead, has a volatility equal to the half of that of underground labor input.

In fact, in the presence of better live conditions in the sunlight sector (positive phases of the business cycle), the workers prefer to have the protection provided by a social security insurance system rather than the risks (accidents, the lack of any form of social protection) related to an underground activity and hence they quickly reallocate themselves into regular economy.

Moreover, all the variables of the underground sector appear to be negatively correlated with the ones of regular economy, showing that they constitute a sort of buffer for the economy, whenever the business cycle is in downturn phases.

The paper is organized as follows. Section 2 presents the model structure, its properties and its optimality conditions derived from the Decentralized Economy Problem. Section 3 describes the calibration of the parameters. Section 4 discusses the dynamic properties of the model resulting from the impulse response function analysis and the simulated time series. Section 5 concludes.

2 The Model Structure

2.1 The Firms

The supply-side of the economy is populated by two kinds of firms, the *sunlight* firm and the *underground* firm that produce the same homogeneous good, i.e. a legal good Y.

There are no barriers to entry, hence there exists a perfect competition market regime.

The firms are owned by households who earn profits in the form of dividends,[1] as we will show in the next section.

Total production Y is allocated to these two sectors according to a percentage α for *sunlight* production and β for *underground* production, so that the sum of the firms' shares is equal to unity:

$$Y_t = (\alpha + \beta) Y_t$$
$$\alpha + \beta = 1$$

The production functions have constant returns to scale and use as inputs labor, n, and capital, k i.e.:

$$\alpha Y_t = Y_t^s = \lambda_t^s \left(k_t^l\right)^\gamma \left(n_t^l\right)^{1-\gamma}$$
$$\beta Y_t = Y_t^u = \lambda_t^u \left(k_t^l\right)^\delta \left(n_t^l\right)^{1-\delta}$$

The superscripts s and u stand for sunlight and underground whereas λ_t^s and λ_t^u represent total factor productivities (TFP) in these two private sectors. The law of motion of the TFPs is described as follows:

$$\Lambda'_{t+1} = \Sigma * \Lambda'_t + v_t$$

where $\Lambda_t = \left[\lambda_t^s, \lambda_t^u\right]$ is a stochastic disturbance vector including TFP and v_t is a vector of the shocks' innovations; the autocorrelation coefficient matrix Σ and the covariance matrix Ξ are defined as follows:

$$\Sigma = \begin{bmatrix} \varphi_{\Lambda^s} & 0 \\ 0 & \varphi_{\Lambda^u} \end{bmatrix} \text{and } \Xi = \begin{bmatrix} \xi_{\Lambda^s} & 0 \\ 0 & \xi_{\Lambda^u} \end{bmatrix}$$

[1]Because in each sector there is a perfect competition among the firms, in the long term there are zero dividends as a consequence of the equality between prices and average costs.

Notice that in our model firms differ in productive structure and in expected profit level. Profit crucially depends on the probabilities of being detected when a firm belongs to the unobserved sector.

Define a price vector for this economy as $\left[p_t, w_t^s, w_t^u, r_t^s, r_t^u\right]$ where p_t is the final output price, w_t^s and w_t^u are sunlight and underground wages, r_t^s and r_t^u are the prices of sunlight and underground capital.

Normalizing next price p to unity, the normalized price vector supporting the equilibrium equals $\left[1, w_t^{s*}, w_t^{u*}, r_t^{s*}, r_t^{u*}\right]$ where $w_t^{s*}, w_t^{u*}, r_t^{s*}, r_t^{u*}$ denote equilibrium prices (see below).

The *sunlight* firm is subject to distortionary taxation on sales, τ_s, on labor wages w_t^s in the form of social security contributions s, that are a percentage of the wages payed.

The sunlight firm's net profit structure is:

$$\pi_t^s = \left[\alpha\left(1-\tau_s\right)Y_t - \left(1+s\right)w_t^s n_t^s - r_t^s k_t^s\right]$$

where n_t^s is the labor offered in the sunlight sector and k_t^s is the capital invested in the sunlight firm.

The *underground* firm evades any form of taxation, and hence profits are higher than those of the *sunlight* firm, but only if it is not detected evading, that happens with probability d; if, instead, the underground firm is detected evading, with probability $1-d$, it is fined with the same amount of taxation as the *sunlight* firm **plus** a penalty factor, $\vartheta^u k_t^u$ with $0 < \vartheta^u < 1$, that is a fraction of the capital invested in the underground firm. The underlying idea is that tax evasion is relatively more costly for society if it is undertaken by a big-size firm. Thus, the sanction should be greater in this case than for the small-size firm.

The underground firm's expected profit structure is:

$$E(\pi_t^u) = d\underbrace{\left(\beta Y_t - w_t^u n_t^u - r_t^u k_t^u\right)}_{\pi_{nd}^u} + (1-d)\underbrace{\left[\beta\left(1-\tau_s\right)Y_t - \left(1+s\right)w_t^u n_t^u - k_t^u\left(r_t^u + \vartheta^u\right)\right]}_{\pi_d^u}$$

Notice that the first part of the sum identifies underground firm profits in the case of not detection $\left(\pi_{nd}^u\right)$, whereas the second part represents profits whenever the underground firm is detected evading $\left(\pi_d^u\right)$.

2.2 The Households and the Government

The demand-side of the economy is populated by an infinite number of infinitely-lived households with preferences defined over private consumption C, with share

η, public consumption G_t, with share $1-\eta$, and labor services N_t. These latter are allocated to regular production $\left(N_t^s\right)$ and underground production $\left(N_t^u\right)$.

Public expenditure is entirely financed by taxation and considered exogenous by consumers, so that in each period public budget is balanced.

Each agent aims to maximize the expected value of an intertemporal utility function, i.e.:

$$E_0 \sum_{t=0}^{\infty} \rho^t U_t \left(C, N_t^s, N_t^u, G_t\right) \tag{2}$$

with ρ^t corresponding to the subjective discount factor.

We assume that there is an idiosyncratic cost in supplying labor in the underground sector, $B^u > 1$ (similarly to Busato and Chiarini 2004; Argentiero et al. 2008). We rationalize these costs as the lack of social protection for those workers who decide to work in the underground economy.

Let the period utility function assume the following form:

$$U_t = \eta \frac{(c)^{1-q_1}}{1-q_1} + (1-\eta) g_t - \frac{\left(n_t^s\right)^{1+\psi}}{1+\psi} - B^u \frac{\left(n_t^u\right)^{1+\omega}}{1+\omega}$$

There are three resource constraints in our model; the first two regard the allocation of labor and capital services (sunlight and underground), i.e.:

$$n_t = n_t^s + n_t^u$$
$$k_t = k_t^s + k_t^u$$

The third one is typically an intertemporal budget constraint, stating that the total flow of consumptions and investments, indicated with x_t^s and x_t^u, cannot exceed disposable income, net of taxes[2]:

$$\begin{aligned} c + x_t^s + x_t^u \leq & \left(1-\tau^n\right) w_t^s n_t^s + \left(1-\tau^k\right) r_t^s k_t^s + \\ & + d\left(w_t^u n_t^u + r_t^u k_t^u\right) + \\ & + (1-d)\left[\left(1-\tau^n\right) w_t^u n_t^u + \left(1-\tau^k\right) r_t^u k_t^u\right] + \\ & + \pi_t^s + \pi_t^u \end{aligned} \tag{3}$$

where τ^n and τ^k are tax rates on wages and capital rents.

Capital accumulation constraints are:

$$x_t^s = k_{t+1}^s - (1-\Omega)^s k_t^s$$

[2]For the sake of simplicity, we do not consider the share of social security contributions payed by the workers, that in general is much lower than the one payed by the firm.

$$x_t^u = k_{t+1}^u - (1-\Omega)^u k_t^u$$

where Ω indicates the rate of capital depreciation.

2.3 Equilibrium Characterization

In this section, we derive optimal conditions characterizing firms and households, given a set of parameters whose value will be discussed in the next section.

Each firm faces the following profit maximization problem:

$$\max_{k_t, n_t} [E(\pi_t)]$$

First order conditions are summarized in the next two groups of relationships

$$w_t^{s*} = \frac{(1-\tau_s)\lambda^s (k_t^s)^{\gamma}(1-\gamma)(n_t^s)^{-\gamma}}{1+s} = \frac{\frac{\partial Y_t^s}{\partial n_t^s}(1-\tau_s)}{1+s}$$

$$r_t^{s*} = (1-\tau_s)\lambda^s (k_t^s)^{\gamma-1}\gamma(n_t^s)^{1-\gamma} \qquad \text{(sunlight firm)}$$

$$r_t^{s*} = \frac{\partial Y_t^s}{\partial k_t^s}(1-\tau_s)$$

$$w_t^{u*} = \frac{\frac{\partial Y_t^u}{\partial n_t^u}[1-\tau_s+d\tau_s]}{[1+s-ds]}$$

$$r_t^{u*} = \frac{\partial Y_t^u}{\partial k_t^u}[1-(1-d)\tau_s] - \vartheta^u(1-d) \qquad \text{(underground firm)}$$

From these preliminary results, we are able to make some considerations:

- For the sunlight firm, real wages and interest rates are equal to their marginal productivities reduced by the tax levy on sales, τ_s, and, only for the real wages, also by the tax wedge, here represented by the social security contributions.
- For the underground firm the level of real wages and interest rates, given the tax rates and social security contributions, depends crucially on the probability of not being detected: in fact the higher is d the higher will be real wages and interest rates. It's easy to show that in the polar case of $d = 1$ (zero probability of being detected by the fiscal authorities):

$$r_t^{u*} = \frac{\partial Y_t^u}{\partial k^u}$$

$$w_t^{u*} = \frac{\partial Y_t^u}{\partial n_t^u}$$

that represent standard first order conditions for a firm using labor and capital as inputs in the absence of any form of taxation.

In the other polar case of $d = 0$ (maximum probability of being detected by the fiscal authorities), real wages and interest rates first order conditions collapse to:

$$r_t^{u*} = \frac{\partial Y_t^u}{\partial k_t^u}(1-\tau_s) - \vartheta^u$$

$$w_t^{u*} = \frac{\frac{\partial Y_t^u}{\partial n_t^u}(1-\tau_s)}{1+s}$$

that, for real wages are equal to the sunlight firm first order conditions, while for real interest rates are lower than the sunlight firm first order conditions due to the weight of the fine, ϑ^u.

Let us now analyze the representative household's behavior.

Each consumer aims to maximize the discounted sum of his expected utility (2) subject to the intertemporal resource constraint (3). Moreover we assume that the initial capital stock is positive, $K_0 > 0$ and given, and that the following inequality constraints hold $C > 0$, $N_t^s > 0$, $N_t^u > 0$, $N_t^c > 0$, i.e.:

$$\max_{\substack{\{C\}_{t=0}^{\infty} \\ \{N_t^s, N_t^u, K_{t+1}\}_{t=0}^{\infty}}} \mathcal{L}_0$$

$$= E_0 \sum_{t=0}^{\infty} \rho^t \left\{ \begin{array}{c} \eta \frac{(c)^{1-q_1}}{1-q_1} + (1-\eta) g_t + \\ -\frac{(n_t^s)^{1+\psi}}{1+\psi} - B^u \frac{(n_t^u)^{1+\omega}}{1+\omega} + \\ +\phi_t \left(\begin{array}{c} (1-\tau^n) w_t^s n_t^s + (1-\tau^k) r_t^s k_t^s + \\ +d(w_t^u n_t^u + r_t^u k_t^u) + \\ +(1-d)\left[(1-\tau^n) w_t^u n_t^u + (1-\tau^k) r_t^u k_t^u\right] + \\ +\pi_t^s + \pi_t^u - c - x_t^s - x_t^u \end{array} \right) \end{array} \right\}$$

and the following transversal condition holds:

$$\lim_{t\to\infty} \rho^t \phi_t K_t = 0 \tag{4}$$

3 Calibration

Before describing the equilibrium behavior of our economy under the framework illustrated above, we need to parameterize the model.

Our calibration is based on quarterly data of Italian economy (1974:01–2011:02).

The system of equations we use to compute the dynamic equilibria of the model depends on the following parameters:

Parameter	Value
φ_{Λ^s}	0.95
φ_{Λ^u}	0.95
ρ	0.99
γ	0.3
δ	0.25
Ω^s	0.05
Ω^u	0.05
τ^s	0.2
τ^n	0.4
τ^k	0.3
s	0.33
ϑ^u	0.3
η	0.8
B^u	2
d	0.3
q_1	0.5
ψ	6.0
ω	3.0

Parameter q_1 is set to 0.5, a value able to match a marginal propensity to consume equal to 0.8, that is the correspondent value for the Italian economy (source: ISTAT) we use to calibrate the preference for private consumption in the utility function, η.

The sunlight capital share γ is set to match the share of total output belonging to capital, whereas for underground sector the corresponding value, δ is supposed slightly lower under the hypothesis that these firms are less capital intensive than the sunlight one, due to the fine linked to capital held that they have to pay in the case of detection. The parameters B^u and B^c represent the disutility of supplying labor specifically to unobserved activities. This is intended to be typically risky, both in terms of lack of social insurance and sanctions received in the case of detection; hence the disutility for consumers is high. Technically, this can be seen as a free parameter and is calibrated to 2 for underground economy, that is consistent with a Frisch labor supply elasticity for underground sector $\left(\frac{1}{\omega}\right)$ equal to 0.3.

These Frisch elasticity values are much higher values than in the sunlight sector, 0.16,[3] to stress that the absence of any form of regulation in the underground labor market makes this productive input more flexible than in the sunlight economy. Moreover, the Italian Frisch labor supply elasticity is in general lower than the

[3]Source: our calculations on ISTAT data.

standard value calibrated for the US economy (i.e. Kydland and Prescott 1982; Cooley and Prescott 1995; Prescott 2004).

The probability of success in tax evasion d is set to 0.70, that corresponds to an average probability of being audited[4] by the Italian fiscal authorities for the firms and self-employed of 0.3 in the period 2001–2009 (source Corte dei Conti, Relazione Annuale 2010).

The values of tax rates are consistent with the same implicit tax rates in Italy: tax rate on capital τ^k is set to 0.3, tax rate on labor τ^n is set to 0.4 and tax rate on sales equals to 0.2.

The rate for social security contributions s is set to 0.33, that is the Italian average legal rate for social security contributions paid by the firms.

Following the real business cycle literature (King and Rebelo 1999), we suppose high values for the persistence coefficients of total factor productivity $\varphi_{\Lambda^s}, \varphi_{\Lambda^u}$ (0.9) and for the subjective discount factor ρ (0.99).

The capital depreciation rates Ω are set equal to the ratio between capital depreciation and gross capital stock for the regular economy, i.e. 0.05.

Finally, following Busato and Chiarini (2004), we set the penalty factor ϑ^u to 0.3, that is the surcharge on the standard tax rate that a firm must pay when detected employing workers in underground sector, according to the Italian Tax Law (Legislative Decree 471/97, Section 13, paragraph 1).

Because the model does not provide a description of the trends in the series, we focus on the cyclical component by using the Hodrick and Prescott filter.[5]

4 The Model Results and Policy Analysis

4.1 The Impulse Response Function Analysis

The steady state values of the model consistent with the parameterization discussed above indicate for Italy a dimension of underground economy equal to 23 % of total GDP; the Italian official estimates[6] of underground economy share in GDP are 17 %. However despite this latter value corresponds to an upper part of a confidence interval, and hence could overestimate the phenomenon, it does not consider the

[4]Although we are aware that the probability of being detected in belonging to underground economy is not the same as the probability of being audited, we can refer to this latter information because is the only publicly available as a good proxy of the phenomenon.

[5]The model generates time series at a quarterly frequency; after log linear transformation of the series, the trend is computed setting the smoothing parameter to 1600, as the standard value in literature. The cyclical component is obtained as the difference between the actual (raw) series and the computed trend component.

[6]Source: ISTAT.

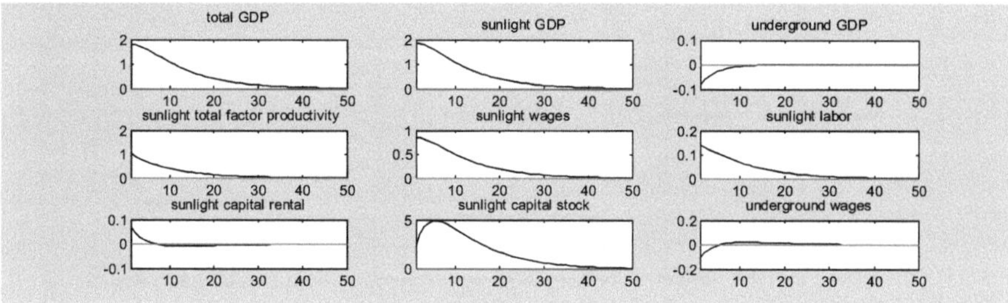

Fig. 1 Impulse response functions for an orthogonalized shock to sunlight TFP

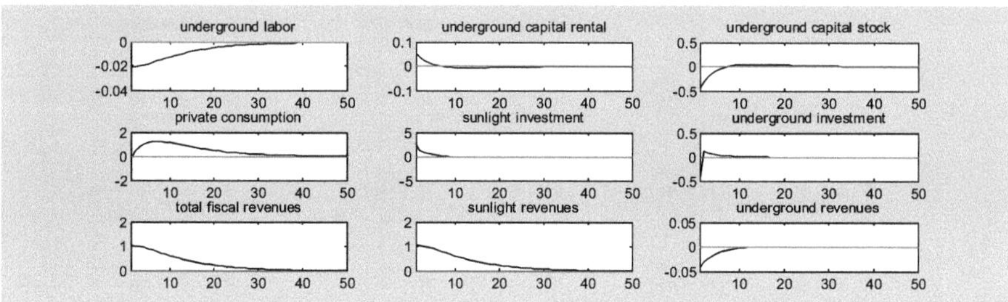

Fig. 2 Impulse response functions for an orthogonalized shock to sunlight TFP (cont.)

role of capital in underground economy and the probability of being detected in belonging to underground sector.

We analyze the impulse response functions of model variables in the presence of technology shocks on both the productive sectors.

When a unitary positive technology shock hits regular sector (Figs. 1 and 2), sunlight GDP increases two percentage points above its steady state value, whereas the reallocation of labor and capital stock from underground to sunlight sector determines a underground GDP reduction. Increase in regular TFP yields sunlight real wages and capital rents rise with a consequent increase in input demand and supply. Nevertheless there is also a slight increase in the underground rental rate; this is due to the positive effect on private consumption generated by the technology shock. In fact the increase in private consumption leads to a reduction in its marginal utility that generates a capital rental rate rise, through the Lucas asset price equation. Sunlight fiscal revenues increase, whereas underground revenues decrease, but the overall government revenues increase.

When a unitary positive technology shock hits underground sector (Figs. 3 and 4), effects on underground inputs and their prices are similar to those for sunlight variables, although smaller in size.

Notably, underground GDP increases but response value is less than one. This happens because there is a probability of being discovered in undertaking an underground activity and because supplying labor in this sector is risky for the worker in (lack of any form of social security insurance). Sunlight indi-

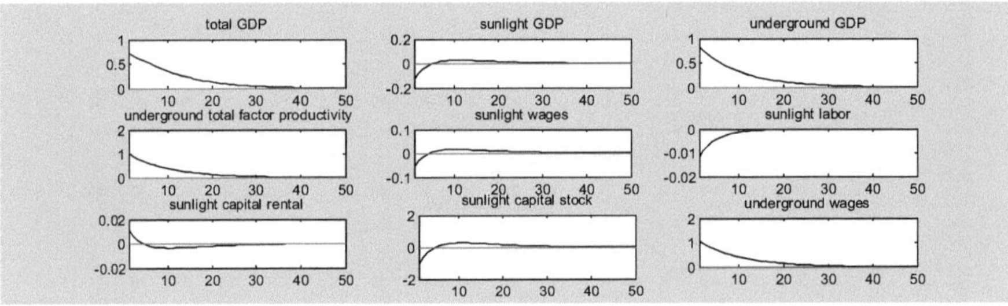

Fig. 3 Impulse response functions for an orthogonalized shock to underground TFP

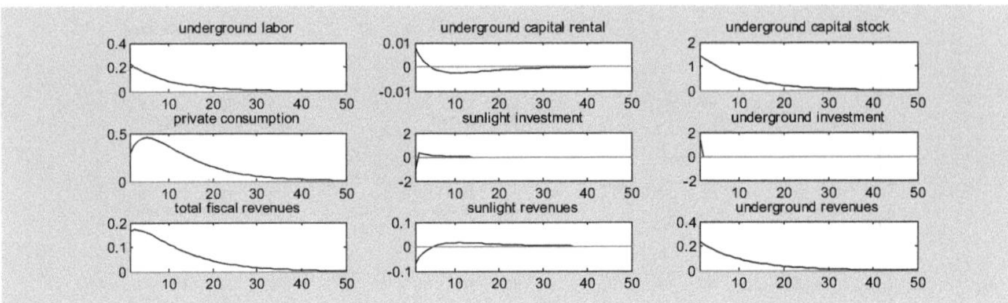

Fig. 4 Impulse response functions for an orthogonalized shock to underground TFP (cont.)

cators decrease with the exception of capital rental that increases in order to balance Lucas asset price equation.[7] Total fiscal revenues increase as a consequence of underground revenues increase (although smaller than sunlight revenues increase).

4.2 *The Numerical Simulations*

The model is simulated for Italy by generating time series of length 150 quarters, over the sample 1974:01–2011:02.

Comparison between the simulated time series with the HP-filtered values for underground GDP and the actual ones is reported in Fig. 5.[8]

The comparison between our simulated time series of the underground economy and the one of ISTAT shows a correlation of 0.32; note that while our series is quarterly and defined over a large period, ISTAT series is annual and publicly available only for 8 years (2000–2008).

[7] Also in this case, private consumption raises but less than in the case of sunlight technology shock.

[8] To compare the series with different frequency we empirically convert low frequencies into high frequencies.

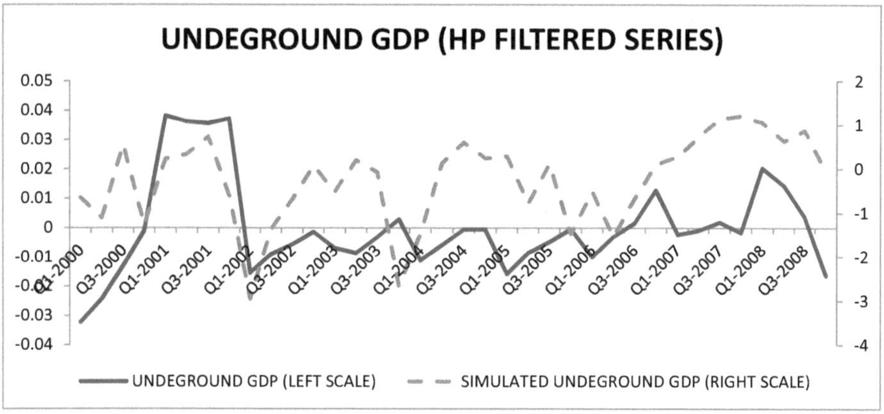

Fig. 5 Actual and simulated HP-filtered time series for Italian underground economy

Table 1 Volatilities and relative volatiles of the simulated series

σ sunlight	*σ underground*	*σ**
$y^s = 2.21$	$y^u = 1.10$	0.50
$\lambda^s = 1.11$	$\lambda^u = 1.24$	1.12
$w^s = 1$	$w^u = 1.42$	1.42
$n^s = 0.15$	$n^u = 0.31$	2.07
$r^s = 0.08$	$r^u = 0.05$	0.63
$k^s = 5.27$	$k^u = 2.26$	0.43
$x^s = 2.92$	$x^u = 1.70$	0.58

In Table 1, instead we summarize the volatilities of sunlight and underground series: in the first column we indicate the volatility of sunlight series, in the second column we put the standard deviation of underground series, whereas the third column measures the relative volatility of underground series with respect to the corresponding sunlight ones.

The analysis of the second moments of the simulated series indicates a relative lower volatility of the underground GDP with respect to sunlight one: this result is in line with the literature (Busato and Chiarini 2004; Orsi et al. 2014).

A possible explanation of this fact can be found in the high tax burden[9] level present in Italy, that has made possible the formation of a stable parallel economic structure, i.e. the underground economy. Hence, the survival of this sector over time has to be understood as a reaction to difficulty of some firms in paying taxes and social security contributions. Nevertheless, a strong presence of underground economy reduces the possibility for a Government of decreasing taxation.

On the other hand, underground labor input shows an higher relative volatility compared with sunlight labor, because whenever the business cycle moves from a downturn phase to an expansion there is a quick reallocation of labor input towards

[9]For 2012 in Italy this value is almost 44 %.

Table 2 Correlation matrix

Variables	y^s	y^u	n^s	n^u	k^s	k^u
y^s	1	−0.10	0.99	−0.11	0.8	−0.2
y^u	−0.10	1	−0.12	0.99	−0.35	0.95
n^s	0.99	−0.12	1	−0.12	0.76	−0.21
n^u	−0.11	0.99	−0.12	1	−0.41	0.98
k^s	0.8	−0.35	0.76	−0.41	1	−0.44
k^u	−0.2	0.95	−0.21	0.98	−0.44	1

sunlight sector. The better living conditions insured by the regular economy (social security contributions and insurance against accidents at work) make it convenient for workers to supply labor in a sunlight firm.

Capital stock, instead, is much more volatile in the sunlight sector than in the underground one.

Moreover, our simulations show that the hidden feature of the underground economy generates less variations in its productivity than the regular economy.

Finally, from the correlation matrix of our simulated time series (Table 2) it emerges a weak negative correlation between the sunlight GDP and the underground GDP: this result is similar the one found by Busato and Chiarini (2004), Orsi et al. (2014), and Argentiero et al. (2008) for money laundering. We think that a relatively larger GDP could mean greater opportunities, better living conditions and hence a deterrent in being a member of the underground sector. In this respect, unobserved activities would be seen as a "buffer" that economic agents use whenever the business cycle is in downturn phases. Therefore, the increase of regular GDP could weaken the origin of unobserved economy.

We find that there exists negative correlation between sunlight and underground labor and capital, although for capital the negative correlation is higher due to the sanction in the case of detection that drives capital stock outside the underground sector when the sunlight sector grows up.

These results are quite robust to a sensitivity analysis on the parameters varying them in a neighborhood of $\pm 5\,\%$.

5 Conclusions

This paper has derived an alternative methodology, but complementary to existing ones, to build and analyze the phenomenon of the underground economy.

This technique is based on a DSGE model considered consistent, both in its structure and in the parameter calibration, with the dynamics of the variables involved in the analysis.

The advantage of this scheme is to generate high frequency data for non observable quantities and to study their relationships on the economic system.

The method used can be considered as a sort of indirect method based on "top-down" estimate which, although not starting from empirical aggregate data it is based on a theoretical macroeconomic model able to generate data qualitatively consistent with the stylized facts.

The simulations are carried out for Italy, but they can be repeated for any other country.

The steady state values of our theoretical model show a dimension of the underground economy on total GDP of 23 %, which in absolute value means more than 300 billions of Euros. Such data are in line with similar models (Orsi et al., 2014) and slightly higher than the official estimates that, however, do not consider the role of capital stock and the probability of being detected by fiscal authorities.

This high presence of underground economy in Italy can be explained by an high level of tax burden that pushes some firms in the underground sector, thus generating a decrease in sunlight fiscal revenues (Laffer effect).

The dynamic properties of the model state a negative correlation between underground economy and regular one due to the reallocation of inputs towards the more productive sector. This means that in downturn phases of the business cycle fiscal policy should create the right conditions to not give incentives to firms to join the underground economy together with a strong fight to fiscal evasion.

The proposed analysis is not intended to be a substitute for econometric modeling, but to complete it and integrate it in some aspects as well as borrowing from econometrics some results, as the calibration values of the parameters.

Acknowledgments We are especially grateful to Alessandro Piergallini and Barbara Annicchiarico for many conversations and precious advice. We thank specially Luigi Paganetto and the participants of "XXV Villa Mondragone International Economic Seminar" held in Rome in June 2013, for comments on previous versions of the paper. Of course, all errors are ours.

References

Argentiero A, Bagella M, Busato F (2008) Money laundering in a two-sector model: using theory for measurement. Eur J Law Econ 26(3):341–359

Bagella M, Busato F, Argentiero A (2009) Money laundering in a microfounded dynamic model: simulations for the U.S. and the EU-15 economies. Rev Law Econ 5(2):4

Bajada C, Schneider F (2009) Unemployment and the shadow economy in the oecd. Rev Écon 60(5):1033–1067

Busato F, Chiarini B (2004) Market and underground activities in a two-sector dynamic equilibrium model. Econ Theory 23(4):831–861

Cagan P (1958) The demand for currency relative to the total money supply. J Polit Econ 66:303

Cooley TF, Prescott EC (1995) Economic growth and business cycles. In: Cooley TF (ed) Frontiers of business cycle research, Princeton University Press, Princeton, NJ, pp 1–38

Feige EL, Pearce DK (1979) The casual causal relationship between money and income: some caveats for time series analysis. Rev Econ Stat 61(4):521–533

Feige EL (1990) Defining and estimating underground and informal economies: the new institutional economics approach. World Dev 18(7):989–1002

Feige EL (1994) The underground economy and the currency enigma. Public Financ [Finances publiques] 49(Suppl.):119–136

Giles DEA (1999) Measuring the hidden economy: implications for econometric modelling. Econ J R Econ Soc 109(456):F370–F380

Ingram BF, Kocherlakota NR, Savin NE (1997) Using theory for measurement: an analysis of the cyclical behavior of home production. J Monet Econ 40:435–456

Kaufmann D, Kaliberda A (1996) Integrating the unofficial economy into the dynamics of post-socialist economies: a framework of analysis and evidence. Policy Research Working Paper Series 1691, The World Bank

King R, Rebelo S (1999) Resuscitating real business cycles. In: Taylor JB, Woodford M (eds) Handbook of macroeconomics. North-Holland, Amsterdam

Kydland FE, Prescott EC (1982) Time to build and aggregate fluctuations. Econometrica 50(6):1345–1370

Orsi R, Raggi D, Turino F (2014) Size, Trend, and Policy Implications of the Underground Economy. Rev Econ Dyn [Elsevier for the Society for Economic Dynamics] 17(3): 417–436

Prado M (2011) Government policy in the formal and informal sectors. Eur Econ Rev 55(8):1120–1136

Prescott EC (2004) Why do Americans work so much more than Europeans? Q Rev Fed Reserve Bank Minneap 28:2–13

Schneider F (2005) Shadow economies around the world: what do we really know? Eur J Polit Econ 21:598–642

Shneider F, Buehn A, Montenegro CE (2010) Shadow economies all over the World new estimates for 162 countries from 1999 to 2007. World Bank Policy Research Working Paper 5356

Tanzi V (1980) The underground economy in the United States: estimates and implications. Banca Naz Lav Q Rev 135(4):427–453

Tanzi V (1983) The underground economy in the United States: annual estimates 1930–1980. IMF Staff Pap 30(2):283–305

Zizza R (2002) Metodologie di stima dell'economia sommersa: un'applicazione al caso italiano. Banca d'Italia, Temi di Discussione, n. 463

Trade Relations Between Latin American Countries and the European Union

Miguel Ruíz-Cabañas Izquierdo

Abstract In discussing this topic, I would like first of all to provide some background information on the current scenario of finance and trade in Latin American and Caribbean countries.

I will then briefly comment on the European economic situation and its impact on our region in terms of trade and investments and the prospects for economic relations which will open up between the two regions over the next few years. After that, I would like to comment on the situation in the Asian Pacific region and on the opportunities they offer to Latin American and Caribbean countries.

Finally, I propose that relations between the EU and AM should not cease to be important, but that they should be regulated according to the logic of new global economics and, consequently, that we should promote trade and investment agreements which are mutually more favourable.

1 Where Is Latin America today?

In Table 1, we can see that with an area of 20.4 million km^2, Latin American countries cover 15.2 % of the world's total territory. Our population of 586 million, for the most part young people, represents 8.44 % of the world's total population. In 2012, the average pro capita GNP exceeded $12,000 and our economies grew at an average rate of 3 % last year. Our trade with the rest of the world, totalling about $2,238.6 billion, represented 6.07 % of world trade, which, according to the United Nations Conference on Trade and Development (UNCTAD), came to about $36,890 billion.

M. Ruíz-Cabañas Izquierdo (✉)
Italo-Latin American Institute (IILA) and Mexican Embassy in Rome, Rome, Italy
e-mail: ofna.embajador@emexitalia.it

L. Paganetto (ed.), *Wealth, Income Inequalities, and Demography*,
DOI 10.1007/978-3-319-05909-9_12,

Table 1 Main Latin American and Caribbean economic indicators in 2012

Indicators	LA & C	World
Territory (km^2)	20,419,640	134,236,058
Population (by millions)	585.8	6,940.7
Unemployment (EAP %)	6.4	n.d.
Real GNP	3.0	3.2
GNP (MMDD)	5,765.6	71,707.3
Pro-capita GNP (PPP, international dollars)	12,332	n.d.
Inflation %	5.6	3.9
Direct foreign investments (MMDD)	216.9	684.4
Exports (MMDD)	1,111.5	18,323
Imports (MMDD)	1,127.1	18,567
Total trade (MMDD)	2,238.6	36,890.0

Sources: IMF, CEPAL and UNCTAD; MMDD: billions of dollars

Table 2 Main LAC economic integration mechanisms

Mercosur (Argentina, Brazil, Paraguay, Uruguay and Venezuela)
SICA (Belize, Guatemala, Honduras, El Salvador, Costa Rica, Nicaragua, Panama)
ALBA (Bolivia, Cuba, Ecuador, Nicaragua and Venezuela)
CARICOM (Anglophone Caribbean countries and Haiti)
The Pacific Alliance (Chile, Colombia, Mexico and Peru)

Latin American countries today manage their economies prudently with low fiscal deficits and significant monetary reserves. We have at our disposal many natural resources, although some countries are extremely vulnerable to climate change, with the risk of prolonged droughts and flooding.

It is important to note that, as opposed to Europe which relies on the European Union, the Latin American and Caribbean countries do not have a single economic integration system. Although the Community of Latin American and Caribbean states, CELAC, uniting all Latin American and Caribbean countries for the first time in history was launched in 2010, its function is to promote political dialogue and cooperation with other regions, such as the European Union, and it lacks mechanisms to foster economic integration between its members. At this time, as can be seen from Table 2, there are at least five important groups in the region promoting economic integration and sub-regional political cooperation.

2 Economic Growth Prospects for Latin America in 2013

At the end of 2012, economic growth in the region came to 3 %. Factors impacting on the region's economic growth were the weakness of the global economy due to the recession in Europe, as well as the slowdown of growth in China, and modest growth in the United States.

Table 3 Latin America and the Caribbean: real growth in GNP

Country	2010	2011	2012	2013
Total: Central America	**4.0**	**4.9**	**5.0**	**4.2**
Mexico	5.6	3.9	3.9	3.5
Belize	2.7	2.3	5.3	2.7
Costa Rica	4.7	4.2	5.1	3.5
El Salvador	1.4	1.5	1.6	2.0
Guatemala	2.9	3.9	3.0	3.2
Honduras	2.8	3.6	3.3	3.3
Nicaragua	3.1	5.1	5.2	5.0
Panama	7.6	10.6	10.7	8.0
Total: South America	**6.5**	**4.5**	**2.5**	**3.5**
Argentina	9.2	8.9	1.9	3.5
Bolivia	4.1	5.2	5.2	5.0
Brazil	7.5	2.7	0.9	3.0
Chile	6.1	6.0	5.6	5.0
Colombia	4.0	5.9	4.0	4.5
Ecuador	3.3	8.0	4.8	3.5
Paraguay	13.1	4.4	−1.2	10.0
Peru	8.8	6.9	6.2	6.0
Uruguay	8.9	5.7	3.9	3.8
Venezuela	−1.5	4.2	5.6	2.0
Total: Caribbean	**3.0**	**2.6**	**2.6**	**3.0**
Antigua and Barbuda	−7.9	−5.0	2.3	2.4
Bahamas	0.2	1.6	2.5	2.4
Barbados	0.2	0.4	0.0	0.7
Cuba	2.4	2.7	3.1	3.5
Dominica	0.9	−0.3	−1.5	1.1
Granada	0.0	1.0	1.2	3.3
Guyana	4.4	5.4	4.8	4.9
Haiti	−5.4	5.6	2.8	6.0
Jamaica	−1.5	1.3	−0.3	0.4
Dominican Republic	7.8	4.5	3.9	3.0
San Cristobal and Nieves	−2.4	2.1	−1.1	2.9
St. Vincent and Grenadine	−2.8	0.1	1.5	1.1
Santa Lucia	0.4	1.3	−3.0	2.7
Suriname	7.3	4.4	4.5	4.3
Trinidad and Tobago	0.0	−1.4	0.4	2.5
Latin America and Caribbean	**5.9**	**4.3**	**3.0**	**3.5**

Growth rates. *Source*: CEPAL

In 2013, (see Table 3), a moderate global economic recovery is forecast, despite a climate of uncertainty and the volatility of international financial markets. The FMI predicts that global economic growth will be at 3.3 % compared to the 3.2 % recorded in 2012. On the other hand, the United Nations is predicting an even lower worldwide growth rate: 2.4 % in 2013.

The economies of developing countries and emerging markets will continue to be the main drivers of the global economy, in particular, the Asian countries (China could record an 8 % growth rate, slightly higher than its 7.8 % rate for 2012). The U.S. will grow at 1.9 %, a slightly lower rate than in 2012 (2.2 %), while the countries in the eurozone will record, for the second year running, an economic recession, which in 2013 will come to – 0.3 %. The crisis in the zone will continue to be one of the principle risk factors for the global economy and for those of Latin America and the Caribbean.

In this scenario, CEPAL (the Economic Commission for Latin America and the Caribbean), estimates that in 2013, Latin America and the Caribbean will record a recovery in economic growth, with a growth rate of approximately 3.5 %, which, though slightly higher than the rate in 2012 (3.0 %), is still far lower than the one recorded in 2010 (5.9 %). This significant growth will be driven mostly by the recovery of the economies of Argentina and Brazil, as well as the growth predicted for Mexico.

At the level of sub-regions, Central America is expected to have an average GNP increase of 4.2 % in 2013, highlighting Panama (8.0 %) which continues the dynamic trend we have observed over the last few years. The South American countries will achieve a growth of 3.5 %, attributable to the improved economic results of Brazil (3.0 %), Argentina (3.5 %), and the strong growth of Colombia (4.5 %), Chile (5.0 %) and Peru (6.0 %). The Caribbean countries will record an increase of 3.0 %, slightly higher than for the previous year due to Cuba's improved economic vitality and the recovery of the economies of Trinidad and Tobago, and Jamaica.

3 The Weight of the European Union in World Trade and Investments and Its Impact on Latin America and the Caribbean

Notwithstanding the economic stagnation of the last few years, the 27 countries comprising the European Union are still the most important exporters and importers of goods and services at a global level, as well as the main providers and recipients of foreign investments worldwide, surpassing the United States, China, and Japan. According to the European Commission, the European industrial base remains very strong, allowing it to achieve a surplus of 300 billion euros annually. At the same time, the European Union is competitive in the services sector, which accounts for its trade surplus of 100 billion euros. The EU has also greatly improved its competitiveness in the agricultural sector, moving from a deficit to a surplus.

The EU has always been a very important trade and investment partner for Latin American and Caribbean countries. In the last 10 years, Europe has invested approximately 40 % of the total direct foreign investments received by our region. By the same token, the EU is the second or third most important trade partner of

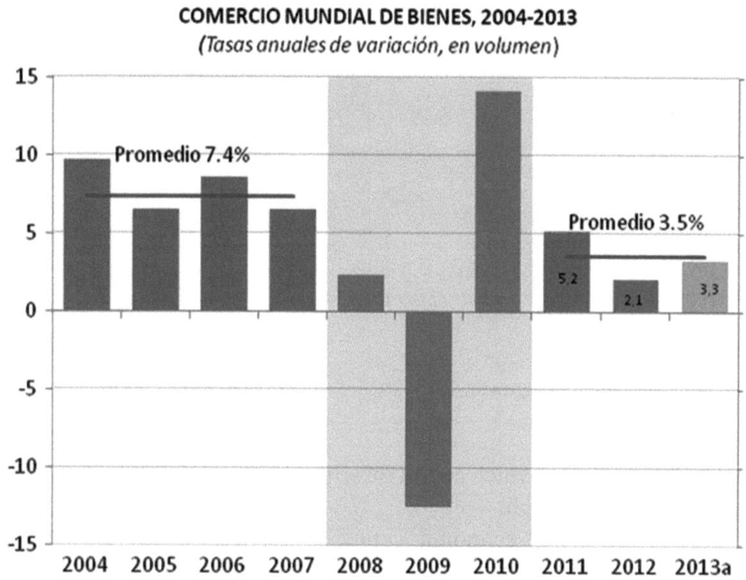

Fig. 1 Global trade in goods, 2004–2013 (variation in yearly rates). *Sources*: UNCTAD, CEPAL

Latin American countries, after the United States, or China, depending on each single country.

Nonetheless, analysts predict that the EU will record negative economic growth for the third consecutive year. This situation will have an impact on the exports of Latin American countries. Experts estimate that it will take another 2–5 years to see economic recovery in the European Union. In reality, the economic stagnation of the EU, added to slow growth in the United States, has had repercussions on international trade, which underwent a slowdown in 2011 and 2012, even though a modest recovery is expected in 2013, as can be seen from Fig. 1.

In the meantime, the Asian Pacific economies have managed to maintain dynamic growth over the last 10 years and in 2012, grew 7.5 % on average. For 2013, the growth rate is expected to be 7.9 %. China grew by 7.8 % in 2012, 1.4 % less than in 2011, but is expected to grow by 8.2 % in 2013. The growing importance of Asian economies, in particular the Chinese one, for the global economy, is forcing Latin American countries to rethink their strategic options. According to the most important international analysts, Asia will continue to drive global growth over the next decade and Latin America will contribute more than Europe, as shown in Fig. 2.

In this context, it is expected that China and the other economies of Asia and the Pacific, such as India, Korea, Taiwan, Hong Kong, Indonesia, Malaysia, Singapore, Vietnam, the Philippines, and Thailand will continue to increase at a faster pace, exceeding 6 or 7 % on average. The demand for raw materials in these economies will help to keep their prices high over the next few years, which will in turn allow

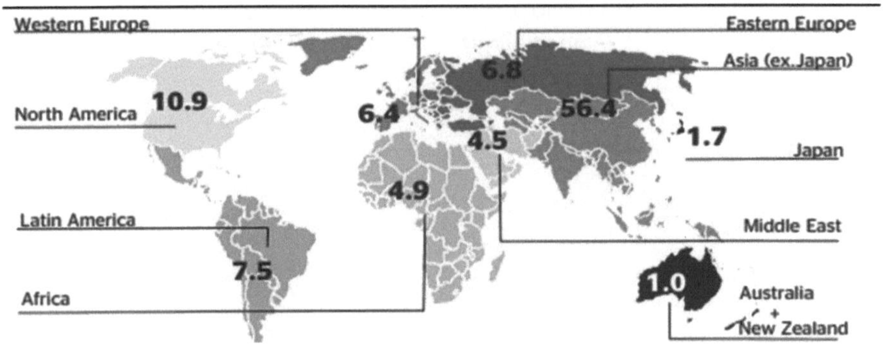

Fig. 2 Regions with the most growth, 2013–2022. *Sources*: UNCTAD, CEPAL

Latin American countries which export these products, mainly from South America, to keep export revenues high.

The shift of the global economic centre of gravity towards Asia has induced some countries and groups of countries to take various strategic decisions over the past few years to attempt to respond, or position themselves, to compete better and benefit from the new global scenario. It is in this sense that we can explain the initiative of the United States and other countries to initiate talks for a Trans-Pacific Partnership for free trade (TTP) which includes several Asian economies, Canada, the U.S.A., Mexico, Chile, and Peru on the American continent. The negotiations for this agreement began in 2011. Their complex nature would lead us to expect that it will take some time before they are successful.

Furthermore, just one week ago, at the conclusion of the G8 summit in Northern Ireland, the leaders of the United States and the European Union announced that, this coming July 8, talks will begin in Washington D.C. for a free trade pact between the European Union and the United States. The European Commission had stated some time ago that this partnership was a top priority for European trade strategy. It is expected that this agreement will be finalized by the end of 2014. Undoubtedly, if the talks are successful, this agreement will have trade and economic repercussions for the rest of the globe, for the simple fact that taken together, the United States and the European Union represent about 52 % of global GNP. Nevertheless, considering that the duties between these two players are already very low, it is expected that the most important effect will be to adopt measures aimed at favouring trade even further through the adoption of standard regulatory systems and common controls.

In Latin America, the vitality of the Asian economies has been the determining factor in the creation of a new group, the Pacific Alliance, which unifies Chile, Colombia, Mexico and Peru. The Pacific Alliance does not seek to offset any other regional or sub-regional integration mechanism. Its aims are to: (1) build, in an active and consensual manner, a highly integrated zone in order to move progressively towards the free movement of goods, services, capital, and people; (2) promote the increased growth, development, and competitiveness of its partners in order to achieve increased well-being, overcoming socio-economic inequalities, and the social participation of its populations, and (3) become a platform for political bodies, for economic and trade integration, opening up towards the world, especially towards the Pacific area. Several countries in the region have asked to join the Alliance as observers, such as Costa Rica, Guatemala, Panama and Uruguay. Furthermore, also some countries outside the region, such as Spain, Canada, Australia, Japan, and New Zealand, have been accepted as observers.

As an economic bloc, Colombia, Chile, Mexico and Peru have a population of more than 210 million people, about 35 % of the total population of Latin America and the Caribbean, with a pro capita GNP of approximately $13,000. In addition, the Gross National Product (GNP) of countries in the Pacific Alliance make up 35 % of the total for Latin America and the Caribbean and the average growth rate was 5 % in 2012, exceeding the global growth rate by 2.2 % this year. The four countries that comprise the bloc are characterized by a high level of macro-economic stability and the potential to increase their market annually.

4 Options for Latin American Countries and the Caribbean

Faced with this new international scenario, it is only natural for countries in the region to seek increased trade and investment ties with Asian countries. Nevertheless, the situation of each country in the region differs according to its productive structure, its capacity to export, and the type of goods and services it exports.

While the European Union economy continues to stagnate or achieve low growth rates, it is unlikely that Latin American countries will increase exportation towards this market. Therefore, it is predicted that over the next few years, Latin American countries will increase trade with China and the Pacific area. This trade will continue to yield significant exportation revenues.

However, these strategic choices do not imply, by any means, that the EU market will be less important for the countries in this region. On the contrary, as has happened in the past few years, the EU countries may increase their investments in all productive sectors of the region's economy, for example, in the railcar and car parts sectors, aerospace, infrastructure projects, biotechnology, the production of new materials, chemical and petrochemical industries, and renewable energy projects.

Between the EU and various Latin American countries, there is already a consolidated institutional structure as evidenced by agreements for strategic cooperation with Brazil and Mexico, free trade agreements with Chile, Colombia, Peru, and Mexico and cooperation with Central American countries, or the CARICOM states. The European Union will continue to negotiate with MERCOSUR, while the absence of an agreement has not restricted trade or investments in these countries. Argentina, Brazil, Uruguay, Paraguay and even Venezuela, are important EU trade partners.

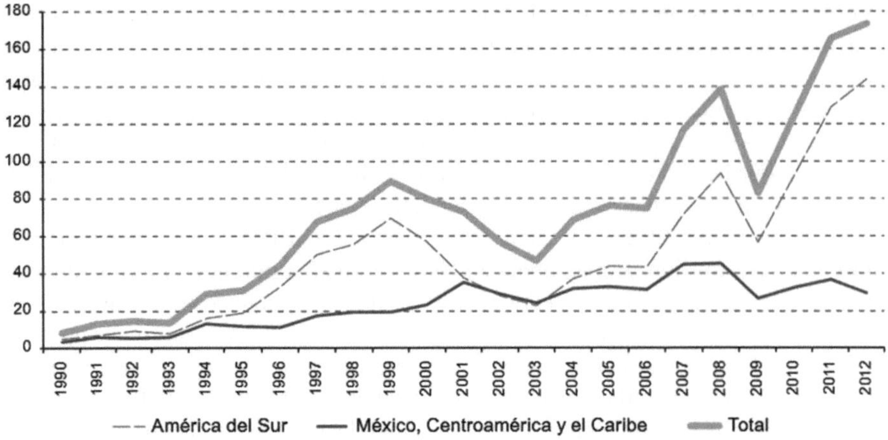

Fig. 3 Direct foreign investments in Latin America and the Caribbean. *Sources*: UNCTAD, CEPAL

Table 4 Amount of European Union investments in LAC, 2008–2011

Regions and Countries	2008	2009	2010	2011
Central America	**310.8**	**390.4**	**404.1**	**449.8**
Mexico	*51.8*	*61.0*	*75.1*	*76.7*
South America	**207.0**	**229.3**	**314.4**	**352.9**
Argentina	*40.8*	*41.7*	*48.1*	*44.3*
Brazil	*108.5*	*139.7*	*200.2*	*238.9*
Chile	*15.3*	*19.5*	*24.9*	*25.0*
Venezuela	*17.3*	*16.3*	*18.9*	*24.0*

Source: European Commission

Through new investments in the region, the EU will benefit not only from the economic growth of Latin America, but will also foster new opportunities for the exportation of intermediate goods and services that can benefit their service manufacturing industries. The European Union can promote a policy of increased internationalization of its companies, above all medium-sized, but also small ones, that are suppliers of large companies already present in the region.

Actually, I believe that this trend began some time ago, as we can see from Fig. 3. Indeed, in 2012, Latin America and the Caribbean received \$173 billion in direct foreign investments: 6.7 % more than in 2011, as shown in Fig. 3.

Approximately 40 % of these investments came from EU member states, as shown in Table 4, that provides the amount of European Union investments in Latin America between 2008–2011.

5 Conclusions

The global scenario is rapidly evolving. China and the Asia Pacific region will be the most important drivers of the world economy in the next decade. The United States, Europe, and Latin America are re-defining their economic strategies in light of this fact. As in other regions, Latin America and the Caribbean will seek to strengthen their trade and investment ties with the Pacific area. Nevertheless, the EU will not cease to be a key partner for Latin American countries in terms of trade and investments. Europe must increase its investments in Latin America and the Caribbean, because it is a region that will continue to grow in the coming decade. This will make exportation towards our countries possible, creating new jobs in both regions. While focussing its attention on talks with the United States, Europe must not forget the opportunities offered by Latin American and Caribbean countries.

Acknowledgments I would like to thank the organizers of the XXV Villa Mondragone International Economic Forum, and above all Prof. Luigi Paganetto, for his kind invitation. I would also like to thank Ambassador Luigi Marras, Director General for the Globalization of the Farnesina.

MIX
Papier aus verantwortungsvollen Quellen
Paper from responsible sources
FSC® C105338
FSC
www.fsc.org

If you have any concerns about our products,
you can contact us on
ProductSafety@springernature.com

In case Publisher is established outside the EU,
the EU authorized representative is:
Springer Nature Customer Service Center GmbH
Europaplatz 3, 69115 Heidelberg, Germany

Printed by Libri Plureos GmbH
in Hamburg, Germany